African Catholic

African Catholic

DECOLONIZATION AND THE TRANSFORMATION
OF THE CHURCH

Elizabeth A. Foster

Harvard University Press

Cambridge, Massachusetts   London, England

2019

LIBRARY OF CONGRESS CATALOGING-IN-PUBLICATION DATA
Names: Foster, Elizabeth Ann, 1976– author.
Title: African Catholic : decolonization and the transformation of the
Church / Elizabeth A. Foster.
Description: Cambridge, Massachusetts : Harvard University Press, 2019. |
Includes bibliographical references.
Identifiers: LCCN 2018028302 | ISBN: 9780674987661 (alk. paper)
Subjects: LCSH: Catholic Church—Africa—History. | Catholic
Church—History—1965– | Decolonization—Africa, French-speaking—
History. | Decolonization—Africa, Sub-Saharan—History. | Christianity
and culture—Africa, French-speaking—History. | Christianity and
culture—Africa, Sub-Saharan—History.
Classification: LCC BX1675 .F67 2018 | DDC 282 / .670917541—dc23
LC record available at https://lccn.loc.gov/2018028302

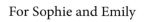

For Sophie and Emily

CONTENTS

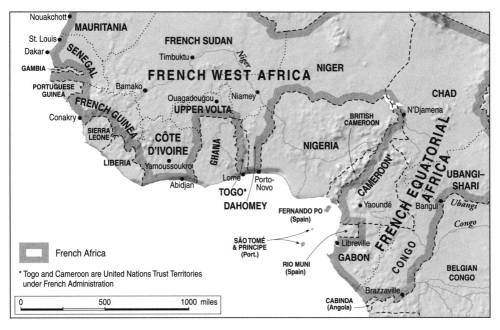

French Africa

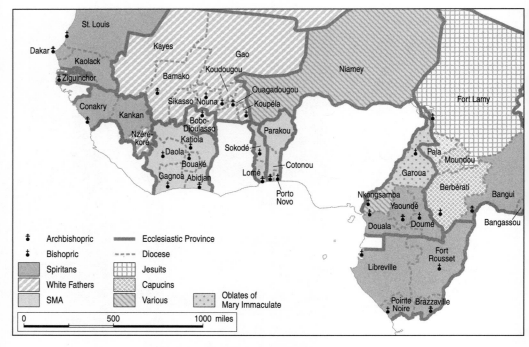

Legend:

- ♯ Archbishopric
- ♯ Bishopric
- Spiritans
- White Fathers
- SMA
- ━━━ Ecclesiastic Province
- ------ Diocese
- Jesuits
- Capucins
- Various
- Oblates of Mary Immaculate

0   500   1000 miles

Ecclesiastical boundaries in French Africa

INTRODUCTION

Catholic Conversations at the End of Empire

IT WAS PRECISELY WHAT the Vatican had long feared might happen in French sub-Saharan Africa: an acrimonious divorce between metropole and colony that jeopardized Catholic interests. In 1958, Guinea became the first, and at that time the only, French Overseas Territory in sub-Saharan Africa to accede to independence. Its citizens, both inspired and coerced by their charismatic leader Sékou Touré, voted overwhelmingly in a referendum to reject membership in the French Community, Charles de Gaulle's replacement for the French Union that accorded member territories more sovereignty under a French umbrella.[1] French officials were incensed by Guinea's defiance and worried it would lead other African territories to regret their "yes" votes for the Community. France retaliated by immediately withdrawing all financial aid from Guinea, ceasing work on ongoing development projects, rerouting ships bound for Conakry with food and vital supplies, taking medicines off hospital shelves, ripping phone lines out of government offices, and wreaking havoc with Guinea's currency reserves.[2]

In the aftermath of this bitter exchange of blows, Touré and his allies in the Democratic Party of Guinea (PDG) assumed a hostile stance

The archbishops of French Africa, 1958. *From right to left*: Joseph Cucherousset, CSSp, archbishop of Bangui; Michel Bernard, CSSp, archbishop of Brazzaville; Jean-Baptiste Boivin, SMA, archbishop of Abidjan; Émile Socquet, MAfr, archbishop of Ouagadougou; Louis Parisot, SMA, archbishop of Cotonou; René Graffin, CSSp, archbishop of Yaoundé; Marcel Lefebvre, CSSp, archbishop of Dakar and apostolic delegate to French Africa; Gérard de Milleville, CSSp, archbishop of Conakry; Joseph-Paul Strebler, SMA, archbishop of Lomé; Pierre Leclerc, MAfr, archbishop of Bamako; Victor Sartre, SJ, archbishop of Tananarive.   From *Horizons africains*, no. 102 (May 1958): 1. Courtesy of ACSSp.

toward the Catholic missions in Guinea, which they accused of complicity in French colonialism. From their perspective, it was an easy case to make. The missions, which catered to a small African Catholic population and ran over seventy schools throughout the country, were still almost exclusively staffed by white French men and women, despite efforts to train more local clergy. In 1958, there were seventy-nine European priests in Guinea and only six Guinean clergymen, while sixty-two European nuns labored alongside seventeen Guinean sisters.[3] Moreover, financial ties between the missions and the French government had intensified in the postwar period. Beginning in 1946, French prelates in

Guinea had received generous support from the French government Fund for Economic and Social Development (FIDES), primarily to expand their network of schools.[4] In 1954, for example, French missionary bishops in Guinea had requested and received over seventy million metropolitan francs from the FIDES to realize ten different school construction projects.[5] The missions were thus vulnerable to Touré's onslaught, and church officials, who feared Touré was a communist at heart, fretted that he would inspire other emerging African leaders to mount similar attacks.

In the years that followed, Sékou Touré repeatedly found the Catholic Church to be a useful political scapegoat, as well as a source of the conspiracies he increasingly imagined, or pretended to imagine, around him.[6] Mission schools were among the first targets: in 1959, the PDG announced its intention to nationalize all Catholic schools in Guinea over the following three years. When the French archbishop of Conakry, Monsignor Gérard de Milleville, denounced this ongoing process from the pulpit in 1961, he was immediately ejected from the country.[7] Touré then insisted on the appointment of an African archbishop to replace de Milleville. The Vatican acquiesced in 1962, nominating Monsignor Raymond-Marie Tchidimbo, a priest of Guinean and Gabonese parentage who had been friendly with Touré as a young man. Tchidimbo had already been serving in an uncomfortable role as a mediator between his French missionary colleagues and Touré's government. His appointment tamped down tension for a time, but in 1967 Touré abruptly expelled all French Catholic missionaries from Guinea. As they were still the majority of clergy in the country, Tchidimbo was left without essential personnel to staff Guinea's parishes. Finally, in 1971 Touré turned on Tchidimbo, accused him of participation in a plot to overthrow the government, and threw him in prison. Narrowly escaping execution, the archbishop did nearly nine years of hard labor before his release in 1979.[8] This "Calvary" of the Catholic Church in independent Guinea turned out to be both painful and protracted.

[Guinea offers the most dramatic example of a new African state targeting the Catholic Church as a bastion of colonialism in the former French colonies of sub-Saharan Africa.] Yet Sékou Touré did not have a monopoly on scathing views of the church's role in French Africa in the

turbulent years just before and after independence—some French observers attacked it for the exact opposite reason. In 1956, François Méjan,
a French Protestant lawyer and civil servant with socialist ties, expertise in religious questions, and administrative experience in Africa,
published a lengthy article in *L'année politique et économique* entitled
"L'Église catholique et la France d'Outre-Mer."[9] The following year, it appeared with Fischbacher as a stand-alone book with the more provocative title of *Le Vatican contre la France d'Outre-Mer?*[10] Though the title
ended in a question mark, there was no doubt in Méjan's mind that the
Vatican was systematically undermining France's control of its overseas
possessions just as much as, if not more than, "'British intrigue,'" "'American propaganda'" or "'Communist agitation.'"[11] Méjan felt compelled
to write the book "out of a duty to my country and out of fear for the
future of its language and culture." He was outraged by what he called
the church's "new missionary doctrine," which he saw as diametrically
opposed to its "classic" missionary policy.[12] In Méjan's view, this novel
orientation was characterized by rhetoric of "de-occidentalizing" the
church, Vatican insistence that French missionaries renounce any loyalty to France, and the promotion of indigenous bishops over Frenchmen
in French-controlled territories. In his mind, this constituted an "abandonment of Western civilization."[13]

Méjan's criticism of the Catholic Church cannot be ascribed to his
Protestantism; in fact, he accused Protestant missions in French Africa
of pursuing similar policies.[14] His outrage instead stemmed from his devotion to state secularism or *laïcité,* a cause he tried to further throughout
his professional career, as well as his firm conviction that France's culture, language, and values were a boon to the African populations under
its rule. His perception that the church was openly repudiating French
civilization was all the more galling to him because the French government, via the FIDES program, was heavily subsidizing church endeavors
across the Overseas Territories.[15] "Will France continue to pay for the
clergy (missionary and autochthonous) and its projects when they no
longer recommend a French presence (even in a federal arrangement
with internal autonomy in the African territories and Madagascar), but
instead favor nationalist claims of total independence?" he asked his
readers.[16] Méjan "condemned" colonialism and racism, declaring that

they were nonexistent in the French Union, which he imagined as a beneficent force in the lives of its peoples. He bristled with resentment of both internal and external critics of French rule, remarking that certain anticolonialist "Powers" (e.g., the United States) practiced racial discrimination at home. He likewise declared, "I hate all fanaticism and intolerance," while lambasting the anti-Western and "anti-white xenophobia" that he discerned in some new "Afro-Asiatic" states, which he accused of "totalitarianism."[17]

Despite the hysterical edge to his arguments, Méjan was no quixotic voice in the wilderness. His book was widely reviewed and debated in a host of Catholic and Protestant periodicals, mainstream French press organs, and prominent media outlets abroad, including *Der Spiegel* and *Time* magazine.[18] He also sent copies of his work to dozens of French ambassadors, legislators, ministers, generals, scholars, and civil servants.[19] Acknowledgments of receipt in his files include signed notes from General de Gaulle; Minister of Justice François Mitterrand; French Socialist Party leader and recent prime minister Guy Mollet; legislator and recent governor general of Algeria Jacques Soustelle; Protestant legislator and antislavery activist Emmanuel La Gravière, and the outgoing and incoming French ambassadors to the Vatican, Wladimir d'Ormesson and Roland de Margerie.[20] In his letter of thanks to Méjan, d'Ormesson opined, "we are showered with ingratitude on all sides. We have spread civilization far and wide and now this civilization pushes us away in the very name of the doctrine that gave rise to it . . . it is a bitter cycle."[21]

Thus, while Méjan and like-minded French people felt that the church was forsaking a generous French civilizing mission in Africa at midcentury, Sékou Touré believed it was perpetuating a harmful one. Though Méjan and Touré probably never crossed paths, their contrasting perspectives comprise a virtual "conversation" about the historic role and the future of the Catholic Church in Africa at midcentury. The church found itself at a crossroads in the postwar period, as the inhabitants of its vast mission fields in Africa began to question and reject European political and cultural dominance. Taken together, Touré's and Méjan's views illustrate the delicacy of the Vatican's position at the end of French rule in Africa. On the one hand, the church was attacked by Africans, including a bevy of devout Catholics, for being Eurocentric, insensible to African culture, and too often personified by racist French missionaries who looked down upon fellow African believers. On the other hand, critics such as Méjan and conservative French clergy felt that church attempts to make Catholicism more attractive to Africans constituted a betrayal of France, of Western civilization, and of the legions of French missionaries who had made sacrifices and continued to work to anchor it in African soil in the first place.

It was not merely the Vatican that was caught between these poles, however. In fact, the most compelling drama was taking place in the hearts and minds of the constituents of a Franco-African Catholic world forged by conquest, colonization, missions, and conversions, and knit together by Catholic faith, Catholic education, Catholic press, and Catholic charities. These constituents included French missionaries in Africa, their superiors in France, African Catholic students in France destined to become leaders in their home countries, French and African Catholic intellectuals, young African clergymen, and French donors to Catholic endeavors in Africa. Many of these people found themselves in spiritual crisis as they tried to reconcile their Catholicism with the political and cultural shifts taking place around them. Young Catholics in Dakar, for example, turned to their deputy to the French National Assembly and fellow believer Léopold Senghor in 1947 because they were fed up with a racist French priest in their community. In Saumur, France, in 1952, a pair of newly arrived African Catholic students advised their peers to nurture their faith despite painful social isolation and their horror at the lack of Catholic observance in the metropole. The same year, in Koumi, Upper Volta (Burkina Faso), embarrassed French missionaries complained to their superiors because their religious vows precluded them from eating with priests who did not belong to their congregation, which forced their African deacons and seminarians to sit at separate tables at mealtimes and provoked accusations of racism. In Paris, in 1954, a young French chaplain to Catholic students from the colonies earned the wrath of his superiors when he publicly endorsed his charges' radical calls for decolonization.

Thus, at midcentury, these denizens of the Franco-African Catholic world were preoccupied with the future of France's African colonies, the place of Catholicism in Africa, and the extent to which their personal loyalties should lie with the Vatican, France, or emerging African states. They discussed the church's historical relationship to its Western heritage, its role in a French "civilizing mission" in Africa, and whether Catholic theology endorsed or repudiated the idea of colonization. Moreover, they debated how to reconcile Catholicism with African culture, how best to train African clergy to replace French priests, how to keep Africa's Catholic elite devout, and how Catholics should relate to Muslims and communists.

Giving equal weight to French and African voices, both prominent and obscure, this book recaptures conversations and heated arguments between Catholics on the future of France, Africa, and Catholicism itself from the end of World War II through the Second Vatican Council (Vatican II) and shows how they mattered deeply in the broader political, intellectual, and cultural movements of the time. The book's protagonists include the long-suffering Archbishop Tchidimbo, whose French missionary superiors derided his precocity and intelligence until he became their precious ally in their dealings with Touré and, subsequently, a near martyr in Guinea's labor camps. Monsignor Marcel Lefebvre, the most powerful French prelate in Africa for most of the postwar period, also figures frequently in these pages. A conservative, Lefebvre would later reject Vatican II in a spectacular revolt against the papacy, but he was no stranger to controversy during his tenure in Africa. Opposed to Lefebvre was a younger generation of French missionaries with a more leftist bent, such as Father Joseph Michel, the chaplain to colonial students in Paris who adopted their critical views of French rule, and Father Luc Moreau, a Dominican who advocated for Catholic rapprochement with Muslims in Africa.

Besides Tchidimbo, other leading African actors include Alioune Diop, a Senegalese Catholic convert from Islam who founded the renowned journal *Présence africaine*. Diop served as the behind-the-scenes architect of the negritude movement, while moving in the most rarified European intellectual circles and getting Pope John XXIII's ear about making the church less European and more truly universal. He shared convictions with Albert Tévoéjdrè from Dahomey and Joseph Ki-Zerbo from Upper Volta, African students in France who became

African Catholic intellectual leaders. They campaigned furiously (albeit unsuccessfully) for a no vote in the 1958 referendum on the French Community, demonstrating that African Catholics were not necessarily quiescent allies of France. In addition to the trajectories of these individuals, evidence from numerous other African students, French missionaries, African clergy, and French and Vatican officials elucidate how Catholics on both continents navigated and shaped the crucial political and religious transformations of the era.

This study brings Europe, Africa, religion, and empire together in innovative, original ways. It provides new perspectives on decolonization, on black internationalism, and on the reform of the Catholic Church in the 1960s. France, its sub-Saharan African territories, and the Catholic Church were all in crisis at midcentury, as dramatic changes unfolded within and around them. French and African Catholics participated in and grappled with these simultaneous and often related shifts, which reoriented their political, intellectual, and religious horizons.

Four significant, interrelated developments combined to shape the Franco-African Catholic world in the postwar period. The first was the ongoing dissolution of the French Empire. While few thought its liquidation was inevitable or even probable in the early postwar period, opinions changed gradually over time. In May of 1954, France lost its nine-year struggle to keep Indochina. Just several months after that war concluded, another erupted in Algeria, a conflict that would polarize the French public between 1954 and 1962 and bring down the Fourth Republic in 1958. In 1956, Tunisia and Morocco achieved independence from France and the so-called *loi-cadre* devolved more authority to territorial assemblies in French West Africa and French Equatorial Africa, effectively giving Africans more say in their own government.[22] Indeed, though France had started aggressively investing in its sub-Saharan African possessions in 1946 via the FIDES mechanism, it was unable to stem mounting African demands for more autonomy.

By 1958, de Gaulle's new regime was offering sub-Saharan African territories the choice between complete independence, effective immediately, and increased autonomy within a French Community of mutual assistance. Touré's Guinea was the only one that opted out in 1958, but by the end of 1960 the rest of French sub-Saharan Africa had gained full independence.[23] After the departure of Algeria in 1962, France's once vast empire was reduced to a clutch of scattered possessions, including Guyana, Djibouti, and islands in the Caribbean, the North Atlantic, the Indian Ocean, and the South Pacific. This protracted process of dismantlement, which was particularly violent, sordid, and painful in Algeria, rocked a French public haunted by the humiliation of defeat and occupation at the hands of the Germans, wracked by extreme political divisions between a newly empowered Communist Party and a Gaullist right, and anxious about the country's diminished place in the new, polarized Cold War world dominated by the American and Soviet superpowers.[24]

The second important development was the emergence of a more robust Catholic left in France. The backdrop of imperial crisis informed how reactionary French Catholics like Lefebvre confronted African independence, yet it also stimulated progressive Catholic currents that had emerged just before and during World War II. While Catholicism had long been the almost exclusive property of the conservative right wing in France, the trials of the occupation and the persecution of Jews during the war, followed closely by violent colonial conflicts and revelations of the French use of torture in Algeria, galvanized left-leaning French Catholic activists who tended to support the aspirations of colonial peoples for independence.[25] These people should not automatically be conflated with France's new postwar Christian Democratic party, the Mouvement républicain populaire (MRP), whose leadership included many staunch French imperialist patriots fervently opposed to decolonization.[26] Instead, they increasingly popped up in French pulpits, Catholic charities, and missionary organizations in the course of the postwar period and allied themselves with Africans to challenge colonialism and conservative French Catholic paradigms.

The third crucial factor was the rise of a vocal and determined French African political and cultural elite, which was disproportionately Catholic. On the cultural side, Alioune Diop was a vital leader. In *Présence africaine,* in the books that came out of his publishing house, in international conferences of black intellectuals that he convened, and in his own writings, he devoted significant space to the relationship between Africans and Catholicism and the delineation of a Catholic negritude. On the political front, though Catholics were in the minority in French Africa, seven of the fourteen French territories of sub-Saharan Africa, including the Trust Territories of Togo and Cameroon, had Catholic heads of state at independence. These included Félix Houphouët-Boigny of Côte d'Ivoire, Hubert Maga of Dahomey, Léon M'Ba of Gabon, Sylvanus Olympio of Togo, Léopold Senghor of Senegal, Maurice Yaméogo of Upper Volta, and Fulbert Youlou of Congo (a former priest). Of course, the place of faith in politics and governance varied greatly for each of these men. What was even more significant was the emergence of a young militant African Catholic elite, who pushed their political and intellectual elders (including Diop and the statesmen listed above) to more radical stances. Beginning in the late 1940s, African students began traveling to France for higher education in greater numbers. Catholics were heavily overrepresented in their ranks, because of the ongoing importance of mission schools in the African territories. In the metropole, some of these young Catholics lost their faith, but others married their Catholicism to the causes of African self-determination and making the Catholic Church less "European" and more hospitable to Africans.

Last but not least, the final decisive element in the mix was the brewing tension within the Catholic Church itself. Like France and Africa, the church was at a crossroads at midcentury. It faced a recurring dilemma in stark new terms: would it be the beacon of the poor and oppressed masses of the world, or an institution aligned with the rich, the powerful, and the status quo in colonial empires and Latin American dictatorships? The specter of decolonization in the French Empire, which was the largest remaining European colonial empire primarily evangelized by Catholics, provoked internal challenges for the church that were emerging in various forms around the globe. As some African Catholics were clamoring for political independence from France and demanding church ceremonies that employed their languages and reflected their cultures, a Catholic theological movement (later christened liberation theology) began to take shape in Latin America, critiquing the crushing social inequality there.[27] Europe, too, had versions of this ferment, illustrated by the worker-priests in France, Belgium, and Italy who donned laymen's clothing and labored in factories alongside the men and women they hoped to reach.[28] The Cold War context gave these Catholic innovations new urgency in the eyes of some church leaders, who feared that if the church did not respond to its radical constituencies, activists would turn their backs on Catholicism and embrace communism instead. Moreover, Africa was particularly important to the Vatican from a strategic perspective, as it was one of the few places left on the globe where mass expansion of the faith appeared feasible, if communism and Islam could be kept at bay.

As this book explores the turbulence produced by the unique conjuncture of these four developments, it challenges existing, disparate literatures on decolonization, negritude, and Catholicism, and fills blind spots within and between them. In the first place, "decolonization" is a broad term in these pages. Half a century after many sub-Saharan African countries gained independence from European rule, the historical literature on decolonization in Africa is still dominated by studies focusing on political transitions from European colonial regimes to African states, although recent scholarship has challenged the teleological assumption that nation-states were its inevitable outcome.[29] This book, however, begins from the premise that processes of "decolonization," defined as the ending or limiting of European hegemony and power, touched private institutions and mentalities that lay well outside state apparatus.[30] It thus offers a new account of late colonialism and early independence in French sub-Saharan Africa by viewing them through the prism of religion.

Indeed, Catholicism was one of the most important mediums of contact between Europeans and Africans in the colonial era, and Catholic institutions and charities have formed one of the most enduring links between France and its former colonies. Moreover, as today's burgeoning African Catholicism is one of the most tangible legacies of European expansion in Africa, it is time that scholars paid closer attention to Catholic activities and their impacts in this crucial era of transition. For a long time, historians outside the church neglected the importance of Catholicism and the ongoing relevance of Catholic faith and institutions in modern France and the French Empire. While missionaries have recently attracted more scholarly attention, researchers have been most interested in whether they were "handmaidens" who paved the way for French rule abroad, or independent agents who undermined it.[31] Very few historians have considered how missions, missionaries, and indigenous believers navigated the departure of European governments from former colonial territories.[32] This book foregrounds neglected connections between religion and decolonization in the francophone world by investigating how both French and African actors thought about the disentanglement of Catholic institutions and theology from the colonial order, as well those actors' impact in France, Africa, and the Catholic Church itself.[33]

Africanists who focus on the colonial period in French Africa were quicker than secular historians of France and its empire to recognize both the value and the pitfalls of missionary sources. Yet in many cases, with some significant exceptions, African Christians have not been the targets of their inquiries.[34] In African history, the celebration of nationalism as a rejection of colonialism long dominated the historiographies of many individual countries.[35] In this paradigm, "European" religions appeared as suspect holdovers from the colonial era and their believers as colonial "collaborators" or "traitors" to African culture. Historians attracted to "authentic" Africans, or to uncovering African resistance to colonial rule, nationalist or otherwise, have thus not been overly interested in African Christians. Even in the case of prominent and celebrated figures such as Léopold Senghor, much of the scholarship tends to downplay his faith and its impact on his politics, writing, leadership, and worldview.

The example of Senghor also illustrates that religion is largely missing from the study of negritude and black internationalism. This may be because scholars with secular bents are less interested in religion, or because the Christian faith of some of negritude's key figures appears to disrupt their status in the intellectual pantheon.[36] Yet, as this book shows, in addition to the professed Christianity of some of its key figures, there was an avowedly Catholic strand of negritude composed of leading black Catholic intellectuals and priests. Led by Alioune Diop, they argued for a truly universal Catholicism that embraced black people and African cultures. Moreover, the evidence presented here shows that powerful figures in the Vatican heard their message and heeded it.

African Catholic thus tells a new story of Catholic reform, showing how decolonization was a pivotal factor in the reorientation of the church in the mid-twentieth century. Some historians have claimed that the 1940s and 1950s were "the hour of the Church"—a golden age of Catholicism before the turmoil of the 1960s left it shunned by former believers. Indeed, the Catholic Church was the only "traditional" European religion gaining adherents in Europe in the 1940s and 1950s, not least because of the new prominence of its affiliate Christian Democratic parties in France, Germany, the Netherlands, Belgium, Italy, and Austria.[37] In his influential book *What Happened at Vatican II?* John O'Malley claims that in contrast to many previous ecumenical councils, "no obvious crisis troubled the Catholic Church" on the eve of Vatican II. Rather, he argues, setting aside Communist persecution of the church behind the iron curtain, "the church in the decade and a half since the end of World War II projected an image of vigor and self-confidence."[38]

That story makes most sense if one is viewing the church primarily in the context of Western Europe and the United States. A wider lens suggests, however, that the fates of Catholic missions and their converts amid the dismantling of European empires—and the French one in particular—were crucial background to Vatican II, on both cultural and political fronts. As both Touré's and Méjan's words illustrate, the church was closely linked to the reigning order in the French Empire, and the church hierarchy thus faced the prospect of French decolonization with a host of conflicting impulses. On the one hand, it was eager to maintain, secure, and grow its following in colonized regions in the event of a French exodus, which pointed toward a policy of backing indigenous independence movements. On the other, it did not want to lose the support of the French missionaries it would have to continue to rely on, as well as conservative French Catholics who were emotionally and financially invested in empire. Moreover, it feared that communists and Muslims would gain influence at its expense in the newly independent countries once French power and influence were removed. Yet even in the cases where the French were actively fighting Muslims (in Algeria) and communists (in Indochina), church officials ultimately became dismayed by the violence and wary of the divisions it sparked among French Catholics at home. At the same time, they became increasingly aware of, and receptive to, the calls of African Catholic intellectuals and clergy for a church that was truly universal, and not Eurocentric.

Under Pius XII, the Vatican muddled along by promoting unity and gesturing to its constituencies on both sides of the colonial divide. In his 1951 encyclical on the promotion of Catholic missions, *Evangelii praecones,* Pius had high praise for missionaries, yet reiterated earlier popes' warnings about divorcing evangelism from national interests. "It is in keeping with your apostolate," he told them, "not to be hampered by any national frontiers." Moreover, he claimed, "Christian faith and universal charity transcend all opposing camps and national boundaries and reach out to the ends of the earth."[39] In his 1955 Christmas message, Pius explicitly addressed anticolonial agitation head on, trying to strike a balance between support for self-determination for colonized peoples and respect for a paternalist conception of a European civilizing mission: "Let not [colonial] peoples be denied a fair and progressive political freedom, nor hindered in its pursuit," he said. "To Europe, however, they will give credit for their advancement, to that Europe without whose influence, extended to all fields, they might be drawn by a blind nationalism to plunge into chaos or slavery."[40] By 1957, demonstrating the Vatican's preoccupation with Africa in particular, he was issuing another encyclical on missions, *Fidei donum,* that focused on the continent. Acknowledging and celebrating the fact that Africa was on the cusp of self-determination, he nonetheless called for Europeans to redouble their missionary efforts in Africa by sending any money and clergy they could spare, betraying his fears that the window for "civilizing" was closing.[41]

Pius died in 1958, just days after the referendum on the French Community took place across Africa. His successor, John XXIII, who initiated Vatican II, had been nuncio to France and a Vatican observer at UNESCO, so he had a unique understanding of the questions roiling the Franco-African Catholic world. These were, in fact, questions for the church as a whole, and they showcase the difficult dilemmas it faced as it confronted a new geopolitical landscape in which European influence was waning and people in the "developing world" were asserting themselves. The awkward dance of the church hierarchy as it tried to find a position between Catholic advocates of political and cultural decolonization and devout champions of the French Empire was just one instance

Pope John XXIII and Bernardin Gantin, archbishop of Cotonou, 1960. Courtesy of
ASMA, Rome.

of its halting attempts to define its place in the world in the shifting political and social landscapes of the mid-twentieth century. The path to
change at Vatican II was not a straightforward one: this book show-
cases the inability of the church hierarchy to stake out a clear position
on questions of colonization and decolonization, or to contain the dissension of the faithful around them in the postwar period. Despite
these challenges, however, the trajectory of Catholicism since the 1960s
suggests that the church proved much more successful at negotiating

"decolonization" in sub-Saharan Africa than holding on to its be-lievers in Europe. ⌉

This book lies at the intersection of political history, social history, intellectual history, and the history of religion. It marries exhaustive research in the archives of Catholic missions and of various arms of the French state with the published work of French and African Catholic intellectuals. Though Vatican archives remain closed for the period in question, many documents from the Sacred Congregation for the Prop-agation of the Faith or Propaganda Fide, the arm of Vatican bureaucracy dedicated to evangelism, surface in missionary archives. Indeed, mis-sions and missionaries occupy a privileged place in this research, as they were the fulcrums of the Franco-African Catholic world and served as transmitters of faith, money, and education from French to African pop-ulations, while communicating ideas about Africa to French Catholics. Missionaries' various priorities, prejudices, and blind spots played an important role in how Africans encountered Catholicism, and how French Catholics understood Africans and Africa.

At the same time, the book highlights the experiences and contribu-tions of a crucial generation of African Catholic students and clergy who came of age in the postwar period. While it casts a broad net geograph-ically, drawing on examples from across French sub-Saharan Africa, this book does not treat the role of Catholics or Catholicism in each specific French African territory at independence. What it does do is delineate, for the first time, the importance of French and African Catholics in po-litical and cultural processes of decolonization in French Africa and in reorienting the Catholic Church as a whole at midcentury.

The complex political and ecclesiastical landscape of postwar French sub-Saharan Africa requires a brief explanation. While the first French outposts on the coast of Senegal dated to the seventeenth century, the vast majority of France's holdings in the region were ac-quired and "pacified" in the late nineteenth and early twentieth centu-ries. They were then incorporated into two large administrative struc-tures known as the federations of French West Africa (AOF) and French Equatorial Africa (AEF), which were each headed by a governor general who oversaw the executives of each component colony. French West Af-rica, established in 1895, included the colonies of Côte d'Ivoire, Dahomey (Benin), Guinea, Mauritania, Niger, Senegal, Sudan (Mali), and Upper Volta (Burkina Faso). French Equatorial Africa, set up in 1910, was comprised of Chad, Congo-Brazzaville, Gabon, and Ubangi-Shari (Central African Republic). Prior to World War II, nearly all of the African inhabitants of these federations were French subjects, not citizens. The only important exception, aside from a miniscule number of notables, was the small group of full-fledged citizens in Senegal's Four Communes of Dakar, Rufisque, Gorée, and Saint-Louis, whose right to vote and send a deputy to the French National Assembly had been confirmed during World War I.[42] At the end of that conflict, France added two more territories to its sub-Saharan African holdings: portions of defeated Germany's former colonies of Togo and Cameroon. Designated mandates under the supervision of the League of Nations, these territories were governed much like the rest of French Africa, though France was technically not sovereign in them and their residents never had French nationality (see map 1).[43]

At the close of World War II, the new French regime began referring to the French Empire as the French Union and to its colonies as Overseas Territories. Recognizing the important role of the colonies in the triumph of Free France, as well as growing internal resistance to and international opprobrium for the perpetuation of the same old colonial rule, French officials sought to reimagine and reconfigure their vast, heterogeneous holdings around the world. According to the "Lamine Guèye law" of May 7, 1946, known for the Senegalese deputy who proposed it, the populations of France's Overseas Territories—including those of West Africa and Equatorial Africa—became French citizens. Ambiguities as to what exactly this meant persisted in France's Constitution of 1946, but Africans had gained the fundamental "right to have rights." Colonial forced labor was abolished and Africans were empowered to vote for representatives in territorial assemblies and the French National Assembly, while retaining the ability to regulate civil affairs according to their "customs" and not the French Civil Code.[44] Meanwhile, the mandates of Togo and Cameroon became Trust Territories under the auspices of the new United Nations, but were still administered by French officials. As noted earlier, the political ground in French Africa shifted again in 1958 with the advent of the Fifth Republic and de

Empire → Union → Comm unity

Gaulle's referendum on replacing the French Union with the French Community. The Community proved to be short-lived, as all of the French holdings in sub-Saharan Africa, including the Trust Territories, acceded to full independence in 1960.

Meanwhile, over the course of the late nineteenth and early twentieth centuries, Catholic ecclesiastical jurisdictions in French Africa gradually came into alignment with colonial political boundaries, though there were some exceptions. As in the case of their French temporal counterparts, the earliest Catholic presence in coastal regions was centuries old—Portuguese Franciscans had first tried to evangelize parts of present-day Senegal, Gambia, and Guinea-Bissau in the fifteenth century—but the most far-reaching missionary expansion took place much later.[45] Beginning in the mid-nineteenth century, the Holy See entrusted most of what became the colonies of French West Africa and French Equatorial Africa to three principal French missionary groups: the Fathers of the Holy Spirit (Spiritans), the Society of African Missions (sometimes called the Fathers of Lyon), and the Society of the Missionaries of Africa (White Fathers).[46] Together, they occupied nearly all of the episcopal seats, which were known as apostolic vicariates and prefectures before they became official archdioceses and dioceses when the church hierarchy was instituted in French Africa in 1955. The Spiritans evangelized Senegal, most of Guinea, Gabon, Ubangi-Shari, and the French Congo; the White Fathers held almost exclusive sway in Sudan and Upper Volta; and the Society of African Missions were most active in Côte d'Ivoire, Dahomey, and Togo (see map 2). In each territory, the leading missionary society controlled the executive decisions about Catholic undertakings such as schools and new mission stations, staffed the parishes and missions with its own priests, and founded seminaries to train up African clergy.

Of course, these dominant French missionary groups did not work alone. They were assisted by numerous congregations of French nuns, and, over time, by African sisters. In the postwar period, they increasingly relied on other male missionaries for help, particularly in specialized domains like education. They also began turning to secular clergy (i.e., priests who had not taken extra vows to abide by the rules of a congregation or apostolic society), including their own African seminary graduates and French diocesan priests recruited by *Fidei donum*, to man their parishes. Yet in almost all cases their members remained at the helm of African dioceses and archdioceses until they turned them over to African prelates. The research presented here thus draws most heavily on their archives, rather than those of groups that made smaller contributions, or those of female missionaries.[47] This means that this book is largely, but not exclusively, populated by French and African men. The Catholic Church was and remains a patriarchal, male-led institution in Europe and in Africa. Moreover, the African political and intellectual elite examined here was also overwhelmingly male. The book evokes the experiences of female African Catholic students in France and offers glimpses into how some African women perceived Catholicism, but many fruitful avenues on Catholic women in postwar Africa remain to be explored.[48]

Meanwhile, reception of Catholicism in French Africa varied widely from place to place and depended on a host of factors, including missionary methods, African perceptions of French rule, ethnic and social

Table I.1 African Catholics in French Africa, 1955

Territory	Total Population	African Catholics	% Catholic
Senegal	2,684,660	78,319	2.9
Sudan	3,510,219	8,458	0.2
Upper Volta	3,242,379	89,314	2.8
Guinea	2,247,318	17,941	0.8
Côte d'Ivoire	2,498,236	160,606	6.4
Dahomey	1,985,698	181,039	9.1
Niger	2,561,506	4,461	0.2
TOTAL AOF	18,730,016	540,138	2.9
Congo-Brazzaville	755,575	213,360	28.2
Gabon	378,290	150,550	39.8
Ubangi-Shari	1,134,092	76,482	6.7
Chad	1,950,000	21,822	1.1
TOTAL AEF	4,217,957	462,214	11.0
Togo	1,045,348	156,847	15.0
Cameroon	3,330,287	587,362	17.6

Source: Adapted from Délégation apostolique de Dakar, *Statistiques annuelles des missions catholiques en Afrique française, année 1954–1955* (Dakar: Imprimerie Mission Catholique), ACSSp 2F 1.3 a5.

Note: There are no statistics for Mauritania, which did not have a Catholic population. While these church statistics are not 100% accurate for total population, they convey the varying rates of conversion across French sub-Saharan Africa.

divides in particular communities, and the presence of Islam. Islam was particularly strong in the northern regions of French sub-Saharan Africa but was making increasing inroads in its southern reaches at midcentury. Church statistics from 1955 demonstrate that missionaries had more success where Islam was not as much of a factor: in Côte d'Ivoire and Dahomey in French West Africa; in Gabon and Congo-Brazzaville in French Equatorial Africa; as well as in the Trust Territories of Togo and Cameroon. Overall, missionaries counted 540,138 African Catholics in a total population of 18,730,016 in French West Africa, which amounted to 2.9 percent, whereas in French Equatorial Africa they counted 462,214 Catholics out of 4,217,957 for nearly 11 percent, a significant difference.[49] In Togo, Catholics made up 15 percent of the African population and in Cameroon, they accounted for almost 18 percent. Yet, as noted, Catholics were greatly overrepresented in the ranks of the African political and intellectual elite at midcentury.

This book is organized thematically, so there is some chronological overlap between chapters. The first two provide the political and intellectual landscape before the rest turn to the key constituencies and urgent questions that animated the Franco-African Catholic world between World War II and Vatican II. The book highlights forces that knit that world together—and others that threatened it—through its close examination of relationships and dialogues across political, racial, and religious differences. Pessimistic French missionaries like Marcel Lefebvre worried that a Catholic future for Africa was in danger of being lost amid decolonization and church reform in the 1950s and 1960s. Yet the great irony is that the seismic shifts of the era had quite a different outcome. In their aftermath, European Catholicism began hemorrhaging believers, while African adherents grew apace. As a result, the Franco-African Catholic world endures today, but its dynamics have changed. Now African priests come to France in droves to fill empty pulpits, a striking reversal from colonial times.

1

POSTWAR WINDS OF CHANGE

Church and State in French Africa

IN JANUARY 1947, Léopold Senghor, who was then representing Senegal as a deputy in the French National Assembly, penned a letter of complaint to Monsignor Louis Le Hunsec, the superior general of the Spiritans, the French missionary congregation that controlled the Catholic hierarchy in Senegal and provided most of the colony's priests.[1] Senghor, a Catholic who had excelled in Spiritan mission schools as a boy and had considered joining the priesthood, was very respectful toward Le Hunsec, who had served in Dakar as the apostolic vicar of Senegambia from 1920 to 1926.[2] Yet the deputy nonetheless forwarded an angry petition from "a group of his young Catholic constituents" concerning a French Spiritan, Father Charles Catlin. They had implored Senghor to see Le Hunsec and make sure that Catlin, then on leave in France, was not sent back to Dakar, where he served as chaplain general of French West African forces.[3] "This priest is a first-class negrophobe," they complained, "and we do not want him anymore. In his conversation, in his entire attitude, in many instances, he displays his complete contempt for those with black skin." They closed their missive with a threat: "If he comes back, he may regret it. We cannot answer for what might happen to him. It would be better not to give us the opportunity to act."[4]

threat

Senghor agreed wholeheartedly with Dakar's bellicose Catholic youth. As a student, he had clashed with Father Albert Lalouse, the director of the Spiritans' seminary in Senegal, who Senghor felt discriminated against his African pupils. Senghor later described Lalouse as a "pious man, but a harsh one, whom we accused of colonialism. He constantly emphasized our flaws as blacks and denounced our lack of civilization."[5] In a follow-up letter to Le Hunsec in March of 1947, Senghor drew the superior general's attention to the "seriousness of the religious situation" in postwar Senegal. "Unfortunately," the deputy observed, "missionaries, who were the most liberal Europeans [in Africa] before the war, fail to comprehend the Revolution the war has wrought in minds and in fact."[6] Senghor meant that the experience of the war, in which hundreds of thousands of France's colonial soldiers had fought to defend the metropole, had raised African expectations for more say in their own affairs, both in the realm of politics and, in the case of African Catholics, within the church.

As a result, Senghor urged French clergy in Africa to advocate for change within the new French Union established by the 1946 constitution, which had made France's African subjects into citizens of their respective territories.[7] "Missionaries should not simply approve, but rather advocate for a radical shift in relations between Europeans and Africans, and especially in political institutions," he advised. "They must refrain, above all, from anti-Socialism or anti-Communism. I permit myself to speak frankly about this as I am neither a Freemason nor a Communist, and I call myself a Catholic in public," he wrote. In addition, he felt it was imperative to fill the post of apostolic vicar of Senegambia, left vacant after the 1946 resignation of the Pétainist Spiritan Augustin Grimault, with someone who "accepts the revolution brought about by the new constitution."[8]

The words of Senghor and of Dakar's militant young believers reveal significant currents of rebellion among African Catholics in the wake of World War II. These Catholics worshipped, married, and baptized their children in a missionary church still overwhelmingly staffed by white French clergy. Moreover, many of them felt that French missionaries reinforced the colonial order by equating Catholicism with "superior" French civilization. The fact that Grimault and other prominent

French Catholic figures in Africa had publicly supported Marshal Pétain's collaborationist Vichy regime while African soldiers, including Senghor himself, languished in German prisoner-of-war camps or died fighting for Free France, only fueled African ire toward the missions.[9] Their growing frustration with the church reflected their broader irritation with French administrative and military authorities, who seemed to want to return to the colonial status quo without recognizing or rewarding African sacrifices in the war. Such tensions ran particularly high in Dakar, the sprawling administrative capital of French West Africa. The brutal French repression of a 1944 protest at nearby Camp Thiaroye, which killed dozens of African soldiers demanding their rightful pay after fighting to liberate metropolitan France, was still fresh in many minds there.[10]

Yet while some French clergymen such as Monsignor Grimault or Father Catlin apparently did not comprehend the mounting African desire for postwar change, there were in fact new forces at work both within and upon the Catholic missions in French Africa in the mid to late 1940s. Together with the activism of a militant African Catholic elite, these new currents would ultimately bring about important transformations in the missions in the two decades that followed. They included novel collaborative efforts between rival missionary congregations to pool resources across territorial borders, a strong Vatican push for the training of more African clergy, and French secular authorities' adoption of what they termed a "positive religious policy," which reversed a forty-year-old administrative stance by fully embracing Catholic missions as valuable allies. Indeed, beginning in 1946, state funding flowed freely to Catholic schools and healthcare initiatives all across French Africa, enabling a vast expansion of Catholic infrastructure and social services.

Of course, these new developments did not all point in the same direction. Vatican initiatives, though halting at the outset, aimed to extricate Catholicism from the prevailing colonial order and create a church manned by African clergy. And while some missionary executives tried to act in the spirit of the Vatican's directives, French priests often had a hard time divorcing themselves from the political, social, and racial structures that shaped their daily lives in French Africa. Moreover, the bracing new state support for missionary activity effectively tied Catholic institutions more closely to the French regime. A French government report from 1945 or 1946 contained the telling observation that there was an important difference between Catholic and Protestant missionaries in French Equatorial Africa: "The Catholics consider themselves French and want to be French; while the Protestants, due to their universalist and international tendencies, confuse the spiritual and the temporal," the author observed.[11] This administrative conflation of French and Catholic aims perfectly corroborates Léopold Senghor's 1947 critique of the church in French Africa. He felt it was not truly catholic in the universal sense, but French, and therefore "colonialist," often racist, and paternalistic toward its African believers.

This chapter examines the immediate postwar maneuvers of the missions, the Vatican, and the French administration vis-à-vis the future of the Catholic Church in French Africa. In doing so, it explores the genesis of a critical tension that underpins the rest of the book. Just at the moment when the French government began funding missions to act as subcontractors in the service of its development goals in Africa, the Vatican launched a sustained push toward a future African church freed from compromising colonial ties. These divergent aims mingled on the ground in daily mission practice and within the consciences of individual missionaries. They sowed confusion and controversy within French and African Catholic communities, whose members seized on and touted visions of the church that aligned with their respective worldviews. Educated, politically engaged African Catholics like Léopold Senghor looked to the church to use its message and its influence to dismantle the racial hierarchies of colonial French Africa as soon as possible, yet conservative missionaries reveled in their conclusion that state authorities had finally recognized the value of their French Catholic "civilizing mission" in Africa. As we will see, the nature of Catholicism's relationship to European colonialism in Africa only became more fraught as critics within and outside of Africa increasingly challenged the legitimacy of the French colonial order.

MISSIONS AFTER THE WAR

Some French missionary bishops did see a need to adapt to new postwar circumstances in Africa, though their thinking did not necessarily align with Senghor's recommendations. Their chief concern was evangelization, which had suffered during the war. The military mobilization of missionaries and of Africans, the interruption of contact with Europe, and attendant material hardships had all taken a toll on the missions' ability to proselytize. Wartime political divisions had not helped matters: while French Equatorial Africa had rallied to de Gaulle in 1940, Pétain's Vichy regime had prevailed in French West Africa until 1943 and had provoked strong disagreements among both French and African Catholics. In addition, missions feared that the newly ascendant French Communist Party was a dangerous rival for African hearts and minds. As a result, at the instigation of White Father and apostolic vicar of Ouagadougou Joanny Thévenoud, the prelates of French West Africa (with some glaring abstentions) met in Bobo-Dioulasso between November 26 and December 1, 1945 to engage in an unprecedented discussion of common challenges that crossed political and ecclesiastical jurisdictions. In response to those challenges, they formulated an ambitious program to combine their forces that resulted in significant new Catholic initiatives and institutions in French Africa.

The disruption of the war had exposed the limitations of the existing model of missionary evangelism, in which the dominant congregation in each jurisdiction treated its territory much like a fief, jealously guarding its control and eyeing its neighboring counterparts with suspicion. Thévenoud and others felt it was high time to try to create federal Catholic institutions across all of French West Africa, though not everyone agreed. The prominent Spiritan bishops Raymond Lerouge in Guinea and Grimault in Senegal refused to go to the meeting, exemplifying rivalries between congregations that would persist for years to come. Apostolic prefect of the Casamance Joseph Faye, the only other Spiritan and the only African prelate in French Africa, also did not attend, but sent a European Spiritan to represent him.[12] Faye, a quiet would-be monk who despaired in his role as superior to missionaries who openly displayed their racist contempt for him, likely did not want to sit around the table with his French counterparts.[13]

The assembled bishops treated a wide variety of subjects, but the most important outcome of their meeting was their creation of joint efforts designed to bolster Catholic influence in three key domains in French West Africa: education, the press, and social activism or, as they termed it, Catholic Action. They expressed their desire to create a training school in Côte d'Ivoire for African teachers and monitors for all the West African missions, as well as to invite the Society of the Sacred Heart of the Child Jesus to found a cross-federation secondary school for promising Catholic students, perhaps also to be located in Côte d'Ivoire.[14] To make their efforts truly collaborative, they proposed sharing the executive positions for federal organizations among their various congregations. Thus, Father Jacques Bertho of the Society of African Missions continued as federal director of Catholic instruction, a post originally created in 1942, and the White Fathers headed up the new federation-wide Catholic newspaper *Afrique nouvelle,* which was headquartered in Dakar as of 1947. Thévenoud hoped to find a Spiritan to be a director of Catholic works, to coordinate Catholic Action initiatives throughout the federation.[15]

The bishops also highlighted the training of African clergy, which, they pronounced, "should be among the first of our preoccupations." In their official report of the meeting, they painted an overly rosy picture of the status of the African clergy in their missions, congratulating themselves that "indigenous priests effectively fulfill the same functions in the ministry as their European counterparts," and noting that in Dahomey and Togo some of them were directors of schools or in sole charge of entire districts. Moreover, they claimed that "everywhere [African clergy] live the communal life of the missionary congregations that trained them."[16] A Vatican representative would see things quite differently when he toured French Africa a few months later, but it is clear that the bishops knew even before his arrival that Rome had high expectations on this front. They formally asked the pope for permission to admit seminary students born of illegitimate marriages and of non-Catholic parents, and to dispense such students from any "irregular" status as a result. "The reason for this," they wrote, "is that these missions have a great need for a numerous indigenous clergy and recruitment among legitimate children of Catholic parents is insufficient, and sometimes we meet with excellent children who would be barred for these reasons."[17]

They thus indicated their commitment to increasing the African clergy to their superiors at the Vatican. In the next several years, they would attempt to expand and improve their training of African priests, though racial tensions within the clergy would persist.

Monsignor Grimault, the conservative Pétainist who represented an important strand of old guard missionary thinking, was incensed by the conclusions reached in Bobo and interpreted the new spirit of cooperation as a direct assault on his authority in Dakar. "So they have decided to create a newspaper in Dakar," he wrote to superior general Le Hunsec. "By what right? Do you see me founding a newspaper in Ouagadougou? What authority could the conference of bishops in Ouagadougou have in Dakar or over Dakar? In whose name did Monsignor Thévenoud invite and preside over this meeting?"[18] Le Hunsec agreed with Thévenoud on the importance of federal initiatives and wanted the Spiritans to do their part, but he did not have the power to force Spiritan bishops, who derived their ecclesiastical powers from Rome, to participate. For example, several months later, when he tried to appoint a young Spiritan to take up the post of federal director of Catholic works in Dakar, Grimault refused to accept the man into his jurisdiction.[19] Grimault also unleashed his indignation on the Vatican, complaining of the White Fathers' newspaper plans to Pietro Cardinal Fumasoni-Biondi, the prefect of the Propaganda Fide.[20] At that moment, Grimault did not yet know that the Vatican's forthcoming emissary to Africa would support Thévenoud's efforts and view Grimault himself as an obstacle to Catholic progress in French Africa that had to be removed.

Indeed, the model of missionary unity and cooperation won out as the way forward for the missions, bitter opposition notwithstanding. *Afrique nouvelle,* for example, became the most important independent press organ in all of French Africa, though its White Father leadership continued to clash with the Spiritan hierarchy in Dakar for years to come. By the fall of 1946, Thévenoud was only more convinced that collaboration was the only possible course of action. "I do not think I am wrong to believe that the church in French West Africa has the greatest interest, in the current climate, in our combining all of our ideas and efforts," he wrote to Le Hunsec. "Because of the rapid evolution here, we must face up to new necessities."[21] The 1945 conference served as a template for future meetings and a model for other regions. Under the aegis of Monsignor Marcel Lefebvre, appointed as the Vatican's apostolic delegate to French Africa in 1948, the French missionary bishops of Africa held numerous conferences in the succeeding years, including an important meeting on Islam in 1955. In 1949, the bishops of French Equatorial Africa and Cameroon also took up the practice of regularly conferring and collaborating.[22] This novel spirit of intermissionary cooperation, and the newly created federal mission posts, provided a degree of hitherto unimaginable organization that allowed the church to take better advantage of the funding opportunities that the French colonial state began to send its way after 1946.

FATHER PROUVOST GOES ON TOUR

Meanwhile, as the war ended, the Vatican moved swiftly to assess the situation in French Africa. Many missions had not been able to send their regular annual reports to Rome during the conflict, and church officials wanted to get a clear sense of what was happening on the ground. Moreover, at the Propaganda Fide, Fumasoni-Biondi and his second-in-command, Monsignor Celso Costantini, were eager to resume efforts they had launched just before the war to promote the development of an indigenous clergy for the church in Africa. The experience of the war, together with mounting anticolonial violence in Asia and elsewhere, only reinforced their resolve.

In fact, the Vatican had been contemplating the dangers of Catholicism's close identification with Europe's colonial regimes around the world for over two decades. In 1919, Pope Benedict XV warned missionaries not to conflate their national interests with evangelism—they were supposed to be the messengers of God, not the imperial shock troops of their earthly countries.[23] In his 1926 encyclical *Rerum ecclesiae,* Pius XI specifically raised the question of how to safeguard Catholic interests in the event of anticolonial revolt. "Suppose that . . . the inhabitants, to render themselves independent, should wish to drive from their territory both the ruling officials and the missionaries of the foreign nation under whose rule they are?" he asked.[24]

To ward off this possibility, Pius called for the energetic cultivation of an indigenous clergy and the distancing of the church from colonial rule through a truly catholic commitment to universality.[25] Monsignor Faye's appointment as apostolic prefect of the Casamance in 1939 had represented a bold symbolic move toward the creation of an African church run by Africans, in the face of vociferous protests of French Spiritans on the ground and Faye himself. Yet it was just a baby step toward a goal that would require a much greater effort, and it would be a gross exaggeration to portray Vatican policies in interwar or postwar Africa as uniformly anticolonial or progressive. For example, only three years prior to Faye's elevation, in a gesture that appeared to cement ties between the French colonial state and the church in Africa, Pius XI had sent Archbishop of Paris Jean Cardinal Verdier to perform the consecration of the cathedral of the Souvenir Africain in Dakar, a building conceived by the Spiritans as an overtly patriotic monument to French colonization.[26]

Moreover, the Vatican had been much slower to insist on the training and promotion of indigenous clergy in French Africa as compared to Southeast Asia, reflecting widely held European prejudices that Africans were particularly backward and uncivilized, as well as the lower numbers of African converts they had to draw on. Still, its executives grasped the importance of change sooner, and more completely, than many French missionaries did. The challenge from their perspective was that the dearth of African clergy only exacerbated their deepening colonial conundrum in the rapidly evolving postwar landscape. Fumasoni-Biondi and Costantini had no alternative but to continue to rely on French personnel who tended to believe in the superiority of French civilization and were prone to confusing French aims with church interests. This difficulty was evident in their very first postwar initiative vis-à-vis French Africa: the sending of an official Vatican representative to assess the state of the missions and communicate Rome's postwar priorities *viva voce* to French clergy.

Their choice of emissary epitomized the tension between the Vatican's desire to change course in Africa and its ongoing dependency on French missionaries. In 1945, they selected Father Henri Prouvost of the Foreign Missions of Paris (MEP) to travel to Africa, bestowing on him the title of "Visiteur apostolique," which gave him wide-ranging power to speak and act on behalf of the pope.[27] He was thus simultaneously a Vatican representative and a French missionary of a certain vintage: born in 1895, Prouvost had left seminary in 1914 to serve in World War I, sustaining serious wounds in 1916. He returned to his studies in 1919, was ordained in 1921, and left for a mission in Bangalore that same year, where he became the director of a school. Returning to France in 1937, he founded an MEP junior seminary at Ménil-Flin, in Meurthe and Moselle, where he remained amidst the German invasion and the fighting accompanying the liberation until he received the Vatican's instructions to embark for Africa.[28]

Rome needed someone like Prouvost who could communicate easily with French missionaries, but whose outsider status enabled him to offer advice and criticism. As the MEP worked exclusively in Asia, he was a stranger to the petty rivalries between the French congregations in sub-Saharan Africa. Moreover, he brought firsthand knowledge of the Asian context, where the training and promotion of indigenous clergy was more advanced than in Africa. Yet like that of many of his colleagues in Africa, Prouvost's position was ambiguous. He was a patriot who felt that French colonization was entirely justified, and he harbored the racist, paternalistic impulses of a European who considered himself superior to Africans. Nonetheless, he also denounced reactionary bishops, called for renewal in the missions, and critiqued French priests' discrimination against African clergy.

Prouvost's tour was quite an undertaking: he spent over a year on the move between August 1945 and October 1946 and then two months debriefing in Rome. Following a grueling itinerary in slow-moving airplanes and trains on sparse, irregular schedules and bouncing over dirt roads in rickety, temperamental, interwar cars, he went from Algeria to Madagascar to Réunion, then to French Equatorial Africa and Cameroon, and finally crisscrossed French West Africa, Togo, and Morocco before returning to Europe. He compiled a detailed report for the Vatican, but as any extant copies are currently beyond the reach of historians, one must cull his personal correspondence, a few articles he composed for the MEP's *Echos missionnaires*, and records of the African missions for clues about what he thought of what he saw.[29] The richest source is a trove of private letters he wrote to his friend and MEP colleague Father Joseph Jean-Baptiste Cuenot, in which he grouched vociferously about his packed schedule, his angry intestines, sweating through his cassocks in overwhelming heat, the logistical difficulties of African travel, and some of the awkward situations he had to deal with, including trying to oust the unrepentant Grimault from Dakar.[30]

Prouvost's writings make it clear that he believed that the missions and the colonial state would benefit immensely from a more effective partnership, evincing little of the caution that Pius XI had urged in this domain in 1926. "When will the State comprehend that the best agents of civilization are our missionaries?" he wrote to Cuenot from Madagascar. "In general, the state leaves them alone, but does not help them! No, that would be contrary to the sacrosanct principles of *laïcité*."[31] In his magazine articles, he extolled the atmosphere of cooperation between French authorities and missionaries in Brazzaville: "If only we could say the same for all the French colonies!" he lamented.[32] In his opinion, such collaboration resulted in "the greatest good for the natives and for religion." Though he admitted that "collaboration" was a frightening word in postwar Europe, he argued that in Africa "collaboration" between missionaries and administrators should have no such unpleasant connotation, because it "assured the well-being, the prosperity of our dear blacks."[33] He clearly felt that French rule benefited Africa, most especially if deployed in conjunction with French missionaries.

Moreover, Prouvost viewed Africans in the condescending terms typical of Frenchmen his age. Stereotypical missionary portraits of Africans as exotic and dim-witted barbarians or as innocent, spiritual foils to debauched Europeans emerge from the articles he wrote for the *Echos missionnaires*.[34] "I even saw," he confided to his readers, "villages in Cameroon where no one wore a stitch of clothing, people wore belts decorated with pearls or women tore leaves off the trees each morning, which permitted them to change their dresses daily, like our elegant European fashionistas." When describing worship in an unspecified village, Prouvost drew a contrast between the ardor of the half-clothed, poor, yet devout African congregation which joined in the chants, and "many a mass in France, where the faithful leave it to a paltry choir, if not a sole cantor, to sing the praises of the Good Lord." Yet, describing a nocturnal celebration in this same village, he observed, "People here seem to wake up at the hour when we are going to bed. They are singing, dancing, clapping their hands, and the party goes on into the middle of the night, because Blacks never tire of turning in circles while incessantly repeating the same expressions."[35] Prouvost thus did not think outside dominant French narratives of African people, and generally felt that French rule over them was justified and beneficial.

Nevertheless, Prouvost rejected aspects of the missionary status quo in French Africa and recognized that French and missionary aims did not always align in the new postwar climate. First of all, he agreed with Léopold Senghor on the need for new blood in the missions. Towards the beginning of his journey, while still in Madagascar, he wrote to Cuenot that "Everywhere there is a need for rejuvenation of missionary personnel."[36] He later observed from Cameroon, "When I listen to the Spiritans, I cannot believe that so many old men still cling to old methods."[37] And despite a dislike of "delicate" situations, Prouvost was harsh when he felt it was warranted, and characterized himself as very frank on more than one occasion. "I say what I think and I call a spade a spade," he told Cuenot.[38] Exasperated by Bishop Henri Friteau, the Spiritan apostolic vicar of Loango in the French Congo, Prouvost counseled him to resign.[39] And as his visit to Dakar approached, Prouvost wrote to Cuenot that Grimault should have resigned before his arrival, because he would not be "soft" on the bishop when he got there.[40] "Occasionally I hear of the resignation of an apostolic vicar, which makes me think that maybe my arguments were persuasive," he reflected at the end of his tour. "Thanks be to God. Everywhere one senses the need for new men."[41] Missionary renewal was thus in his thoughts throughout the trip.

And despite his ardor for collaboration with the administration, Prouvost was also capable of recognizing that it could backfire for missions. During his trip, he was forced to think about the challenges facing French missionaries in postwar colonial settings due to the litany of bad news he received regarding MEP missions in Asia, and because of rumblings of anti-French sentiment that he witnessed himself in Madagascar and in Cameroon. The years 1945 and 1946 were particularly grim for the MEP, which lost numerous priests due to famine and privation in Korea and Manchuria, and to violence at the hands of Viet Minh rebels and the Japanese. For example, while in Africa, Prouvost learned that Father Adolphe Keller had been arrested by the Viet Minh and then killed ("probably eviscerated," according to the *Echos missionnaires*), while Fathers Jean Chauvel and Louis Gabillard were gunned down in a rebel ambush in between the Djiring plateau and Phan-Thiêt.[42] In addition, Father Cuenot reported that Father Jean Fraix had been decapitated in Laos, Fathers Jean Chevalier and Noël Tenaud had been killed by *"annamites,"* and Father André Vacquier had been kidnapped from Tonkin.[43] Cuenot complained that nationalism had ravaged the indigenous clergy, many of whom were siding with the Viet Minh and preventing French priests from exercising their ministry.[44] Though some of these reports turned out to be erroneous, they shocked and horrified Prouvost.

Indeed, Prouvost cited the tense situation in Southeast Asia as he instructed the French missions in Africa to accelerate the development of indigenous clergy on Rome's behalf. "For me it is a reason to urge the training of this black clergy, so that if xenophobia prevails someday, perhaps soon, the Christians here will not be left all alone," he wrote to Cuenot.[45] He prioritized visiting seminaries during his trip and did not usually like what he saw. "Everywhere there is a lack of personnel," he complained, "and in general everyone has shied away from making the necessary sacrifices, so Band-Aid solutions prevail. This is not the way to train a good indigenous clergy."[46] He also characterized the seminaries in French Equatorial Africa as "abominable with respect to their buildings, professors, and regulations."[47] In Cameroon, where he detected "negativity" in the context of "rapid evolution," he observed that the African clergy had often "rebelled against the whites." He also had the perspicacity to observe, however, "it must be said that certain rules that are imposed on them can only be shocking to them."[48] He saw clearly that his fellow French missionaries were making the situation worse through their racist disdain for their African colleagues.

In Madagascar, Prouvost found another reason to be wary of close missionary alignment with French authorities, when he realized that postwar unrest there was due in part to continued administrative reliance on forced labor. "French Catholic missionaries are in a very awkward situation," he observed. "As Frenchmen, they suffer because of the errors of the administration. If they defend the rights of their faithful, they risk being accused of fighting against the state. If they keep quiet, the Christians reproach them for being 'whites' as opposed to defenders of the oppressed and weak. Let us hope that those in high places hear their requests, inspired by a thirst for justice and a love of their mother country." He wrote in the *Echos missionnaires* that steps needed to be taken right away to ameliorate the situation before it degenerated into "hatred and revolt."[49] He hoped for administrative reform that would appease angry Malagasies and allow evangelism to continue without interference.

Prouvost thus embodied the contradictions in the church's postwar position in French colonial territories, even as he diagnosed them. He saw the need for new men and methods in the missions and the advancement of African clergy, yet his vision of the church still fit largely inside the existing structures and justifying ideas of French colonialism. In the cases of Madagascar and Indochina in 1945 and 1946, he confronted the reality that the Vatican had warned of in the 1920s: harsh and/or unwanted colonial rule could be a disaster for missionaries of the ruling country and thus for Catholic evangelism. Yet his first instinct was to try to fix wayward French administrators and partner with them, rather than distance the church from colonial rule and stake a claim for catholic universality over European superiority. And the reality was that for some years to come the Vatican had no choice but to rely on Frenchmen like Prouvost to staff and expand the church in French sub-Saharan Africa, much as it hoped to see African clergy rise to positions of leadership and prominence.

ADMINISTRATIVE AND MISSIONARY RAPPROCHEMENT IN WARTIME GAULLIST AFRICA

While Senghor felt that the war had wrought a revolution in African minds, the conflict also brought about significant shifts in French thinking about Africa, including the prevailing administrative approach to Catholic missions. "The war revealed the *fait africain*," wrote Minister of Foreign Affairs Georges Bidault in a circular to French diplomats in 1946. "It shone a light on the strategic and economic importance of the entire Black continent. . . ."[50] Bidault, a former Catholic youth organizer and wartime resistance activist, founded the French Christian Democratic Mouvement républicain populaire in 1944, and became a key power broker in the early Fourth Republic.[51] His words capture Africa's crucial role in the ultimate triumph of the Free French: without the support of Félix Éboué, the black Guyanese governor of Chad who rallied to de Gaulle and went on to be the wartime governor general of French Equatorial Africa, the general's movement would not have had a French territory to establish its legitimacy in 1940.[52] As a result, some of Éboué's policies, including his embrace of Catholic missions, were influential in the immediate postwar moment and enjoyed a long afterlife. In the words of Éboué's close collaborator Henri Laurentie, "a new atmosphere of confident cooperation between the state and the Catholic missions was established in the colonies of Fighting France, which spread to the entire reassembled empire."[53] Moreover, deep French concern about American Protestant missions and whether Muslim hostility to France in North Africa would move south also contributed to shaping new official support for French Catholic missions in the sub-Saharan African colonies.

It is perhaps surprising that Éboué, rather than the senior administration in French West Africa, which aligned itself with Pétain's Vichy regime, took the earliest and most dramatic steps to effect rapprochement between French colonial officials and Catholic missionaries in wartime Africa.[54] In the metropole, Vichy's renunciation of the Third Republic's anticlericalism and its conservative social program attracted the support of much of the church hierarchy, though its collusion in the persecution of Jews ultimately undermined its support among French Christians.[55] Moreover, Éboué was himself a Freemason, if not an overly ardent one.[56] Yet during his administrative career, Éboué had a record of trying to make peace with missionaries, even if he sometimes felt he had to defend African customs and culture against their disruptive innovations.[57] As one Spiritan who worked in Brazzaville in the 1940s later recalled, "There was no Freemasonry in his actions toward or his relationships with the missions . . . there is no doubt that when he died, the Lord considered him as one of the men of goodwill."[58] Éboué's stance on missions reveals his practical approach to government, which became ever more necessary in the uncertain days of 1940–1941, when French Equatorial Africa was the territorial home of the precarious Gaullist movement. To maintain his grip on power, Éboué needed to conciliate various French interests, including some prominent Catholic prelates who had preferred Vichy in 1940. This also made sound political sense because he governed a significant Catholic minority: missionaries had been more successful at converting Africans in French Equatorial Africa, especially in Gabon and the French Congo, than in French West Africa, where Islam was more prevalent.[59]

In addition, Éboué's missionary policy was shaped by his trusted lieutenant, the Catholic idealist Henri Laurentie. Indeed, Laurentie was personally largely responsible for the extension of that "new atmosphere of confident cooperation between the state and the Catholic missions" beyond French Equatorial Africa after the war. Laurentie had administered a district in Chad under then-governor Éboué, who subsequently made him an unofficial secretary general in Fort-Lamy and then took him along to Brazzaville in 1940. Rejecting Pétain's capitulation to Germany, Laurentie influenced Éboué to support General de Gaulle after the fall of metropolitan France.[60] A product of a Catholic family (philosopher and politician of the Bourbon Restoration Pierre-Paul Royer-Collard was an ancestor), Laurentie was well-known among peers in Chad for his religious conviction, though also for his vast library, his "wit," his "disarming modesty," and his "emotional patriotism."[61] In 1943, he went from serving as Éboué's secretary general to the post of director of political affairs in the French Committee for National Liberation's Commissariat for the Colonies in Algiers and then became "France's senior official colonial policymaker in the key period from early 1944 to March 1947."[62] In these various roles, he was in a strong position to encourage Catholic-friendly policies across French Africa.

Together, Éboué and Laurentie reached out to court individual Catholic leaders who had rejected Gaullism, and invited loyal ones to help shape policy. Monsignor Louis Tardy, the widely respected Spiritan apostolic vicar of Libreville, Gabon, was an example of the former. Tardy had refused to rally to de Gaulle in August 1940 and, along with some timber magnates, had helped persuade Governor Georges Masson to stay loyal to Pétain after Masson had initially declared for de Gaulle.[63] Gaullist forces subsequently invaded Gabon to bring it into their fold. When they won, Masson committed suicide, while Tardy refused to preside over a mass of celebration and was detained. In the spring of 1941, Éboué visited Gabon and tried to mend fences with Tardy, and though the bishop never renounced his ardent support of Pétain, he adopted a public pose of political neutrality.[64]

By contrast, Monsignor Paul Biéchy, apostolic vicar of Brazzaville and also a Spiritan, worked closely with Laurentie and Éboué, a personal friend.[65] Éboué invited Biéchy's collaboration on his influential circular on indigenous policy of November 8, 1941, which set the precedent for the administration's postwar relationships with missions. In 1944, when Laurentie organized the Brazzaville conference on the future of French Africa, Biéchy also took part, serving on the committee on family and social customs and fueling Protestant complaints of a pro-Catholic bias at the proceedings.[66] Correspondence between the two men reveals their warm working relationship: for example, in 1944, Laurentie intervened on Biéchy's behalf to convince René Pleven, a devout Catholic and the director of the French Committee for National Liberation's Commissariat for the Colonies, to include a large subsidy for the construction of a new cathedral in Brazzaville in the state budget.[67] "I still harbor great friendship for those I worked with in Brazzaville," Laurentie wrote to the bishop, "including yourself, with whom it is so easy and useful to fight the good fight."[68] There is thus no question that Catholic missionaries loyal to de Gaulle in French Equatorial Africa had new opportunities to be heard in administrative circles during and after the war.

Éboué's 1941 circular on indigenous policy is worth analyzing in detail, as it illustrates his administration's innovative stance vis-à-vis Catholic missions, which was deeply influential after the war. In November of that year, Éboué and Laurentie hosted a consultative commission in Brazzaville, composed of notable Europeans in French Equatorial Africa, including the Catholic bishops.[69] The document that emerged from these talks, drafted by Laurentie but presented in Éboué's voice, advocated administrative collaboration with missions, particularly in the domain of education.[70] Contrary to the dominant interwar administrative stance in much of French Africa, which criticized missionary

Governor General Félix Éboué and Monsignor Paul Biéchy, apostolic vicar of
Brazzaville, 1944.   Courtesy of ACSSp.

activity for destroying the social fabric of African society (and thereby
creating headaches for French officials), the circular argued, "Should we
see missionary instruction as one of those initiatives which, by straining
custom, risks throwing indigenous society off balance and destroying
it? I think not."[71] This provided a stark contrast to a 1933 circular of governor general of French West Africa Jules Brévié, who had pursued legal
limitations on missionary activity and had required African minors to
obtain parental permission to convert because he felt that proselytism
was dividing and destroying African families and communities. Christianity penetrated African society imperfectly, Brévié had claimed, and

resulted in "social groups with ill-defined status and muddled aspirations who tend to try to free themselves from their roots before they have sufficiently adapted to their new milieu."[72] These *déracinés,* Brévié had felt, were a threat to stability and French control.

Éboué's circular instead expressed boundless optimism about the effects of Christianity in Africa. Claiming that Christianity could "improve African society without denaturing it," it posited that monogamy, free consent of both parties to marriage, and the impossibility of divorce would ultimately uplift African society, yet not change its fundamental character. It could even, the document argued, reinforce chiefly authority, rather than undermine it. The circular parroted missionary arguments that it had taken more than three centuries for Christianity to conquer Gaul and to convert its existing institutions, and that the evangelization of Africa had only just begun. It also made the extraordinary assertion that in Gaul, "social life and the character of the family were respected, and Christianization came about by an almost imperceptible movement such that no rupture occurred in tradition until the moment when people noticed that the work was complete and the Church of France was completely in bloom."[73] It is highly likely that Laurentie was entirely responsible for projecting this remarkable assessment of the European past onto the African future in Éboué's directive. He made similar claims in a lecture course for aspiring colonial administrators at the École nationale de la France d'Outre-Mer (ENFOM) in 1945, while stating his conviction that "it is important, at the present time, that the administration [in Africa] favor religious missions, and lets them accomplish their educative mission." Though wary of "bizarre" manifestations of Christianity, often linked to foreign Protestants, that he believed "destabilized the indigenous mind," Laurentie told his students that the advantages of Catholic and mainstream Protestant missionary activity in French Africa were evident.[74]

There was also a more practical aspect to the circular's support of missions. A separate section on education in French Equatorial Africa was bluntly critical of the status quo, bemoaning the lack of African secretaries, accountants, and clerks, let alone doctors, veterinarians, engineers, and editors. The state itself was not equipped to remedy the situation, so Éboué asked for the missions' help and, in turn, funded them for their efforts. "I found that they completely understood our failings and harbored the sincerest desire to help me to correct them," he declared. "Thus we came to the conclusion that the instruction of the public schools and of the Christian schools, having the same goal and similar methods, should receive equal assistance from the government." Yet Éboué also made it clear that the state was not taking over mission schools: "As an enemy of everything authoritarian and anything that restrains initiative, I do not intend to make the mission schools into state schools . . . we are creating mutual support and harmony in freely given effort," he stated.[75]

This too was a substantial departure from previous official policy in Africa. While the colonial administration had occasionally funded mission schools in interwar Africa, officials had always insisted that such measures were out of the ordinary. In the words of Minister of Colonies Marius Moutet, who agreed to subsidies for Catholic schools in Côte d'Ivoire in 1936, "liberalities of this nature should not occur except in very limited measure and only on a temporary and exceptional basis." Furthermore, he concluded, the granting of subsidies should "permit tighter control of these establishments, and in their application of the official program of education."[76]

By contrast, Éboué and Laurentie equated mission goals with those of the French colonial state, made subsidies widespread and permanent, and yet left clergy considerable discretion within their own institutions. These policies were a delight to missionaries who had been arguing for decades that they were the real (and often only) agents of "civilization" in the empire.[77] Éboué's unimpeachable status as a republican and a Gaullist gave the missions new credibility in official circles that tended to be skeptical of religious enterprises. As an admiring voice (perhaps Laurentie) put it in an administrative report: "This black man, Antillean, humanist in ways that people are not anymore, of pure African stock, a career administrator known for his republican opinions, a dignitary of Freemasonry, did not fear to outline a program of French civilizing in close collaboration with the evangelical doctrine of missionaries as civilizing agents and indispensable collaborators of the administration."[78] Indeed, Éboué's pragmatism in the early days of Gaullism, combined with Laurentie's fervent Catholicism, truly revolutionized the nature of administrative and mission relations in Africa during and after the war.

MUSLIM AND AMERICAN THREATS?

Éboué's example and Laurentie's influence were crucial to the French colonial state's postwar shift on Catholic missions, but geopolitical circumstances also reinforced the change in orientation. For example, new fears about pan-Arabism and Muslim hostility to France were a factor in administrative rapprochement with Catholic missions, though policy on the ground toward Muslims in sub-Saharan Africa remained a complex mix of alliances, accommodations, and surveillance.[79] Catholics in high-profile positions in the early postwar colonial and diplomatic corps identified Islam as a threat to French rule in the African colonies, particularly as unrest in North Africa mounted. Laurentie, for example, was a staunch opponent of any action, such as building mosques or madrasas, that would encourage the spread of Islam in sub-Saharan Africa, where, he felt, it was more of a political than a religious force. He told his students at ENFOM in 1945 that "we do not have a shred of interest in favoring Islam in the French colonies" and that "French administrators in Africa do not adequately grasp the Muslim threat." Citing widespread African conversions to Islam in Guinea, which he tied to the French presence and policies, Laurentie warned that both negligence of or favoritism of Islam could have negative consequences for French Africa. Tellingly, he also instructed his students to keep this part of his lecture absolutely secret, and not to preserve written traces of it, as "it cannot be publicly known that France could have a policy vis-à-vis Islam."[80]

For his part, Georges Bidault acknowledged that in the past administrators had felt it was easier to let Africans embrace Islam than Christianity. But, he cautioned in 1946, Islam had become very strong, was descending south of the equator, and was everywhere serving as a basis of dangerous pan-Arabism.[81] Similarly, Monsignor Biéchy claimed that René Pleven had agreed with him "that we must construct a barrier against the invasion of Muslims from the North [in Chad] . . . which would be in the interest of France: the most recent events in Algeria clearly show where our Muslim policy has gotten us."[82] Laurentie was in favor of this, as was de Gaulle.[83] Heightened fears of pan-Arab Islamic agitation "contaminating" sub-Saharan Africa thus provided a backdrop that prompted powerful French officials, many of them Catholic, to look on missions with greater favor.

Yet by far the most important geopolitical factor that shaped the administrative shift in mission policy was a deep French distrust of American intentions in postwar Africa and, more specifically, fears that American Protestant missionaries were actively undermining France's control of its African colonies. In his 1946 circular to diplomats, Bidault, who had led the French delegation to the 1945 San Francisco conference that founded the United Nations, noted that the Americans had recently created an "African Division" and a "Division of Dependent Areas" at the State Department. He surmised that they were after raw materials for their industry, including uranium from the Belgian Congo, as well as markets for their goods, which, he claimed, were already flooding into the continent. French diplomats felt that these economic interests were motivating an American doctrine of "trusteeship," which they feared would replace French sovereignty in Africa with international oversight, to ultimate American advantage. "In striving for the creation of numerous Trusteeships, Washington is seeking to extend the principle of the 'open door,'" Bidault contended.[84]

Bidault went on to claim that the Americans were also interested in cultural power in Africa, and that their numerous Protestant missionaries on the ground were their most important ambassadors in this regard.[85] Moreover, he was so concerned about how American public opinion might be brought to bear on the fate of Africa that in 1947 he personally instructed the French ambassador to Washington to place articles praising French Catholic missionary work on the continent into the most important Catholic periodicals in the Unites States.[86] And foreign affairs officials were not the only ones concerned about these missionaries and their ability to influence Africans, the American public, and the United States government. Secret communications reveal that even as the American-led liberation of France unfolded in 1944, French colonial executives were carefully watching American Protestant missionaries within the African colonies.[87]

Just after the war, in a secret 1946 circular that Laurentie drafted to solicit information on missions from the governors general and governors of the African colonies, Minister of Colonies Paul Giacobbi illustrated French perceptions of American Protestants and their sway over their government, and, by extension, the wider world.[88] He claimed that "evangelical churches and their missionary organizations played a considerable, if unofficial part" in American preparatory work for the conferences of Hot Springs in 1943, Dumbarton Oaks in 1944, as well as Yalta and San Francisco in 1945, all pivotal meetings in the development of the United Nations. Moreover, he argued, "it is thanks to their direct or indirect intervention that the conferences at Hot Springs and San Francisco broached the colonial question, and, by having posed it to the civilized world, transformed it into a question of international law." He also cited the 1942 Church Conference on African Affairs at Otterbein College in Ohio as producing some recommendations that suggested the "internationalization of the colonies." To both Laurentie and Giacobbi, it was clear that wealthy "Anglo-Saxon" missionaries, "more or less opposed to French colonization" and "imbued with internationalist ideas" were going to try to take an even greater role in the evolution of African societies in the coming years.[89]

A lengthy report on both French and foreign missions in French Equatorial Africa, drawn up in response to this circular, reveals similar views among French missionaries and administrators on the ground. It described American missionaries as "partial and critical observers, with a wide audience and possessed of enormous resources," claiming that "it is from their judiciously located missions that the order could come for an extended trusteeship and the opening of an enormous economic market."[90] Officials accused American missionaries of making films in Africa that fueled criticism of French colonization by an American public who "knew little of conditions of life in the colonies but took a political interest in them." The report also quoted an assertion by Monsignor Pierre Sintas, apostolic prefect of Berbérati, that "a smear campaign has been underway for several months in America and I have precise information on the fashion in which they are discussing the work of our administrators and French missionaries over there, as they accuse us of the same incompetence and fault us both equally for the slow progress of education and the evolution of the peoples of this colony; moreover I know that the shamelessly declared goal of this propaganda is to replace French Catholic missionaries with American missionaries and also French administrators with American ones, forthwith."[91] Father Prouvost also noticed this prevailing attitude on his tour, observing that French authorities in Brazzaville were very distrustful of American missionaries and were hoping to be able to deploy French missions against them.[92]

French officials' breathtaking distrust of their American allies in wartime and postwar Africa completely dwarfs any concerns about Soviet-inspired communism in the archival record. Moreover, it was based on largely groundless distortions of American aims and capabilities. There were dissenting voices, but their objections only confirm the dominant trend. For example, in a 1946 letter to Étienne Dennery, director of American affairs at the Ministry of Foreign Affairs, Marcel J. Brun, a French Protestant minister who had left his adopted city of Philadelphia to become a chaplain in de Gaulle's army, observed with frustration, "French policy, particularly on colonial questions, gives the impression of being animated by fear." When he wrote to Dennery, Brun had just conducted a lengthy interview with John Foster Dulles, the US secretary of state, and was adamant that "America is not at all in favor of the colonial powers abandoning their responsibilities, but on the contrary, that they become more conscious of them and lead the people they administer to their cultural, economic, and political maturity."[93] Brun, who complained vociferously of Catholic bias at the Brazzaville conference to senior French officials, certainly harbored sympathy for his fellow Protestants, but that did not prevent him from seeing the American government's position more clearly than some of his contemporaries.[94]

The veritable French paranoia about American designs on postwar Africa was certainly born of a sense of weakness and diminishment in the face of American military and material might, but it also had deep roots in interwar suspicions of American Protestant missionaries, as well as colonial officials' longstanding ambivalence about international agreements pertaining to Africa. As part of the Paris Peace process ending World War I, France signed the Protocol of Saint-Germain, which required the signatory powers "to protect and favor, without distinction of nationality or of religion, the religious, scientific or charitable institutions or undertakings created or organized by nationals of the other Signatory Powers and of States, Members of the League of Nations, which may become parties to the present Convention, which aim at leading the natives in the path of progress and civilization." Furthermore, it explicitly stated, "Missionaries shall have the right to enter into, and to travel and reside in, African territory with a view to practicing their calling." It specified that a colonial power could only restrict such activity if it threatened public order or security, or if it contradicted its constitutional law.[95] The agreement thus effectively opened the African empires of its signatory powers to missionaries of varied nationalities and faiths. French colonial authorities reacted to Saint-Germain with frustration, because they already feared an invasion of wealthy "Anglo-Saxon" missionaries who might spread the English language and anti-French propaganda in Africa.[96]

The Protocol of Saint-Germain resurfaced in the postwar moment, and the hegemonic fear of American intentions heightened officials' anxiety about French obligations under the agreement. French authorities sought to determine whether they could reconcile the terms of the protocol to "protect and favor" missionaries of all nationalities with their desire to thwart "Anglo-Saxon" Protestant missionary activity. They consulted legal experts, researched the relevant policies of the Belgian, Portuguese, and British governments, and looked back to interwar precedents. They knew these explorations were delicate: a deliberately anonymous handwritten note in the political affairs files of the Overseas ministry underlined that all related documents were *"confidential"* and must never be allowed to damage French interests vis-à-vis the United Nations or the Holy See. Moreover, the note advised, "American sensitivities must be handled carefully" and French Protestants must be "protected."[97] The 1946 circular to the governors and governors general of French Africa also acknowledged that, given American assistance in the war and an international climate that was incubating opposition to colonialism, it would be politically impossible to erect legal barriers against foreign missions in France's African territories. The governor of Chad's proposed solution, which carried the day, was to combat the anglophone Protestant foreigners by boosting French Catholic missionaries. "To protect ourselves," the governor continued, "we must put [foreign missions] under surveillance and foil their efforts with French missionaries working in the same places."[98] Officials ultimately concluded that this policy could coexist with their commitment to Saint-Germain.

It should also be emphasized, however, that there was an undercurrent of Catholic favoritism in postwar French colonial circles that went well beyond the simple equation of foreigners with Protestantism. Though officials insisted that French Protestants must be "protected," some of them felt that Protestantism was intrinsically detrimental to the maintenance of French authority in Africa. For example, the exhaustive report on missions in French Equatorial Africa clearly endorsed the work of French Catholic missionaries over Protestants of any background. Officials argued that the diversity of Protestant sects suggested a sort of religious relativism to Africans, who felt they could pick and choose what to believe. In French authorities' eyes, this amounted to a "degradation" of Christianity and its descent from universalism into warring particularities. Moreover, the report faulted Protestantism for its spirit of "*libre examen*," which, its authors argued, led African believers to "reject all discipline" including "laws, regulations, and chiefly power." Officials worried that sectarianism and disagreements over religious beliefs heightened political risks by inciting Africans to quarrel with each other and to challenge administrative authority, thereby sowing "anarchy and insurrection." Indeed, concluded the report's authors in a strident tone, "In this particular respect, local indigenous policy has no worse enemy, and, more generally, this instinct of fragmentation and division is directly contrary to the spirit of the French Union, i.e. the great national community." While these administrators did not fault Protestants personally for this, they saw it as a natural outcome of the diversity of Protestant teachings and practices in Africa.[99] By contrast, Catholicism appealed to many French authorities because they felt that Catholic conceptions of hierarchy and authority mirrored their own administrative structure and were more conducive to order than the chaotic jumble of Protestant sects.

A "POSITIVE RELIGIOUS POLICY" AND MONEY
FOR MISSIONS

French officials' concerns about the future of their African territories, especially in light of perceived Muslim and American threats, and Éboué's wartime precedent of seeking missionary collaboration resulted in what Henri Laurentie termed a "positive religious policy" in French Africa, understood privately as "help for French missions, above all Catholic ones."[100] Though officials refrained from openly speaking in favor of any particular confession and downplayed conflict with laic principles, the administration's predilections were clear.[101] Missionaries themselves recognized Laurentie's Catholic influence in the government and saw him as a champion. In February 1946, Father Prouvost wrote to Father Cuenot from Brazzaville, "It seems Laurentie wants to inaugurate a policy friendly to French missionaries. Will his government agree?"[102] It did: beginning in the mid-1940s, French officials funded and favored French missions on an unprecedented scale. Suddenly, French Catholic missionaries found themselves enjoying an unexpectedly close, formal, collaborative relationship with the French state.

In particular, Éboué and Laurentie's wartime contention that the state needed to make use of missionary assistance in education proved influential in French Africa after 1946, when French colonial authorities were eager to mobilize all available resources to promote development in their domains. Their hope was that developing the African territories would stimulate the French economy, and also improve France's image in international forums, where they felt defensive about their colonial holdings.[103] French officials also wanted to steer the newly enfranchised African citizens of the Overseas Territories in politically palatable directions. They saw French missionaries, already present on the ground throughout the colonies, as ready-made allies who could provide salutary education on the cheap.

In 1948, for example, a ministerial circular addressed to the governors of the Overseas Territories echoed the spirit of Éboué's missive of 1941, stating that "the diffusion of instruction / education in our Overseas Territories is now a more pressing duty and necessity than ever, because of the political evolution of these territories and their need for qualified personnel, which is growing as they develop economically." Yet, the document acknowledged, state-run education was not up to the task: it lacked the personnel, the buildings, the materials and the funds to keep pace with the demand. Moreover, it was not likely to catch up anytime soon. "This is why," the ministry explained, "the Administration is duty-bound not to neglect any help in this domain, in particular that of religious missions."[104] Indeed, the ministry argued, the tight budgets of the Overseas Territories were actually an argument for missionary subsidies, not against them. State money, when combined with mission funds, personnel, buildings, and materials, would go much further than it would on its own.

The main mechanism of financial aid for missionary education and health initiatives in Africa (and the Overseas Territories more broadly) was the Fund for Economic and Social Development (FIDES), approved by the French legislature in 1946.[105] The FIDES channeled billions of francs to a wide array of infrastructure and social programs, and funding to missionaries was only a small part of its total expenditure. From the missions' perspective, however, the FIDES was a windfall that enabled rapid, vast expansion of their educational and healthcare endeavors. Both Catholics and Protestants benefited, and even foreign Protestants received funding occasionally, but the vast majority of recipients were French Catholic missions.

Hitherto unimaginable infusions of cash from the FIDES utterly transformed Catholic missionary work in French Africa in the postwar period. Between 1948 and 1950, the program expended 252 million metropolitan francs on private (usually synonymous with missionary) education in French West Africa, and 41 million francs in French Equatorial Africa. While missions had to put up some of the money for new schools or healthcare initiatives, the state often chipped in at least half the cost. Final decisions were made by the FIDES director's office in France, in consultation with representatives of state and private education. To make sure projects stayed on budget, building plans were carefully reviewed and followed by public works and education officials in each territory. In fiscal year 1950/51, every single request for assistance for private education that received funding in Africa was from a Catholic bishop, including the apostolic vicars or prefects of Libreville,

Ubangi, Chad, Sassandra (Côte d'Ivoire), Conakry, Ouagadougou, and Ziguinchor.[106] All were seeking to increase Catholic education rapidly by building new schools or expanding existing ones. There was sympathy at the top: in 1950, the director of the FIDES was none other than Louis-Paul Aujoulat, a staunch Catholic doctor, European MRP deputy from Cameroon, and a founder of Ad Lucem, a lay association of Catholic students and missionaries that aimed at "the fraternal union of the races."[107]

The effects were swift and dramatic. According to FIDES records, Monsignor Prosper Dodds, the métis (mixed-race) Senegalese apostolic prefect of the Casamance, expanded Catholic schools in his vicariate from forty students in 1948 to 1,257 in 1950. As 1,037 of those students were boys, the administration endorsed his subsequent request for ten million francs to build a primary school for girls, complete with a dormitory for boarders and instruction in household management. The total cost would be eighteen million francs—the mission would kick in eight million, but the government would pay the lion's share. The administrators who held the purse strings saw Dodds's rapid expansion of Catholic education as a boon, not a threat.[108] Similarly, officials were enthusiastic about plans by Monsignor Émile-Joseph Socquet to construct an "*école ménagère*" for girls in Ouagadougou, Upper Volta. Socquet asked for 50 percent of his budget of thirteen million francs, which was granted. Officials observed that approximately 6,000 of the paltry 14,500 school students in the entire territory attended Catholic school—staggering evidence of the limited reach of French education in the colony, private or public. Moreover, they noted, "the necessity of an institution for post-school training and instruction for young girls is now being felt." It is clear from their remarks that they were wholly aligned with the Catholic idea that the key to "evolving" African society meant influencing women to become managers of monogamous Christian households. "This will enable," they wrote, "the more complete education of young girls and the evolution of the family and thus of African society."[109] The FIDES thus gave Catholic missions the means to carry out the social and educational vision they had not been able to afford on their own.

Funding for Catholic endeavors only grew over time, and some Protestants got in on the action too. Requests multiplied: in 1950–1951 there were forty submissions for aid for private schools across the entire empire, and by 1956–1957 there were over two hundred.[110] By 1956, FIDES had distributed a total of over 4.4 billion metropolitan francs to support private education endeavors in the empire, and 674 million metropolitan francs to support private public health installations, the vast majority of which went to missions in Madagascar and sub-Saharan Africa.[111] For fiscal year 1956/57, private initiatives in French West Africa submitted 120 requests for educational subsidies, of which ninety-one were approved at a cost of 415 million francs.[112] Eighty-five of those were projects proposed by French Catholic missions.[113] In French Equatorial Africa, the program accepted thirty-five out of thirty-eight total requests, totaling over 260 million metropolitan francs.[114] Of these thirty-five funded projects, six were Protestant, including one in Gabon by the "Anglo-Saxon" Christian and Missionary Alliance, but the rest were Catholic. Often, FIDES paperwork designated missionary education projects as "integrated into the overall education plan for the territory."[115]

Bureaucratic adjustments underscored the new friendly official approach to French missions. Internal memos from the Ministry of Overseas France made the case that Christian Merlo, the official charged with managing relationships with missions in the 1950s, be exempt from decrees limiting the length of administrative tours of duty.[116] "In the beginning," noted Deputy Director of Political Affairs Pierre Jean Marie Delteil, "a civil servant without any particular training was sufficiently competent to deal with questions of missionary policy amid other topics, but since 1949, the development of and increasing complexity of missionary policy in the national and international spheres made it necessary to redistribute the workload."[117] Managing this policy was not merely a matter of applying texts, but rested on knowledge of African societies and religions, of missionary problems, and of the myriad missionary societies, as well as the cultivation of liaisons with their leaders in the metropole. This relationship management, with both Catholic and Protestant organizations, was "a complex and delicate task" that senior officials felt could not be entrusted to a new person every few years.[118] The "positive religious policy" was thus considered important enough to bend the in-house rules at the ministry.

The upshot of all of this evidence is crystal clear: the administration's new "positive religious policy" backed missionary activity to the hilt in postwar French Africa. It encouraged and enabled an enormous expansion in Catholic social services in France's African territories after 1946, particularly in the realm of education. It gave missions an effective stranglehold on instruction in regions where public schools were inadequate and allowed them to put state money in service of their particular social vision for Africa. All in all, it was a striking about-face from prevailing interwar policy toward missions. It reflected French officials' postwar conclusion that missions bolstered their efforts to develop their African domains and to keep them out of the clutches of the Americans and / or international organizations.

KEEPING CATHOLIC MISSIONS FRENCH

This French government support for Catholic missions did have some strings attached, however. Chief among them was French officials' insistence that missions be staffed exclusively by French nationals. They wanted Catholic missions to remain vectors of French language and culture in Africa, and never to become conduits for foreign influence. As a result, administrators expressed concern when French missionary congregations sent foreign-born missionaries to French territories, and French diplomats tried to exert control over Vatican appointments in French Africa, to be certain that missionary bishops would be French. French wrangling with the Vatican over nominations of francophone foreign prelates for posts in French Africa reveals the emerging dissonance between Vatican and French goals in postwar Africa, even as French missions benefited from state monies like never before. The church wanted to prioritize evangelization above all, while French officials cared most about preserving French hegemony in Africa, and saw missions primarily as a tool to do so.

Whether French officials realized it or not, the state money that allowed French Catholic missions to expand their work and influence in Africa also forced many missionary prelates to call upon new personnel and new congregations to staff their mushrooming schools, clinics, and shelters for African women. This necessarily meant asking for help from some non-French Catholics. Even well before the war, there had been a trend toward internationalization within the major French congregations that worked in Africa. For example, in 1880, forty-three of the White Fathers' forty-five members had been French, but that proportion dropped steadily over the succeeding decades. In 1947, 473 of 1,491 White Fathers were French and by 1951 the numbers were 584 out of 1,882, or just under a third, though of course many of the French ones were working in French African territories.[119] Moreover, the trend toward internationalization of congregations only continued as French vocations plummeted in the postwar period. Between 1950 and 1964, ordinations in the leading French missionary congregations fell by 60 percent, and the steepest part of that plunge took place before 1958.[120] Even someone as fiercely patriotic, and possessing, in the admiring words of French ambassador to the Vatican Wladimir d'Ormesson, such "eminently French qualities" as Monsignor Marcel Lefebvre, found it impossible to meet the needs of growing Catholic enterprises in French Africa with exclusively French personnel.[121]

To make sure Catholic missions would stay aligned with administrative goals in the postwar period, French diplomats pushed for a written accord stipulating that the Holy See would always consult French authorities prior to the appointment of prelates in French Africa, and that appointees would always have French nationality (which would not preclude French African candidates). This grew out of administrative opposition to the 1949 nomination of Father Jacques Teerenstra to the post of apostolic vicar of Doumé in Cameroon. This remote area had been manned for several years by Spiritans of Dutch background, of which Teerenstra was one. To appease French officials who unofficially but strongly opposed the elevation of a foreigner to the rank of bishop on French territory (though technically Cameroon was a UN Trust Territory), the Holy See initially made Teerenstra an "auxiliary" to Monsignor René Graffin, the French apostolic vicar of Yaoundé, and charged Graffin with representing Doumé vis-à-vis the French administration. This embarrassed Graffin, and irritated Teerenstra and his Dutch clergy, who conducted their ministry and their schools in the French language, and considered their country an ally of France.[122] In 1950, this case came to a head when Lefebvre met with François Mitterrand, then minister of Overseas France, about the question of foreigners leading Catholic missions in Africa.

Lefebvre explained to Mitterrand that because of the scarcity of French missionaries, the church had to ask foreigners to help in French Africa, and as more of them came, the more likely they were to ascend to leadership positions. Lefebvre comprehended that this might worry some administrative authorities, but he felt that a xenophobic stance by the French government vis-à-vis such prelates "risked alienating foreign Catholics" and wanted administrative officials to adopt a more broad-minded view that would "do honor to France and immediately assure her sympathy and respect."[123] Mitterrand allowed Teerenstra to be recognized, but he held a firm line on appointing foreign prelates "on the Republic's territory," arguing that Teerenstra's case should not be seen as setting a precedent for such appointments, but as a particular exception. In fact, Mitterrand wanted a 1921 agreement that the Vatican would consult the French government about its nominees for French bishoprics extended to the entire French Union. He suggested to his foreign affairs counterpart that perhaps the French ambassador could use French accommodation to Teerenstra's case as a tool to exact Vatican cooperation in the matter of appointing prelates in France's Overseas Territories, "a domain," he wrote, "which very closely concerns our sovereign rights and our constitutional principles, according to which the Overseas Territories are included in the French Republic."[124]

Formal negotiations followed between d'Ormesson and Pius XII's secretary of state, Monsignor Domenico Tardini, with mixed results from the French point of view. According to d'Ormesson, while the Vatican was sympathetic to the French position and willing to agree to consult on such appointments, the pope would not consent to the production of any formal document that other states might get wind of, thus compromising his ability to name bishops elsewhere.[125] Tardini provided a piece of paper, which he titled "Oral Communication" and signed in his own hand, that promised the Vatican would give the French administration advance warning of any appointments of non-French nationals in France's Overseas Territories. It also spelled out, per postwar Vatican priorities, that "*indigènes*" were French nationals.[126]

There were limits, however, to the diplomatic pressure French officials could bring to bear on the Vatican, despite their newfound favor for Catholic missions. Just a few weeks later, the accord was put to the test when Rome named Eugène Maillat, a Swiss White Father, to lead the isolated apostolic prefecture of Nzérékoré in southeastern Guinea. D'Ormesson reported to Paris that the Holy See had asked him if the French government had any political objection to the nomination. "Since this is the first time that the accord we just reached has been used in practice and the Propaganda Fide did its part with perfect exactitude," he telegraphed on July 9,1951, "I would be grateful to the Department to make sure to reply to me as quickly as possible."[127] His superiors replied on July 21 that the French government did not oppose the nomination, commenting, "Please let your interlocutor know that we are grateful to the Holy See for having obligingly consulted us before making this designation."[128] Pleasantries thus abounded, but in August, a chargé d'affaires in the French delegation to the Holy See noted that the *Osservatore Romano,* the official mouthpiece of the Vatican, listed May 4 as the date of the decree nominating Maillat to Nzérékoré. "One can conclude from this," he pointed out, "that this nomination had already been made when the Vatican Secretary of State used the new procedures and asked us if we had any objection to make."[129] France ultimately had little power to sway the Vatican, but officials' efforts to police Rome's appointments in the most far-flung outposts of French Africa nonetheless reveal how closely they equated French Catholic missions with French state interests in postwar Africa and looked upon the arrangement as a quid pro quo.

The diplomatic wrangling about foreign-born bishops illustrates the fact that France and the Vatican were ultimately pursuing different goals in Africa at midcentury. At the end of the day, the church cared more about conversions than French sovereignty in Africa, whereas the state naturally prioritized the latter. Yet this underlying dissonance was not at all readily apparent to many observers on the ground, who experienced Catholicism via missions directed primarily by French personnel and, increasingly, funded by the French state. It is not hard to see why some Africans critiqued the church for being too close to the colonial order of things.

In the mid-1940s, Léopold Senghor was frustrated with the French missionary church in Africa and concerned that it would not adapt to a postwar world in which Africans, particularly the educated elite, were weary of French racism and condescension, and wanted to have more of a hand in their own destinies. In the short to medium term, his fears were more than justified. His advice about Father Catlin was not heeded by the Spiritans in Senegal. Catlin remained in place in Dakar as military chaplain general, and Grimault's successor, Monsignor Lefebvre, made Catlin his secretary general in 1948. In 1951, Catlin took on an additional responsibility that put him in a leadership position vis-à-vis young African Catholics when he took up a post at the new regional seminary at Sébikotane. Catlin thus reprised the role that the prejudiced Father Lalouse had played in Senghor's own education, though he was only present at the seminary a couple of days a week because he shuttled back and forth to fulfill his other duties in Dakar. All in all, it is clear that his previous clashes with African Catholics did not persuade his superiors to remove Catlin from sensitive and influential posts.[130]

The Spiritan leadership disappointed Senghor in other ways too, though in the course of the 1950s and 1960s he witnessed a changing of the guard, as young French and African priests replaced their more conservative forbears. Lefebvre did not keep quiet about communism, as Senghor had suggested missionaries do in his 1947 letter to Le Hunsec. As Lefebvre wrote to his parishioners in his pastoral letter of 1955, "The Church of Senegal will not intervene in politics except in the case of completely perverse doctrines that are radically opposed to the laws of God, the Church, the family, and the human person, such as communism."[131] Indeed, though he was a shrewd and capable administrator who vastly expanded Catholic works in Africa, Lefebvre stirred up multiple controversies about communism, Islam, and other subjects during his tenure as apostolic vicar / archbishop of Dakar (1947–1962) and papal delegate to French Africa (1948–1959).[132] Yet on Lefebvre's watch eighteen African priests were ordained in Senegal between 1949 and 1961, while twelve French Spiritan missionaries there passed away between 1948 and 1959, including Catlin, who died in 1957. Most of the deceased had arrived in the African colonies before World War I—some even before the turn of the century.[133] They had spent their careers living and working in a paternalistic and racist colonial milieu, where African leadership of the state or the church was well nigh inconceivable. Their younger successors, both French and African, were better able to imagine and work toward a different future.

There is a final ironic twist to Senghor's dealings with French Catholic missionaries in Africa, which took place during his tenure as the first president of independent Senegal. Just over twenty years after he had complained to Monsignor Le Hunsec of the racism and political conservatism of French missionaries, and demanded that they refrain from criticizing socialism and communism, he angrily faulted French Dominican friars who served as chaplains at the University of Dakar for encouraging Communist-inspired student violence in the spring of 1968.[134] Outraged by protests against his regime, Senghor complained to the apostolic nuncio in Dakar, Monsignor Giovanni Mariani, "Alas, instead of directing the Catholic students, the priests are letting the students lead them in subversive undertakings, which are remote-controlled by Peking." He believed that the disturbances at the University of Dakar were related to those at the Sorbonne in Paris, which he also saw as Maoist in origin. He also accused the Dominicans of telephoning his office and falsely reporting that multiple students had died in the disturbances. "When one is a director of conscience and a priest," he admonished, "one does not behave so thoughtlessly." Senghor wanted the French Dominicans out of Dakar and appealed unsuccessfully via Mariani to Pope Paul VI to make that happen.[135]

Senghor's clash with the Dominicans emphasizes the central importance of dramatic generational change within the Catholic Church in French Africa in the middle decades of the twentieth century, a theme that reappears throughout this book. The missionary church appeared to be getting closer to the conservative colonial order in the late 1940s and early 1950s, but by the late 1960s, Dakar had an African archbishop and the archdiocese's young French personnel proved far too radical for Senghor, who had bemoaned the backwardness of their forerunners twenty years earlier. The incidents of 1968 and Senghor's reaction to them thus illustrate the striking shifts that had taken place in the Franco-African Catholic world in the two decades following the war. They also provide one of many examples of the church's ambiguous relationship to political power in French Africa, under both the colonial regime and its successors. In France, Africa, and many other places, institutions of the Catholic Church have served both as pillars of a conservative ruling order and a source of radical dissent—often simultaneously. This was particularly true of the church in Africa in the years following World War II. Even as missions became ever more closely linked to the colonial state financially and bureaucratically, some of the faithful within them increasingly looked to an independent future for Africa and its Catholics.

2

A TRULY UNIVERSAL CHURCH

Alioune Diop and Catholic Negritude

WHILE FRENCH OFFICIALS and Catholic missionaries were working out a new modus vivendi in Africa in the immediate postwar period, African intellectuals in France were at the forefront of the development and expansion of the pan-African negritude movement. In recent years, negritude has enjoyed enthusiastic scholarly attention. Studies of black artistic and literary innovations, of global black cultural networks and their political ramifications, or of one or more members of negritude's famed triumvirate of Senegal's Léopold Senghor, Martinique's Aimé Césaire, and Guyana's Léon-Gontran Damas are multiplying on library shelves.[1] Yet Alioune Diop, the man who arguably did more than any other person to coordinate and sustain the postwar international black cultural movement, remains largely in the background.[2] Indeed, one of the few books devoted to Diop denotes him in its title as "The unknown builder of the black world."[3] By founding the journal *Présence africaine* and the Parisian publishing house and bookstore of the same name, organizing groundbreaking international conferences of black culture in Paris in 1956 and Rome in 1959, cofounding the African Society of Culture (SAC) in 1956 and serving as its secretary general, Diop created the institutions that were essential to negritude's lasting impact. His personal efforts to build and maintain networks between black writers, artists, students, scholars, philosophers, and priests, and to link them with their European counterparts, forged solidarity among black intellectuals and gave them an international audience from the 1940s onward. Moreover, his intellectual contributions are notable in their own right, and had particularly important ramifications in the Franco-African Catholic world explored in this book.

If Diop has been neglected by researchers, so too have important Catholic strands of black thought, which he actively encouraged and developed. It is not merely that scholars have tended to discount or disregard the Catholicism of leading lights in the black cultural movement, such as Senghor or Diop himself, but also that they have ignored explicitly Catholic engagement with pan-Africanism and colonialism in the pages of *Présence africaine* or in the books that issued from the eponymous publishing house. This Catholic negritude, which became explicitly anticolonial, insisted on a "de-occidentalization" of the Catholic Church. It demanded that the church embrace African peoples and African culture, and cease to privilege white people and European culture, so that it could incarnate its own universal premise. It provided a crucial intellectual engine for the changes taking place in the church at midcentury.

The Catholic presence at the heart of negritude is a reminder that *Présence africaine* had a robust Catholic audience encompassing both French intellectuals and African elites. In the words of the Guadeloupian French writer Daniel Maximin, who came to know Alioune Diop and the circle of intellectuals around *Présence africaine* in his student days and later served as the journal's literary editor, "People forget that Présence was a movement that started with leftist Christians."[4] Indeed, a contemporary Marxist African critic, the Guinean playwright Condetto Nenekhaly Camara, went so far as to charge in 1961 that *Présence africaine* was founded by African Catholic intellectuals "with the covert sponsorship of French Catholic intellectuals." Camara argued that the colonizing powers, realizing their days were numbered in their overseas possessions, used Christianity as part of a backdoor effort to "stimulate cultural movements" that denounced some Western values but "remained

Catholicism at the heart of the negritude movement. A group including (*from right*) Jacques Rabemananjara, Jean Price-Mars, Émile Saint-Lôt, Édouard Glissant, Alioune Diop and (*from left*) Father Robert Sastre. From Femi Ojo-Ade, *Analytic Index of Présence Africaine (1947–1972)* (Washington, DC: Three Continents Press, 1977).

attached to others which were given a halo of universalism, to conserve western-European influence in Africa."[5] Diop probably bristled at these statements if he read them, as Camara's evocation of veiled, "colonialist" French Catholic influence at *Présence africaine* unfairly diminished his own personal initiative, anticolonial activism, and commitment to representing a wide range of viewpoints in his publications. *Présence africaine* welcomed and showcased the writing of contributors of various religious backgrounds who held divergent political views, including communists.[6] Yet Diop would have likely ruefully acknowledged Camara's perspective as the result of the church's failure to denounce colonialism and divorce itself more emphatically from Europe in the postwar period.

Camara was right insofar as Diop served as a link between European thinkers and African intellectuals, though there was absolutely nothing "covert" about this engagement. Diop was deeply interested in European culture and he believed wholeheartedly in the importance of dialogue and the exchange of ideas with people of various races, cultures, and religions. He both borrowed from European intellectuals and challenged them in a variety of ways, not least about their understandings of Christianity. The most prominent and influential French Catholic intellectual that Diop introduced, literally, to Africa and Africans was Emmanuel Mounier, a leading exponent of Catholic personalism, who visited Diop in Senegal in the spring of 1947. Personalism was an anti-materialist "third-way" philosophy that celebrated the human person in his or her community, simultaneously denouncing the individualism of capitalism and the negation of the individual in communism. Mounier had a great influence on African Catholic students, intellectuals, and clergy who found personalist ideas useful as they struggled to reconcile their Catholic faith with its European origins and their critiques of French colonialism. Yet the relationship between Diop and Mounier also demonstrates that while Diop found elements of French Catholic thought persuasive and seductive, he rejected the paternalism of even his most supportive French interlocutors.

Indeed, over time, Alioune Diop became an increasingly strident and vocal critic of the church's identification with Europe and of European intellectuals whose concepts of "universalism" and Catholicism he found self-referential and limited. By the mid-1950s, he was authoring pieces in *Présence africaine* accusing European Catholics of "religious racism" and calling on them to embrace a truly catholic commitment to universality. His increasingly militant public stance on the necessity of decoupling the Catholic Church from the "West" grew in part out of interactions with provocative European intellectuals, including Umberto Campagnolo, the founder of the European Society of Culture (SEC). In the course of the 1950s, Diop engaged in a public and private dialogue with Campagnolo about the meaning of a "civilization of the universal," a broad concept that had implications for Christianity. Diop grew increasingly frustrated by Campagnolo's Eurocentric mindset, and his anodyne view of colonialism. Diop admired European civilization, but he hoped Europeans, especially Catholics, would likewise appreciate and accept African contributions to dialogue and exchange. Their frequent failure to do so, whether conscious or not, irked him and prompted his adoption of a more radical tone on questions of religion and of culture more broadly.

Diop's advocacy for change in European Catholic mindsets and institutions was also influenced and buoyed by younger African Catholic students and clergymen whom he mentored and encouraged. Moved by their conviction, he used his publishing platforms to air their ideas, experiences, and concerns, thus multiplying the African voices that were calling on the church to reset its approach to the non-European world. Indeed, throughout his life, Diop maintained that Africa had ideas and values to offer the world at large and the Catholic Church in particular. In the articles, book prefaces, and books on Catholicism that he either authored or published, he made the case that Africa could help make the church truly universal. These efforts were not in vain: by 1963, Diop was repeating his message on Vatican radio and lauding the early results of Vatican II. Though he remained critical of the persistent discrepancies between his vision of the church and its daily reality, he had done much to move the pendulum on the church's approach to Africa and the developing world more broadly.

ALIOUNE DIOP'S CATHOLIC JOURNEY

It seems as though Alioune Diop knew everybody in postwar intellectual circles in France, francophone Africa, and the black diaspora. He occupied a unique position at the nexus of French and African political, cultural, and Catholic worlds, and he facilitated the connections between them. He joined the prestigious European Society of Culture in 1952 and was a founder and perennial secretary general of the African Society of Culture.[7] He counted Albert Camus, Aimé Césaire, Léon Damas, Father Jean-Augustin Maydieu, Emmanuel Mounier, Jacques Rabemananjara, Léopold Senghor and many other European, Caribbean, and African intellectual luminaries as good friends. He knew the surrealist writer and ethnographer Michel Leiris, the Islamophile Catholic thinker Louis

Massignon, the naturalist and explorer Théodore Monod, Pablo Picasso, Jean-Paul Sartre, and many other leading scholars, artists, and writers. A lengthy volume of some eighty written tributes to Diop by friends, collaborators, and mentees the world over, assembled by the Italian Friends of *Présence africaine* in 1977, testifies to his astonishing, far-reaching impact in the cultural sphere.[8]

Diop also moved easily in circles in Paris and Dakar that ranged far beyond the purely intellectual realm. In 1946 he took up the post of chief of staff for René Barthes, the new governor general of French West Africa, becoming the first African to hold that position.[9] At the end of that year, he was elected on a French Section of the Workers' International (SFIO) list to represent Senegal in the French Senate and served a two-year term, while launching *Présence africaine*.[10] Wherever he went, Diop assembled diverse groups for conversation and exchange, by reaching out to a variety of people, many of whom later testified to his friendliness, "elegance," and open, generous nature.[11] When he was working with Barthes in Dakar, Diop invited Georges Balandier to live with his family while the young scholar was doing his early ethnographic fieldwork in Senegal.[12] Balandier described Diop's home as the headquarters of an informal salon that warmly received a constant stream of local political notables, imams, Islamic scholars, and African intellectuals, including Lamine Guèye, Léopold Senghor, and Amadou-Mahtar M'Bow, a future director-general of UNESCO.[13] When he was back in Paris for work, Diop accessed the top of the missionary hierarchy in Senegal by reaching out to Spiritan superior general Le Hunsec to discuss education and culture, and to solicit works on Africa to review in *Présence africaine*.[14]

In some respects, Diop's position at the intersection of these various webs made perfect sense: he grew up in the cultural, religious, and linguistic crossroads of Saint-Louis, Senegal, where the Muslim Wolof majority had rubbed shoulders with French traders and a devout Catholic métis population for centuries.[15] Diop's extended family exemplified the town's religious and cultural complexity. In the 1830s, Alioune's great-grandfather, then a young child, had been adopted (apparently without his parents' permission) by a French trader named Mathurin and taken to France, where he was raised a Catholic. Upon his return to Saint-Louis as an adult, he married a local woman and raised two daughters in the church, including Hélène Fatou, Alioune's grandmother. When Hélène married Alioune's grandfather, she then converted from Catholicism to Islam.[16] Thus, although his parents were both Muslim, Alioune had Catholic Mathurin kin, as well as a family history of conversion and tolerance. Moreover, as an *originaire* of Saint-Louis, Alioune Diop enjoyed French citizenship, which helped him access pathways to the metropole that were closed to African subjects. In going to France, he followed in the footsteps of his older cousin Adolphe Sar (Valentin) Mathurin, an interwar activist for black rights in Paris.[17]

Nonetheless, Diop's ascendance to a position of vast influence, particularly in the Franco-African Catholic world, is remarkable. Diop's family could trace its roots to the Wolof aristocracy of the precolonial kingdom of Kajoor, but did not occupy a position of particular prestige in Saint-Louis society.[18] His father was not highly educated, and his mother was an illiterate and deeply pious Muslim who raised him, as he put it, "in the love of God and of the Good."[19] Like many Wolof boys in Saint-Louis, he began attending a Koranic school run by a local *marabout* around the age of five, and spent the first several years of his formal education memorizing the Koran in Arabic, a language he did not understand.[20] A future as a leading Catholic African intellectual would have then seemed highly unlikely.

For Diop, as for most of his African intellectual peers at midcentury, French education was the route to the metropole and its opportunities. At age ten, his parents sent him up the Senegal River to Dagana to attend a French school run by an uncle. He excelled academically, becoming the only African student in his class to go on to secondary school at the Lycée Faidherbe in Saint-Louis, where he encountered more European classmates. He continued his pattern of achievement there, becoming a tutor for younger boys. Upon graduation, he studied Greek independently and then went to the University of Algiers in 1933, where he prepared for a *licence* in Classical Letters and first crossed paths with Albert Camus, who would become a friend and ally.[21]

Diop made his move to the metropole in time for the *rentrée* of 1937, and began to forge connections with more French, black, and Catholic intellectuals. In France he met Césaire, Damas, and Senghor, who, along with the Cameroonian dancer, nightclub owner, and man about town

Vincent Eyoum Moudio, would facilitate his relationship with prominent French intellectuals such as Mounier, André Gide, and Sartre, and help convince them to contribute to *Présence africaine*.[22] Initially, Diop worked as a housemaster for boarding students at schools in the Parisian suburbs, while pursuing a Diploma of Advanced Studies (DES) in Classical Letters. Mobilized in 1939, he was discharged in 1940, and after a year in Marseilles, spent two years in the heart of occupied Paris at the Lycée Saint-Louis and the Lycée Voltaire between late 1941 and late 1943.[23]

This period in wartime Paris was particularly important for Diop's development as a cultural leader of the black diaspora and for his religious life. This is when he met Father Maydieu, who became a close friend and mentor, both in a religious sense and in general. Maydieu, a Dominican, had been a youthful adherent of the reactionary, anti-Semitic, fervently Catholic, and monarchist *Action française* and had even served as a "cudgel-bearing" bodyguard for its leader, Charles Maurras, before parting ways with the extreme right and adopting quite a different brand of Catholicism.[24] Diop was inspired to convert to Catholicism and to pursue his life's work of promoting African culture and cross-cultural dialogue by Maydieu's Christian certitude, as well as what Diop described as the priest's love for and profound interest in his fellow human beings, regardless of race, philosophy, or creed.[25] The context of war and occupation was also very significant: having a ringside seat to Europe's self-destruction prompted Diop and other young African intellectuals in France to study Europe's failings, as well as to reflect on their own societies and values. This, Diop later wrote, was the germination of the idea for the journal *Présence africaine* in 1942–1943, though it would not come to fruition until 1947.[26]

At this time, Alioune Diop also emerged as an elder brother figure to younger black students in France, as Césaire had returned to Martinique in 1939 and Senghor languished in a German prisoner-of-war camp between 1940 and 1942.[27] He organized meetings of colonial students in Paris, which became known as the "cercle du Père Diop," and he continued these rendezvous after the war, inviting Sartre and Mounier, among others, to address them.[28] He remained a stalwart and sympathetic supporter of black students in the metropole throughout his life, contributing to their publications and giving them a voice in *Présence africaine,* as in a 1953 issue devoted to students. In later years, African

and Antillean students enjoyed a warm reception at the Présence africaine book store in the Latin Quarter's rue des Écoles, where Diop and
other leading lights of negritude welcomed them as friends and equals,
encouraged them, and listened to their ideas and dreams.[29] In turn,
Diop's younger mentees would push him and his peers to take more
radical stances vis-à-vis colonialism, African self-determination, and
the church's approach to Africa in the years that followed.

Diop's study of and attachment to Catholicism deepened in the course
of the war, resulting in his baptism on Christmas Day, 1944. He wrote
in 1943 that he had been convinced since 1935, when he had been to Algeria but not yet to mainland France, that Christianity was the "salvation" of Europe, though it appears that he did not yet think that his personal salvation lay in that direction.[30] In the fall of 1943, he was afforded
more time for self-reflection and introspection when the French authorities, wary of his activities in Paris, exiled him to the provinces to take
up his first real teaching post at the prestigious Prytanée militaire de La
Flèche.[31] Alioune was quite isolated in this town of 10,000 in the Loire
Valley, where the appearance of an African teacher was quite an extraordinary event.[32] He worked hard at his job, attended mass almost daily,
and followed a plan of Catholic catechism designed by Maydieu.

In the course of this introspection and study, Diop grappled contin-
ually with the relationship between Christianity, race, and colonialism,
honing positions that characterized an African vision of Catholicism
that he would publicize widely in the postwar years. Some of the core
elements of Diop's Catholicism, including his engagement with personalism, his belief that true Christianity was colorblind, and his conviction that the church had to lead the way to purify European Christianity
and save the continent from itself, appear already in a 1943 letter he wrote
from La Flèche to Marguerite Marteau, a Catholic mentor who would
be his godmother at baptism. Diop believed wholeheartedly that genuine Christianity had the power to heal the problems posed by colonization. If Europeans "behaved and lived" as true Christians, he wrote,
"everything would be well for the people of the colonies (to whom their
destiny is henceforth tied)."[33] He thus drew a line between Christianity
as it was often invoked or practiced in Europe and colonial settings, and
a true commitment to Christian values, which, he intimated, would

bring about a sea change in relations between Europeans and colonized populations.

Diop's parenthetical assertion that the destinies of colonized peoples were henceforth linked to those of Europeans was a key underlying assumption of his thought. For him, there was no going backwards from the increased contact between Europeans and their subject peoples, yet genuine Christianity was a path to reimagining these intertwined destinies in a much more positive way. Dialogue was key: he felt that colonized people had much to teach Europe, including about the true nature of Christianity. As he wrote to Marteau, "Europe has the rest of the world at its disposition. More riches than it needs to live. However, it is tearing itself apart. The wish of the most sensible among us is that the message of peace come from these younger children who are the colonized of all parts of the world." He recognized, however, that Europe might not be receptive to such a message, so he felt the church must take it up and deliver it: "And that is where I see the role of the church. To inform and train the indigenous peoples? Fine. But also to purify the faith of Europeans, in calming their fever, in winning them over one by one by example."[34] He wanted to harness the institutional church to the propagation of this vision of just and pure Christianity, which developed in the crucible of the black experience of colonization and discrimination in the French Empire. Like the African Catholic student activists that he encouraged and mentored, or the black priests whose reflections he published, Diop thus hoped to change Catholicism from the inside.

Diop acknowledged that he had not arrived at this optimistic and constructive vision without struggle. He himself questioned whether it was "utopian" and he did not think the work of "purifying" European Christianity would be easy. Racism was a towering impediment, for Europeans and Africans alike. Diop labeled race as an "impersonal" and meaningless category, arguing that for him, "races did not exist." What counted was the interior of a person, not the exterior. "On the interior, we are inexpressibly singular and unique. It is not a question of racial superiority, but rather for each man to take his particular destiny in hand." Yet he also hinted that he had not always felt this way or had been so certain of the value of his contribution: "I still have traces of the painful era when I had an inferiority complex," he admitted. "And the attitude of certain Europeans does not calm me nor cure me."[35]

Regardless of any such residual pangs, and despite his profound understanding of the daunting obstacles littering the path to the future he envisioned, Diop forged ahead after the war and, notwithstanding ongoing paper shortages, launched *Présence africaine,* the centerpiece of his project to promote African culture and initiate a black conversation with the "Occident."[36] In his introductory article to the first issue in 1947, entitled "Niam n'goura or the raisons d'être of *Présence africaine,*" he described its central goal as "defining African originality and hastening its insertion in the modern world."[37] Amid the ruins of postwar Europe, he wrote of "recreating a humanism on a truly human scale," which would necessarily incorporate contributions of all men, including Africans, who would "signify their presence" by participating. In his view, the future must be built on dialogue and mutual respect between peoples and cultures: "it is certain that we cannot attain authentic universalism," he wrote, "if only European subjectivities play a part in its formation."[38]

For Diop, this statement about humanism applied equally well to Catholicism, and he often connected the two. For believers, he wrote in 1953, "dialogue means love," citing Father Maydieu as a European who embraced that love.[39] In a *Présence africaine* editorial on education that same year, Diop invoked love again while linking humanism and Christianity. "Would it be best, humanists and Christians of Europe, to limit the development of culture and the expansion of love?" he asked rhetorically, calling on European readers to reject the path of Western superiority for that of dialogue with and appreciation of non-European peoples.[40] His views on Catholicism and his hope to purge it of vestiges of colonialism thus reflected and animated his broader goals in the cultural sphere.

ALIOUNE DIOP, EMMANUEL MOUNIER, CATHOLIC PERSONALISM, AND AFRICA

In practice, Diop's interactions with European Catholic intellectuals were both extraordinarily fruitful and, at times, deeply frustrating. Such was the case of his close relationship with Emmanuel Mounier, one of the French intellectual eminences whom Diop placed on the original patronage committee of *Présence africaine* and whom he invited to contribute to its first issue. Mounier was a devout Catholic philosopher, writer, and the founder of the influential nonconformist review *Esprit*, which Diop saw as a model for *Présence africaine*.[41] It is possible that Diop met Mounier through Léopold Senghor, who had first come to France in 1928 and was drawn to the Catholic intellectuals at *Esprit* in the 1930s.[42] Diop and Mounier were probably acquainted, and perhaps already well known to each other, by the time Diop was leading the "cercle du Père Diop" in occupied Paris between 1941 and 1943.[43] They embarked on a robust dialogue in the mid-1940s: shortly after the liberation Mounier addressed Diop's group as part of a lecture series on "Encounters with Europe," and in 1947 he journeyed to Dakar to visit Diop and embark on a speaking tour of French West Africa.[44] Diop and like-minded Africans found Mounier's Catholic thought inspirational and helpful, but they also bridled at his patronizing paternalism.

Mounier's fame, then and now, was as a leading intellectual exponent of Catholic personalism; he was "the man who made its intellectual fortune" in interwar and postwar France before his premature death in 1950 at the age of forty-four, though he did not invent it.[45] Personalism, though always a bit ambiguous, was an antimaterialist philosophy that rejected both the rampant individualism of unbridled capitalism and the complete subordination of the individual to the collective in communism. As Mounier put it, the "central affirmation" of personalism was the "existence of free and creative persons." The person was "precisely that which in each man cannot be treated as an object," or what made each individual unique, aside from whatever social categories into which he or she might fall.[46] Though not overtly Catholic in its origins, personalism became attractive to interwar Catholic intellectuals who were dismayed by what they saw around them in society and politics—as Mounier termed it, "the established disorder."[47] Mounier countered both bourgeois individualism and communism with a vision that celebrated the "dignity" of the whole person, spiritual and physical, embedded in his or her community.[48] Personalism was thus one articulation of a "third way" that many disaffected intellectuals sought in the turbulent interwar years.

Personalism was thus not the exclusive property of the right or the left, nor, indeed, of Mounier, but a capacious tent that proved attractive to a motley assortment of thinkers, believers, and activists. In settings far removed from Mounier's intellectual circles, it became a favored concept among French Catholic missionaries, who, beginning in the interwar years, liked to describe their work as recognizing and promoting the dignity of the African person. A variety of characters in this book, including Monsignor Marcel Lefebvre, Sister Marie-André de Sacré-Cœur, and the conservative Dominican executive Father Joseph-Vincent Ducattillon, invoked personalism in their writings and correspondence. Marshal Philippe Pétain also employed the language of personalism in 1940 when he expressed his desire to revamp French education in the wake of the German defeat: "'Individualism has nothing in common with respect for the human person. . . . The French school of tomorrow will teach respect of the human person, the family, society, the fatherland,'" he wrote.[49] Mounier initially shared the marshal's belief that obsessive French individualism had been a primary cause of the disaster of 1940, and Mounier wielded significant, though unofficial, influence over Vichy's youth policy before his break with the regime and imprisonment in the autumn of 1941.[50] Indeed, the inherent vagueness of personalist doctrine allowed it to accompany Mounier from his nonconformist origins and right-wing flirtations to the postwar left.[51] And immediately after the war, Catholic personalist thought, deployed by Pétain's strident critic Jacques Maritain, played a crucial role in the elaboration of human rights doctrines in Europe.[52] It was thus flexible enough to inspire people with a wide variety of visions, politics, and programs.

Indeed, personalism also surfaces frequently in the context of the political and / or cultural decolonization of the francophone world in sub-Saharan Africa, Vietnam, and even Québec.[53] However, just as Mounier's engagement with Africa and his impact on African intellectuals and clergy scarcely surface in studies of his life and work, personalism's role in decolonization remains understudied.[54] In the African case, Mounier's dual rejection of rampant individualism and communism struck a chord with African Catholic intellectuals who did not see the political or social future of Africa developing along either path. Critical, like Mounier, of the materialism they saw all around them in Europe, they too were seekers of a third way and appreciated his intellectual project. Moreover, they felt that Africa had unique contributions to make in the elaboration of alternatives to individualism and communism, as well as to Catholicism itself. Senghor, for instance, who would later cite Mounier as the sole contemporary who had a great influence on him, saw a role for African values and spirituality in "rescuing" French culture and "restoring the primacy of the human personality and community," as Mounier and his disciples aimed to do.[55] Diop did too—his entire project at *Présence africaine* was to publicize, celebrate, and validate African culture, values, and spirituality, both for the uplift of Africa and for the redemption of a decadent and hypocritical Europe, including the Catholic Church. Mounier's specific personalist thought thus became central to the visions and interpretations of Catholicism that African intellectuals like Diop and others were developing at midcentury. It became a tool in their repertoire for critiquing colonialism both within and outside of the church, and for reconciling their Catholicism with their African selves.

It would be overly simplistic, however, to suggest that African intellectuals such as Diop or Senghor merely kowtowed to Mounier and imbibed his ideas uncritically. Diop and his allies had a complex relationship with Mounier. They found his thought illuminating for their own intellectual projects, and he tended to be critical of colonialism, though sometimes weakly so. He was also genuinely interested in Africa and Africans, as evidenced by his 1947 trip. Encouraged by Diop, Governor General Barthes, and the African Association of Friends of *Esprit* magazine, Mounier undertook a speaking tour of French West Africa funded by the Alliance française, and assisted by the government.[56] He was there for Easter, which he passed joyfully in the company of Diop's friends in Dakar.[57] He spent the most time in Senegal, but also briefly visited Mauritania, Côte d'Ivoire, Dahomey, Guinea, French Sudan, Cameroon, and Togo, as well as Liberia and British Sierra Leone. He produced a significant body of writing related to the trip, including a travel journal, which was published in two installments in *Esprit* in July and September 1947, and a series of ten articles that appeared in May 1947 in *Combat,* the left-leaning resistance newspaper then edited by Camus.[58] When *Présence africaine* launched later that year, Mounier contributed a "Letter to an African friend" (Diop) to the first issue. One year later, he published all of these writings together in a book entitled *L'éveil de l'Afrique noire.*[59]

There is thus little doubt that Mounier's engagement with Africa was deeply meaningful to him. He delighted in making African friends and wrote to Diop: "how excited I am for the future of these bonds we are trying to create between living France and living Africa."[60] In the course of his journey, he discovered things that resonated with him. For example, he was taken with the idea, whose formulation he attributed to Diop and Diop's friends in Dakar, that "the key to the Black is his total lack of individualism," which insulated Africans from the "esprit bourgeois" that Mounier so detested (though he also noted that individualism was the "greatest temptation" for the African elite, an idea he would explore in his letter for the first issue of *Présence africaine*).[61] Moreover, his writings reveal that he was attuned to and interested in the unique place of francophone African intellectuals positioned between their homelands and France. In addition to enjoying a "punch" with Diop and his friends in Dakar, Mounier sought out other African notables on his own, including ethnologist, author, and fellow Catholic Paul Hazoumé in Cotonou.[62] And at the end of his African sojourn, Mounier refused an invitation to join the official retinue of French president Vincent Auriol, who was then touring French West Africa, opting instead to journey to Senegal's Sereer country to see Senghor's hometown of Joal.[63]

Yet, despite this genuine and sympathetic interest, Mounier's writings about Africa, Africans, and elite African intellectuals in particular, assumed a paternalistic tone that many of them found grating and supercilious. He embodied a figure they encountered with some regularity in postwar circles in France, French colonial Africa, and the Vatican: a sensitive and supportive European who saw some of the shortcomings of his contemporaries and yet nonetheless often thought, wrote, and acted within the categories of the extant colonial order. These were the people, African activists learned, who could be hardest to convince that they were perpetuating aspects of that hegemony.

Mounier was not an apologist for colonialism and he recognized European failures to comprehend the experience of colonized peoples, but he was often ambivalent about it, and clearly believed that a French civilizing mission in Africa was justified. Under his guidance, *Esprit* had been critical of French rule in Southeast Asia as early as the mid-1930s, and in 1937 he wrote a scathing denunciation of French journalists who were traveling to Tunisia "not to get to know and resolve Tunisians' problems, but to verify an ideology conceived in European situations and in European terms."[64] In his writing about his 1947 trip to Africa, Mounier derided brutal French exploitation of African labor and the petulant, selfish, and hypocritical *colons* who crossed his path.[65] However, in his last diary entry from the trip, he compared colonization to the airplane he flew from Dakar to Casablanca, which missed the runway in the fog and got stuck in the sand. "It was necessary to change planes," he wrote, using the word "*appareil*" for plane. "It was, nonetheless, a fine machine." He then made the analogy to colonization, suggesting it had good and bad sides to it, though its time had passed: "Europe is also getting stuck in the sands of colonization. She does some great things with it, others not so great. But history has changed and it is necessary to change systems," he wrote, reusing the word "*appareil*" for system.[66] This was hardly a scathing indictment of French colonial rule in Africa, though it posited, as many of his contemporaries did not in 1947, that colonialism had to end.

Moreover, some of Mounier's critiques of French colonialism suggest that he felt the worst thing about it was that the French had failed to execute a civilizing mission. Upon his arrival in Senegal, he wrote, "Fifteen hours from Paris to Dakar. To Dakar? No. To get to Dakar one must first cross Medina, the African city; it is necessary to go back two centuries in time, to walk along these streets without light and hovels without hope, to be seized by the throat by the unforgettable odor of filth, misery, and the tide mixed together, and immediately afterwards see the feats of the colonizer, to feel the first so as not to forget the odor of his sin."[67] Mounier thus communicated the de facto segregation in Dakar, and evoked, in Catholic terms of sin and error, a botched civilizing mission.[68] Moreover, he conveyed a dim view of African neighborhoods, equating them primarily with suffering and squalor.[69]

Indeed, the theme of African misery recurs over and over in Mounier's writing from the trip, as do his startling depictions of a powerful and baleful natural environment that he saw as the chief cause of it. "Ah!

would that each traveler could awaken Europe to the knowledge of this enormous tumor of misery . . . this stinking tumor, reeking of suint, earth, filth, and illness," he wrote from Senegal.[70] He constantly returned to the idea of Africans struggling against nature and scarcely prevailing—contending, for example, with fantastically gigantic cockroaches in Saint-Louis, Senegal, or endlessly having to beat back encroaching wildlife and forests in Côte d'Ivoire.[71] He was deeply appalled by the natural landscapes he observed: of the scenery during his car trip between Rufisque and Sébikotane, Senegal, he wrote, "the ghastly baobabs (still without leaves) are eyesores on this misery."[72] He explicitly rejected racism in these dire evocations of African misery: "Nothing permits us to talk of racial inferiority," he wrote, arguing instead that Africans were miserable because of their "exceptionally inhumane" natural environment.[73]

However, although Mounier eschewed racism, it surfaced in his writings nonetheless. He occasionally deployed the basest stereotypes of Africans—describing, for example, fields he passed in Cameroon as being tended by "entirely naked, heavy and bestial women, stoutened by generations of working the earth."[74] Yet this particular observation did not prevent him from resorting to the European cliché that Africans tended to shirk manual labor and were "slow" workers. "It is true," he wrote in *Combat,* "that the African does not like work and manages only mediocre productivity."[75] He also made the arresting comment in an article in *Combat,* condescendingly entitled "Is Africa reaching maturity?," that "African psychology" contained a tendency to use words too lightly. "Nothing compares to the facility with which a Black will say anything: alternately yes and no, to please, to avoid moving, to avoid recognizing a wrong, and sometimes very gratuitously," he wrote, adding that young educated Africans had to be put on guard against the temptation to engage in the hyperbolic, pompous, redundant, and hollow speech that he found rampant in the African press.[76]

This paternalistic, patronizing, and haughty tone of Mounier's vis-à-vis the rising African elite irked Alioune Diop and sowed discontent among African Catholic intellectuals—even more so, perhaps, than Mounier's ambivalence about colonialism and a French civilizing mission. All of these frustrating tendencies were present in the letter Mounier addressed to Diop as his contribution to the first issue of *Présence afric-*

aine, for which he drew on his travel journal entries and articles, some-times verbatim.[77] Mounier, speaking directly to Diop and educated African readers in the essay, decided to focus "on the dangers of your path, as opposed to its hopes" in this piece for the magazine's seminal first issue. Assuming a position of authority and knowing superiority in relation to his African interlocutors, he stated, "Every new movement is threatened by many childhood illnesses. This volume affirms the maturity of the African elite: it is therefore the moment to eliminate the fevers of youth."[78]

Mounier then took it upon himself to put the African elite on their guard as to what he saw as the pitfalls of their position, in a manner that suggested he thought they were already falling prey to the foibles that he cautioned them against. He warned them: "yours is not a triumphant generation, it is and will stay a torn generation." According to him, theirs was also a sacrificial generation—they had to subordinate their individual achievements and goals to the greater good of their collective peoples. He advised them against distancing themselves from their African roots and pursuing brilliant individual careers, urging them not to become "a bourgeoisie cut off from its roots, a caste of parvenus without contacts with those who pushed you ahead so you could lift them." He claimed that in the course of his visit to Africa he had had to defend African culture and learning in the face of skepticism on the part of his African student auditors in the elite schools of French West Africa. In closing the letter, Mounier wrote, "To those who read us, my dear Alioune, we put forth our common wishes. I would like your voice to be stronger than mine, because it will carry farther."[79] Mounier thus assumed the voice of his friend, harnessing Diop to his provocative tone and message.

Diop, for his part, preferred Mounier's personalism without the paternalism, and apparently resented Mounier's appropriation of his voice in the essay. Diop was probably annoyed all the more by the fact that Mounier had taken much more trouble than most French intellectuals to comprehend his point of view, by traveling to Africa and engaging in conversations with Africans. Mounier had arguably developed a profound understanding of many elements of Diop's position and project, though he retained maddening blind spots as well. Twenty years later,

Diop's brother-in-law Iwiyé Kala-Lobé claimed that both "the tone and the content" of Mounier's letter greatly irritated Diop, who did not want to publish it. According to Kala-Lobé, "it took all the tact" of several friends, including Thomas Diop, a former priest, to change Alioune's mind and avoid a potentially messy conflict with one of the stars of the patronage committee.[80] Literary scholar Salah Hassan has suggested that the positioning of Mounier's contribution as the eighth essay in the issue, sandwiched between pieces by Georges Balandier and Pierre Naville, two younger men who were "less established" intellectuals at the time, may have reflected Diop's displeasure.[81] And while Diop left Mounier's name on the masthead of *Présence africaine* for four years after the philosopher's premature death in 1950 (until he did away with the European-dominated patronage committee altogether in 1955), Mounier never made another intervention in its pages. Moreover, the magazine, in contrast to Diop's emotional avant-propos upon Father Maydieu's death in 1955, did not remark on Mounier's passing.[82]

Mounier's early death meant that he never weighed in on the political debates surrounding the decolonization of sub-Saharan Africa in the decade that followed, but he remained a touchstone for African Catholic intellectuals. Some remained true devotees to his person as well as to his thought. Among them was Raymond-Marie Tchidimbo, the Spiritan Gabonese-Guinean priest who became the first African archbishop of Conakry. Tchidimbo called Mounier "an African by vocation" and felt deeply indebted to him: "All men of color who had the good fortune of coming into contact with him would express what the intelligentsia of the black continent owes him," he wrote.[83] Tchidimbo, who studied in Europe in the 1950s, penned an article for Diop's special 1953 issue of *Présence africaine* on students entitled, "The African student confronts Latin culture" in which he invoked Mounier repeatedly on the internal struggles of African students to reconcile their African identities with the European education they were pursuing.[84] And his commitment did not waver: in 1963, after ascending to the post of archbishop, Tchidimbo published a book entitled *L'homme noir dans l'Église* with Présence africaine that argued, among other things, that the church was not inherently Western, and that it should embrace more African clergy.[85] Mounier was everywhere in the book: Tchidimbo opened with an epigraph quoting Mounier's letter to Diop on how educated Africans should honor their African selves, and he devoted a special section of the bibliography entirely to Mounier's work. He clearly felt that Mounier's personalism supported "Africanization" of the church, and was apparently untroubled by the Frenchman's paternalism.

And even those African Catholic intellectuals who rebelled against Mounier's condescension, including Diop, built upon the personalist vision of Catholicism that he did so much to diffuse. Critics of Mounier included members of the rising generation of African Catholic student radicals, especially their most prominent spokesman, Joseph Ki-Zerbo of Upper Volta. In 1955, Ki-Zerbo took vehement issue with Mounier's characterization of his cohort in *Tam-Tam,* the magazine of Catholic African students in France. "Certain people claim that this is a sacrificial generation," he wrote, and mocked Mounier's paternal tone, "'Little one, you feel impatient, boiling, torn? Nothing extraordinary there! It's your fate to live at this moment in African history. There is nothing you can do about it.'" Ki-Zerbo rejected this line of thinking, arguing instead that the story of his generation was not one of sacrifice, but one of pride to be able to make a difference at such a key time. Yet it is noteworthy that even as he rejected Mounier's paternalistic overtones, Ki-Zerbo echoed one of the philosopher's core messages, steering his student readers away from individualism to "the good of the community."[86]

Indeed, in spite of Mounier's divisive interventions, personalism became central to African understandings of Catholicism and of their place within the increasingly global community of the faithful. Alioune Diop's Catholicism was personalist, and rested on the "primacy of the free and creative person."[87] Indeed, for Diop, true dialogue could only happen between free and creative persons—thus Africans had to be free to engage on equal terms with their European interlocutors, something that was nearly impossible within the confines of colonialism. In the years that followed the launch of *Présence africaine,* he returned time and again to the themes of dignity and respect for the human person in his determined campaign to de-occidentalize the church and make it truly universal. In doing so, he and his fellow anticolonial African Catholics leveraged personalism in the service of decolonization and thus played a role in its ascension within the church as a whole.

THE MEANING OF UNIVERSAL: ALIOUNE DIOP, UMBERTO CAMPAGNOLO, AND CATHOLICISM

In the course of the 1950s, Alioune Diop grew increasingly outspoken and critical of colonialism in general and of the European equation of Christianity with the West in particular. As his 1943 letter to Marguerite Marteau illustrates, these were not new ideas for Diop, but they took on fresh urgency for him a decade later. His sharper tone emerged as major political shocks succeeded one another in a heady rush: the defeat of France in Indochina in 1954, the outbreak of war in Algeria later that year, followed by the independence of Tunisia and Morocco and the *loi-cadre* devolving more power to French sub-Saharan Africa in 1956. These events suggested that the peoples of the French Overseas Territories were going to have more of a say in their political destinies sooner than many had supposed. Meanwhile, the Bandung conference of 1955, which gathered representatives of twenty-nine African and Asian states determined to resist foreign domination in the context of the Cold War, showed the strength of anticolonial sentiment worldwide.

In 1955, in the midst of these developments, Diop and his collaborators at *Présence africaine* scrapped the magazine's vestiges of deference to the French intellectual elite by removing the patronage committee from the masthead and launching a "new series" by restarting their numbering of issues at 1. They replaced the patrons with a *"Présence africaine* committee," which was an egalitarian, alphabetical list of the black intellectuals who did the actual editorial work.[88] The following year, Diop organized the first international congress of black artists and writers, held at the Sorbonne. It was the "cultural Bandung"—an assertion of the independent creative genius of black peoples throughout the world.[89] The French police, who spied on Diop intermittently between the late 1940s and mid-1960s, took notice of this shift. "From a national point of view," one police report noted, "we have never considered Diop to have particularly kindly sentiments towards France and its policies in its Overseas Territories. Yet several months ago, he seems to have taken a clear position in favor of extremist groups and particularly nationalist movements."[90]

While the ambient political effervescence and the attendant mobilization of African Catholic students certainly played a role in Diop's changing tone in these years, his ongoing dialogues with European intellectuals were also key to his radicalization, particularly regarding his thinking about Catholicism. One of his main interlocutors in the 1950s was the Italian philosopher of law Umberto Campagnolo, who founded the European Society of Culture in 1950.[91] Campagnolo's Eurocentric idea of a "civilization of the universal" provoked some of Diop's most forceful writing, in which he confronted the problem of the "universal" Catholic Church's Western heritage. In rejecting the idea that Europe had given rise to a "civilization of the universal," he passionately articulated a personalist vision of Catholicism that would truly incarnate the universal by embracing cultures, peoples, and races outside of Europe.

As had been the case with Mounier, Diop had a lot in common with Campagnolo intellectually. Indeed, even while furiously denouncing Campagnolo's ideas in 1957, Diop recognized him as "an eminent mind" and a fellow believer in the "authority of culture."[92] The two men shared a belief in the importance and power of culture to traverse borders and to counter political divisions. Campagnolo founded the SEC primarily in response to the Cold War and the partition of Europe, which pained him greatly. Many of the leading lights of European cultural and intellectual life on both sides of the communist divide joined the SEC, including the bulk of the French intellectual elite.[93] Indeed, it was French members of the SEC, including Father Maydieu, who facilitated Diop's connection to the group. In 1952, Alioune attended the second general assembly of the society in Venice and subsequently solicited membership in a letter that Campagnolo published in *Comprendre,* the society's magazine, in September 1953.[94]

Diop was eager to engage with the European intellectuals in the SEC, but he was nonetheless suspicious of the group's approach to the non-European world and was determined to disrupt their thinking about it. At the 1952 meeting, he warned his audience that they were in danger of being "trapped in a worldview in which only 'Eastern and Western Europe existed'" and that they would be "cultural imperialists" themselves if they did not take the world's non-European majority into account and cease a "'mission of managing the world and assuming everyone's destiny.'"[95] While Diop's message fell on some very sympathetic ears, it did not sway Campagnolo, who responded the following year by elaborating his definition of the civilization of the universal in starkly European terms in an essay entitled "European responsibilities."[96]

Thanks in large part to contestation by Diop and Europeans in the SEC who sided with him, the term "civilization of the universal" ultimately had a much more inclusive meaning.[97] The term was an organizing principle of UNESCO's programming under René Maheu between 1961 and 1974 and became a favorite concept of Léopold Senghor, who found inspiration for his vision of it in the writings of Pierre Teilhard de Chardin.[98] Yet Campagnolo did not see it that way. He argued that "Europe, taken in its largest extent, is the place where the civilization of the universal was born" and, moreover, "the civilization of the universal continues to have its deepest roots in Europe and finds there the most favorable conditions for its blossoming." This civilization, he argued, never closed itself off within its creations, or stayed satisfied with its conquests. It invented the notion of progress and was in a permanent state of revolution. Science and philosophy, because they were never static and ever striving for deeper understanding, were its hallmark disciplines. For Campagnolo, this explained why Europeans, as opposed to other peoples, "discovered the world, conquered the skies, unlocked the secret of matter," and so forth.[99]

Europe's relationship with the rest of the world was thus key to Campagnolo's elaboration of the civilization of the universal, and he anchored his vision in a benign reading of the motives of European colonial activity. While he did not deny the violent and exploitative effects of Europe's global expansion in many instances, he was determined to retain a redemptive notion of the spirit in which it was undertaken, which he felt Europeans themselves, caught in a frenzy of self-flagellation at mid-century, no longer perceived. "Without the reasons which are at the origins of its most important undertakings, [the history of Europe and the world] is no more than a monstrous series of errors and crimes," he wrote, unable to fathom such a conclusion. To his mind, Europe's beneficent approach toward other civilizations was one of the hallmarks of its identity as the civilization of the universal. "The civilization of the universal is the only one that seeks to enter into contact with other civilizations for reasons that are not born of immediate necessity or of purely selfish or casual interest," he wrote, "it is the sole one that wishes to know them, whether they are past or present, that wishes to understand them, that is ready to appreciate them." Moreover, he claimed, the experiences and works of those civilizations took on a deeper meaning once they were exposed to the light of the civilization of the universal. Neatly reserving all agency for Europeans, Campagnolo argued that the civilization of the universal "discovered" other civilizations and "revealed them to themselves" while integrating them into broader human civilization.[100] It is noteworthy that this essay appeared in the very same issue of *Comprendre* in which Campagnolo published Diop's letter seeking membership in the SEC, and thus frames the way Campagnolo thought about his relationship to Diop and other Africans.

While Christianity's universal pretentions were implicit in Campagnolo's thesis, he also specifically marshaled religion as evidence of Europe's unique development of the civilization of the universal. The dynamic and restless character of this civilization, he claimed, explained why "its religion was the scandal of the cross, a religion of love and not of authority, a religion of struggle and not of peace." Moreover, he invoked religion when he argued, in paternalistic fashion, that non-European peoples' "attempts to free themselves from Europe take forms and are often undertaken in the name of principles and according to aspirations which are implicated in what they are repulsing, and not only in the political and economic domains, but also in the spiritual domain."[101] Here he was undercutting Diop and other peoples from the colonized world who sought engagement and dialogue with Europeans by citing their adoption of "European" education, institutions, and faith as evidence of the truth of his argument about the civilization of the universal. He was doing exactly what radical African Catholic students would beg French Catholics not to do in a public declaration in 1956—making it harder for Africans to be Catholics by associating Christianity with Europe in a way that was intolerable for them and alienated them from their fellow Africans.[102]

Campagnolo's conception of the civilization of the universal became a foil that Alioune Diop returned to repeatedly in his writings in the mid-1950s. These included a spurt of interventions about Catholicism, encompassing several articles in *Présence africaine* as well as prefaces to books brought out by his publishing house—books that were themselves refutations of Campagnolo's views. For Diop, the self-centered, "unconsciously *racist*" arrogance of Europeans who were convinced that what was European was universal went hand in hand with their misinterpretations of Catholicism: "What we reproach [these men of culture] for," he wrote in *Présence africaine* in 1955, after citing Campagnolo at length, "is their implicit acceptance that they will decide the destiny of bound and blindfolded peoples who lack memory and imagination—that the authority of their judgment could not perceive nor enact the fact that there are no peoples without culture nor peoples who are ignorant of the vocation of the universal. There are thus no peoples who cannot be both fraternal and worthy of love. The serenity of intellectual Europe is betrayed, at the heart of its glorious certainty, by a desire for assimilation, or racism. And thus the fate of culture is tied to the colonial problem. And so is the fate of Christendom (of its habits of thought and its spirituality)." Moreover, Diop argued, Christianity was not a civilization and should never conflate its destiny with that of a particular people, that is, Europeans.[103] The problem lay not with Christianity itself, but with the insufficient charity and faith of its European adherents.

In contrast to Campagnolo's portrait of European expansion undergirded by laudable motives, Diop presented a thoroughgoing condemnation of colonialism, and called European Christians to account for not having done more to oppose it. "Colonization leads to spiritual as much as to economic and biological extermination," he wrote in the foreword to a 1955 issue of *Présence africaine*. "That is why it is astonishing that the intuition and authority of European Christianity did not detect or combat the colonization of Africa and Asia sooner, and did not break more openly with the colonizers."[104] He was eager to convince European Christians that their values aligned with anticolonialism, regardless of the religion of the peoples struggling to free themselves: "the people of the colonies have waited a long time for the Christian West to join in an alliance against colonialism, even with non-Christian colonized peoples, because they are spiritual nonetheless," he observed in a 1956 article in *Présence africaine* entitled "The Christian West and us."[105] Here, as part of his call to action, were the ecumenism and interfaith dialogue that Diop held very dear.

Catholic missionaries occupied a privileged place among the European Christians whom Diop called on to assist Africans in the fight _politics_ + _unity_

against colonialism. In his eyes, this struggle involved two things: respect for African culture and support for African political self-determination. He rebuked missionaries' "desire to 'civilize,' that is to say, to replace civilizations, customs, cultures, and local laws with their customs, cultures, and European laws, which, however, are so independent of Christianity."[106] By 1955, when the Vatican instituted the hierarchy in French Africa by substituting dioceses and archdioceses for missionary apostolic prefectures and vicariates, Diop was unequivocal that the time had come for a sea change: "From now on, missionary work must choose: it can continue to make Christianity the spiritual institution of a single civilization, or it can lean on the autonomous wisdom of peoples capable of organizing, thinking, and living their churches."[107] And the following year he again observed in _Présence africaine,_ "Let us be careful to respect the liberty of peoples. Adherence to Christian values is not imaginable if it does not rest on the liberty to not adhere to Western values. If not, the chances of dialogue will be compromised, and spiritual dirigisme will only have mediocre results that fail to take root."[108] Christianity thus had to be able to incarnate itself in the cultures and civilizations of all peoples if it was going to be true to itself. ~ _important_

On the political front, Diop accused European missionaries of feeling as though they had to favor colonialism over the national aspirations of the people they ministered to. "Everything seems to have unfolded as if colonialism were a supernatural link between the Church and the peoples of Africa, a major condition of the Christianizing of the blacks," he observed. Acknowledging that many missionaries preferred to sidestep politics altogether, he argued that, at a minimum, they had to be sure they did not betray the political aspirations of the peoples they worked among. "If the missionary has the right to lose interest in politics," Diop wrote in _Présence africaine,_ "he cannot legitimately do so without an initial heroic effort that consists of conceptualizing and organizing his life in the colonies, his habits, his means of expression in such a way that they do not betray the national and political-cultural liberties of the people he wants to serve." This was ultimately in the interest of the church, he argued, "because these liberties are themselves the soil in which the seeds of evangelization must germinate."[109] The future of the church in the wider world depended on both the Vatican's and missionaries' ability to see that the era of European dominance within Catholicism needed to end, even if European men of state and culture were trying to preserve their superiority over colonized peoples at midcentury.

In keeping with his vision of an African church developing along African lines, Diop called for African priests to assume direction of African spiritual affairs. He also wanted African archbishops to run the newly minted archdioceses, citing the "painful embarrassment" of black Christians "by this ongoing possible confusion between colonial and church policy."[110] Moreover, he wanted Africans to see themselves reflected in the church both physically and spiritually. On more than one occasion, he decried the lack of African saints in the church in *Présence africaine,* citing the example of the "Ugandan martyrs," a group thirty-two African converts to Catholicism and Anglicanism who were burned to death by King Mwanza II of Buganda between 1885 and 1887.[111] Beatified in 1920 by Benedict XV, the pontiff who had issued a stern call for European missions to divorce nationalism from evangelism in his 1919 apostolic letter *Maximum illud,* they had not yet progressed to sainthood by the 1950s.[112]

As he defined what he believed Catholicism truly was in his own writings, Diop was vigilant about countering Europeans who equated Christianity with the West, or who voiced the opinion that the church was betraying its European "base" by cultivating African clergy or manifesting support for anticolonial movements. In *Présence africaine* in 1956, he denounced an article in the Algiers-based French magazine *Eurafrique* that worried about African or Asian Christianities making common cause with anticolonial nationalism. He also heaped ire on a piece by Father André Bonnichon in the Jesuit magazine *Études* that attacked Canon Jacques Leclercq's laudatory biography of Father Vincent Lebbé, a Sinophile Belgian Lazarist, which Bonnichon read as hostile to the "European" church.[113] The next year, in a blistering *Présence africaine* editorial entitled "Can they set the Vatican against peoples of color?" he denounced a clutch of European authors from a variety of political backgrounds for their Eurocentric approaches to Christianity. These included François Méjan and Joseph Hours, the wartime editor of the resistance newspaper *Témoignage chrétien* and cofounder of the Christian Democratic MRP, whom Diop faulted for suggesting that non-Catholic French people would blame French Catholics for "destroying their own country" through their "devotion to the Holy See" in the context of decolonization.[114]

In this same editorial, Diop also circled back to Campagnolo's "cultural racism" in the 1953 essay on "European responsibilities" before fiercely indicting him and *Comprendre* for "religious racism" in its 1957 issue on the theme of "Civilizations and Christianity." While admitting that some of the articles in the issue, such as the ones by the Vietnamese author Van Ky, the Chinese priest François Houang, and Louis Massignon were more in line with his own thinking, Diop charged that the contributions of Campagnolo and others, such as the eminent French Jesuit Jean Daniélou, "tended to show that they cannot dissociate Christianity from the universalizing vocation of the Occident." Campagnolo, he charged, suggested by asserting that Socrates, Aristotle, and Plato were Christians before Christianity existed that "The Church is the West and the West is the Church." Daniélou, Diop complained, "contented himself with arguing that political emancipation does not signify cultural emancipation" and only affirmed the "universalism of science (which would be Western) and the Christian concept of man (also Western)." The bottom line, for Diop, was that the biggest obstacle facing the diffusion of Christianity was not the political and cultural awakening of colonized peoples, but rather "colonial paternalism" and colonialism itself.[115]

In addition to his own writings about the future of Catholicism in a decolonizing world in the 1950s, Diop associated his name with others making similar efforts, either by prefacing their work or bringing it out with his publishing house.[116] Examples include his collaboration in the publication of a volume of essays by black clergy entitled *Des prêtres noirs s'intérrogent* in 1956, and his prefacing and publication of Albert Tévoédjrè's fervent 1958 denunciation of colonialism, *L'Afrique révoltée*. In 1957, Diop also authored the preface to François Houang's *Âme chinoise et christianisme*, observing that Houang's assessments of Christianity were very similar to those of African clergy. "The "Christian West," Diop continued, "through inadequacies or egoism, has aroused the same malaise in Asia and in Africa."[117] Houang's work on China thus enabled Diop to emphasize his message about the true nature of universality.

Houang and Diop had followed somewhat similar itineraries. Although China had never been a formal French colony, French missionaries had been active there for generations and were protected by a treaty with the Qing.[118] Born one year after Diop, Houang, son of a Buddhist mother and Confucian father, converted to Catholicism at the same age Diop did, in 1945. He too pursued pathways of French education to the metropole and studied in Lyon and Paris en route to obtaining a doctorate in philosophy in 1954. Like Diop, he joined the European Society of Culture, and participated in critiques of Campagnolo's Eurocentric idea of the civilization of the universal at the 1953 general assembly in Paris.[119] Unlike Diop, however, he became a priest, eventually serving as the vicar of Saint-Eustache near Les Halles in Paris.[120]

Diop used his emotional preface to Houang's book to argue that by dint of their insensitivity to the peoples of the colonized world and their cultures, European Christians had forsaken the role of transmitting the Christian message. Europe, he charged, had not known how to "diminish itself in the face of Christ," but instead had asked other peoples to worship it alongside Christ, in the same way. It was therefore no wonder, he thought, that evangelization had proceeded slowly in Africa and Asia—Europe had ended up being an obstacle to the development of national churches. "Our Christianity is most often nothing but a varnish on the fragile scaffolding of a cultural community built by the stranger and placed under his guard," Diop asserted. Borrowing imagery from Houang, he inveighed that Christian universalism could not be conceived of as a train where some would be in first class and the rest in third class, but instead as a "rose window whose rays of light reached all races and cultures equally."[121] Without a profound shift in Europeans' understanding of universalism, he feared that the future expansion of Christianity was very much in doubt.

Diop repeated these themes even more caustically in his preface to Tévoédjrè's *L'Afrique révoltée* the following year. Tévoédjrè, a Catholic Béninois born in 1929, attended the SMA's St. Gall seminary in Ouidah before seeking higher education in Dakar and France.[122] A member of the younger student generation that followed Diop's to France, he got into trouble with colonial officials during a stint as editor of *L'étudiant d'Afrique noire,* the periodical of the Federation of Black African Students in France (FEANF).[123] The same year that *L'Afrique révoltée* appeared, Tévoédjrè cofounded the African National Liberation Movement

(MLN) with fellow Catholics Joseph Ki-Zerbo, Ahmadou Dicko, and Jean Pliya, and campaigned heavily in Africa against de Gaulle's proposed French Community.[124] The tone of his book was aggressive: he drew on his own vast travels and experience to critique French rule in Africa in many domains, including education, economics, and health. He also included a chapter on "The church and the colonial problem in black Africa," which Diop took up in the preface.

Diop used this opportunity to reiterate his call for European Catholics, and missionaries in particular, to show that they were ready to embrace universality in what he saw as its truest sense. He criticized European leaders for trying to figure out how to "assure their world dominance in cultural and spiritual matters, in order to maintain economic colonialism."[125] Adapting a maxim of the famed American Catholic radio personality Monsignor Fulton J. Sheen, Diop argued that the "peoples of color" of the world had "shouldered the Cross without Christ," while European colonizers had "adopted Christ without the Cross."[126] Emphasizing that colonized populations of color had truly suffered, often to the benefit of Western peoples who were nominally Christian, Diop called for a "new balance" in world Christianity. It could no longer speak solely to Western societies and cultures, and had to allow peoples of color in Africa and Asia the freedom to "orient" the church toward "new cultural and sociological structures." European Christians had to realize that, "The salvation of people who are weak and underequipped demands from both missionaries and lay Christians *a jealous attention to their vulnerability and to the freedom of all of their initiatives.*" In Diop's view, the fate of the church as "the greatest moral and spiritual authority" rested on the ability of Western Christians to grasp this reality. If they failed, they would compromise that authority in the eyes of the majority of peoples of the world, thus betraying the church's universal vocation.[127]

Diop did not mention political freedom specifically in this preface, but implied it when he called on Western Christians to allow peoples of color "freedom in all their initiatives." In the main text of the book, however, Tévoédjrè confronted the church directly with African aspirations for self-determination. "Either our religion is tied to the fate of French colonialism, and thus we will be liquidated along with French hegemony," he wrote, "or the church will be African in Africa and Christians must work toward African political independence."[128] Noting that many African congregations sang canticles like "Queen of France, pray for us . . ." and "Save France in the name of the Sacred Heart," that French flags adorned many African altars on July 14, and that students in African Catholic schools saluted the French flag and sang the Marseillaise before they prayed to God to bless their daily schoolwork, Tévoédjrè argued that the incipient Catholic identification with France and neglect of Africa was growing increasingly absurd for many Africans.[129]

Tévoédjrè shared the conception of a personalist, activist, anticolonial Catholicism that Diop had been elaborating over the course of the decade in exchanges with his various European interlocutors. Like Diop, Tévoédjrè believed that "in *principle,* it is strictly impossible for the church to be a vassal of a system of domination," though, he pointed out, current practice was far removed from this ideal. Both men believed it was the duty of African Catholics to be the conscience of the church and confront its colonial hypocrisy, along with colonialism itself.[130] Personalism, with its emphasis on human dignity, was a way to do this, both within the realm of religion and more generally. Tévoédjrè, for example, claimed that African Christians "remain very much attached to the value of the human person, renewed by the suffering of Christ" and insisted to themselves, in the shadow of colonial rule, that "'God does not want man to humiliate man.'"[131] Similarly, Diop's writing about Guinea's rejection of the French Community and subsequent independence in 1958 was pregnant with personalist language. "Dignity," he argued, "the basis of African personhood, manifests itself essentially by the action of national sovereignty."[132] For Diop and other African Catholic intellectuals, the church was betraying itself if it did not advocate for African sovereignty, oppose colonial exploitation, and embrace non-European cultures.

ALIOUNE DIOP AND THE VATICAN

When Alioune Diop wrote about Catholicism in *Présence africaine,* he reached devout readers in the Franco-African Catholic world, as well as members of the broader European and African intellectual circles that he moved in. He hoped to influence French missionaries to change their approach to the peoples they evangelized in Africa and Asia, and to bolster young African clergymen who were embarking on their careers. Yet he also wanted to get his message through to the Catholic leadership at the Vatican. While internal Vatican documents from the period remain largely inaccessible, there were public occasions when Diop and his allies were able to get the ear of the Vatican bureaucracy, including Pope John XXIII. And the record shows that by the time of Vatican II, Diop's thought had gained a great deal of traction at the very heart of the church.

The first major francophone African Catholic sally to Rome occurred at Easter 1957, when the Association of Catholic African Students in France undertook a pilgrimage there as their second annual convention. In Catholicism's world headquarters, the students asked the church to adapt its message to Africans, calling on European missionaries to embody catholic universality and cease promoting their own cultures.[133] The students, led by Joseph Ki-Zerbo, met with Pietro Cardinal Sigismondi, the secretary of the Propaganda Fide. Ki-Zerbo did not beat around the bush, telling the cardinal outright that the church should "take a solemn position against colonialism" and support the political aspirations of its African adherents.[134] The Vatican met these demands with some circumspection—Sigismondi responded with a call for "realism" and moderation.[135] Moreover, Pope Pius XII did not deign to meet with the students, but sent them a brief paternalistic statement, subsequently printed in the *Osservatore Romano* and *Tam-Tam,* exhorting them to prepare "seriously" for their future social, professional, and political roles, all while assiduously obeying their bishops, who were then almost exclusively French.[136] Moreover, Pius chose the same weekend to release his encyclical *Fidei donum,* which recognized the rapid political evolution in Africa, but was primarily a desperate call for more European missionaries to go to Africa before it was lost to the church.

Two years later, leading African intellectuals were back in Rome on Easter weekend for the Second Congress of Black Artists and Writers, organized by Diop.[137] A lot had changed since 1957: the French Union had become the French Community, Guinea had become fully independent by voting "no" in the referendum of 1958, and the Mali Federation would be founded just days after the congress concluded. There was also a new pope: John XXIII, the former Cardinal Roncalli, had acceded to the throne of Saint Peter the previous October. Just nine weeks prior to the congress, Pope John had surprised Catholics with his intention to call a council, eschewing the role of an elderly caretaker pope.[138] Though they were officially the guests of the Italian government, the black intellectuals at the congress were meeting in the heart of Christianity's holy city on its most holy days, a context which the numerous Catholics among them, especially Diop, used as a means to reflect on the church's universal claims and its relationship to African culture.[139]

In his opening address to the conference, Diop set the tone by hammering on his cherished theme of de-occidentalizing. Using the language of personalism, he evoked the "dignity" of the black race and insisted on the liberation of African "personhood" from a Western grip. It is our "duty," he told the assembled men of culture, to "save the universal from the egoism and the inadequacies of the occident." Theology was on a list of domains he declared to be dominated by European perspectives: "law, sociology, and theological thought suffer in their universal vocation in having to find their expression in references taken solely from Western experience," he said.[140] His thought was echoed in the conclusions of the congress's subcommission on theology, whose members stressed the importance of tolerance, universality, and respect for African culture. "We must open our hearts and our minds to everything that is universal in the values of *whatever culture* or *religious expression,* distinguishing in them what is universal and consequently valuable for every man," they declared. They also insisted on the value of dialogue between faiths, something that was dear to Diop: "we want to institute a *dialogue* between the various religions in the Negro-African world, a dialogue which should not result in an insurmountable opposition between religions, but rather a mutual enrichment that will permit each religion to express itself via Negro-African culture." Their list of final motions included one that urged missionaries to try to "comprehend African culture" and "use it in the transmission of their message."[141]

This time around, the new pope was ready and willing to meet the African Catholic intellectuals assembled on his doorstep. Roncalli had served as papal nuncio to France between December 1944 and January 1953 and was intimately aware of the political and Catholic contexts in which many leading African intellectuals had lived and studied in France. He had observed firsthand, he told the visitors, that Paris, "a city particularly dear" to him, attracted the intellectual elite from everywhere and particularly from Africa.[142] John also had long had an eye on the developing world, as he had served as the Vatican's first official observer at UNESCO beginning in 1951. In the words of his biographer Thomas Cahill, Roncalli was "impressed by this international project, which seemed to him to embody many of the aims of Christianity without its official vocabulary. He encouraged Catholics working for UNESCO to enter into dialogue with both unbelievers and other kinds of believers."[143] By virtue of his experience and his values, John was much better equipped to understand the concerns and demands of African Catholic intellectuals than Pius XII had been.

During the papal audience, Jean Price-Mars, the elderly Haitian president of the SAC, delivered a very brief allocution expressing the group's "respect and veneration" for the pope, and then John XXIII addressed his guests in French. Ever the diplomat, he extolled Western culture, yet also conveyed that he comprehended the mission of the congress.[144] There was definitely some European paternalism in the speech: in choosing Paris and Rome as the sites for their congresses, he told the assembled intellectuals, "you insisted on affirming your esteem for the great values of the spirit, which, for centuries, have found their home in Europe and from which you have yourselves received the inestimable benefits." But John understood his audience and indicated his support for their work: "You apply yourselves to the study of the unity and responsibilities of a Negro-African culture," he noted, continuing, "you affirm yourselves united by your race of origin and by common responsibilities to your ancestral patrimony." He stated that the church "appreciates, respects, and encourages such work of investigation and reflection" and asserted that "the church is ready to favor this work of intellect everywhere where authentic values of art and thought are likely to enrich the human family as a whole," thus embracing Diop's fundamental contention that African people had viable contributions to make to human knowledge in general.[145]

Finally, John reaffirmed the church's universality and its independence from any particular culture, while acknowledging that its history was very much bound up with European civilization. "The church," he asserted, "in the bloom of a youth ever renewed by the breath of the spirit, remains willing to recognize, to welcome, and even to nourish everything that honors human intelligence and the human heart on beaches of the world other than this Mediterranean basin which was the providential cradle of Christianity." He insisted that the church had a "universal point of view" that was attentive to the "human resources of all peoples."[146] If he had not put things exactly as Diop would have, John had clearly digested what African Catholic intellectuals were after. Though he would not live to see the end of it, their ideas would gain broader acceptance at the great council he convened.[147]

Indeed, Alioune Diop saw the Second Vatican Council as an unparalleled opportunity to press his claims for a truly universal Catholicism, and he took it upon himself to make sure that John XXIII would follow through on his promise to be attentive to the "human resources" of Africa. At his instigation, the SAC convened two days of study and reflection in Rome in May 1962 on "The presence and the expression of African personhood in Catholic life" to prepare for the council.[148] The participants divided themselves into three commissions which asserted African ideas and experience in multiple domains: the first examined spirituality, liturgy, and theology, the second tackled ecumenism, and the third discussed laity and social problems. In the wake of these discussions, Diop led an effort to reach out, by mail, to hundreds of African priests, bishops, and lay Catholics, as well as non-Catholic African intellectuals, to solicit their thoughts on these issues and to send their opinions on "African personhood" in the church.[149] Though fewer responded than he hoped, in 1963 Présence africaine was able to publish a volume of contributions entitled Personnalité africaine et catholicisme, largely but not exclusively by black clergy. It made Diop's case that Africa, long on the receiving end of Catholic instruction, should now have the chance to "GIVE" its wisdom to the rest of the church.[150] Présence africaine sent a copy to every African bishop attending the council, and Diop organized a standing "lobby," the "Catholic group" of the SAC, which remained in Rome during the entire length of the council, and diffused its ideas in a bulletin entitled "Africa at the Council."[151] Diop was bound and determined to make himself and his fellow Africans heard at the epicenter of the Catholic world.

He enjoyed a measure of success: by March of 1963, Alioune Diop was delivering his message in his own words on Vatican Radio's "Literary Tuesdays" program. Vatican Radio was an increasingly powerful tool of the papacy in the late 1950s and early 1960s—John XXIII had built on technical improvements initiated by Pius XII to widen the station's reach, inaugurating daily broadcasts to Africa in late 1961.[152] A French diplomatic observer noted that Diop spoke in "emotional" terms to a sizable audience of black seminarians, and began by underlining "the great satisfaction that the council's convocation and initial results had brought Africa."[153] Yet Diop also suggested there was much more work to do to make African Catholics truly at home in a church where they still had to "borrow theological thought, spirituality, liturgy" from the West. The solution, he declared in personalist terms, was for Africans to be able to "express their African personhood at the very heart of Catholicism." It was now Africans' turn to give to the Occident. They wanted to bring their own "original creations," cultural traditions, and unique experiences as Africans to the church. "Our fervor will build a spirituality which will be authentically and entirely devoted to the church, yet be no less the fruit of our own experience and our own genius," he said. One concrete way in which he suggested African experience and reality could impact the wider church would be to extend the conciliar spirit of ecumenism aimed at Protestants and even atheists in Europe to Islam and indigenous religions of Africa. He also thought that Africa presented unique opportunities for mobilization of the laity, because they were better equipped, he thought, to express the "fundamental values of African civilization."[154]

In this talk, Diop explicitly equated African Catholics' particular concerns and aspirations with those of the "poets of negritude" and African intellectuals who were trying to bring African culture and African voices to Western consciousness. Yet he also singled out African Catholic intellectuals for a "special, delicate, and very serious" mission to fulfill on behalf of the church in Africa. They would have to "approach" their non-Christian compatriots—the majority—not to convert them, but to "justify and heighten the moral authority of the church in the world." Diop saw the moral authority of the church as a kind of "security deposit for the dignity of man in the Third World," which would ensure the "social and cultural advancement" of its peoples. Calling on the church not to disappoint the people of the Third World, he urged it to come to know and to help save their civilizations.[155]

This snapshot from Rome in 1963 illustrates how far Alioune Diop had come on his personal Catholic odyssey, and how the ideas he and his African Catholic allies honed in the postwar period had moved from the periphery of the church to its very core. In his unorthodox journey from a Muslim Wolof boyhood in Senegal to broadcasting to Catholic audiences from the Vatican, Diop had confronted prejudice, criticism, and opposition from Europeans and Africans alike. The key to his self-realization had been his engagement in dialogue and exchange with peoples of all religions and races, his commitment to retain what he valued from their input while firmly rejecting what he found to be destructive, and his unflagging celebration of his African cultural heritage. Indeed, respectful open-minded dialogue was the essence of what he sought to get the church to undertake in Africa. By the time of Vatican II, the increasing profile of his ideas illustrated the developing reality that Catholicism's future lay not in Europe, but in the mission fields of Europe's former colonies.

3

THEOLOGIES OF COLONIZATION

Debating the Legitimacy of Empire

AFRICAN INTELLECTUALS SUCH AS Alioune Diop were not the only ones wrestling with the relationship between Catholicism and Europe's colonial endeavors abroad in the postwar period. In June of 1956 an extraordinary meeting took place at the headquarters of the Jesuit periodical *Revue de l'Action populaire* in Paris. At the urgent request of Archbishop of Paris Maurice Cardinal Feltin, a small coterie of distinguished French Catholic thinkers and teachers assembled around a large conference table. The purpose of their gathering was to resolve a bitter public feud over church teachings on colonization between two vocal and influential French priests: Father Joseph Michel, a Spiritan missionary who served as chaplain for students from the colonies in the metropole, and Father Joseph-Vincent Ducattillon, the provincial superior of the Dominican order in France, a former professor, and author of several books. Troubled by Catholic bickering over questions of colonization and decolonization that were taking center stage in France and its empire, the cardinal hoped the meeting would reconcile the two men. Feltin wanted them to issue a jointly signed publication that would present a united front on the interpretation of church teachings on colonization, leaving no room for further ambiguity and discord.[1]

The prelude to the meeting in Paris was a public two-year-long debate between Michel and Ducattillon over the writings of the sixteenth-century Spanish Dominican Francisco de Vitoria and their application to France's colonial empire in the 1950s. In his work, Vitoria, a philosopher and jurist who lectured on theology at the University of Salamanca during the Spanish conquest of the Americas, grappled with legal and theological questions provoked by colonization, in particular the rights and duties of both indigenous peoples and colonists.[2] Remarkably, Michel and Ducattillon both recognized Vitoria as the preeminent church authority on colonization, but they drew radically different conclusions from his work. In early 1954, Michel found an imperative call to decolonize in Vitoria's teachings, which he presented as a controversial lecture entitled "The duty to decolonize" and subsequently published as a text. A year later, Ducattillon responded with a reading of Vitoria that rejected Michel's interpretation and instead called for a just and vigorous defense of French colonists and French imperial interests abroad. After that, they and their respective supporters continued their quarrel in various press outlets, as the French Empire disintegrated around them.

The feud between Michel and Ducattillon was a prominent example of the tense conversations developing between Catholics throughout the French Empire in the 1950s. Their debate took place at a pivotal moment when France's relationship with its Overseas Territories was evolving rapidly. Just three months after Michel's lecture, France lost the decisive battle of Dien Bien Phu in Indochina, and by the end of that year the war in Algeria had begun. Tunisia and Morocco achieved independence from France a few months before Feltin convened the summit at the *Revue*'s offices in 1956. And the very week that the meeting between Michel and Ducattillon took place, the French government, fearful of possible unrest in sub-Saharan Africa, pushed the *loi-cadre,* which expanded the autonomy of the region's territorial assemblies, through the National Assembly.

Thus, as Cardinal Feltin's anxious intervention makes clear, the theological debate between Michel and Ducattillon was no mere academic dispute about a long-dead Spanish philosopher's views on colonization. It captured the fraught situation of the church—and of Catholics in

France and the French Overseas Territories in particular—as the possibility of the total collapse of the French Empire became increasingly imaginable in the 1950s. The battle between Michel and Ducattillon both reflected and heightened the deep divisions among believers in the French Empire and within the church establishment over the future of the French colonies. Both men experienced the rapidly changing world around them as Frenchmen and as men of the church and found diametrically opposed answers to the challenges they faced in both capacities in the same historical text.[3] Michel hoped to force the church to adapt to and even lead the process of dismantling empire, while Ducattillon firmly resisted it.

Michel's and Ducattillon's arguments each appealed to key segments of the francophone Catholic world. Michel's radical thinking was shaped by elite African students he mentored in France. Many of these students were products of Catholic mission education who were destined to be prominent citizens in their future independent countries, and some of them were closely connected to the negritude intellectual circles surrounding Alioune Diop and *Présence africaine*. Ducattillon's position resonated with conservative French Catholics who identified themselves as patriots and supporters of the French Army, and especially European Catholics in Algeria who felt under siege in the Muslim-led rebellion there.[4] A "theology of colonization" mattered very deeply to Catholics on both sides: they wanted the comfort and the empowerment of knowing that the church endorsed their views and their actions regarding the future of the colonies.

The meeting arranged by Cardinal Feltin to resolve the differences between Michel and Ducattillon was a failure—a lasting, meaningful agreement between the two sides proved unattainable. Feltin hoped that the church could somehow dodge its decolonization predicament and stay above the attendant political and social conflict by maintaining a position of benevolent neutrality. Instead, the meeting amply illustrated the inability of church leaders in France and its colonies to stake out a clear position on questions of colonization and decolonization in the 1950s. Their inconsistencies and indecision in the face of a crumbling empire reflected the church's complex historical entanglement with French colonialism.

VITORIA AND COLONIZATION

Given their stark differences of opinion, Michel's and Ducattillon's firm accord that four-hundred-year-old Spanish texts were the most relevant Catholic sources for guidance on French colonialism in the 1950s is in itself astonishing. It reveals the staggering lack of sustained, learned, or critical Catholic engagement with modern imperialism and colonization, which is symptomatic of how closely Catholic evangelism and European expansion were aligned in the modern era. During the height of European imperialism in the late nineteenth and early twentieth centuries, the Vatican energetically promoted missionary vocations among Europeans, exhorting them to go forth and found missions that would grow to be indigenous churches in Africa and Asia. In some cases, Catholic evangelism preceded the establishment of European colonial rule, and in others missionaries followed in the wake of armies, but by World War I most missions abroad were operating within colonies. The church ultimately conformed most of its jurisdictions to those colonial boundaries in an accommodation of the status quo. And despite the Vatican's interwar admonitions against missionary patriotism and its subsequent exhortations that European missionaries train indigenous clergy to run local churches, the church never fully distanced itself from European imperial projects. Indeed, Catholic missions' embrace of state funding in the postwar FIDES program only blurred fuzzy lines even more in French sub-Saharan Africa. And while there had long been friction on the ground in the French colonies between missionaries and administrators over the treatment of indigenous populations, no persuasive Catholic voice had emerged with a thoroughgoing theological critique of colonization per se.

Thus, when the entire edifice of European colonialism began to appear fragile in the 1950s, Catholic thinkers had to cast their nets widely to find teachings and texts that responded to contemporary circumstances. In his lecture on "The duty to decolonize" that initiated the debate with Ducattillon, Michel began by asking whether there was such a thing as a Christian colonial ethic. There was indeed, he asserted, and it had existed since the first half of the sixteenth century, though secular European powers dependent on the profits brought in by colonization had acted to stifle it for three hundred years. The first people to define it, he claimed, were the missionaries who accompanied the Spanish to the New World, whom Michel, who had served as a missionary himself in the French Congo, cast as defenders of the indigenous people against Spanish depredations. The most famous was Bartolomé de Las Casas, who had traveled back and forth from the Americas to Spain, and had published pamphlets detailing Spanish abuses of the Amerindians. Such reports moved Spanish theologians to examine the legality of such expansion and Michel identified Vitoria as the most important one, calling him "the Doctor par excellence of the Law of Colonization," though Vitoria never actually used the word colonization himself. Michel then asserted that the world was still waiting for an updated, truly Catholic treatment of colonization that could be addressed to colonizers and colonized of good faith alike. By "truly Catholic" he meant "not written by white men for white men," nor tainted by racial or national bias.[5]

Ducattillon was in complete agreement with Michel as far as the relevance and importance of Vitoria were concerned, calling the Spanish theologian "the grand master of Catholic thought on colonization" and likewise noting that "no one preceded him and no one has yet succeeded him."[6] Ducattillon also concurred with Michel that Catholic intellectual engagement with the idea of colonization in general, and Vitoria's contribution in particular, had remained dormant for three centuries.[7] He even explicitly cited Michel to the effect that a new synthesis of Catholic thought on colonization was urgently needed in the contemporary context. Ducattillon warned that the international and "psychological" conditions were vastly different than in Vitoria's time and the problems posed by colonization much more "complex," yet he felt nonetheless that any Catholic treatment of the phenomenon of colonization had to be rooted in Vitoria's thought. That was the extent of his alignment with Michel, however. Though they relied on the same source base, their interpretations of it diverged sharply.

A DUTY TO DECOLONIZE?

Joseph Michel was a rather unlikely radical in some respects. Born in 1912 to a large farming family in Brittany that produced nine religious vocations among its ten surviving children, he grew up in a region famous for its conservative Catholic royalism. Many of his peers at school were ardent adherents of *Action française,* the right-wing antirepublican movement that grew out of the anti-Dreyfusard campaigns at the turn of the century. Yet his father cultivated an independent streak that he passed on to his son, and thus while Michel fervently embraced Catholicism, he turned toward missionary endeavors abroad rather than conservative politics at home.[8]

Over time, Michel developed a desire to reclaim and reorient the church as a defender of the oppressed, colonized populations of the French Empire. He became intimately acquainted with and influenced by the postwar political aspirations of the populations of France's Overseas Territories, particularly Africans. While serving as a missionary in Dolisie, Congo, between 1946 and 1950, he founded the Étoile de Niari, an association of so-called *évolués,* or educated Africans, most of whom were Catholic. The association, which held meetings to discuss pressing issues and ideas such as socialism, Marxism, and polygamy, boasted over three hundred members in its first year and drew the attention of suspicious French authorities.[9] This experience working with the emerging African elite is likely what moved Monsignor Lefebvre, in his capacity as papal delegate to French Africa, to post Michel to Paris in 1950 as head chaplain to colonial students studying in France.[10]

To Lefebvre's chagrin, Michel's Parisian headquarters, in the rue Thibaud in the fourteenth arrondissement, became a hub of radical African Catholic student activism. Michel assisted the students in both spiritual and temporal matters, providing religious counsel as well as helping them plan their studies and locate housing. He also served as editor of and regular contributor to *Tam-Tam,* the magazine by and for African Catholic students in France, which gained a wide readership in the 1950s and 1960s.[11] *Tam-Tam* regularly tackled thorny subjects surrounding the future of France's African colonies and Catholics' place in them, as well as day-to-day matters of interest to students such as the

Joseph Michel in his office in the rue Thibaud, 1950s. Courtesy of ACSSp.

difficulty of finding affordable housing in Paris or suitable employment when they returned to Africa. As Michel witnessed the struggles his students faced in the metropole and absorbed their desire for political change in Africa, he began to adopt some of their views, especially their contention that the church should lead the charge against colonialism. Indeed, in 1952, one of his African mentees, Sébastien Abessolo, published a brief article in *Tam-Tam* on theology and colonialism that prefigured the chaplain's position in his 1954 lecture on "The duty to decolonize."[12]

Michel hoped to persuade French Catholics and church officials to embrace a contemporary role as opponents of the maintenance of empire by reminding them of the church's past record of critiquing colonization, however spotty. In his lecture, he wove a historical narrative of a church that had shielded vulnerable colonized populations, casting missionaries as his central protagonists. Though he acknowledged that missionaries had not always effectively combated the abuses of European colonization and slave trading, he cited their subjugation to secular powers that did not brook dissent.[13] Eight months later, Michel amplified his case for the church as a historical advocate for colonized peoples by publishing a special issue of *Tam-Tam* entitled "The Catholic hierarchy and colonial ethics." This issue, which stretched to over ninety pages, assembled a number of texts from the 1890s onward that demonstrated how the Catholic hierarchy, and missionary bishops in particular, had served as critics of colonial practices from racism to forced labor and as champions of oppressed indigenous women.[14] Most of the citations emerged from the French colonial context, though there was a sprinkling of other examples in the compilation.

Like many of the missionaries he lionized, however, Michel himself was a product of his time, and his arguments, while bold for the era, also reflected the limits of French Catholic thinking about racial difference and the rationales for colonization in the 1950s. On the one hand, Michel tenaciously and publicly trumpeted the cause of independence for colonized peoples and critiqued French colonial rule, which made him a radical among his French colleagues. On the other, like Emmanuel Mounier, he exhibited a measure of the paternalism so commonly displayed by French people in their relations with Africans.[15] Furthermore, Michel based much of his theological argument for decolonization on Eurocentric notions of a "civilizing mission" and a colonizer's "duty to tutor" the colonized. Like many of his devout countrymen, his thought was still deeply rooted in the logic of colonialism, advocating decolonization as the natural outcome of a successful "civilizing mission" that was both European and Catholic.[16]

Michel's 1954 lecture, given at Pax Christi headquarters in the sixth arrondissement of Paris, perfectly captures both his firebrand radicalism and the Eurocentric mindset that underlay his views. It reached a wide audience, as he subsequently released it as an article in various French and colonial Catholic student publications and published an abridged version in the Catholic magazine *Actualité religieuse dans le monde*.[17] His choice of the title "The duty to decolonize" was deliberately provocative, as was his central claim that Vitoria pointed the way to an understanding of decolonization as one of the primary obligations of a colonizer. In fact, he said, the duty of decolonization was the "inseparable corollary" of the right to colonize: "the goal of colonization is decolonization." Michel based this claim on the so-called right of tutelage of

Interesting POV

more advanced countries—the right to "teach" more "savage" ones. In Michel's formulation then, the colonizing nation was a tutor and the colonized peoples were its pupils. In this conception, the colonizer was supposed to put the needs of its pupils first and to subordinate its own interests to theirs. It would see to the "education" of the colonized and prepare them to assume control of their own affairs. As a result, colonization was necessarily temporary in nature, and its entire action, if conducted legitimately and properly, was supposed to be geared toward the emancipation of the colonized.[18]

The most strident and radical messages of the talk included Michel's denunciation of colonialism and his brief evocation of the right of colonized peoples to revolt. Michel argued that colonialism, which he defined as the "violation of the principles which should regulate the relationship between colonizers and colonized," was a sin in the eyes of the church.[19] Moreover, he asserted, it was virtually impossible to find a historical example of colonization where Christian principles, such as the right of tutelage, were ever enacted. Thus, Michel allowed for the possibility of an ideal, justifiable colonization governed by a civilizing mission in accordance with Christian teachings, yet he also posited that it was unattainable in the real world of men. In practice, colonization was inextricably bound to the sin of colonialism—yet another reason that colonizers (e.g., the French) should take up the duty of decolonization rather than shirk it. Michel went on to suggest that Catholic teaching sanctioned the revolt of colonized populations in particular circumstances. He quoted a 1933 thesis on "The right of colonization" by the Catholic sociologist and journalist Joseph Folliet, who argued that such revolt was legitimate under four conditions: 1) the metropole governed tyrannically in its own interest and its rule was insupportable; 2) colonial subjects had tried all peaceful means of protest and remonstration; 3) public opinion, or at least "the opinion of the wise," dictated revolt; 4) those who revolted had "moral certitude of success."[20] Michel, perhaps because the topic of revolt strayed onto very controversial ground, added very little of his own to his citations of Folliet, though he inserted a long passage from William Gladstone lamenting British errors that had sparked revolt in the American and Canadian colonies. It was still "cruelly" relevant, Michel wrote, suggesting by analogy that France was in

Colonization vs colonialism [handwritten marginalia]

danger of repeating mistakes made by metropoles in the past, sparking colonial revolt and thereby damaging its own interests in the long run.[21]

All in all, according to Michel's interpretation of Catholic teaching, there was no doubt that the church was on the side of colonized populations and their desires for autonomy. His lecture immediately sent ripples throughout the Franco-African Catholic world, delighting some and appalling others. He was not the very first French clergyman to grapple with how the church approached colonization and decolonization, but he was a major actor in a nascent, fragmented movement within the French church that had begun seriously to entertain decolonization as a moral imperative during the war in Indochina. In June of 1954, for example, a group of intellectual clergy in Lyon finally issued a public declaration in favor of peace in that nine-year-old conflict.[22] Yet Michel's bold statement of his case went beyond what most within the church establishment had been willing to say up to that point and touched nerves on both sides of the issue. While his students applauded his work, Michel's denunciation of colonialism as a sin in the eyes of the church and his claim that decolonization was the only moral way forward disgusted many prominent French Catholics with colonial ties. Monsignor Adrien Bressolles, a high-ranking church official and president of the Sainte-Enfance, the pontifical charity organization that assisted French missions in educating children, ostentatiously walked out in the middle of the talk.[23] Just weeks later, Monsignor Lefebvre wrote to Spiritan headquarters that the ministry for colonial students was a "serious problem" and that a replacement should be found for Michel, whom he deemed "incapable of collaboration."[24]

Michel's lecture also outraged François Charles-Roux, the president of the Comité central de la France d'Outre-Mer, the leading imperial commercial lobby.[25] Charles-Roux, a devout Catholic, career diplomat, and prolific writer, had served as French ambassador to the Vatican between 1932 and 1940. At the time of Michel's presentation, Charles-Roux was already in the midst of publishing a series of articles in the Comité's magazine, Nouvelle revue française d'Outre-Mer, defending France's civilizing mission in the empire against mounting skepticism among Catholics.[26] He was aghast that a French priest in a position of influence and authority over students from the Overseas Territories appeared to be stoking their anti-French nationalism instead of reminding them that they owed their instruction and cultivation to France. He denounced Michel in a biting article entitled "Is there a 'sin of colonialism' and a 'Christian duty to decolonize?'" and followed up with several more diatribes against Catholic critiques of colonization.[27]

Charles-Roux objected to many elements of Michel's presentation, including the contention that Christian principles had never really been applied in a colonial situation. He rattled off a standard list of French colonial heroes, including Joseph Gallieni, Hubert Lyautey, Christophe de Lamoricière, and Louis Faidherbe, whose actions, he claimed, refuted that premise. Like Michel, he claimed that evangelism and colonial expansion were intertwined, but in his narrative the missionaries were not the conscience of the colonial effort, shielding indigenous populations from the depredations of secular powers. Instead, he wove a tale of close cooperation between missionaries and heroic French colonizers, who together bestowed light and civilization on the benighted populations of Africa and Asia. Indeed, Charles-Roux contended, Michel had overlooked all the benefits France had brought and continued to bring to its colonies, which had been backward and barbaric before the French arrival. "France can only be proud of the difference between a black student at the Sorbonne and a subject of [African military leaders] Samory or Rabah, and one would not expect to hear regret at this metamorphosis from the chaplain of these students," he chided.[28] Charles-Roux did not refute the idea that France should eventually emancipate its colonies, but it was clear to him that it was not the moment to do so. He painted Michel as a traitor whose rhetoric was advancing the Communist cause and inciting acts of violence and terror in the empire.

Charles-Roux did not make his case only to the business people and colonial officials who read the Comité's magazine; he also sent his article directly to a number of French bishops in the metropole and in the colonies, causing a stir in the church hierarchy. To address the controversy, the president of the Secretariat of the French Episcopate, Monsignor Jean-Marie Villot, issued two strictly confidential circulars to all French bishops in November of 1954.[29] The first note explained the individuals and institutions involved and their respective stances. The second examined some of the themes related to the controversy in more detail, compiling relevant statements and writings by church fathers and Catholic intellectuals on nationalism and colonial independence, the historical relationship between French missions and the French colonial endeavor, and the students' position.[30] It quoted and explicated many of the sources that Michel had relied on in his piece. According to Michel, Villot called upon churchmen sympathetic to Michel's position to draft the explanations to the bishops, but the notes maintained a factual tone that was not overly skewed toward his viewpoint.[31] Nonetheless, the fact that the hierarchy felt it necessary to communicate the information to all French prelates in such a detailed and thorough manner showed that it took Michel's intervention and the ensuing controversy very seriously.

Charles-Roux denounced Michel to colonial professionals and forced the French episcopal hierarchy to reckon internally with the tensions surrounding colonization and decolonization. Yet Michel's most ardent and persistent opponent, Father Ducattillon, came from within the church itself, which posed a new quandary for the leadership of the French church. Ducattillon, perhaps feeling proprietary toward his fellow Dominican Vitoria, countered Michel's provocative piece with his own reading of the Spanish theologian in a 1955 article entitled "Theology of colonization" in the Jesuit *Revue de l'Action populaire.*[32] Ducattillon's retort in the press made the debate an open one. The French Catholic reading public thus became party to a bout between two men located within the church establishment who were fighting, albeit in scholarly language, over one of the most important issues of the day. From the French Catholic hierarchy's perspective, this acrimonious public dispute could only do harm to the church as a whole, by alienating elements of its metropolitan or overseas constituencies.

A "THEOLOGY OF COLONIZATION"

Between the time Michel gave his "Duty to decolonize" speech at Pax Christi in February of 1954 and the publication of Ducattillon's refutation of it in the summer of 1955, the situation in the French Overseas Territories had grown dramatically more acute. In particular, Catholic debates over decolonization took on new urgency with the onset of violence in Algeria. On November 1, 1954—All Saints' Day—Algerian rebels orchestrated a series of attacks on French targets, beginning what would become a long and ugly armed conflict characterized by terrorism and atrocities. The nascent unrest there was particularly alarming to many French people, who had become accustomed to the notion that Algeria was an extension of mainland France. In the mid-1950s, many prominent French leftists who supported decolonization elsewhere rejected the idea of Algerian independence because they did not see Algeria as a colony like the others.[33] The Europeans in Algeria, over a million strong, enjoyed full, unadulterated citizenship in metropolitan France. Though they were a minority amid the nearly nine million indigenous inhabitants, some of their families had been there for generations and considered it home. From a Catholic perspective, the conflict had an additional edge to it, as the indigenous population was predominantly Muslim, and the National Liberation Front (FLN), which emerged as the leading rebel party, utilized Islam as motivation and discipline among its own ranks. Settlers, on the other hand, were predominantly Catholic, though religious commitment among both Muslims and Christians varied widely, of course.

It is clear that Ducattillon had the Algerian situation, and the position of European settlers in the colony in particular, in mind as he formulated his response to Michel. He rejected Michel's "right of tutelage" reasoning as an illegitimate reading of Vitoria and instead offered a competing interpretation that justified the colonist presence in Algeria, and French protection of that presence, though he did not mention Algeria by name.[34] Despite his scholarly tone, his focus on theology, and an apparent desire to appear academic and neutral, Ducattillon acknowledged the political import of the debate: "We are not posing a question of pure erudition but that of a justifying principle of colonization, and, in consequence, shaping the conception of it and the attitude people must adopt toward it," he wrote.[35]

There is nothing obvious in Ducattillon's background to suggest that he had a particular interest, such as a family connection, in defending settlers in Algeria, though his age and his trajectory through the world wars may have contributed to an outlook that privileged the maintenance of French power and prestige in the world. The son of a manufacturer, he was born in 1898 in Hem, a town close to the Belgian border in the heavily industrialized Nord region of France.[36] Fourteen years older than Michel, he came of age during the German military occupation of his home region in World War I. In 1918, he entered training at the Dominican establishment at Kain, Belgium, which had been founded just across the French border after the dissolution and expulsion of many French Catholic congregations in the wake of the 1901 Law on Association.[37] Bright and gifted, he attained his doctorate in theology in 1927, rose to positions of leadership within the Dominican community in the 1930s, and reached a wider public through books and lectures.[38] In 1933, he published *Le vrai et le faux patriotisme*, in which he displayed his ardent love for France and sympathy for the French Army, themes he would revisit again and again in the decades that followed.[39] In 1938, preoccupied with France's place in the world, he gave lectures on the "Spiritual conditions of a French renaissance" at the Madeleine, which were broadcast on Radio-Paris.[40] During World War II, Ducattillon did not experience the pain of the German occupation of France firsthand. He was on an annual extended preaching tour of North America during the French defeat of 1940, so he spent the war in exile in New York, Canada, and Latin America, joining the "spiritual resistance" with lectures and a book entitled *La guerre, cette révolution*.[41] In it, he argued, employing the language of personalism that Africans would take up after the war in the service of very different ends, that there was no real difference between communism, fascism, and "Hitlerism." All were systems that attacked the basis of Christian civilization with their focus on the mass rather than the individual, "repudiating the eminent dignity of the free and responsible human person."[42]

Many Dominicans were at the forefront of the grassroots movements challenging the status quo in the church in the postwar period, but Ducattillon was not among them. They were central actors in the European worker-priest movement, and some radical French worker-priests who had come into contact with Algerian laborers in the metropole in the early 1950s went on to become staunch opponents of French rule in Algeria.[43] When the Vatican acted to suppress the worker-priests in 1954,

Father Joseph-Vincent Ducattillon. Courtesy of ADPF.

Ducattillon proved to be an eager helper. Second-in-command of the Dominicans in France in the early 1950s, he was promoted to the top job after his superior, Father Albert Avril, was forced to resign over the worker-priest crisis.[44] Ducattillon was willing to follow directions from Dominican executives and crack down on his radical brethren, institute censorship, and try to steer the order back into good standing with the Vatican. He displayed "rigidity" and deference to central authority that displeased his leftist colleagues.[45]

Ducattillon apparently first visited Algeria in 1933, on the occasion of the Semaine sociale, an annual Catholic conference. In 1956, in his position as provincial superior, he returned to Algeria to inaugurate a Dominican installation there, speaking of the "necessity of deepening the implantation of Christian doctrine in Algeria." His writings on Vitoria and on patriotism in the 1950s, described below, endeared him to the European community in the colony. After his sudden death from injuries sustained in a car accident in Paris in 1957, an admiring obituary in the *Cahiers religieux d'Afrique du Nord* noted that "we have lost a defender." The obituary, skirting the controversy surrounding his leadership during the worker-priest movement, claimed he had earned a "reputation for wisdom" and was seen as "perhaps a little too prudent by the adventurous spirits of 1945–1955." He was a company man: demonstrating Pope Pius XII's appreciation of Ducattillon's service, apostolic nuncio to France Paolo Marella asked to give the absolution at the Dominican's funeral.[46]

In his 1955 "Theology of colonization," Ducattillon characterized Michel's "duty to decolonize" as a "paradoxical and willfully provocative" phrase. Contending not only that Michel had misinterpreted Vitoria's position on tutelage, the Dominican argued that tutelage was a red herring, amounting to an afterthought in Vitoria's work. In his view, tutelage could not really justify colonization because it necessarily had to follow colonization, already held to be legitimate. Using tutelage as a justification for colonization (and then decolonization) was putting the cart before the horse.[47]

To justify colonization in theological terms, Ducattillon felt it was necessary to examine Vitoria's handling of *jus communicationis,* the "natural right of communication and society," which Ducattillon also defined as the right of "universal circulation and universal transmigration." Here, like Umberto Campagnolo and Alioune Diop, Ducattillon appropriated Catholic claims to universality for his argument. He asserted the primacy of a "universal human community that is anterior to and underlies all other human communities," essentially arguing that no people could legitimately violate the greater good of all to protect their own interests. In a discussion of sixteenth-century Spaniards that evoked the situation of present-day French colonists in Algeria, Ducattillon claimed, following Vitoria, that the earth belonged to all peoples and no people had the right to ban another people from any part of it. The only limit on a person's (or a people's) right to travel was the rights of others. To this, Ducattillon added a "right of free commerce between nations." Goods had to be able to circulate just as people did, for the benefit of the greater human community. Exploitation of natural resources such as gold in rivers or fish in the sea should be open to all. As members of the universal human community, newcomers to a land had a right to these riches, provided their exploitation did not "affect" local inhabitants.[48]

From here Ducattillon drew his central conclusion, which squarely favored French expansion overseas, and French colonists in particular. There was no doubt, he argued, that the "natural right of communication and society, as conceived by Vitoria, fully legitimized colonial expansion, defined as the need of abundant and evolving peoples, brimming with vitality, to spread, to swarm, to pour out, to find spaces and new countries where they can exercise their spirit of adventure and enterprise." Ducattillon qualified this with the caveat that this expansion could not inflict injury on the indigenous inhabitants and the "dignity of their persons must be respected and nothing should be unjustly taken from them." Yet he argued that the indigenous peoples had no right to object to colonization if these conditions were met. Indeed, they would be "guilty of grave injustice" if they opposed the "colonial expansion of peoples more privileged than they." Indeed, by resisting, they would be violating both the rights of the colonists and those of the wider universal human community, which stood to benefit from the development of the colonized lands.[49] This amounted to a thinly veiled condemnation of the Algerian rebellion.

For Ducattillon, then, Vitoria's writings did not point to a "duty to decolonize"; rather, they justified colonization and defended the maintenance of the French Empire, by force if necessary. The Dominican went so far as to argue that the political domination by a colonizing people of an indigenous people was legitimate, thereby sanctioning the French state's involvement in the Algerian conflict. While he qualified his discussion with the caveat that Vitoria was primarily thinking of individuals in his discussion of the right of communication and society, he nonetheless argued that states had the "right and even the duty" to involve themselves in colonization and that it was a truly "national" undertaking. A government should support the colonizing energy of its people and use its power to protect and defend them. If indigenous people mounted opposition, their political liberty could be forfeit to the state of the colonizing people. Ducattillon emphasized that Vitoria urged the use of great care, persuasion, and negotiation in such a circumstance. The use of force could only be justified in self-defense, and as a last resort. Even with these qualifications, however, Ducattillon felt confident concluding that Vitoria had outlined "principles and rules by which colonial expansion, including its political aspects, could be legitimate."[50] The Dominican thus used Vitoria to draw conclusions completely opposed to those of Father Michel.

Ducattillon's article did not go unnoticed by Michel and his allies. Michel contacted Jesuit Fathers Pierre Bigo and Philippe Laurent, the editors of *Revue de l'Action populaire,* and asked them to publish something that would offer another point of view on the same questions. According to Michel, Bigo and Laurent invited him to respond, but he refused to do so without meeting Ducattillon face to face, which the Jesuits proved unable to arrange.[51] Michel also telephoned Father Albert Perbal, a member of the Congregation of the Missionary Oblates of Mary Immaculate, who, in a varied career as an author, teacher, and administrator of his congregation, had taught at the Missiological Institute of the Propaganda Fide and at the Institut Catholique in Paris.[52] Perbal, then living in Rome, had met African seminary students in his professorial role and followed their subsequent progress in France and in Africa with interest.[53] He read *Tam-Tam* and applauded its positions on colonial questions.[54] Michel urged Perbal to obtain a copy of Ducattillon's piece and communicate his thoughts, which he did in a lengthy letter. In his detailed analysis, Perbal characterized Ducattillon as "a real dialectician, who challenges the meanings of words and slips between dilemmas." Using Vitoria in turn, Perbal denounced both Ducattillon's reading of *jus communicationis* and his rejection of Michel's tutelage argument.[55] Michel saved this letter and deployed it publicly at the next stage of the debate, after Ducattillon upped the ante by publishing an article on patriotism that reprised and extended key themes of his "Theology of colonization."

PATRIOTISM, COLONIZATION, AND CATHOLIC FAITH

In the spring and summer of 1956, tensions over the fate of the colonies within the Franco-African Catholic world reached new heights. Father Michel, his student allies, and Father Ducattillon made fresh, forceful public declarations of their positions. Their contributions took place against a dramatic backdrop of increasing French military involvement in Algeria and political change in France's sub-Saharan African colonies. In February, a frenzied mob of Algerian settlers threw tomatoes at Guy Mollet, the socialist French prime minister, to emphasize their hardline position against indigenous rebels and their frustration with the metropolitan government. Their violence worked: Mollet, a socialist and a pacifist, radically scaled up France's military commitment in Algeria, lengthening military tours and committing tens of thousands of conscripts and reservists to the conflict.[56] The reliance on conscripts, who had not been used in Indochina, ensured that the war would impact households all across France. Then, during the summer, fears of unrest in sub-Saharan Africa led France to grant its territorial assemblies more scope for self-government. Rather than seeming arcane, the theological justifications of colonization and decolonization appeared ever more immediate and relevant to a broader Catholic audience. The continuing controversy, which reverberated in both Catholic and mainstream media outlets, provoked anxiety within the Catholic hierarchy, which attempted damage control.

African Catholic students in France fired the first salvo in April 1956, issuing a radical public declaration in favor of decolonization that emphasized their Catholic faith and tried to persuade their French coreligionists of the justice of their cause. This text, which we will explore in greater detail later, reached a wide audience, via a range of media that included *Le Monde,* the leftist Catholic paper *Témoignage chrétien,* the prominent sub-Saharan Catholic weekly *Afrique nouvelle,* and, of course, *Tam-Tam.*[57] In it, the students made several controversial statements and demands, including that a "duty to decolonize" existed for all colonized countries, including Algeria, and that France should stop using sub-Saharan African troops in the Algerian conflict. Likely with Ducattillon in mind, the students condemned "the complicity of certain Catholics, who make the peaceful attainment of independence by colonized peoples dangerously difficult, by their writings, by their words, and by their influence more generally, and who nourish an unfortunate conflation of missionary evangelism and the colonial system."[58] This manifesto was a student initiative and it is unclear whether it went beyond Michel's comfort zone, but as it employed his catchphrase and he published it in *Tam-Tam,* it seems likely that it had his blessing.

Though it is impossible to know if Ducattillon was reacting specifically to the students' declaration, on May 29 he issued his own missive
to French Catholics, entitled "The state of patriotism," in the leading
French Catholic daily *La Croix*.[59] His message, of course, was radically
different. The Dominican pronounced that Catholic faith and patriotism
had long been closely linked in France but that there was now a deep
"crisis of patriotism at the heart of French Catholicism," which he presented as a problem of imperial conscience. French Catholics, formerly
so openly patriotic, had celebrated the growth of missionary endeavors
alongside the expansion of France in the world. In what was an indictment of a younger generation, he asserted that most French Catholics
were now suspicious of ultra-nationalism, so they shied away from patriotism. While they supported missionary work, they wished to divorce
it from French influence. When discussing colonization, they tended to
focus on its abuses, often exaggerating them. They wanted to view colonization as a gift or act of charity on the part of the colonizing power,
refusing to admit that it could rest on a right or a genuine interest of
the colonizer. The result, Ducattillon claimed, was one of the "most
acute and serious" crises of the day. "The future of French Catholicism
and that of our country itself depends on how it evolves," he wrote. He
asserted that patriotism in fact demanded the support of French citizens and even the blood of their sons to maintain France's overseas
possessions.[60]

Ducattillon's article aimed to bring the "rights" of France and the
French, particularly in the colonial context, back into focus for Catholics. The situation of the European population in Algeria was clearly foremost in his mind as he remounted his spirited defense of colonization
based on his understanding of Vitoria. Asserting that the right of im-
migration and emigration was "the most fundamental principle of
human rights," he went on to argue that migrants' home country (i.e.,
France) should protect them if their "security" or "legitimate interests"
were "gravely threatened" and that it was legitimate for their country to
establish political domination over the colonized one to ensure that protection. Moreover, he wrote, it was a violation of justice for a colonized
people (i.e., Algerian rebels) to pursue a political emancipation that
would be detrimental to the most recent immigrants among them. Finally,

it was never permissible for a people to resort to terrorism, even if they had legitimate claims to political emancipation. The use of terrorism only provided further justification for colonial rule, as the repression of such "abuses" was the fundamental basis of what gave one people the right to hold authority over another. To be sure, a colonizing people had to be just and charitable, even to "the guilty," and they had a duty to help the colonized people toward full participation in civic life. Yet colonizers would be remiss and would violate the tenets of justice and charity if they did not exercise their right to rule. "It is the duty and the honor of a fecund and prosperous country to be at once the defender of its own interests and a beneficial agent of civilization," he argued.[61]

Ducattillon's scathing attack on the "defeatism" and "pacifism" of French Catholics and his proxy defense of French military action in Algeria provoked widespread debate across boundaries of metropole and colony. Deluged by letters both supporting and condemning Ducattillon's exposition, the editors of La Croix published a sampling of the reactions, which they dryly categorized as "diverse," on June 12.[62] A fellow theologian, who applauded Ducattillon for delivering a balanced assessment of the issues, declared himself "shocked" by the protests the article evoked, accusing those clergy who opposed it of pandering to indigenous nationalism for "so-called apostolic" ends. He equally deplored clergy in Algeria who aligned themselves with the extreme politics of the colons in order to keep them in the fold: "the role of the apostle is not to win the masses by flattering them, but to enlighten them to the truth by approaching questions with a spirit of lofty impartiality," he wrote. A notable letter by Paul Buttin argued that given the vast injustices of colonialism on the ground, which did not conform to the ideal theoretical situations Ducattillon had described, "The state of patriotism" was in fact "the most straightforward condemnation of colonialism as it has been practiced." Buttin, a respected lawyer, journalist, and lay Christian activist who had lived in Morocco since 1920 and had advocated a measured transition to independence there in his 1955 book Le drame du Maroc, asserted that Ducattillon's abstract theories ultimately condemned lived reality because "military colonialism had almost always preceded political colonialism, which, for its part, had preceded and prepared economic colonialism."[63] The editors of La Croix, who seemed mildly anxious to defend Ducattillon, noted in a footnote to this letter that the Dominican was "logical in his principles and did not challenge this condemnation."[64]

In their handling of the controversy, the editors of *La Croix* were apparently trying to delineate a position of impartiality and Catholic respect for "human dignity" on all sides of the Algerian conflict, though their proposals reflected the muddled and tendentious thinking that characterized public discussion of the topic. Just a few weeks before Ducattillon's article appeared, the paper's editor-in-chief, Father Émile Gabel, had visited Algeria and subsequently published a series of three front-page editorials in the paper that explored the situation there and possible ways forward. Gabel's first observation was that there were no simple, formulaic solutions and that extremist answers on either side were misplaced.[65] While recognizing the legitimate frustration of the Muslim majority vis-à-vis their lack of political rights and a long string of broken French promises, Gabel maintained that *colons'* fears of a Muslim-dominated future were also well founded.[66] In his final installment, in which he too invoked Vitoria on the concept of just war, he argued that French young people were suffering from a general moral collapse. Gabel saw French intervention to protect its citizens in Algeria as justified and claimed that it was clear that France was in a better position to assure the material well-being of the populace than the rebels who wished to take over. Mutinous French youth had a duty to serve their country in Algeria, he claimed, "out of love for all of the inhabitants of Algeria, whatever their status, race, or religion." Their service was an act for peace, he claimed, and a step toward the establishment of solidarity between the estranged communities there.[67]

French Catholic youth did not necessarily agree with Gabel on this last point: some French Catholic university students rejected Ducattillon's position on Algeria and pointed out how objectionable the Dominican's argument sounded when applied to France during World War II. Marie-José de Saint-Marc and Jean-Louis Monzat of the secretariat général of the French Jeunesse étudiante chrétienne (JEC), the French Catholic student youth organization, wrote Ducattillon a personal letter, which they also sent to Father Gabel, deploring the impact of "The state of patriotism" in the university milieu and conveying the "disappointment" of many young Catholics who read it. "We have the duty to tell you," they wrote, "of the exploitation that is already beginning of your article," which they characterized as a "personal reflection without theological justification." The fact that the article appeared in *La Croix,* they argued, had led many young Catholics to believe that it represented the church's point of view. Already a committee of students was busy distributing flyers outside Parisian university cafeterias with excerpts from the article alongside slogans such as "Algeria is France." "We do not doubt that you would reject the utilization of your point of view in the service of a political cause that is, at the very least, debatable," they wrote. They wondered how Ducattillon's pronouncements that "a country can deserve, through its own fault, to be stripped of full political autonomy" and that "the repression of terrorism is the basis of the right of a people to exercise its authority over another" would have been understood in France between 1940 and 1944. They closed their letter by evoking the "disastrous effect" of the article on non-Catholic students, and particularly on students from the colonies, who found in it a "disavowal" of French Catholics who professed to share their "profound desire for justice, advancement, and friendship."[68]

Indeed, to the Catholic students from the colonies and their mentors, Ducattillon's article was completely unacceptable. They reacted swiftly and furiously to marginalize Ducattillon, painting his position as extreme and not representative of the church as a whole. Like the leaders of the JEC, they labeled Ducattillon's writings as personal opinions with no basis in theology. Four days after the article appeared, the chaplains who served Catholic African, Antillean, Guyanese, Malagasy, and Vietnamese students in Paris, including Father Michel, composed a protest against Ducattillon's article. They sent this document, along with Father Perbal's denunciation of Ducattillon's use of Vitoria in the earlier article "Theology of colonization," to Cardinal Feltin, *La Croix,* and *Le Monde.*[69] *Le Monde,* which had reproduced part of "The state of patriotism" in its edition of May 30, printed a small excerpt from the protest and noted Perbal's disapproval of Ducattillon's interpretation of Vitoria in its issue of June 3–4.[70] The chaplains characterized Ducattillon's point of view as a "personal opinion, which nothing in the traditional teachings of the church suggests adopting," and stated that his arguments "contradicted the colonial teachings of the church." They also scolded, "in the current climate, such an opinion, expressed by an eminent theologian, can only cast doubt on the Catholic Church's claims to supranationality and confirm suspicions of collusion between the church and the colonial system."[71] Seizing the moral high ground, they "deplored any partisan use, conscious or not, of theology or religion in the service of a contestable colonial policy, when everything should be done to find peaceful solutions to the colonial problem." They closed by invoking the "human and Christian future" of colonized peoples and called for a "spirit of justice and charity" in approaching the problem in order to avoid driving Catholics and others alike toward extreme positions.[72]

The echoes of the controversy continued to ripple outwards in the media. In its issue of June 16, the weekly digest *Informations catholiques internationales* published a press review entitled "'Traitors' or 'patriots'?" It led with a lengthy discussion of Ducattillon's article, followed by some of the reactions to it published in *La Croix* and the chaplains' manifesto. To these, the editors added summaries of articles from *Témoignage chrétien, La France catholique,* and *Revue de l'Action populaire,* which presented varying opinions on the question of whether it would be a treasonous abandonment to negotiate with the Algerian rebels. The compilation purposefully included a wide range of Catholic opinion on the colonial situation without clearly endorsing any point of view. Readers presumably came away with the troubling sense that there was no easy "Catholic" stance to take on colonialism or the Algerian War, despite Ducattillon's and Michel's assertions to the contrary.

Meanwhile, the church hierarchy became increasingly anxious about the acrimonious and public row between Ducattillon and Michel. French Catholic leaders in both the metropole and the Overseas Territories did not want to see colonial troubles divide the church, sully its reputation, or get in the way of its work. On June 5, Monsignor Lefebvre wrote to Michel from Dakar, admonishing him for his "extreme" positions. Revealing his own prejudices toward Africans, Lefebvre observed that "to work with students, and with black students whose sentiments dominate their reason, is not an easy task." Nonetheless, he continued, Michel had gone too far and had expressed opinions that were not doctrines of the church. "You wanted to prove," he wrote, "that decolonization is imperative. There is some truth in that, but it is not entirely true." Lefebvre critiqued Michel for insisting on principles and overlooking the wide range of situations in the French Union. The archbishop did not "completely approve" of Father Ducattillon's stance either, which he characterized as "going too far" and as "based on fairly indefensible motives." Nonetheless, he agreed with Ducattillon that the "colonizing powers had acquired some legitimate rights," especially in cases of mass migration such as Algeria. Lefebvre, who was extremely pessimistic about the future of Africa in the 1950s, felt that Europe still had an important role to play there as a guarantor of peaceful evolution. The choice, he wrote, was between anarchy, a "return to savagery," or a continued foreign presence. Above all, Lefebvre sought to remind Michel that his loyalty should lie first and foremost with the church. Catholicism could have an important impact in Africa, but not in an atmosphere of anarchy, fanatical Islam, or communism, he warned.[73] Leaning on Michel's invocation of the "right of tutelage," Lefebvre asserted that it was not time to decolonize: the period of tutoring was not over and premature departure would be bad for Africa and, most importantly, for the church.

In Paris, Cardinal Feltin also found the controversy unseemly and potentially harmful to the church. Feltin's approach to the war in Algeria was very cautious in 1956. Earlier, on April 20, he had addressed a large gathering of Parisian parish representatives on how Catholics should regard the situation in Algeria, mixing recommendations and observations in a somewhat awkward blend of Michel's and Ducattillon's positions. Feltin had begun by reminding his audience of the complexity of the conflict in Algeria and of how hard it was to ascertain the reality on the ground from afar. He then reiterated the official line that the church stood above all political parties and factions and was concerned only with "the moral aspect of the problem." He listed several key principles that guided the church's position on the subject. The first was that the church desired peace and an end to violence. The second was that the church opposed racism and had always argued, he claimed, that all men were brothers. Yet Feltin also declared that within this universal brotherhood, individuals owed a special allegiance to their own country, their "veritable mother." Finally, he argued, true colonization was a service to the colonized. Races were all equal, he said, but civilizations were not. Peoples who enjoyed cultural and technological superiority had a "duty" to help less privileged peoples—that is, a civilizing mission. In a line that Ducattillon might have written, Feltin claimed that colonization benefited the human community by helping colonized people exploit material, intellectual, and spiritual treasures that would otherwise be lost to humanity as a whole. He also said that it would not be fair for the colonized to seize goods from colonizers who had acquired them honestly. Yet, following Michel, Feltin warned that colonization could not continue indefinitely. The point was to help colonized people realize their potential, and it was the colonizing people's duty to "prepare and realize a progressive emancipation of the colony." The cardinal, who had tried to say something to nearly every constituency, closed by calling for "all useful reforms to allow Africans to take progressively more responsibility in the social realm" and for the cooperation of all for peace, an end to police actions, and the establishment of viable treaties.[74]

After receiving the manifesto that the chaplains had sent to the press, Feltin wrote to Michel on June 8. Michel's response indicates that Feltin was displeased by their decision to publicize their denunciation of "The state of patriotism." Michel defended their actions by citing the widespread diffusion of Ducattillon's article beyond the pages of La Croix to L'Aurore and Le Monde, where the students from the colonies encountered it. Had it just been a question of an article in La Croix, Michel claimed, the group would have been content to ask Father Gabel to revisit the question in a subsequent issue of the paper. That was the approach they had taken regarding Ducattillon's "Theology of colonization" in Revue de l'Action populaire in 1955. Yet the visibility of Ducattillon's ideas, and the students' "extraordinary" reactions, demanded a more vigorous and immediate course of action. Michel was not afraid to indict his superiors in self-defense, noting that skeptics saw the article as "proof of the truth of their accusations against the church hierarchy." Still, he hoped that the church could find some good in the situation and deepen the dialogue between metropolitan and overseas Catholics.[75]

Feltin's subsequent decision to orchestrate the face-to-face meeting between Michel and Ducattillon in late June was an attempt to force a united Catholic front on the question of colonization. It was not just a discussion between the two men: it was a sort of mini-summit attended by a contingent of Jesuits, including faculty members of the Institut d'études sociales at the Institut Catholique such as Fathers Bigo, Robert Bosc, Alfred de Soras, and Stanislas de Lestapis, as well as Father (and future cardinal) Jean Daniélou and two Malagasy priests.[76] Father Laurent presided. When the meeting began, Laurent gave Ducattillon the floor, and the Dominican reprised the main points of his 1955 article "Theology of colonization" but said nothing about Algeria. When it was his turn, Michel summarized his points from "The duty to decolonize" and then closed with a selection of quotes that he believed undermined Ducattillon's reliance on *jus communicationis,* sending the listening Jesuits into a frenzy of page-flipping in their copies of Vitoria. The key citation was, "if the barbarians do not offer us any just cause for war, and if they do not consent to recognize the Spanish princes, our entire establishment in their lands must cease, to the great detriment of Spain."[77] Michel's point was that if modern-day French theologians followed Vitoria, they had to recognize that French colonization was potentially illegitimate and could not be maintained by force without just cause, even if that would mean a loss of power, wealth, and prestige for France.

Michel subsequently presented the meeting as a victory for his point of view, though it did not result in the reconciliation that Feltin had hoped for. After the initial statements, discussion ranged freely about whether Vitoria's thought was still relevant (those present agreed that it was) and how it would apply to Algeria, which provoked a long and lively debate. In a question designed to weigh the strength of his French patriotism against his Catholic faith, Father Ducattillon was asked whether he would give absolution to a Christian Algerian rebel who rejected torture. Ducattillon asserted he would, apparently concluding that Catholicism should trump patriotism, however much he sympathized with Algeria's *colons.* According to Michel, Ducattillon agreed to write a new article that he and Michel would co-sign, which would smooth over their differences.[78]

Yet the hoped-for conversion of the Dominican did not take place, and Ducattillon never wrote the allegedly promised piece. Instead, the following year he released a book on patriotism and colonization that reprinted his 1955 article on the "Theology of colonization" and his *La*

Croix article on "The state of patriotism."[79] Furthermore, in May 1957, he gave a speech on "The Christian meaning of the military vocation," celebrating the French Army's role in the country's civilizing mission throughout the world. He critiqued those who questioned the continued relevance of patriotism, armies, and colonies as "'public criminals and perverters of the Christian conscience they invoke.'"[80] Ducattillon apparently remained unapologetically firm in his views until his sudden death a month later.

The dispute between Michel and Ducattillon over Catholic teaching on colonization encapsulated multiple, related, and simultaneous confrontations occurring in the turbulent French Union in the 1950s. It was first and foremost a battle over the future of French possessions overseas, which had important ramifications for France's standing on the world stage. Each man spoke to and for the aspirations and concerns of particular constituencies within the empire: Michel to young Africans desiring their independence and Ducattillon to settlers in Algeria and devout French patriots who were unwilling to countenance any loss of territory.) —o *different audiences*

Secondly, their feud captured the broader ideological fragmentation among, and the increasingly radical urges of French Catholics at midcentury. Vast political fissures had opened up within a metropolitan French Catholic public that had been largely conservative before World War I, and a robust Catholic left had crystallized under German occupation.[81] In many respects, Ducattillon thought and wrote like traditional, conservative, right-wing French Catholics, though he claimed to reject some of their fanatical and "pagan" patriotism.[82] Michel, on the other hand, had more in common with a newer cohort of French believers such as the worker-priests, who embraced leftist positions on social justice and the winding down of empire.

Finally, Michel's and Ducattillon's politics also reflected the fact that their feud was generational. Though only fourteen years apart, they belonged to different eras. Ducattillon, who remembered World War I, espoused a firm and fervent brand of French patriotism that did not resonate with many who came of age amid the moral ambiguities of the German occupation and the colonial wars that followed. Michel, who spent his time with students, was constantly hearing, and to an extent adopting, the perspective of an African youth that was increasingly disenchanted with imperial France and the older generation that governed it.

Meanwhile, the awkwardness of the French church hierarchy as it tried to find a position between Michel and Ducattillon, and between Catholic advocates of decolonization and devout champions of the French Empire more broadly, was emblematic of the church's colonial problem at midcentury. Cardinal Feltin believed in the superiority of French civilization and felt that colonization had largely been a boon for indigenous peoples in the colonies. Yet he did not want church interests and opportunities among Africans or his left-leaning compatriots to be damaged by a damning association with colonialism, especially as communists were standing by at the ready with an alternative ideology. He hopefully imagined that there was a way for the French church to exist safely on a higher plane, above the colonial controversies plaguing the metropole and its Overseas Territories. Yet this proved to be a pipe dream, as African Catholics and their French allies continued to hammer on the "unchristian" nature of colonialism, increasingly bypassing the French hierarchy and taking their message directly to the Vatican.

4

ENTIRELY CHRISTIAN AND ENTIRELY AFRICAN

African Catholic Students in Postwar France

IN THE SPRING OF 1956, as the dispute between Fathers Michel and Ducattillon built to its climax, the Association of Catholic African Students in France held its first annual convention in the southern university town of Pau.[1] In its wake, the students issued the strident public declaration mentioned earlier, which appeared in a variety of major media outlets including *Le Monde*, *Témoignage chrétien*, and *Afrique nouvelle*. It began, "We, the Catholic students of black Africa in France, reaffirm our desire to stay simultaneously entirely Christian and entirely African; we cannot, in any circumstances or under any kind of pressure, choose between these two loyalties."[2] Yet the rest of the statement reflected how difficult it was to maintain this dual identity as tension over the future of the French African colonies mounted. Though conceived for a broader public, the declaration was aimed primarily at French Catholics and the missionary wing of the Catholic Church in French Africa. Through rhetoric that emphasized their Catholic faith, the students hoped to persuade French believers and missionary clergy of the evils of colonialism and enlist their support for African autonomy. "We affirm our attachment to the natural right of African peoples to self-determination," they announced. "Rather than diminishing this attachment, our faith reinforces it, because it aims at the liberation and the spiritual blossoming of man." The students argued that French Catholic support of their endeavors would help them resolve the tension between their potentially conflicting allegiances: "We ask French Catholics to make the necessary effort to understand the demands of this double loyalty to the church and to Africa," they affirmed. "Their refusal to make this effort will only reinforce the impression of some of our compatriots that we risk being less African because we are Christians."[3] They thus highlighted the delicacy of their position between French and African publics, while calling for change in French Catholic attitudes.

The students closed their declaration with four statements that were highly controversial in 1956, when the majority of the French public did not support Algerian independence. First, they "solemnly reaffirm[ed] that a 'duty to decolonize' exists for all colonized countries, including Algeria," which, they claimed, rested on the right of self-determination of all peoples. Second, the students "deplore[d] the complicity of certain Catholics, who make the peaceful attainment of independence by colonized peoples dangerously difficult, by their writings, by their words and by their influence more generally, and who nourish an unfortunate conflation of missionary evangelism and the colonial system." Third, they "declare[d] with emotion that the use of so-called *'tirailleurs sénégalais'* (African soldiers) in a colonial war such as that in Algeria poses a grave moral problem; clashes profoundly with our Christian spirit and our African consciousness; creates a hostile atmosphere between brother peoples; and goes against the basic respect and justice due to African populations." Finally, they "demand[ed], in consequence, that all those exercising political, social, or religious power in France and Africa try as hard as possible to end such a pernicious abuse."[4] This attack on French colonial rule and particular elements within the Catholic Church was radical in all of its dimensions. Its stridency is all the more striking considering that its authors were a group of devout Catholics, when communists are best known for critiquing colonialism and the Catholic Church in midcentury France.

The 1956 declaration was only one example of public dialogue initiated by militant African Catholic students in France in the turbulent postwar years. These students were at the forefront both of denouncing the persistence of French rule in Africa and of pushing the Catholic Church to distance itself from colonial regimes.[5] They cultivated a critical stance vis-à-vis colonial and church authorities that was born of their intertwined struggles as Africans, Catholics, and students in the oft-inhospitable metropole. Indeed, many French believers did not "make the necessary effort" to reach out to or comprehend the unique position of the African Catholics in their midst. Instead, the students frequently found their French coreligionists to be racist, paternalistic, and unsympathetic to African aspirations for autonomy. At the same time, however, the students encountered clergy and Catholic intellectuals in the metropole, of both French and African origin, who were more supportive of decolonization than many French missionaries in Africa. The students pushed many of these mentors, such as Joseph Michel and Alioune Diop, to more radical stances as they worked together to convince French Catholics and the church hierarchy to support African independence. Their activism was part and parcel of their deeply personal quest to harmonize their Catholic and African identities as they self-consciously molded themselves into an elite that would return to Africa to lead.

Just as Catholic strands of negritude have been neglected, African Catholic student activism is largely missing from the existing literature on African students in midcentury France. French and African scholars have produced several studies of African students in France in the 1950s, and in particular of the secular Federation of Black African Students in France (FEANF), the largest student group active in the metropole. Yet they rarely mention the Association of Catholic African Students, though it disseminated its ideas quite effectively via *Tam-Tam*.[6] By 1955, *Tam-Tam* was circulating 5,000 copies, but many of those were passed around among multiple readers, and a variety of press outlets reproduced much of the magazine's content.[7]

Moreover, when Catholic students do surface in accounts of the period, they have been almost uniformly characterized as moderates. Charles-Edouard Harang, for example, describes them as "members of an elite focused on modernization and compromise that looked more towards emancipation within the colonial context than to veritable independence."[8] In their assessment of *Tam-Tam,* Nicolas Bancel and Jean

Devisse label its tone as "moderate."[9] In his history of the FEANF, Amady Aly Dieng reproduces this conclusion, while Charles Diané also calls *Tam-Tam* "more moderate" but does note that it was "firmly supportive of African liberation and African unity."[10] The insistence that the Association of Catholic African Students in France was moderate in orientation, which is contradicted by much of the evidence, seems to result from a conception of politics that equates radicalism primarily with communism. It may also reflect a persistence of the perception, which the students highlighted in their declaration, that Catholics were somehow less authentically "African."[11] In actual fact, however, the association's students consistently assailed French colonialism and the Catholic Church in the mid-1950s. Indeed, their 1956 statement declaring the duty to decolonize and denouncing the war in Algeria preceded a joint declaration in support of Algerian independence by the FEANF and activist students in Dakar by two months.[12]

Not every African Catholic student in France became a militant, of course, but most of them encountered a particular set of challenges that stemmed from their distinctive situation as Africans, Catholics, and students in midcentury France, which radicalized an influential, vocal group among them. Both church and state attempted to steer and monitor African students in postwar France, but such efforts often did not turn out exactly as either set of authorities imagined. African Catholic students' experience in the metropole between the mid-1940s and late 1950s informed their views of France, Africa, and Catholicism. Catholics shared many of the hardships of their non-Catholic African peers, including social isolation, racism, worries about money, difficulties navigating French institutions and bureaucracy, scarce and expensive lodging and food, and frequent illness. While Catholicism could serve as a source of strength in the face of adversity, Catholic students also often grappled with crises in faith inflected by these challenges and by the sheer shock of the differences in material and spiritual life between Africa and France. After exploring students' physical, social, and spiritual lives in the metropole, we will examine the activism of highly articulate radicals among them, showing how, alongside African Catholic intellectuals and clergy, they pushed to change the church from the inside. Their activities reveal that conservative French Catholic authorities were increasingly reacting to, rather than leading, their African student "protégés" in the years prior to independence.

STEERING AN AFRICAN ELITE

In the interwar period, a very few sub-Saharan Africans made their way to France to seek higher education. Among them, of course, were Alioune Diop and some other *originaires* of Senegal's Four Communes, who enjoyed the privilege of full French citizenship. According to historian Amady Aly Dieng, there were twenty-five sub-Saharan African and fifty Malagasy students in France in 1926, and twenty-one sub-Saharan Africans and nineteen Malagasies in 1932.[13] While these statistics may underestimate the total numbers somewhat, they are unlikely to be wildly incorrect, and indicate that a critical mass had not yet developed. Paris police archives indicate that an "Association des étudiants ouest-africains" was officially founded in January 1934, dissolved soon thereafter because of a lack of adherents, and then reappeared in 1938.[14]

After the war, this diminutive trickle began to swell rapidly: there were 2,000 black African students in France in 1950, 4,000 in 1952, and 8,000 in 1960.[15] Though Paris was the most popular destination, many were scattered in high schools, technical schools, and universities across the country. In academic year 1951–1952, for instance, the French government estimated that 429 individuals from French West Africa were studying in Paris, while 711 were dispersed in the provinces.[16] A disproportionate number of these students were Catholic, because mission schools were more common and sometimes more effective than state schools across large swaths of French Africa. For example, out of fifty-one students who embarked from Lomé, Togo for France in 1947, thirty-two were Catholic.[17] Togo was not heavily Muslim like other parts of French-controlled sub-Saharan Africa, but even when Muslim areas are factored in, Catholic students still predominated in the ranks of Africans who pursued education in France. In 1951, fully half of the African students in France were Catholic, though, according to church statistics, Catholics composed just under 6 percent of the entire population of French West Africa, French Equatorial Africa, Togo, and Cameroon combined.[18]

Though their numbers were growing, the Africans studying in France nonetheless composed a tiny elite, as many African children, especially in rural areas, did not have the opportunity to attend school at all under French rule. As late as 1958, for example, out of an estimated 2.9 million children in the colonies of French West Africa, only 427,000 were in primary school, 22,000 were in secondary or technical school, and 1,000 attended the University of Dakar, which was only founded the year before.[19] State and church authorities, as well as the students themselves, were thus very conscious of the fact that they would likely play an outsized role in the future of their homelands because of their educational attainments. As Bernard Cornut-Gentille, high commissioner in French Equatorial Africa from 1948 until 1951 and then in French West Africa between 1951 and 1956 wrote to his subordinate governors in 1954, "I have already, on multiple occasions, underlined the attention I am giving to the problem of students and the importance I attach to the development of an autochthonous elite. The evolution of Africa depends in large part on the care we take in preparing these future leaders and in giving them the training they expect from us."[20] Under his leadership, the administration expanded its budget to provide grants to promising African students to study in the metropole. As a result, in the early 1950s, just over half of them supported their studies with state-sponsored scholarships dispensed by their home territories.[21]

The French government tried to make sure that African students would repay the state's investment with meaningful service in their territories of origin. Those who prepared for careers in teaching and administration on government scholarships signed contracts committing themselves to ten years of work in Africa after the completion of their studies.[22] Cornut-Gentille also tried to create attractive and suitable employments for educated Africans to return to. Senegalese deputy Abbas Guèye wrote to the high commissioner in 1952, thanking him for measures that would "permit the Federation to recuperate its intellectual elites, who, left to themselves, would be definitively lost to the territories that currently support the costs of their studies."[23]

This fear of "losing" educated African students who migrated to the metropole to study was not unique to Guèye or to French administrative authorities. French Catholic missionaries in Africa had the exact same anxieties. Church authorities dearly hoped that educated Catholic students would bring their faith back to leadership roles in Africa. Yet they also worried that the students would abandon Catholicism in France, which might have negative consequences for the future of the church in Africa. As one missionary put it, "one cannot exaggerate the influence they will have, for good or bad, on the spiritual orientation of their homelands."[24] In 1954, Father Joseph-Roger de Benoist, then a young White Father working on the staff of *Afrique nouvelle* in Dakar, was profoundly pessimistic about African students coming back from France and injuring the church. "In the coming years," he wrote, "we are going to see the return of the students currently studying in France. Everything we know about them suggests that these years are going to be very hard and that the missions are going to be subjected to assaults by young people bursting with communist, nationalist, anticolonialist, and anti-Christian slogans. Some of them will have more serious training and will rapidly become the opinion leaders in AOF and replace the current legislators."[25] De Benoist was far from conservative—a few years later, when he became editor-in-chief of *Afrique nouvelle* in Dakar, he supported African self-determination and clashed repeatedly with Archbishop Lefebvre.[26] His thinking in 1954, however, reveals that even relatively progressive French Catholic missionaries believed that African students posed a potential threat to the church in French Africa.

Like Cornut-Gentille's administration, Catholic authorities had the impulse to guide African student experience in France to a desirable outcome, which for them meant developing and fortifying Catholic students' spiritual defenses against exposure to materialism, communism, and atheism in the metropole. This was precisely why Monsignor Lefebvre founded the ministry in Paris for Catholic students from the colonies in the late 1940s. Lefebvre conceived of this initiative as an investment in the future—by safeguarding the Catholicism of the emerging African elite, he would ensure a lasting place for the church in Africa.[27] Lefebvre wielded significant influence in Pius XII's Vatican, and the pope echoed this idea in his 1957 encyclical *Fidei donum,* noting that the "Christian lives" of students from Africa and Asia in France might be "endangered" if they lacked support while they were abroad, which would have serious ramifications for "their present and future careers." He urged "devout and well-equipped" clergy to see to their needs and thus "relieve the anxieties" of their bishops back home.[28]

Other French missionaries in Africa also undertook major efforts to mold young African Catholic students in order to make sure that church projects in postwar Africa had a bright future. In 1947, for example, Monsignor Joseph-Paul Strebler, an Alsatian SMA missionary who served as the apostolic vicar of Lomé, Togo, sent a clutch of promising African students to the Episcopal College of Zillisheim near Strasbourg to study for the baccalaureate and then the *brevet supérieur,* so they could return home to teach in his mission's new Collège Saint Joseph.[29] The vicariate paid the high costs of their education—some 175,000 metropolitan francs per year—but in the late 1940s Strebler and his advisors were convinced that cultivating skilled local personnel was the best way to ensure that their venture would endure.[30] As in the case of state-funded scholarships, students who took money from the mission for education signed a contract committing to ten years of teaching service in Togo at the end of their studies.[31] Strebler and his collaborators also kept up correspondence with a number of other Catholic mentees who were studying in educational establishments all across France, and the SMA province of Alsace, which oversaw the Togo missions, hosted many of these students during school vacations.

These missionary efforts to monitor and mold elite African Catholic students in France often did not have the intended results. Between the late 1940s and mid-1950s, the relationship between African Catholic students in France and the church evolved rapidly, and not necessarily in directions envisioned by French missionaries. African Catholic students turned out to be unpredictable investments: some abandoned their faith while studying in the metropole, while some that remained devout became uncomfortably radical, challenging both the state and the church on colonialism. Still others discovered that they wanted to pursue career paths other than those laid out for them by their missionary mentors. By 1951, Monsignor Strebler had become circumspect about the Zillisheim students, noting the "high probability" that they would "not want to serve the mission," and that they might not even be able to if their grades did not improve.[32] He did not seem overly inclined to hold them to the terms of their contracts either.[33] Meanwhile, Monsignor Lefebvre began to regret his 1950 nomination of Father Michel to the Paris chaplaincy for overseas students, as Michel's office in the rue Thibaud in the fourteenth arrondissement became a hotbed of activism where students decried both French colonial rule in Africa and the elements within the Catholic Church that wanted to maintain it.

AFRICAN CATHOLIC STUDENT LIFE IN THE MIDCENTURY METROPOLE

Much of the dissonance between African Catholic students' trajectories and missionary clergy's hopes for them lay in the myriad material and spiritual struggles the students encountered in France. Even a vocal public advocate for African Catholic students like Father Michel felt privately that too many of them were coming to the metropole in the early 1950s. He worried that the precariousness of their existence in France, particularly for those who lacked scholarships, was doing them more harm than good.[34]

One of the students' most basic difficulties was adjusting to the French climate, particularly if they went somewhere cold. For example, in 1947 a group of twenty-five Togolese students, four destined for veterinary or forestry work and twenty-one as future teachers, embarked for the Lycée de Gap in the Hautes-Alpes region of southeastern France. Gap holds the distinction as the highest departmental capital in France at 750 meters above sea level, and its alpine environment was a rude shock to the Africans. "We are badly situated here," wrote student Victor Tenneroni to Monsignor Strebler in June of 1948, "the climate is one of the harshest in France. . . . How many of us have spent several weeks in the infirmary!" The students demanded to leave for a school in a "better region," though they needed the permission of the administration in Togo, which was paying their tuition. The SMA mission sent Father Aloyse Riegert, the director of Catholic education in Togo, to visit the students, and mailed them copies of *Mia Holo,* a Catholic newspaper in the Ewe language, to make them feel more at home.[35] Even African students in more temperate zones of France battled illness with some regularity. The extant correspondence of SMA missionaries with Togolese students Clovis Olympio and Gabriel Koudry reveal ongoing battles with weight loss and anemia, respectively.[36] And as one African Catholic student journalist noted in *Tam-Tam* in 1953, the many African students who fell sick in Paris in the winter could end up suffering alone for days before anyone noticed.[37]

Indeed, social isolation was a common problem for African students who came to France, both in Paris and in the provinces. Like other students from abroad, they were far from home, family, and friends, yet Africans also had to contend with racism and colonial paternalism, in both blatant and subtle manifestations. As Alioune Diop experienced in La Flèche in the mid-1940s, Africans often had the status of curiosities, rather than community members, in smaller towns in the provinces. In 1947, Vincent Gbikpi, a Togolese based in the commune of Huos near the foothills of the Pyrenees, alluded to his uncomfortable local notoriety in a letter to an SMA mentor. He suggested that his correspondent could simply address letters to 'Vincent at Huos' because "in everyone's mind, Vincent means the Black . . ."[38] Even in bigger cities, students felt the stares of French people who had not encountered Africans before. Joseph Ki-Zerbo, the student from Upper Volta who became the most prominent radical Catholic student leader, wrote an article for *Tam-Tam* in which he described the case of a fifteen-year-old from Dahomey who disembarked alone in Bordeaux and had to make his way northward to school. Overwhelmed and afraid, the young man walked the streets but did not speak to anyone, eventually taking refuge in the welcoming darkness of a movie theater, where he did not feel so conspicuous.[39] In yet another example, two students from Dahomey studying in Saumur testified that they felt very isolated when they arrived, knowing next to no one. They eventually managed to emerge from this loneliness thanks in large part to their African and Antillean classmates at school, which suggests that they either segregated themselves or were shunned by French classmates.[40]

In Paris, anonymity, racism, and widespread indifference contributed to African students' isolation. In a 1953 *Tam-Tam* article, a colonial student using the byline "Toutane" noted that while it looked as though there was a great deal of camaraderie among students at the Sorbonne, in reality, few genuine friendships developed at the university itself. All of the people socializing together on campus had likely met elsewhere. "Someone who does not know anyone, and who is naturally timid, is at great risk of staying isolated throughout the academic year," Toutane wrote. The only way to avoid "getting lost in the flood" was to find a student group to join as soon as possible.[41] It helped to know someone: Gabriel Koudry was lucky that when he moved to Paris from the provinces in 1954, his friend and fellow Togolese student Alex Dosseh was already there, and they took their meals together when they could.[42]

Social isolation was also inextricably intertwined with the severe financial challenges most African students faced in France. A few of the Togolese students affiliated with the SMA missions came from wealthy families that insulated them from this kind of hardship. Clovis Olympio, for example, was a member of Togo's most prominent black family, which produced Sylvanus Olympio, the country's first independent president. Founding ancestor Francisco Olympio Silva, an Afro-Brazilian, left Brazil for Africa in 1850 at the age of seventeen and built up a vast fortune in trade, including slaving, and took seven wives.[43] By the mid-twentieth century, this prodigious family was fabulously wealthy, devoutly Catholic, and its male members were highly educated.[44] Another Togolese Catholic student, Epiphan Seddoh, was the son of wealthy Lomé businessman Patrick Seddoh.[45] Unlike many of his cash-strapped peers, who were often stranded during school vacations without means to travel or easily replace the meals that their institutions provided them in term time, his parents could pay vacation room and board at an SMA facility in Alsace.[46]

The majority of African students, however, struggled financially in France. By 1948, Vincent Gbikpi had moved on from Huos to the École supérieure d'agriculture de Purpan in Toulouse, where he reported he was "having difficulty making ends meet." His state scholarship did not cover his living expenses, plus he had incurred various one-time charges when he entered his new school. "I am starting next trimester without hope because the cost of board and school fees is 25,000 francs per term, but my scholarship is 7,800 francs per month," he wrote to an SMA priest. "Believe me, Father, I have always suffered humiliations in monetary affairs." He hoped to close the looming gap by selling coffee that his relatives sent him from Togo.[47] Similarly, Alex Dosseh found himself in dire straits when his state scholarship was canceled for academic year 1952–1953.[48] Intense lobbying to reverse the decision failed and Monsignor Strebler encouraged him to return home, but Dosseh decided to try to stick it out in Paris.[49] He was one of a fortunate few Africans who were able to find a room in the France d'Outre-Mer pavilion at the Cité universitaire, with a 1,400 franc discount off the usual monthly rent of 5,500 francs. He saved additional money on food by eating cheaply at the Cité a couple of times a week. He was also lucky because his family had enough money to send him some relief, and, as a gifted musician who later composed Togo's national anthem, he had a special set of skills.[50] Through the intervention of Father Michel, he got a partial stipend from the César Franck music school and made money on the side by teaching piano, music theory, and composition to two French students. "I am not terribly unhappy," he wrote to an SMA priest, "I have no time to think of material needs." Nonetheless, he observed, "I am counting on Providence for a future with fewer worries."[51] Dosseh made it through that hard year—SMA correspondence indicates that he was still getting by in Paris in 1956.[52]

As Dosseh's case highlights, affordable housing was a major obstacle for African students, especially in the capital, where the cost of living was highest. Some of the lycées in the provinces and some state scholarships provided housing, but most of the African students in France had to find places to live on their own. By the early 1950s, there were some officially sponsored options, such as the France d'Outre-Mer Pavilion, but they could only accommodate a small portion of the demand. The Pavilion, which catered to students from all overseas possessions, could house 250, but not all of its rooms ended up going to colonial students. In 1953, for example, only 210 of the 4,500 students from the colonies in Paris found accommodation there. Some Overseas Territories, including French West Africa and Madagascar, purchased buildings to house their students in Paris, but they too were insufficient. In 1952, fifty students in the "maison AOF" on the boulevard Poniatowski in the twelfth arrondissement attempted to expel forcibly some thirty other tenants in the building to make more rooms available for students.[53] The following year, there were seventy-four students housed there, only a fraction of the total number of West African students in Paris.[54]

Because of the dearth of official options, many students ended up in cheap and tawdry hotels, or renting rooms from private individuals.[55] At first, Gabriel Koudry rented a room in a private home in the fourteenth arrondissement, but stayed only two months because the room was too small and, as he put it, "did not meet indispensable conditions of hygiene." He was lucky to find a better sublet nearby with friends, a M. and Mme Lemorcier, whom he may have met through Catholic circles or because they had some connection to Togo.[56] Similarly, between 1949 and 1956, before he married a fellow African student, Joseph Ki-Zerbo lived in the seventh arrondissement of Paris at the home of a Mme Masson, the mother of a missionary priest he had befriended.[57] Both young men were fortunate to have kindly landlords—living in a hotel room or in a private room in an indifferent household could be very isolating and conducive to depression.

Housing posed particular challenges for female African students, who, along with their families, were often more concerned about their physical safety in France than men.[58] Women were a small but significant minority of the African students who came to France—an estimated 202 out of a total of 1,401 West African students in France in 1953 were female.[59] Many of them came to study as nurses or social workers, and students enrolled in such programs did not get access to inexpensive university restaurants without special permission.[60] Landlords who rented rooms in their homes tended to prefer male tenants who usually did not ask to use kitchen or laundry facilities and often stayed out all day. Private access to a water source for bathing and laundry or permission to cook were rare in such situations.[61] A hotel room was not ideal either—the cost of a hotel did not include meals, and it could be isolating, especially for the many young women who had come directly from a religious school where they lived with other students. The best option for young African women was usually a "foyer féminin." Often run by nuns or Catholic laywomen, these institutions offered meals but often did not include bread, sugar, drinks, sheets, or cutlery, which the student either would have to provide or pay for.[62] Foyers also often had nighttime curfews, which prevented lodgers from coming and going entirely as they pleased. Yet, they were relatively affordable, typically had laundry facilities, and frequently offered opportunities to learn skills such as sewing on a machine. They provided a community that staved off isolation, assured help in case of illness, and usually had chapels where the devout could worship. Because of these advantages, places in foyers were hard to come by, and female students often had to apply with strong references at least six months in advance to secure a spot.[63]

House hunting also exposed African students to some of the most open, unbridled racism that they encountered in France. In 1954, Father Michel noted ruefully that the *Figaro* newspaper had called his office to complain because its readers were up in arms when African students began to seek housing via its lodging service.[64] Similarly, an administrative report on Senegalese students in France observed of racism in the housing market, "This racism is notorious to the point that the statistics of the Office of Overseas Students emphasize that out of every ten advertisements for rooms to rent at COPAR (Parisian Committee of University Projects), eight to nine clearly stipulate that the landlord will not accept African students."[65] Michel and his collaborators in the rue Thibaud tried to improve African students' access to housing, and to combat the racial prejudices that kept French people from renting to them. In 1954, they assembled a press kit for the JEC, to sensitize French Catholics to the difficulties colonial students faced in this domain.[66]

Several of the documents in the kit exposed the racism of Catholic French landlords in alternately shocking and comic terms. They were essentially fables aimed at steering the conservative Catholic bourgeoisie of France to an attitude of tolerance and respect for African students. In one anecdote, a man came by the office in the rue Thibaud and told the African secretary that he had a room to rent, "but if possible, try to find me a student who is not too black," he cautioned. The secretary, who had just lost a brother fighting for France in Indochina, was deeply insulted and replied, "You are in the wrong place, Monsieur, because all of our students are as black as I am!" The man repeated his request to Father Michel, claiming that his housekeeper would be afraid of someone "too black." Michel finally talked him into relinquishing this condition, and reported that once he had accepted a student, the housekeeper had gotten over her fears.[67]

In similar fashion, Michel related how two elderly French Catholic matrons overcame their prejudices to become surrogate mothers of African students. In one case, the woman in question reacted to Michel's initial proposal to host an African by blurting out, "But I've heard that they bite!" Michel explained that because of her advanced age, the woman had likely been told fanciful stories of cannibals from the early colonial era. Eventually she relinquished her fears, and became very solicitous of her tenant, tending his health assiduously with home remedies. In another case, when a potential French hostess saw that the medical student Michel sent her was black, she turned him away from her door by making up a story about how she had just rented her spare room to a clergyman. Displaying a common fear among potential French housing providers, she worried, "What will the landlord say? The neighbors?" Two days later, however, she called Michel back and said that her grown children had told her she should take the student, whom she admitted she had found very polite. Six months later, when the student moved to be closer to campus, she called Michel to ask if he could find her another African student to take care of.[68]

Allies like Michel tried to alleviate the various hardships that African students faced in France, but sometimes metropolitan clergy were part of the problem, exhibiting the racism, paternalism, and lack of comprehension that the students found in French society more broadly. It is true that African students grumbled more about missionary racism and usually found metropolitan clergy to be more "progressive" on colonial matters than French priests in the colonies.[69] Yet even sympathetic clergy in France, including Father Michel, were not entirely exempt from the prejudices of the era. Early in his tenure as chaplain, for example, Michel was brutally frank about how hard he thought it was for a French Catholic to befriend an African and exercise a meaningful influence on him. "It requires total devotion, a great deal of patience, and tact, because of their touchiness and their inferiority complex: one cannot display any agitation in the face of declarations of territorial independence, or of a social or racist nature (because the black is as ferociously racist as many French people)," he wrote to a colleague in 1951, and "one cannot be surprised by mood swings, childish whims, or the most unexpected wild imaginings."[70] Nonetheless, Michel was a dogged advocate for his students, whereas other young Africans encountered clergy in the metropole who seemed unable to think outside of racist tropes.

Such was the case for the small group of students that Monsignor Strebler's Lomé mission sent to Zillisheim in the late 1940s. The school's director, Canon Paul Aberer, tended to see the worst in some of his charges, whom he referred to paternalistically as "our blacks." Aberer characterized Quirin Feliho, the son of prosperous Lomé trader Vincent Feliho, as a rebel and a troublemaker, writing in July of 1948 that Quirin "was embittered against his teachers" and "would not do anything good."[71] Aberer also described him as "very sensual, judging by his behavior to his white classmates. He likes to caress and to tickle them, especially the younger ones, and he knows perfectly well that he is not being good." This suggestion of improper physical contact was a heavy indictment for a boy who was likely lonely and bewildered, and demonstrably not receiving sympathetic support so far from home. Aberer made no bones about wanting Quirin out of his establishment as soon as possible.[72]

And Aberer's racist fixation on black "sensuality" vis-à-vis whites was not confined to Feliho. In 1947, he opened and secretly read a letter that Clovis Olympio had written to a friend named Folly, which included the line "'Watch out for the hens in Hagenau, no?'" "Does he mean to put his friend gently on his guard?" Aberer worried in a letter to Father Victor Kern, the superior of the SMA province of Strasbourg, "Or do you think Clovis himself is keeping unhealthy company?"[73] In a separate letter, Aberer noted that Clovis, who was older than the other students, needed "careful surveillance," was too fond of "light reading," and took "more interest than he should in girls."[74] Aberer also expressed anxiety regarding the fact that some French students were inviting their Togolese classmates home to meet their families. "I fear precisely the proximity of the sisters of our young people and their female friends," he wrote; "several people have put me on my guard regarding the appetites of Blacks for white girls."[75] By 1950, Clovis had moved on to the Collège St. André in Mulhouse, but it is clear that Father Kern had absorbed Aberer's concern. When Clovis expressed interest in finding a tutor to help him on the weekends, Kern warned the school's director that potential candidates should not have older girl children "to avoid what must be avoided."[76] These worries did not surface anywhere, however, in the deferent letters the mission wrote to Clovis's wealthy father, Christiano Olympio. Two months prior, an SMA priest (likely Father Kern himself) had reported to Christiano that "Clovis is a very good boy, who is loved wherever he goes and who exhibits very good behavior; he deserves to succeed. One can see that he has had a good education; he is very polite and helpful."[77] It seems likely that the students were well aware of the prejudices of these spiritual mentors, even if their parents were not.

Indeed, African Catholic students' encounters with French Catholics and French Catholicism more broadly were often profoundly bewildering and upsetting to them. They were frequently disappointed by the lax observance and apparent religious indifference of many so-called Catholics in the metropole. Basile Mensah, a Catholic student and veteran of the Indochina War from Dahomey, wrote in *Tam-Tam* in 1954 that France seemed predominantly atheist to African Catholic students when they first arrived, which led them to relinquish their own external and internal patterns of religious observance over time.[78] The two Catholic students from Dahomey in Saumur expressed similar disenchantment. They had been forewarned about "corruption" among both French and African students in the metropole, but were still "scandalized" by African Catholic students who had followed the example of their French colleagues and abandoned their religious zeal. They felt obligated to "preach religious renewal" to one such student they met in Marseille. Citing a conversation with a lapsed French Catholic student, one of them wrote, "I have deduced that nearly all of the Christians in France care very little about the Christian religion. We have concluded that the Catholic religion is in decline."[79]

In his capacity as chaplain, Father Michel worried greatly about African Catholic students' ability to maintain their faith in the metropole's hostile spiritual environment. He wrote to a colleague that some of them came to France with a "very deficient" and "very superficial" religious background, which could not survive the "brutal contact with our materialism." He believed that even devout young Africans with excellent religious educations were in danger of going astray in France if not strongly supported by the chaplain of their schools, or a Catholic youth group, which happened all too rarely, in his opinion.[80] In an article entitled "Testimony of a Catholic student" for Alioune Diop's special 1953 issue of *Présence africaine* "Black students speak," Joseph Ki-Zerbo echoed this concern, faulting French missionaries for their inadequate religious instruction of young Catholics in Africa, in particular the future lay elites. He criticized missionaries for focusing too narrowly on training African clergy, and not providing other ardent believers with a sophisticated religious education.[81]

The testimony of a Togolese student who was well into his second year of studies in Bordeaux in the spring of 1947 speaks to Michel's concerns. "I can tell you with joy," he wrote an SMA priest, "that with God's help I still remain a pretty good Catholic. Up until now, I have not had a crisis of faith. But the moral crises! They happen every day, even every hour. You know the world of today, and especially present-day life in France, better than I do. One is enveloped by it! Nonetheless—another divine mercy—I am still holding firm." He went to mass every Sunday, and took communion as often as possible, yet found he had no time for spiritual cultivation, religious reading, or meditation, because he was trying to complete a four-year academic program in half the time. He begged an African priest, Father Jean Gbikpi, to write him and "insist on the moral side of things," effectively asking for the spiritual guidance he needed to remain Catholic in his new surroundings.[82]

Father Michel also lamented how hard it was for African Catholic students to connect with their French counterparts. In his view, instead of providing a common ground, faith often did not overcome cultural divides that hindered the formation of deep friendships. French students tended to keep their religious lives private, and felt they had made a great social effort when they invited Africans to play ping-pong. Meanwhile, Catholic Africans, who tended to seek profound interpersonal connections and intimate exchanges of ideas, found their relationships with French students to be superficial and disappointing.[83] In his 1953 article in *Présence africaine,* Joseph Ki-Zerbo echoed Michel's observation that dissonance between varying approaches to religion and worship created distance between French and African Catholics. Citing African practices of Catholicism that Vatican II would ultimately embrace, such as "prayers, songs, and ritual gestures performed in unison," Ki-Zerbo argued that many Africans found French Catholic services to be cold and sterile, and French Catholics very closed off and private, which flew in the face of the solidarity that Africans wanted and expected to feel in a Catholic community.[84]

These various examples show that while African Catholic students faced the same environmental, social, and financial trials that most African students encountered in France, they often bore the additional burden of wrestling with their Catholic faith in a setting that deeply undermined it. The myriad environmental, social, and financial obstacles they faced, as well as the overarching colonial situation, posed a grave challenge to that faith. As Joseph Ki-Zerbo pointed out in *Présence africaine,* since Catholicism could be considered a "French import" to Africa, it was viewed in some quarters as the "'nec plus ultra' of 'assimilation'" and amounted to "suicide" of an African's "own personality."[85]

Indeed, as the 1956 declaration highlights, the tension between being both authentically Catholic and African was omnipresent for elite African Catholic students in the postwar period. Some individual students, feeling as though they had to choose between their African and Catholic selves, abandoned their faith. On the other hand, that tension was a crucial factor in the development of African Catholic student activism and political agitation. Committed African Catholic student activists worked for better conditions for African students in the metropole, but also championed African independence. For them, it was not enough to sensitize French Catholics to the ugliness and iniquity of racism in the housing market. They needed to go further and persuade French Catholics and the hierarchy of the French church of the righteousness of decolonization, as well as the necessity of making the church an institution in which Africans were valued equals, not subordinates.

AN "AUTHENTIC" ANTICOLONIAL CONSCIOUSNESS

Though their numbers were much smaller than those of the FEANF, the knot of activists who formed the Association of Catholic African Students boasted a stunning array of intellectual firepower. Their ranks included individuals who would go on to make significant professional and political contributions in independent Africa. The most vocal of these was Ki-Zerbo, the first African to become *agrégé d'histoire* in France, who remained politically active and became a distinguished scholar of African history in his native Upper Volta (Burkina Faso).[86] Jean Pliya, the internationally known Beninese author, playwright, government minister, and historian, served as the group's president, as did Nicolas Toufic, who became an eye doctor and a crusader against endemic disease across West Africa.[87] Two other African medical pioneers were part of the Catholic student circle: Alexis Codjia, the first Beninese surgeon at the Centre national hospitalier et universitaire (originally the Hôpital Hubert Maga) in Cotonou and Raymond Messanvi Johnson, who got his MD at the University of Paris in 1961 and became Togo's leading psychiatrist.[88] *Tam-Tam*'s pages feature numerous contributions from Paulin Joachim, the Beninese poet and journalist, who had gone to France to study law at the Catholic University of Lyon, but dropped out for financial reasons in the early 1950s.[89] The group also included Basile Mensah, whose administrative career got caught up in political upheaval in 1960s Dahomey; Paul Kaya, an engineering student from Congo-Brazzaville who later served as a minister in the independent Republic of the Congo; Richard Dogbeh, a famous Beninese writer who also served as a minister in the 1960s; and Emmanuel Olory-Togbe, a Beninese who went on to become a mathematics teacher at the Lycée Behanzin in Porto-Novo.[90]

These militant students interacted with broader secular and religious African and pan-African movements in France. They were in contact with young African clergy who were studying in Europe and who went on to be prelates in Africa, such as Robert Sastre and Raymond-Marie Tchidimbo. They were also connected to Alioune Diop, whom they referred to as an "older brother," and the negritude milieu surrounding *Présence africaine*.[91] Indeed, as the rue Thibaud was also the headquarters of the Catholic student associations of the Antilles and of Madagascar, the Africans were constantly in touch with black students from around the French Union. Each group published its own magazine—the Antilleans put out *Alizés* and the Malagasies *Fehim-Pihavanana*—but there was significant overlap between the publications. Maddy (Madeleine) Lastel, a Guyanese student, served as secretary to the editor for *Tam-Tam* and *Alizés* in the mid-1950s and frequently contributed articles to both.[92] Although there was some friction between Antilleans and Africans in France, which derived partially from longstanding white French perspectives (shared by some Antilleans) that Antilleans were more "civilized" than Africans, Lastel affirmed that the Catholic representatives of both groups had forged fraternity and unity on the basis of their common faith. "We are members of a community that

Catholic African and Antillean students in France, 1950s. Father Joseph Michel is at rear left. Courtesy of ACSSp.

respects and absorbs differences, in which each individual can freely pursue his or her 'fundamental project,'" she wrote in *Tam-Tam* in 1955.[93]

Catholicism was thus not an obstacle, and could even be a pathway to participation in broader pan-African circles. Ki-Zerbo, the leading African Catholic student spokesman in the mid-1950s, did not operate in a Catholic silo. He was also active in the FEANF and helped to found its sub-association of students from Upper Volta.[94] Yet his indefatigable activity for the Association of Catholic African Students revealed that his faith remained a priority as he agitated for change in Africa. He and his allies wanted to change the church from within to bring it into line with their hopes for Africa, thereby resolving the tension between the "African" and "Catholic" aspects of their identities. They insisted that

African Catholic students could be active militants for their church and their continent at the same time.

In this context, African Catholic students' faith was both a liability and a resource for their activism. On the one hand, they felt obliged to fend off accusations that conversion to a "European" faith had diminished their Africanness, especially when French Catholics, or members of the church hierarchy, were insensitive to them personally or belittled African aspirations for independence. On the other hand, Catholic teachings provided student activists, as well as African priests and Alioune Diop, with ammunition to criticize those who did not share their anticolonial views. Catholic rhetoric of universality and justice became a powerful weapon they could deploy against conservative and procolonial interests inside the church itself.

Indeed, as African Catholic students and their mentors drew more public attention to their positions, they had more opportunities to interact with senior members of the church. In December 1954, Cardinal Feltin, the archbishop of Paris, paid a visit to the rue Thibaud. Joseph Ki-Zerbo, who addressed the cardinal on behalf of the assembled students, proudly vaunted the students' accomplishments in their internal spiritual domains, as well as their work to publicize their point of view in the press. Yet the bulk of his speech had an edge to it—Ki-Zerbo presented a fairly negative view of the church and openly challenged the cardinal to expand his point of view. "If the ambition of a true apostle is to be Greek among the Greeks, Jewish among the Jews (and therefore black or Malagasy with us), it follows that one cannot pretend to move toward colonial youth, nor to call them to the Christian ideal, without comprehending the existential climate in which they live," he said, arguing that African Catholic students "lived Catholicism" in a particular economic, sociological, and political context.[95]

Ki-Zerbo went on to present Feltin with a list of the church's shortcomings, as the students saw them. He cited the "problem of the attitude of the church vis-à-vis the fact and law of colonialism." He criticized missionary silence on colonialism, which he defined as "methods of injustice and racism that too often accompany colonization." He raised student concern over how Catholicism was presented and taught to colonized populations—what he called the "adaptation" and "incarnation" of Catholicism in the colonies. Much like the African priests who would soon publish *Des prêtres noirs s'interrogent* in collaboration with Présence africaine, he decried missionaries' emphasis on assimilation, which led them to dismiss and denigrate indigenous culture, instead of finding ways to integrate church practice and teaching with local traditions. Ki-Zerbo also criticized French Catholics for their poor reception of African Catholic students in the metropole. Finally, he evoked the specter of the church as a "harlequin" in colonial lands—wearing a coat of many colors that it adapted to circumstances, such as colonialism, rather than its "divine robe, without embroidery, consistent across time and place." He called for a condemnation "from the highest Catholic authorities" of the "sin" of colonialism, and took aim at the French church in particular. "Certainly, we do not doubt that Our Holy Father the Pope is attentive to these serious problems," he said, "but what of the French church, glorious pioneer of the faith—does it not have a special vocation in this regard?"[96] As Feltin was the most prominent member of the French church, this was tantamount to a personal attack.

In his response to Ki-Zerbo, Cardinal Feltin reproduced the students' strategy by insisting on the justice of Catholic principles. He also tried to blunt their criticism by enveloping them in his portrayal of the church. He was particularly struck, he said, by Ki-Zerbo's suggestion that the church wore a "harlequin's coat." "This accusation makes all of us suffer," he said, "you and me, because we know that it is fundamentally untrue, because we are convinced that the church remains true to herself, and does not vary her Law and her principles according to circumstances." Feltin maintained that the church had always "condemned injustice in all circumstances." He also asserted, in response to Ki-Zerbo's call for better missionary accommodation of African culture, that the church "had always perceived the necessary adaptations," citing as proof "all of the indigenous priests and bishops, that we have had many occasions to meet and admire." Finally, the cardinal claimed that the church had "always" been worried about the reception of colonial students in France, and was working toward improving it. Feltin ended his talk on a cautionary note, warning the students not to take their protests too far into the territory of hate, revolution, and bloody combat, which the church abhorred. While it was legitimate to protest grave injustices, he admitted, one had to guard against exaggeration that would spark extremism. The "constant view and continual instructions" of the church were to work for evolution, rather than revolution, or "change that transforms hearts and minds bit by bit, so men can become brothers."[97] Feltin thus made it clear that he understood the students' frustrations but did not endorse their radical stance in its entirety.

Ki-Zerbo described Feltin's visit to the rue Thibaud as "a consecration" of the ministry's and the students' efforts.[98] It was certainly evidence of the growing importance of African Catholic student activism in France, and an acknowledgment that the French church hierarchy could no longer ignore it, even if Feltin tried to exert a moderating influence. After meeting with the cardinal, the students heightened their public profile. In 1956, they held their first annual convention at Pau, where they issued the declaration for decolonization. At Easter 1957, they turned their second annual convention into a pilgrimage to Rome. Two hundred students from French Africa, Madagascar, and the Antilles descended on the epicenter of Catholicism, where they drafted a set of resolutions regarding the economic, political, social, and religious situation of Africa. Among other things, the resolutions stridently endorsed the independence and sovereignty of black Africa; rejected any French colonial reform initiatives which did not result in complete, unfettered independence; called on Europeans in Africa to stop acting as "masters"; called for the education of African women and the protection of African workers; denounced French economic exploitation of Africa; and argued that the French deployment of FIDES funds was failing to end metropolitan economic subjugation of the Overseas Territories.[99]

The students, who had become public relations experts in the course of their campaigns in France, utilized the Rome trip to bring these causes to the attention of the Vatican hierarchy and to push the highest church officials to endorse their point of view. Their primary Vatican interlocutor was Pietro Cardinal Sigismondi, the secretary of the Propaganda Fide. On the religious front, the students' resolutions called for a Christian message better adapted to Africa, better religious training and support for lay Catholics so that Christianity in Africa would have a more "authentically African" face, and the cooperation and understanding of European missionaries, who would have to realize and enact the true universality of church by divorcing their faith from their own culture.[100] In a speech on behalf of the students, attended by Sigismondi, erstwhile spokesman Ki-Zerbo echoed these themes, calling on "religious authorities" to "second" colonial Catholics in their quest for political autonomy. "We ask from our Mother church more attentive care and more substantial nourishment" for our cause, he said. "The church, which has taken the part of the weak over and over again for centuries, must be an active presence at the side of colonized peoples at this decisive moment," he lectured. "Should not the church take a solemn position against colonialism?"[101]

The students' aggressive stance did not sway their listeners entirely, though the respect accorded them showed that the church felt they could not be ignored. Much like Feltin, Sigismondi responded with a call for moderation, and Pope Pius XII, who did not meet personally with the students, released *Fidei donum* the same weekend.[102] The encyclical acknowledged the rapid evolution of the situation in Africa and called on both Europeans and Africans to behave with restraint as Africans moved toward political independence, but its main thrust was a desperate appeal for more help for the African missions, before the continent slipped out of the church's grasp. It was certainly not the strident endorsement of African autonomy that the students were calling for, but it was a sign that the Vatican was watching Africa, and Africans, very closely.[103]

There is no question, however, that radical African Catholic students played a key role in making the Catholic Church grapple with the pitfalls of its ambiguous relationship with French colonialism in the postwar period. Their determined activism also inspired some of their French and African Catholic mentors to take up their points of view. Moved by the brilliant, devout, and committed students around him, Father Michel ultimately went further, earlier, than many French priests in recognizing the validity of African critiques of the French state and the Catholic Church in Africa. Similarly, Brother Bertrand Duclos, a Franciscan who began serving as the chaplain for students from the colonies in Toulouse in 1951, later wrote to Paul Kaya, a former mentee, "'I thank God for having put people like you, [Jean-Baptiste] Yonké, [Jean] Pliya, [Albert] Tévoédjrè, etc. on my path. . . . You made me make the transition from a triumphalist church that was aligned with the powerful to an evangelical church.'"[104] Duclos became one of the "great figures of the anti-establishment church of the years 1950–1970" thanks to his work with African students.[105] And it appears that the students also pushed Alioune Diop to more critical interventions on Catholicism and colonialism in the mid-1950s. Scholars have pointed out that Diop's student issue of *Présence africaine* in 1953 anticipated and likely influenced the more radical stance the magazine took after its retooling in 1955, and the same holds true for the Catholic threads within it.[106]

In 1958, the seismic shifts in France, French Africa, and the Vatican opened up new possibilities for African Catholic students. In May of that year, the French Fourth Republic collapsed under pressure from military supporters of the maintenance of French power in Algeria. Charles de Gaulle, who had been out of government since 1946, returned to power and oversaw the writing of a new constitution for France and its empire. This constitution reimagined the French Union as the French Community and called for each colony to hold a referendum on joining it on September 28. De Gaulle described the community as "independence" with "interdependence," though full independence was not possible within it. Member states would have internal autonomy, but the French president would be the executive of the Union, and a committee of the members would collaborate on foreign policy, currency, defense, external transport, and telecommunications.[107] De Gaulle carefully lobbied African leaders with promises of assistance if their territories joined, and threats to withdraw technical expertise and financial help if they did not.[108]

The referendum provided some alumni of the Association of Catholic African Students an opportunity for further radical political engagement. As noted, Joseph Ki-Zerbo and Jean Pliya were among the cofounders of the African National Liberation Movement (MLN) with Albert Tévoédjrè, the Catholic Beninese author of *L'Afrique révoltée* who had been the editor of the FEANF newspaper, and Ahmadou Dicko, a student of Spanish literature in Toulouse from Upper Volta.[109] Though many of the leading personalities were Catholic, the movement was not explicitly so, though it employed a lexicon of African personalism that had Catholic roots.[110] Avowedly socialist and nationalist, it looked to build its base among "intellectuals" and peasants while choosing nonalignment over ideological affiliation with either side in the Cold War.[111] Its initial manifesto, which surfaced on August 25, 1958 in Paris and Dakar, called for the "liberation of Africa, United States of black Africa, African socialism."[112] Ki-Zerbo later wrote that the movement (its manifesto rejected the label of "party") privileged independence over unity, as emphasizing unity would delay independence indefinitely, and also served as a way for the colonial powers to "divert attention and sow confusion."[113]

The MLN campaigned furiously against de Gaulle's vision of the French Community, urging Africans to vote no in the referendum. Ki-Zerbo later recalled his intense frustration with the African elite in Ouagadougou, who countered his exhortations for independence with the claim that Upper Volta could not become independent, because "economically we have nothing." Ki-Zerbo, decrying the cowardice and cravenness of African leaders who did French bidding, argued that the fact of "having nothing" after seventy years of French colonization was in itself the best argument for independence. The MLN's rejection of either a Marxist or Catholic identity did not prevent it from being tarred with both brushes, however. Ki-Zerbo noted that some opponents characterized the MLN leadership as crypto-communist, while at the end of his journal detailing the ill-fated campaign, Dicko bitterly denounced the "Marxists-leninists-conséquents" who whispered that the MLN "was a Catholic movement destined to serve the Vatican in Africa."[114] Despite militant African Catholics' anticolonial stance, elements on the left continued to view them as under European thumbs. In the short term, the MLN's effort was unsuccessful: as noted earlier, Guinea under Sékou Touré was the only African colony to declare its full independence from France in 1958.

Despite the MLN's failure in 1958, circumstances evolved rapidly in Africa and in the church immediately afterwards, with results that were both frustrating and pleasing to African Catholic activists like Ki-Zerbo and his colleagues. By 1960, all of French sub-Saharan Africa would be independent, though the MLN's dream of unity and a United States of black Africa would not be realized, and persistent economic and political weaknesses would plague many of these African states for years to come. Change in the church was perhaps more gratifying: less than two weeks after the referendum, Pope Pius XII, who had presided over the Vatican since 1939, died in office. By the end of October 1958, John XXIII took over and began moving the church in new directions: he replaced Monsignor Lefebvre as papal delegate to French Africa, he accelerated the process of appointing African bishops to preside in African dioceses, and he called the Second Vatican Council. The council would wrestle with the central critique that radical African Catholic students had raised: it sought to make Catholicism less European and more universal with liturgy in vernacular languages and new teachings on the place of the church in the modern world. By the mid-1960s, then, African Catholic students saw some of their political and religious hopes fulfilled. Though the next decades would bring reversals in both realms, they were better able to harmonize their African and Catholic loyalties.

5

MEN OF TRANSITION

African Clergy in Postwar French Africa

IN HIS SCREED *Le Vatican contre la France d'Outre-Mer?*, François Méjan cited the Vatican's nomination of indigenous prelates in the French Overseas Territories as a key element of the church's betrayal of France. He was particularly incensed, he wrote, that French missionary congregations, who had been forfeiting blood and treasure for decades to win the church new converts, were having to "sacrifice" territory they had long serviced to "rapidly promoted indigenous bishops."[1] He also criticized the Vatican for what he saw as the repudiation of centuries of cultural identification with Europe by "pushing cultural and religious indigenization to the maximum."[2] Yet his book hit the shelves precisely when radical African Catholic students and intellectuals were taking the church to task for being too closely aligned with colonizing Europe. Indeed, in the eyes of African Catholic activists such as Joseph Ki-Zerbo or Alioune Diop, the church was dragging its feet in decoupling itself from its European heritage and embracing true universality.

Diop, outraged by Méjan's book, composed a direct response as the lead editorial in the October–November 1957 issue of *Présence africaine*, complete with the parallel title of "Peut-on dresser le Vatican contre les peuples de couleur?" ("Can they set the Vatican against peoples of color?"). This same article appeared as a full page feature the following month in the left-leaning Catholic paper *Témoignage chrétien,* where it most certainly reached a broad French audience.[3] Founded as a clandestine organ of Catholic French resistance in the 1940s with the motto "truth, justice, whatever the cost," *Témoignage chrétien* supported decolonization and denounced the use of torture in colonial wars in the 1950s. Diop dismissed Méjan as someone "devoid of any profound cultural concern or sense of moral responsibility," but acknowledged that Méjan represented strands of opinion that ran deep in French government circles, as well as in the European intellectual milieus Diop himself frequented. Arguing that the church could no longer identify itself with the West against the more vulnerable peoples of the world, Diop ridiculed Méjan's thesis, noting, "The [Vatican's] first treachery apparently consists in admitting that indigenous men could be priests. We are stupefied and wondering how anyone can complain about the church conferring priestly dignity on a yellow or a black man."[4]

As Méjan's argument and Diop's refutation of it demonstrate, African priests and prelates lay at the heart of escalating disputes about the church's future in Africa in the postwar period. The Vatican, with an eye toward the possibility of future political decolonization, was eager for Africans to take the reins of the church in their own communities. African Catholic intellectuals and radical African politicians clamored for the elevation of more African prelates to show that the church was truly decolonizing itself and was not a fixture of the colonial order. Some French missionaries, particularly younger ones, collaborated wholeheartedly in efforts to mentor African clergy and submit to new African ecclesiastical superiors. Yet some of their more conservative colleagues disliked the idea that French congregations would lose control of ecclesiastical districts that they had overseen since inception by having to turn them over to secular African clergy.[5] Like Méjan, they worried that this would lead to an "Africanization" of the church as a whole, which would debase its rites and chase French language from its African schools. Moreover, some missionaries, particularly older ones, simply could not stomach the idea of white priests having to obey a black bishop.

Ordinations of African priests, Koumi, Upper Volta. Courtesy of AGMAfr.

As these tensions mounted, a new generation of African priests and prelates emerged in French Africa. Theirs was the first to amount to a sizable cohort, as French missionaries' African seminaries finally churned out meaningful numbers of graduates after decades of failure. In general, their experiences as seminarians and young clergymen embodied the contradictions of the moment: they were often celebrated as the leaders of an emerging church, yet they also encountered daily, petty discrimination among their French colleagues and superiors. Nonetheless, these men are not easily categorized as a group. While many of them resented the racism of some French colleagues and participated in calls to de-occidentalize the church, some of them also remained intensely loyal and even quite deferent to their French mentors. Their politics and theology sometimes overlapped with that of progressive European clergymen, but not always, and they tended to prioritize particular African concerns, such as interfaith dialogue with Islam. Some of them were public intellectuals who participated in the elaboration of Catholic negritude, while others studiously avoided the spotlight. This chapter examines how they contended with divisions within the church and postwar French Africa by exploring their training, their life in missions still dominated by European clergymen, their positioning in Vatican political maneuvering around independence, and their intellectual contributions to negritude. For some of them it was a period of promise, while for others it was a frustrating and, in the case of the eventual archbishop of Conakry Raymond-Marie Tchidimbo, perilous time.

RACE AND AUTHORITY

François Méjan was correct insofar as the Vatican placed new emphasis on the cultivation and promotion of African clergy after the war and that its maneuvers were political in nature. On his tour of French Africa on behalf of the Vatican in 1945–1946, Father Prouvost had carefully observed the status of indigenous clergy and recommended their advancement to the missions. In June of 1948, White Fathers superior general Louis Durrieu wrote to his missionary prelates in French Africa that the Vatican wanted "to assure the foundation of indigenous churches as soon as possible, in order to parry any future developments, especially any possible nationalist crises." Knowing that his men might balk, he urged their "most entire collaboration" in the congregation's efforts to support the Holy See's vision of the future, regardless of the "thousand objections" they might raise in the near term.[6] In October of that year, the congregation's governing council issued the following statement to its priests which reflected the Vatican's view of the continent: "All of Africa is in the midst of disconcertingly rapid evolution, which is economic, political, and cultural. The Holy See anticipates that sooner than many people think, this evolution will reach a natural conclusion: Whites will have to cede the levers of power progressively to the most evolved locals, to govern their peoples."[7]

Indeed, when the Propaganda Fide nominated Monsignor Marcel Lefebvre to the post of apostolic delegate for French sub-Saharan Africa and Madagascar that November, his official instructions were crystal clear on this point: "The Delegate will insist most particularly to the prelates and missionaries that they make an effort to cultivate vocations in young Africans." Each mission was to have its own junior seminary, and

missions were to "give the maximum effort" to erect regional senior seminaries, where "future priests would receive complete instruction and
training." In closing, the directives reiterated, "Would that the Apostolic
Delegate never cease to keep in mind that the missions must aim to
found the church in Africa with an indigenous hierarchy."[8] This Vatican
perspective on Africa's future was the fruit of harrowing experience in
East Asia in the preceding two decades, when European missionaries,
including many French ones, fell victim to nationalist violence.

Lefebvre and his various missionary collaborators had their work cut
out for them to fulfill these Vatican aspirations. Even by the early 1950s,
African priests were still a small minority of the clergy in most of the
French territories on the continent. Statistics compiled by the apostolic
delegation in Dakar (which, though they are likely accurate, would probably err on the side of exaggerating numbers of African personnel)
record that there were seventy African and 640 European priests at
work in all of French West Africa and Togo in 1952. The Trust Territory of Cameroon, which was a particularly fertile ground for missions, had seventy-five African priests of its own by 1952, working
alongside 255 European priests. Meanwhile, there were thirty-five African and 201 European priests in French Equatorial Africa.[9] In practice, this meant that, with the exception of Cameroon, African priests
were very thin on the ground across the vast reaches of French Africa.
Most African Catholic communities did not have exposure to an African

Table 5.1   African clergy in French Africa, 1950s

Territory	1952		1958		% increase 1952–1958	
	European clergy	African clergy	European clergy	African clergy	European clergy	African clergy
AOF	576	65	794	127	37.8	95.4
AEF	201	35	354	42	76.1	20.0
Togo	64	5	77	12	20.3	140.0
Cameroon	255	75	323	114	26.7	52.0

Source: Adapted from Délégation apostolique de Dakar, *Statistiques annuelles des missions catholiques en Afrique française, année 1951–1952* (Dakar: Imprimerie Mission Catholique); Délégation apostolique de Dakar, *Statistiques annuelles des missions catholiques en Afrique française, année 1957–1958* (Dakar: Imprimerie Mission Catholique), ACSSp 2F 1.3 a5.

priest, and at many mission stations African clergymen lived and worked solo among their European colleagues.

Moreover, missionaries' senior seminaries in French Africa were still on shaky ground in the early postwar period. The White Fathers were arguably the most successful congregation when it came to training African priests. In 1952, Superior General Louis Durrieu proudly circulated an effusive letter from the Vatican congratulating the congregation on their efforts in this domain, quoting the pope's praise of the "'fruits of their labors obtained by constant submission to the directives of the Holy See.'" They had produced five hundred seminary graduates across the continent by then, but the vast majority of those men did not hail from or work in French Africa.[10] In the Great Lakes Region of East Central Africa, for example, the White Fathers had ordained the first priests in what are now Rwanda and Uganda in 1913 and went on to train dozens more in the interwar period.[11] By contrast, their only senior seminary in French Africa, located in Koumi, Upper Volta, did not open its doors until the 1930s, and apparently did not graduate any priests before 1942, though it ordained thirty-two Africans in the following decade.[12] In 1952, the apostolic delegation's statistics recorded 116 senior seminarians in French West Africa (Ouidah, Dahomey, home to forty of these, was the most prolific place of origin), ninety-two in Cameroon, and only twenty-six in French Equatorial Africa. Junior seminary enrollments were much higher, totaling 576 students in French West Africa, 220 in Cameroon, and 216 in French Equatorial Africa, though of course not all those students moved on to senior seminary.[13] From the Vatican's point of view, this boded well for the future, but the process of educating priests was not a quick one and there were numerous obstacles facing both the missions and their students in the endeavor.

From the missions' perspective, finding qualified teachers and mentors was the biggest hurdle. As Father Jean Hébert, who taught at one of the White Fathers' junior seminaries at Nasso, Upper Volta, observed in 1947, "within a single vicariate it is very difficult to find personnel competent to provide the education and instruction of the indigenous clergy."[14] This had been a problem for decades, but it became even more acute in the postwar period as the Vatican began demanding a higher standard of preparation for African clergy. "They do not want us to make

African seminarians, Koumi, Upper Volta.   Courtesy of AGMAfr.

third-rate priests, but desire that Africans receive the same training as European clergy, from both a spiritual and intellectual point of view," Superior General Durrieu wrote to the White Father missionary prelates in French Africa in 1948.[15] Moreover, Durrieu and his governing council wanted their seminarians to get an education equivalent to that of other African "*évolués*" so that the priests could command respect within the emerging elite. The congregation's leadership thus insisted that their junior seminaries coordinate their programs and teach at the same level as state-run schools.[16]

Those carrying out the work on the ground did not necessarily agree with this policy. Revealing skepticism of secular curricula, as well as a streak of the racist disdain for so-called *évolué* Africans that was fairly common among European missionaries, a White Father at the junior seminary at Pabre, Upper Volta, complained to Durrieu in 1949. He felt that preparing African seminarians for the French baccalaureate would fill their heads with useless information, distract them from essential progress in Latin and French, and make them "superficial, vain, nouveau-riche in knowledge and, therefore, incapable."[17] Durrieu acknowledged these concerns, but wrote, "if it were not for the current process of evolution in Africa, we could perhaps have skipped the bac, but if our seminarians do not get these diplomas, they will be considered second-rate *évolués*. It is useless to dream of different historical circumstances; they are imposed on us from the outside and we must make the best of them."[18] In addition to the European bac, the White Fathers' leadership also desired that African seminarians receive a thorough grounding in their own language, culture, history, traditions, and customs, as they would be de facto missionaries among their peoples.[19] All in all, it was a challenge to find personnel within the congregations that had the requisite training to teach to these exacting requirements.

Ultimately, the independence and authority of individual French missionary bishops gave way to collaboration in the face of daunting shortages of personnel and money. In 1948, for example, the SMA instituted a ten-year plan of cooperation across its missions in West Africa, with the intention of maximizing the impact of limited resources. While prelates often wanted to set up junior seminaries in their own jurisdictions (and had the right to do so), the SMA mission leaders agreed to create one junior seminary for the districts of Ouidah (Dahomey), Lomé (Togo), Sokodé (Togo), and Niamey (Niger), and another for Abidjan, Sassandra, and Korhogo (all in Côte d'Ivoire). These would in turn feed their senior seminary at Ouidah, which would become a regional institution.[20] The Spiritans and White Fathers followed suit and operated their respective senior seminaries in Senegal and Upper Volta as regional hubs that took junior seminarians from several vicariates.

Moreover, the interests and achievements of individual missionary groups also had to take a back seat to the new Vatican priorities. The loyalty of many French missionaries to their particular congregation (and attendant rivalries with the others) should not be underestimated, as it was a powerful factor in how some of them interpreted the postwar shifts in the church. For example, in the early 1950s, Monsignor Lefebvre, who was then simultaneously serving as the Spiritan apostolic vicar of Dakar and the apostolic delegate to all of French Africa, considered turning the senior seminary the Spiritans had founded in Senegal nearly one hundred years before over to the Fathers of Chavagnes (Congregation of the Sons of Mary Immaculate).[21] As a Spiritan "it would break his heart" to do it, he wrote to his superior general, but "we have too many setbacks with our current personnel to count on them" and he knew that his duty was to do whatever he could to advance the training of African priests.[22] At that time, the seminary was staffed by Father François Morvan, whom Lefebvre characterized as excellent but overburdened, and Father Jules Bourdelet, who, Lefebvre claimed, did not "grasp the natives' psychology."[23] They received part-time assistance from Father Charles Catlin, the priest accused of racism by young African Catholics in Dakar in 1947, whom Lefebvre described as a "good teacher, but not fit to be director."[24]

The Spiritans in Senegal were aghast at the prospect of relinquishing the seminary and wrote the congregation's leadership in desperation: "With the agreement of all the Spiritans here, and also with the authority of Monsignor Lefebvre, I implore you to send us at least one Father with a theological degree this year," begged one of them. "It is not just a question of prestige. In Senegal, the press is already in the hands of the White Fathers and the Marist Fathers have the secondary school—if the senior seminary gets away from us, people will conclude that the Spiritans are merely pioneers and not true organizers of Christian communities."[25] In the end, these emotional pleas had the desired effect: the Spiritan leadership allocated Father Maurice Fourmond, a recently ordained priest who had studied theology in Rome, to the seminary.[26] Nevertheless, the institution's successful operation rested on the backs of just a handful of men who had to remain healthy and do a consistent, competent job—a tall order. Just three years later, Morvan was still at the helm, but Bourdelet and Fourmond had been replaced by Fathers Georges-Henri Thibault and Christian De Mare.[27]

Father Catlin's presence at the seminary despite the earlier accusations of racism against him, and Lefebvre's comment about Father Bourdelet's inability to understand "native psychology" reveal another towering impediment to the advancement of African clergy: the persistence of racial tensions within the Catholic seminaries and mission stations of French Africa well into the postwar era. These tensions had a long history. French missionaries' doubts about Africans' capabilities and their insensitivity to the scope of the demands they were placing on seminarians (separation from family, celibacy, the learning of multiple European languages) had contributed, along with the missions' continual dearth of human and material resources, to staggering rates of attrition in seminaries across Africa in the nineteenth and early twentieth centuries. For example, between the 1850s and the 1920s, the Spiritan seminary in Senegal admitted over three hundred students and graduated only approximately fifteen priests, while its counterpart in Gabon admitted some two hundred Africans over several decades before it produced its first priest in 1899.[28] In Uganda, the White Fathers ordained only two priests out of 160 seminary students between 1878 and 1913.[29] On the eve of World War II, when the Vatican insisted on the appointment of African Father Joseph Faye as apostolic prefect of the remote Casamance region of Senegal, he faced condescension and disobedience from his French Spiritan subordinates. They did not want to submit to a black prelate, while Faye, a product of their instruction and immersed in the racial hierarchies of colonial society, questioned his own ability to lead them.[30]

In the postwar period, when the Vatican was pushing energetically for the advancement of African clergy, blatant racism on the part of European missionaries became more unacceptable and they knew it. In a report to the Propaganda Fide on the apostolic vicariate of Dakar between 1951 and 1955, French Monsignor Georges Guibert (Lefebvre's auxiliary bishop), knowing what his audience wanted to hear, wrote, "*PERFECT HARMONY* reigns between the secular and regular clergy, especially between the African priests and the foreign [European] ones."[31] Guibert's enthusiasm masked a more complex reality on the ground, however. Harmony and collaboration did exist across racial lines in some locales and circumstances, but not in others. Many younger French missionaries, who had not spent decades in colonial Africa, tended not to harbor the same kind of attitudes toward Africans as their older counterparts did.[32] Still, aspiring African clergymen frequently encountered racism on the part of their European teachers, mentors, and peers in the 1950s. Even some of the most sympathetic Frenchmen condescended to their African colleagues, and some Africans remained very deferent to European superiors. Moreover, secular African priests or seminarians often felt excluded or isolated when posted to mission stations where regular European clergy observed rules and rituals unique to their particular missionary societies. And amid the mounting political tensions of the era, and as their congregations were losing status and prestige in areas they had once dominated, some resentful European missionaries, à la François Méjan, accused African clergy of "reverse" racism.

Evidence of racial strife is often half-buried in the archival record, because European clergy knew they were not supposed to be racist and African priests could be reluctant to complain to European superiors about discrimination. In the summer of 1948, for example, Father Antoon Wouters, the White Fathers' procurator in Rome, wrote to Superior General Durrieu to describe a confidential conversation he had had with an African priest who had trained with the congregation in Africa. Wouters explained that the priest in question preferred to remain anonymous, and did not want to cite particular individuals or incidents, but was of the opinion that "a certain number of our missionaries, more so in the field than in the seminaries, are not understanding enough vis-à-vis Africans in general and even the African clergy. He does not claim that the African clergy are blameless, but the fault is not entirely on their side." The African priest's insistence on anonymity and his careful phrasing suggest the difficulties of communicating this kind of criticism to Europeans. He proposed to Wouters that the seminaries address racial tensions head on: "one could try to train [African seminarians] in the flexibility that mutual relations between the two clergies require," Wouters reported to Durrieu. "He would be very grateful if you could keep an eye on this state of affairs, which could hinder in-depth work on the African soul."[33]

Durrieu seemed to take this to heart—he returned to the problem of racial prejudice multiple times in the years that followed, though he was not able to step entirely outside of prevailing European views of Africans either. In October of 1948 he presided over a meeting of mission chiefs at the senior seminary in Kachebere, Nyasaland to discuss the issue. "Profound differences separate us psychologically from the blacks," he observed. "Not having the same atavism nor the same initial education, we do not have the same ideas nor the same sentiments about many things, and our character traits, our qualities or faults, are also very divergent. It is useless to deny this obstacle and impossible to behave as if it did not exist. On the contrary, we must recognize it for what it is and make the seminarians recognize it too." He continued that they should not let such hurdles get in the way of mutual respect, confidence, and collaboration. "It would be lamentable," he observed, "if the African clergy should discover, contrary to what they were told in seminary, that a real gulf exists between them and the White Fathers. And this is inevitably what will happen if the White Fathers, through lack of spiritual conviction and abnegation, or only by inattentiveness and a lack of reflection, show them disdain or indifference. They would surely respond with deep but more or less hidden hostility and an incurable distrust."[34] Durrieu insisted that mission superiors had to remain vigilant to make sure their personnel adhered to these directives.

Durrieu also argued in paternalistic fashion that African deference to Europeans, born of the colonial situation, got in the way of training African clergy. He was opposed to sending African seminarians to study in Rome partly because he doubted that potential instructors fully comprehended the "mentality of our Blacks."[35] "The mentality of these natives is such that they still tend to accept what they are told, and above all they continue to always say yes to whatever a white man tells them," he explained. "The white man decided that an African would become a priest, or at least that he would study to become a priest, so he accepts and says yes." In these circumstances, Durrieu maintained, it was difficult for the directors of Roman seminaries to detect a genuine priestly vocation, to test it, and to admit only those who would be successful priests. Moreover, he worried that African seminarians in Rome would be too afraid to confide in their mentors there if they developed doubts about their calling. They would see it as unbearably shameful to be sent home, and so would be reticent about confessing their difficulties. Durrieu's condescension could not have been clearer when he remarked, "Our natives are so primitive that a difficult and serious work of psychology and constant attention is required of those that guide and judge them."[36] His testimony reveals how the cursus of training for the priesthood lent itself to paternalism and rigid structures of authority that could reinforce racial hierarchies, rather than undo them.

Indeed, to test the vocations of their African seminarians, the White Fathers demanded that students complete a year of probation in the missions between completing seminary and ordination, and they recommended to other congregations that this practice be implemented all

African seminarians, Koumi, Upper Volta, 1940s. Paul Zoungrana seated, front right. Courtesy of AGMAfr.

across French Africa. They found this to be an effective way of exposing a candidate to the temptations and challenges he would face as a priest and of making sure that his conviction would surmount them. The SMA fathers, by contrast, were not convinced of the utility of this practice, and felt it was actually detrimental to African vocations. In their view, it added a year to a very lengthy path that already provided ample opportunity to ascertain a student's calling. Monsignor Joseph-Paul Strebler, SMA apostolic vicar of Lomé, Togo, reported to the Vatican in 1950 that Togolese seminarians dreaded the probation year as a "stumbling block" and suggested that Africans found the very idea of probation to be racist. "As long as the church applies exceptional rules to seminarians of color that canon law does not provide for in the case of other races, 'probation' will not be valued, but suffered with grumbling," he observed.[37]

Moreover, Strebler intimated that racial tensions posed problems during the probation year, when the students, not yet full-fledged priests, joined missionary communities in a temporary capacity. They tended not to find "a climate favorable to their perseverance and happiness" in the missions, he wrote. "I share their apprehensions," he confided, "because I know the milieu in which this 'probation' takes place." Strebler believed that probation should be a truly exceptional practice for cases where seminary leadership or the relevant bishop had doubts about a particular vocation, and should occur in a friendly and encouraging setting. "The seminarian in question should participate in all of the spiritual exercises of the missionary community and be treated as a member of it, not as a 'boy,'" he wrote, indicating the racism and condescension probationers often grappled with on the ground. To second his opinion, Strebler appended a letter from Togolese Father Jean Gbikpi, who concurred that probation, as it functioned in practice, was more likely to hinder young Africans' vocations than encourage them.[38]

Strebler's evocation of African seminarians being treated as servant "boys," as well as Father Prouvost's 1946 observation that "certain rules that are imposed on [African clergy] can only be shocking to them" points to imbalances of power across racial lines in French Africa's missions.[39] This problem was often bound up with the distinction between secular African clergy and the regular European congregations, especially when they lived and worked together at the same stations. Spiritans and White Fathers, for example, who took an additional set of vows mandated by their respective congregations, were supposed to observe strict regulations about spiritual exercises, meals, and precedence in their communities. While a handful of Africans joined the missionary congregations and lived by their rules, most did not.[40] Thus, when the European members of a mixed Euro-African clerical community that shared housing and dining facilities followed to a special regimen that impacted the very minutiae of everyday living, de facto racial segregation occurred, which exacerbated the potential for abuses of power along racial lines and the social isolation of African priests.

In these cases, French missionaries on the ground who were sensitive to the difficulties provoked by the rules were actually more likely to try to alleviate the attendant problems than their superiors in Europe, despite the latter's insistence on racial equity in their instructions to men in the field. In the face of the loss of territory, ecclesiastical offices, and

Catholic institutions to other congregations and to African clergy in what had been their exclusive African domains, these leaders wanted to be doubly sure that their priests adhered to their vows and maintained their particular congregation's unique purpose and identity. In the early 1950s, for instance, Monsignor Durrieu received repeated requests from French Africa to relax the White Fathers' strict rules about communal dining and recreation to allow African seminarians on probation to join their mentors at table and in leisure. At first, Durrieu argued that he could not alter regulations put in place by the congregation's governing council and instructed the local prelates to place African priests on probation in communities with other African priests.[41] Ultimately, however, all of the White Father apostolic vicars and prefects in French Africa, the congregation's two regional executives, and Father Jean Cormy, the superior of their senior seminary at Koumi, co-signed a letter insisting on changes. It was very awkward, they reported, when the clergy emerged from prayer and the sole African on probation had to distance himself from his European colleagues and eat his meal by himself. Moreover, this practice was turning their African Christian parishioners against them. "They have been accusing missionaries of being racists and have been interpreting this rule as a measure of disdain," they wrote.[42] Faced with this reasoning, Durrieu backed down and ordered a temporary suspension of the rules.[43]

The Spiritans in postwar Senegal also struggled with race in community dynamics and a similar disconnect developed between the men on the spot and the distant leaders of the congregation, who were more likely to insist on rules over circumstances. In 1956, for example, Spiritan executives in France protested that secular African priest Father Laurent Sagna was acting as the superior of a mission composed of himself, a Spiritan Father Govers, and a Spiritan Brother Grégoire. According to the congregation's regulations, only a Spiritan could preside over a Spiritan community and enforce observation of the Spiritan regulations.[44] Father Jean Bourgoing, who served in Senegal as religious superior for all the Spiritan missions there, retorted that Sagna was much more "regular" about his exercises of piety than the "ungovernable" Govers.[45] After a further dispute about the disposition of secular and regular clergy in Senegal (including European secular clergy sent in response to the 1957 encyclical *Fidei donum*) that diluted Spiritan residential communities, Father Henri Neyrand, the first assistant to the superior general, wrote a stinging rebuke to Bourgoing. "This manner of doing things is not permitted," he instructed, "and it is your job as religious superior to disallow it." Neyrand insisted that secular priests should be housed with each other, and that Spiritans be organized into exclusively Spiritan mission stations, though that would result in most of the African clergy being grouped together, and not distributed throughout the territory. "We insist absolutely that Spiritans live in a Spiritan community according to the Spiritan rules. This is a sina qua non condition of their being sent to any diocese," he wrote. The rules were "the support of our spiritual life and our calling, and are too often neglected for the so-called profit of the ministry." In Neyrand's mind, politics and / or local exigency were not reason enough to risk weakening the particular vocation of the congregation's personnel, but the men on the ground felt otherwise.[46]

In this climate of racial tension in the missions, power relations between African and European clergy were often delicate. On the one hand, some African priests remained extremely deferent to European clergy. In 1951, Father Cormy observed of his African colleagues, "With regard to a White Father, there is always a sort of instinctive, reverential fear, while they are more likely to accord less importance to directives or remarks from their [African] parish priests." Cormy also claimed that European priests all agreed that the African clergy were "very zealous and devoted," but suggested that "left to themselves they do not have perhaps enough initiative."[47] On the other hand, when African clergy displayed initiative or wielded authority, French priests who expected meek deference from them were often displeased. For example, in 1953 Spiritan Father Bernard Gandner complained that his African superior, again Father Laurent Sagna, "did not let his subordinate Spiritan *Toubab* [white man] forget his station." Using a pun in French, Gandner said he "saw the black side of everything," phrasing that linked race to his negativity about the situation.[48]

Another case in point was that of Raymond-Marie Tchidimbo, the priest of Guinean and Gabonese parentage who joined the Spiritan congregation and eventually became the archbishop of Conakry.

Tchidimbo's career in the church had almost been derailed by his compulsory military service in World War II—he was stationed in West Africa, North Africa, and then participated in the liberation of France in late 1944. To his dismay, he discovered upon his return to Guinea in 1945 that missionaries eyed him warily as a veteran who had seen the world and acquired independent habits, and did not want to admit him to senior seminary.[49] Tchidimbo persevered, however, and in October 1952, he took up his first mission post at Faranah, in Guinea's Kankan region. The station's diary notes, "The mission and the entire town of Faranah are overjoyed to have the first African Spiritan posted to Kankan prefecture."[50] Tchidimbo was very bright, capable, and did not waste time—just weeks after his arrival he founded a Catholic study circle for parishioners.[51] Yet it was not long before his drive and self-assurance rubbed some of his French Spiritan colleagues and superiors the wrong way.

A month later, the Spiritan religious superior in Guinea, Father Georges Cousart, reported deep frustration with Tchidimbo in one of his periodic reports to Spiritan headquarters. According to Cousart, an older missionary who had been working in Guinea since 1920, Tchidimbo had displayed "too much self-importance" in letters to his ecclesiastical superior, the Spiritan apostolic prefect of Kankan, Monsignor Maurice Le Mailloux.[52] Cousart, who wrote that the "painful" situation made him "suffer," claimed that he was not entirely surprised by this turn of events, since he had known Tchidimbo when the young priest had been in junior seminary at Dixinn, and did not approve of Tchidimbo's "character" or his "temperament." Cousart objected to the fact that when Le Mailloux had suggested that Tchidimbo study for a teaching credential in order to serve as the director of a school, Tchidimbo replied that it would be more "'efficient'" for him to pursue a bachelor's degree in theology or canon law. Cousart, referring to Tchidimbo as *ce petit prétentieux*," found this overly aggressive and aspirational. "I must confess that my native priests in the vicariate of Conakry do not have such pretentions, and do not dare to give advice of this kind to their ecclesiastical superior," he sniffed.[53]

In response, a Spiritan at headquarters in Paris, most likely Neyrand, revealed his own racial prejudices when he responded, "It is too bad that

Father Tchidimbo is starting out with such smugness. That often happens to younger priests, and when they are of a certain color it is even worse. But I think that this crisis will pass and that Monsignor Le Mailloux will be patient enough not to antagonize this young father."[54] On a tour of inspection of Guinea two years later, Neyrand would characterize Tchidimbo as "a good priest, very active and intelligent and wields great influence. Very sure of himself, has a superiority complex."[55] Indeed, at various points in his career Tchidimbo would clash with Spiritan authorities, who found him quick to anger and to insist on his rights and prerogatives.[56] Yet such behavior hardly seems surprising given Tchidimbo's wealth of talent and the overwhelming evidence that he had received messages from his French colleagues to be content with his lot and not aspire to more. He rejected the role of the deferent African clergyman by joining a European congregation and demanded treatment commensurate with his capabilities.

Some French clergy experienced African priests' pushback or criticism as racism. This perception mounted as the main missionary congregations lost ground and political tensions over the colonial order increased. In 1954, Father Morvan reported from Senegal that his current seminarians were "full of goodwill, very studious, and deeply pious" but that he had concerns about the junior seminary students who would be coming to the senior seminary at Sébikotane in the fall. "The milieu in which they find themselves is not conducive to their improvement," he worried, "in that environment they naturally become racist and very demanding." He was worried this spirit would infect Sébikotane gradually as new students came every year.[57]

Similarly, Father Albert Delisse, a decorated veteran of World War II who subsequently became a White Father, wrote to Superior General Durrieu in 1952 that he was increasingly annoyed by what he saw as mounting African anti-white racism. Delisse declared that after spending two periods of six months living and working alongside African priests in Upper Volta he was "always edified by their truly sacerdotal conduct." Moreover, he asserted, "I never hid my sympathy for them and I took several opportunities to defend them against Europeans, either within the priesthood or outside it." Yet Delisse had some complaints to air. Chief among them was his perception that African priests were constantly rehashing bad experiences they had had with racist European priests. Secondly, he charged, they were "gradually embracing the [negative] ideas of some *évolués* on Whites."[58]

Delisse did acknowledge that Europeans played a role in growing racial friction in the missions. He pointed to hostility born of the variations between the different sets of rules for the regular and secular clergy. One example was that the White Fathers, who were expected to adhere to quite spartan regulations regarding material possessions, fretted that Canadian donors were spoiling African seminarians with extravagant gifts and trinkets. In addition, and here the superciliousness of some Europeans is patently evident, Delisse noted, "Some missionaries readily adopt the opinion of a local administrator who says, '[African priests] have no class.' This is said to be visible in their apostolate, the way they organize their lives, their projects, their approach to accounting, etc." Delisse felt that he should report all this to his superiors, though he also understood what he was supposed to think: "This does not at all weaken our enthusiastic will to respond to the desires of the Holy See, and yours too, that we work with all our hearts for the extension of the African church," he assured Durrieu.[59]

In his response to Delisse, Durrieu counseled tolerance and charity vis-à-vis young African clergy. "These priests have a right to our affection and our respect, and of course we must have patience because they have flaws, just as we do. It is a long-term project to train priests who are truly worthy and effective. . . . They are not yet 'high class' according to this administrator. Not yet, but they are growing in stature nonetheless. Love them, support them as much as possible."[60] Durrieu repeated these sentiments in a 1952 circular letter to the congregation on the subject of African clergy, "It is thus natural that [African clergy] expect from us the respect, esteem, confidence, affection, and fraternal assistance that priests owe to priests who care for the same flock. Let us be sure not to disappoint their expectations." Moreover, Durrieu reminded his men, all African eyes were on them: "If they notice that we do not treat them as perfect equals, they will conclude that even Catholic missionaries are racists. A chasm will quickly open between White Fathers on one side and African clergy on the other. Nothing could be more disastrous for the present or the future."[61]

In this circular, Durrieu described that future as one in which European missionaries would be subordinate auxiliaries to African prelates, who would not be able to draw on sufficient African personnel to found new mission stations, seminaries, schools, press organs, or Catholic Action initiatives for years to come. "Faithful to our African vocation to the end, we must provide this personnel," Durrieu wrote. "Such is the will of the Holy See and we cannot consider not adhering to it most completely for an instant."[62] This was not necessarily an easy pill to swallow, even for French missionaries who understood why it was imperative. Father Bourgoing, for example, who manifested respect for his African colleagues during his tenure as Spiritan religious superior in Senegal, felt bereft when Monsignor Lefebvre gave his post of parish priest in the railroad town of Thiès to an African, Father Pierre Sock, in 1958. "It is not without regret that I leave this mission where I have been since *1941*," he emphasized to his superior general, "but one must know how to give way to the young and the Africanization of the ranks."[63] Two months later, he reiterated his grief: "Leaving Thiès after seventeen years is quite painful, but I am happy to still have ministry to do . . ."[64] The accomplishment of the Vatican's mission to train African clergy thus involved a sense of loss for many French missionaries, whether they harbored racial prejudices or not.

PRELATES AND POLITICS AT INDEPENDENCE

The year 1958, when Sock took over from Bourgoing in Thiès, was also the year of de Gaulle's referendum on the French Community and Guinea's independence. By then, significant growth in the numbers of African clergy had occurred, but Europeans, the vast majority of whom were French, still dominated the ranks of the church in French Africa. In that year, there were 127 African priests and 794 European clergymen in French West Africa, 114 African and 323 European priests in Cameroon, and twelve African and seventy-seven European priests in Togo, while numbers in French Equatorial Africa were still quite low: forty-two African priests labored alongside 354 European counterparts. Compared to the 1952 numbers, this represented a doubling and near doubling of the African clergy in Togo and French West Africa respectively, a 52 percent increase in Cameroon, and a more modest 20 percent gain in French Equatorial Africa in six years. Yet it is important to note that the numbers of European priests also increased in that interval by over 37 percent in AOF, nearly 27 percent in Cameroon, and over 76 percent in AEF.[65] With the exception of AEF, the overall proportion of African clergy was growing, but in most areas it would take at least another generation before African Catholics could be served predominantly by priests from their own communities.

Moreover, there were scarcely any Africans in positions of church leadership in French Africa by the time François Méjan published his diatribe against the Vatican, though his panicked, angry tone suggested otherwise. In 1955, the Vatican established the church hierarchy across French Africa, transforming many missionary apostolic prefectures and vicariates into dioceses and archdioceses. As it did so, it began elevating a handful of African priests to the episcopate, but when Méjan's book came out there were just four young black African bishops in all of French sub-Saharan Africa, including the Trust Territories of Togo and Cameroon. These were Monsignor Paul Etoga, born in 1911, who became auxiliary bishop of Yaoundé, Cameroon in 1955; Monsignor Thomas Mongo, born in 1914, who became auxiliary bishop of Douala, Cameroon in 1955 (Mongo took over the post of bishop in 1957 upon the death of his French Spiritan superior, Monsignor Pierre Bonneau); Monsignor Bernardin Gantin, born in 1922, who became auxiliary bishop of Cotonou, Dahomey in 1957; and Monsignor Dieudonné Yougbaré, born in 1917, who became bishop of his native Koupéla, Upper Volta in 1956.[66] Moreover, none of these men sat in positions of great influence. Koupéla was quite removed from the seats of political and administrative power, and though Mongo, Etoga, and Gantin worked in major population centers, they were placed in subordinate roles to the Frenchmen Bonneau, Monsignor René Graffin, the Spiritan archbishop of Yaoundé, and Monsignor Louis Parisot, the SMA archbishop of Cotonou, respectively.[67] Nonetheless, this was too much for Méjan. In a 1957 article, separate from his book, he paused to remark on Gantin's elevation to prelate, noting that "*he was only ordained as a priest in 1951,* five years prior to his nomination as bishop" and, to emphasize the decoupling of Vatican and French interests, that Gantin had gone to "*Rome*" and "not metropolitan France" to study theology in 1953.[68]

In the late 1950s and early 1960s, the question of whether to put Africans at the head of the archbishoprics of territorial (subsequently national) capitals, the church's most high-profile positions in French Africa, became more pressing and more politicized. Pressure mounted from within the church and without. In 1960, the year of independence for most of the French African colonies, several Africans took up high-profile posts. In January, Monsignor Gantin replaced the ailing Monsignor Parisot as archbishop of Cotonou.[69] In February, Monsignor Jean-Marie Maury, a Frenchman who had replaced Lefebvre as apostolic delegate (Lefebvre remained in place as archbishop of Dakar), wrote to White Fathers superior general Léo Volker that the nomination of an African archbishop was "IMPERATIVE" in Ouagadougou, Upper Volta.[70] Maury remarked that all the French bishops and all of the African clergy there were demanding that an African prelate occupy the most visible Catholic post in the land. According to Maury, they were seconded by all of the European White Fathers on the ground except four, three of whom subsequently rallied to that position because, in their rueful words, "'now one cannot do otherwise.'"[71] In April, the Vatican announced the nomination of Father Paul Zoungrana, one of the few African members of the White Fathers congregation, as archbishop of Ouagadougou, as well as that of African secular priest Bernard Yago as archbishop of Abidjan, Côte d'Ivoire.

It is a noteworthy commentary on racial tensions within the clergy that the African priests in Upper Volta unanimously voted for Zoungrana over Monsignor Yougbaré, the other African candidate for Ouagadougou, because they considered Yougbaré a "caricature of a White Father" and more "White Father-like" (i.e., more harsh and overbearing) than Zoungrana.[72] In a symbolic move, Pope John XXIII consecrated Yago and Zoungrana himself in a joint ceremony in Saint Peter's basilica on May 8, 1960, demonstrating his personal commitment to the promotion of Africans in the church. The Vatican managed to pull this off just three months before each country marked its official independence in August, so it had an African prelate on the spot to participate in those festivities in both places.[73]

Monsignor Maury noted, however, that the new president of Upper Volta Maurice Yaméogo, himself a Catholic, did not support the nomination of an African to the post of archbishop. Maury's interpretation of this stance was that Yaméogo feared an African archbishop would have too much influence in the new nation, whereas a European "could always be made to feel he was a foreigner" and thus kept on his toes.[74] By contrast to Yaméogo, however, some leading African statesmen of the era called for the appointment of Africans to lead the church on the continent. In 1961, for example, President Modibo Keita communicated to Maury that he desired the nomination of an African prelate in Mali. Maury was concerned that there were still not enough viable candidates in the heavily Muslim country to constitute a valid "terna," or list of three options for Rome to choose from. Nonetheless, he wrote to the White Fathers' headquarters, the question was becoming "more and more urgent."[75]

But by far the thorniest case from the church's perspective was that of Guinea, where Sékou Touré was publicly and vociferously attacking the church and demanding that it appoint an African executive in his country. Touré's campaign against French missionaries and the Vatican's cagey response reveal the church's political liabilities in Africa, as well as its determination to control its own narrative of "decolonization." Moreover, Father Raymond-Marie Tchidimbo's emergence in the crucial and delicate position as a broker on the spot sheds light on some of the daunting challenges African clergy could face between European missions and African politicians in this time of transition, akin to those of African Catholic intellectuals sandwiched between a persistently Eurocentric church and its African critics.

As noted above, under Touré's leadership, Guinea was the only former French colony in sub-Saharan Africa to vote "no" on the referendum establishing the French Community in 1958, thus becoming the first one to attain complete independence. Historians differ somewhat on how long and how seriously Touré was wedded to this outcome, and whether it was the product of his toxic interactions with the imperious Charles de Gaulle or a concession to leftists in Guinea, but in any event the result was dramatic.[76] In retaliation for the no vote, France immediately withdrew all financial and technical assistance from Guinea. French personnel canceled bank loans and a planned hydroelectric project, burned military barracks, cut telephone wires, removed medicines from hospital shelves, and even smashed official state dishware.[77] Moreover, France isolated Guinea diplomatically, thus driving it into the arms of the Communist foes of the North Atlantic Treaty Organization for aid.[78] For

French Catholic missionaries on the ground, this was a harrowing turn of events. They were suddenly vulnerable nationals of a foreign power *non grata* in a political environment that seemed to them to be tilting ever more toward authoritarian communism. To make matters worse from a Catholic perspective, French priests and nuns still formed the veritable backbone of the church in Guinea—without them, it would cease to function. In 1958, in Guinea's three ecclesiastical districts of Conakry, Kankan, and Nzérékoré there were only six Guinean priests and seventy-nine European clergymen.[79] And as of 1960, there was only one Guinean in senior seminary.[80]

It did not take long before Touré openly attacked the church as a relic of the French colonial past. In September 1959, his Democratic Party of Guinea voted that private education in Guinea (which was mostly Catholic) be suppressed in the following three years.[81] At that time, the missions operated approximately seventy primary schools in Guinea, a secondary school for boys in Conakry, a teacher training school near Kankan, and a junior seminary at Dixinn. Over the next three years, the government successively took over Catholic schools, sometimes requisitioning their Guinean employees and threatening them with treason if they refused to serve the state, as well as imprisoning some parents who protested. The *coup de grâce* came in August of 1961, when the government definitively did away with private education.[82] In a statement Sékou Touré opined, "We do not conflate the suppression of private education with the free choice of men and families to practice their religion. But, we nonetheless hope for the total Africanization of all of the religious organizations in Guinea in the future." Moreover, he added, "Why could there not be a Momodouba or a Camara at the head of the Guinean church?"[83]

French missionaries interpreted this last question as a portent of a future mass expulsion of foreign-born clergy, which did in fact take place in 1967.[84] In the meantime, Spiritan Archbishop of Conakry Gérard de Milleville composed a statement denouncing the "injustice" of the PDG's school closures that was read from every pulpit in his archdiocese. In response, Touré immediately threw him out of the country, employing, perhaps intentionally, the language of dignity so common in Catholic personalist circles at the time.[85] "A man who has dignity, who respects himself, knows to respect all dignity, especially that of an entire people incarnated in another man. But a man who does not want to respect, in the person of the head of state, the dignity of the Guinean people, does not belong in the Republic of Guinea," he declared.[86]

In the course of this unfolding crisis, the French episcopate in Guinea came to rely on the capable, energetic Father Tchidimbo to communicate with Touré's regime. Tchidimbo had been friendly with Touré for years—he later claimed to have encouraged Touré's efforts to develop syndicalism in Africa in the early 1950s, in defiance of the colonial authorities.[87] The two men were still on good terms in the late 1950s and early 1960s, a fact that did not go unnoticed by Tchidimbo's French superiors. In the fall of 1960, as the missions felt increasingly threatened by Touré's regime, Monsignor de Milleville summoned Tchidimbo from rural Kankan to serve in a special role representing Guinea's three French prelates vis-à-vis government authorities.[88] The two men developed a close working relationship. De Milleville subsequently wrote to his superiors in France that "I am delighted that I took on Father Tchidimbo as my vicar general and that I put him in charge of relations with the government, because he is precious in the current circumstances and is not afraid to defend the interests of the church."[89] And after his expulsion de Milleville wrote to Tchidimbo, "Make all of the necessary decisions for the functioning of the diocese; I have full confidence in you, because you know the situation well and will be witness to its evolution."[90] He lamented that in his absence Tchidimbo would effectively carry the burden of being bishop without the accompanying title, but concluded that it was a necessary sacrifice for the well-being of the church.

Father Tchidimbo had in fact been considered for a prelature in 1958— the post of prefect of Kankan.[91] The prefecture had fallen into financial disarray under the leadership of Spiritan Monsignor Maurice Le Mailloux, prompting his resignation.[92] As was customary for episcopal nominations, the Spiritan congregation proposed three candidates to the Holy See, including Tchidimbo, even though Monsignor Lefebvre, citing opposition among the French clergy in Kankan, advised against it because of the Vatican's zeal to appoint Africans to positions of leadership. "If you do," he warned, "he will automatically be nominated."[93]

In the end, Lefebvre was mistaken on this point, as the Vatican decided to leave the post open and simply add Kankan to Monsignor de Milleville's portfolio in Conakry. Even though they nominated him, however, the attendant Spiritan evaluation of Tchidimbo revealed persistent prejudices among the European clergy vis-à-vis their African counterparts. Spiritan Superior General Francis Griffin wrote to Rome: "Father Tchidimbo has real qualities, but only six years of experience in the ministry and, moreover, a character that could make relations with his colleagues difficult, to the detriment of the difficult ministry in this prefecture. That is why his fellow priests are very reticent about his possible nomination, in spite of the benefits his nationality might confer. Moreover, Father Tchidimbo, because of his African temperament, seems ill qualified to put Kankan's finances back in order. All of this makes the General Council very hesitant, despite his good qualities, regarding the possibility of his serving as Apostolic Prefect."[94]

This analysis suggests that French priests balked at being led by an ambitious, precocious young African clergyman who was anything but deferent. Griffin's equation of Tchidimbo's so-called "African temperament" with an inability to manage finances is particularly striking, not least because in a 1954 inspection Father Neyrand had noted that Father Tchidimbo "took great care" with the accounting books at Faranah, which were "very well kept."[95] Tchidimbo does not appear to have been involved in the financial disaster at Kankan, yet by 1960 Neyrand was writing that he lacked "any sense of religious poverty and of the value of money. Very persuaded of his own worth, authoritarian, very critical. He has the capacity to be a bishop, but would break the bank and be difficult on his personnel."[96] This evolution in Neyrand's evaluation raises the possibility that some French Spiritans saw Tchidimbo in a more negative light as he moved closer to positions of leadership.

Despite these mixed reviews from his French colleagues, Tchidimbo did indeed stand up for the church when push came to shove in Guinea, and even some of his more grudging peers appreciated it. Neyrand, never disposed to shower Tchidimbo with praise, agreed on his value in the crisis, albeit in a backhanded way. After touring Guinea that year he noted: "As for Father Tchidimbo, he is definitely a person of worth, intelligent, and a good priest . . . he is performing great services in

Conakry through his innumerable acquaintances throughout the government, who respect him and fear him even more than they like him."[97] Neyrand, who continued to regard Tchidimbo as "slippery," overly "independent" and too convinced of his own merit, nonetheless confirmed the vicar's tenacious advocacy for the missions.[98] Similarly, Father Jean Kerloc'h, the Spiritan religious superior in Guinea, applauded Tchidimbo's willingness to defend the church in the tense climate of the time. In the spring of 1959, as Touré's new regime was starting to take shape, Tchidimbo gave a public lecture entitled "Is religion an obstacle to the evolution of peoples?" which was attended by hecklers who came to refute his ideas. Kerloc'h reported to Spiritan headquarters in France that Tchidimbo spoke persuasively and gave his audience a demonstration of how to counter Marxist claims, as well as the confidence to do so. At that moment in Guinea, Kerloc'h noted, "a white man can hardly give a successful public lecture, and among the African clergy, Father Tchidimbo is the only one who has the audacity to do it."[99]

When Tchidimbo took over after de Milleville's expulsion, effectively becoming the acting executive of the church in Guinea, Touré's government rebuffed him repeatedly when he tried to open negotiations regarding the reinstatement of Catholic schools and the junior seminary, which had also been forced to close. Touré made it clear that he would not deal with any representative of the church except a bona fide archbishop, who would have to be African. In a press release he stated, "Let them find him in Dakar, Mauritania, Tunisia, Rao, Congo—it is not a question of racism. But we do not expect to be provoked."[100] Touré meant to force the pace of indigenization of the church in Guinea and bend the Vatican to his will.

Indeed, the Vatican was closely monitoring the rapidly deteriorating situation in Guinea, which had potential implications for the church all across francophone Africa. If, for example, other African nationalist leaders mimicked Touré and scapegoated the church as a colonialist institution, its future in independent Africa could be jeopardized. Shortly after his expulsion from Guinea, Monsignor de Milleville wrote to Tchidimbo from exile in Rome, "I was struck when I arrived here by the interest in our situation and the fact that all doors opened for me. It seems that as soon as a situation threatens the progress of the church, it gets everyone's attention."[101] De Milleville, as the missionary archbishop of a relatively small and isolated African outpost of Catholicism, was not used to solicitous treatment by the princes of the church.

Although it had long stressed the importance of promoting African clergy, the Vatican wanted to remain in control of its own process of "decolonization" and not appear as though it was being forced to act by an upstart African state, lest that embolden other potentially hostile political leaders.[102] In October of 1961, Maury reported that Monsignors Antonio Samorè, a Vatican diplomat, and Pietro Sigismondi, the secretary of the Propaganda Fide, told him, "We are not accountable to Mr. Sékou Touré, and above all we cannot rush ourselves." Similarly, Gregorio Cardinal Agagianian, the prefect of the Propaganda Fide, wrote confidentially to Spiritan Superior General Francis Griffin that, "We must avoid that the nomination of an African in Conakry could be interpreted as an act of weakness by the Holy See in the face of the constraints and threats of the Guinean government: that is what it would look like if we made that appointment first and by itself."[103] Maury was anxious lest French priests in Guinea think he had abandoned them, but Pope John XXIII counseled patience and prudence. Regarding Touré and his regime, the pontiff reportedly observed to Maury, "They are good men, at heart, but they do not know it. One must not cut off relations with them."[104] This suggests that John felt that the French government's angry, punitive stance toward Guinea after 1958 was unproductive.

The Vatican thus delayed a decision for seven months, while the situation continued to deteriorate on the ground. In early February 1962, two French White Fathers in the rural diocese of Nzérékoré were imprisoned without charge and forbidden to say mass, read books, or take communion.[105] Several weeks later, two more missionary priests in Nzérékoré were incarcerated, and then all four were transferred to the central police headquarters in Conakry—a step up from prison, but still confinement.[106] Around the same time, several other White Fathers and a French nun were sent from Nzérékoré to Conakry because of difficulties with their visas, which were subsequently confiscated, while authorities instructed the Spiritans at Kankan not to leave the grounds of their mission, which prevented them from reaching African Christians in surrounding communities.[107] Maury began to worry that Touré's regime would go too far and make it politically impossible for the Vatican to appoint an African to the post in Conakry. In desperation, he met with Maurice Yaméogo, the Catholic president of Upper Volta and a friend of Sékou Touré. Yaméogo composed a letter asking Touré to be more conciliatory and de-escalate the mounting tension with the missions.[108] Finally on April 1, 1962, after multiple interventions by French and Swiss diplomats (one of the priests was a Swiss national), the detained missionaries were freed.[109]

Just a few days later, on April 5, 1962, the Vatican responded in dramatic fashion by nominating a wave of African archbishops for Dakar, Bamako, Lomé, and Conakry simultaneously. These were, respectively, Father Hyacinthe Thiandoum, age forty-one; Father Luc Sangaré, age thirty-six, Father Robert Dosseh, age thirty-six, and Father Tchidimbo, age forty-one.[110] Sangaré and Dosseh immediately became the youngest archbishops in the church. The French Catholic daily *La Croix* noted that these nominations on the eve of Vatican II were particularly significant and portended the importance of Africa at the council.[111] To camouflage their acquiescence to Touré, Vatican officials insisted that Thiandoum be consecrated first in Dakar, since it was the former capital of all of French West Africa and the seat of the apostolic delegate, and then instructed Thiandoum to preside over Tchidimbo's installation in Conakry. In their view, this way of proceeding saved the church some face.

There was still some Spiritan skepticism about Tchidimbo for the post in Conakry in 1962, though there was no other choice from the Vatican's perspective. Tchidimbo was the only African with the requisite qualifications and connections, plus he knew the situation better than anyone. Superior General Griffin did not object to Tchidimbo's nomination this time around, though he was not entirely complimentary, and somewhat condescending when Cardinal Agagianian solicited his opinion. "Father Tchidimbo is intelligent, active, has a strong influence over his entourage and is well regarded by state authorities," Griffin wrote. "Nonetheless, he has a tendency to be authoritarian with his colleagues, to be a bit too demanding, and above all, does not have a good head for money, which he spends without much judgment."[112]

The Spiritan leadership pushed back harder against the Vatican's consideration of the secular priest Thiandoum for archbishop of Dakar, because it would mean that the congregation would lose that episcopal seat after controlling it for more than a century. Griffin expressed doubts to Agagianian about Thiandoum, describing him as a "very good" priest who was "zealous, but rather timid," and suggested that he might lack sufficient character to "resist the numerous exterior influences that would bombard him." Griffin tried to preserve the congregation's authority in Senegal by making a strong case in favor of Spiritan Monsignor Prosper Dodds, a product of Saint-Louis's métis elite who had been serving as a prelate in the Casamance since 1947. Griffin claimed that the Senegalese political leadership was clamoring for Dodds and that Dodds had the necessary qualities to succeed as archbishop; a local son well known by the elite, he possessed "a fine intelligence, strong theological training, experience" and "a firm character tempered by great bonhomie."[113] The Vatican did not agree, however; the hierarchy felt it was imperative to have a black African in Dakar.

On May 31, 1962, Tchidimbo's lavish consecration ceremony took place in Conakry's cathedral, just a week after Thiandoum's installation in Dakar. It was both a joyous celebration and a very carefully orchestrated political dance between the church and Sékou Touré's regime. In contrast to Thiandoum, who was consecrated by his French predecessor, Monsignor Lefebvre; to Sangaré, who was consecrated by Monsignor Maury; and to Dosseh, who was consecrated by the German cardinal Julius Döpfner; Tchidimbo's consecrator was an African prelate. In a nod to Guinea's insistence on Africanization and its troubled relations with French authorities, Thiandoum performed the ceremony, assisted by Monsignor Bernardin Gantin, the African archbishop of Cotonou, Monsignor Bernard Yago, the African archbishop of Abidjan, and Monsignor Maury, the only European in the group. Father Jean Gomez, another Guinean priest, directed the choir. The rest of the French prelates of West Africa, as well as dozens of French missionaries, watched from the audience.[114]

Touré himself stayed away from the official church ceremony, though numerous ministers represented his government in the cathedral. He did come to lunch at the Catholic mission in Conakry following the

Monsignor Raymond-Marie Tchidimbo and President Sékou Touré following
Tchidimbo's consecration as archbishop of Conakry, May 31, 1962. Courtesy of ACSSp.

consecration. When he arrived, the Republican Guard played the national anthem and he and Tchidimbo reviewed a contingent of troops
side by side.[115] After lunch, Tchidimbo traveled to Touré's turf to place a
bouquet of flowers at the Monument to the Martyrs of Colonialism, formerly the French "Monument aux morts" in central Conakry, near the
presidential palace. This repurposed memorial was a totem for the regime, and visiting dignitaries of other former colonies often laid of-
ferings there. In the wake of Monsignor de Milleville's public criticism
of the government in 1961, Léon Maka, a Catholic Guinean politician
and diplomat took the French archbishop to task in the PDG paper
Horoya for the fact that the most recent Corpus Christi procession
through Conakry had not seen fit to pause at the monument and pay respects.[116] Tchidimbo's deference to it was clearly meant to further distance the church from the colonial past and emphasize Catholic acceptance of the new independent Guinea. That evening, Touré and his wife

Expelled French Catholic missionaries waiting for a plane, Conakry, 1967. Courtesy of ACSSp.

hosted a reception in honor of the new archbishop at the governmental palace.[117]

Overall the day went very well, from a Catholic perspective. Father Bourgoing was pleased to report to his colleagues in France that the Guinean government had gone out of its way to make the day special, though there were some causes for concern. He noted some potentially ominous phrases in Touré's official declaration on the consecration, which seemed to place the church at the service of his political agenda. These included, "the revolutionary faith which animates our people enriches theology" and "we are completely satisfied that the keys of the Christian house of Guinea have been placed in the hands of a son of our people, because the unity of Guinean Catholics can only enrich the unity of the Nation, by consolidating the common house of the people."[118] The church hierarchy hoped that this new beginning under Tchidimbo would defuse tension with the regime and firmly disassociate the church from the former French colonial order, though most of the religious personnel on the ground were still French missionaries. It worked for a time. One Spiritan historian subsequently referred to the five years following the consecration as a "reprieve" before Touré lashed out at the church again and expelled all French missionaries from the country in 1967.[119] Then in 1971 Touré accused Tchidimbo of plotting against him and threw him in prison. Narrowly escaping execution, the archbishop did nearly nine years of hard labor before his release in 1979. He finished his career in Rome and spent his retirement in France, but was buried in the cathedral of Conakry after his death in 2011.

While this dire outcome was by no means typical for this first generation of African prelates in former French Africa, elements of Tchidimbo's experience shed light on the paths these men trod in their early years on the job. As African priests and newly minted bishops and archbishops, they navigated racial tensions within the clergy and within the political realm at independence. They coped both with the condescension of European colleagues and the assumptions of African politicians that they would, as Africans, support indigenous regimes, come what may. In addition, along with Alioune Diop and the radical Catholic African students in 1950s Paris, Tchidimbo and some of his fellow African clergymen took part in public intellectual efforts to define a Catholicism that embraced racial and cultural difference, thereby helping to develop Catholic negritude.

INTELLECTUAL CONTRIBUTIONS

African priests who publicly examined and defended Catholicism in the postwar period were often simultaneously critical and celebratory of the church. These men, whose clerical commitments made them perhaps even more personally invested in their faith than passionate laymen such as Alioune Diop or Joseph Ki-Zerbo, were eager to define Catholicism in a way that they could square with their experience as black men, though it was not always easy for them to do so. In a presentation on "Theology and African culture" at Alioune Diop's Second Congress of Black Writers and Artists in Rome in 1959, Father Robert Sastre, who served for a time as a chaplain for colonial students in Paris and editor of *Tam-Tam* alongside Father Joseph Michel and then later became bishop of Lokossa, Benin, explained this dilemma.[120] Acknowledging the profound tensions between his priestly vocation and his forays as a black intellectual, Sastre told his audience, "It is veritably impossible to know how to reconcile the demands of complete and submissive faith with the lucidity of an intellectual who is probing the vicissitudes of the history of his race, to speak in front of men who do not share my faith of things that cannot be fully grasped without faith, and to expose to the faithful cracks in the theological edifice that they consider seamless and solid, and definitively constructed." Yet, he continued, "I must face the challenge in the name of my faith and in the name of my negritude, as I am certain that both of them cannot help but grow in stature from the confrontation that I will engage in before you, and which consti- tutes the heart of my life as an African priest."[121] Sastre chose to see the potential dissonance between Catholicism and negritude as an oppor- tunity for growth and discovery, rather than an impasse that under- mined his faith.

Raymond-Marie Tchidimbo, ridiculed by some Spiritan superiors for his intellectual aspirations, also publicly addressed the challenges of being African in the church in the 1950s and 1960s. He relied heavily on Emmanuel Mounier's personalism and cited the Frenchman frequently in his work, which included the article for Diop's 1953 student issue of Présence africaine entitled "The African Student Confronts Latin Culture" as well as a 1963 volume of reflections on Catholicism, L'homme noir dans l'Église, that appeared with Présence africaine.[122] Like Alioune Diop and other Catholic African activists, Tchidimbo wanted to speak for a church that welcomed all. "The Catholic Church is not the creation nor the property of the West," he wrote, "it is the property of all good souls who wish to watch it, know it, and love it."[123] Tchidimbo called on the church to be true to its own universal values and diversify its ranks for its own sake.[124] He did not shy away from critiquing missionary errors, of which he had bitter firsthand experience: their tendency to subordinate African clergy, their refusal to recognize the transient na- ture of their task, their failure to implement Vatican directives.[125] Yet he also asserted that it was necessary to have the courage to face the fact that colonizing powers were the "providential organs of the trans- mission of the Gospel" in Africa, as they gave rise to "generous mis- sionaries" who brought it with them. In any case, he wrote, "sterile and regretful contemplation of the past" was useless—he wanted to look toward a promising Catholic future in Africa.[126]

Not all of their peers in black internationalist circles were willing to accept these priests' positive spin on Catholicism, however. For example, at Diop's First International Congress of Black Writers and Artists, held at the Sorbonne in 1956, Christianity proved to be a particularly emotional topic during one evening of unstructured discussion. Haitian priest Gérard Bissainthe took some of his fellow attendees to task for their freewheeling use of the term "religious colonialism." It was not surprising, he said, that European missionaries had confused Christianity with the Western culture they inhabited, but he wished to point out that such practice had been condemned by popes since the seventeenth century. Bissainthe insisted, "it is necessary that you make a distinction when you are talking of my church. The catholic church consists of two things: there are men of the church, and there is the Church itself. The Church itself is a spiritual Church, a Church that wants, obviously, the good of the entire world and which intends to bring each person something, something *in his own culture.*" Bissainthe was adamant that his audience "recognize that this Church exists," and that, separately, men of the church also existed who did not always understand the true church.[127]

That same year, a time of great intellectual ferment in the Franco-African Catholic world, a book of essays appeared entitled *Des prêtres noirs s'intérrogent.*[128] A key text of Catholic negritude that was dedicated to Diop's spiritual mentor Father Jean-Augustin Maydieu, it was compiled by Bissainthe and overseen by the editorial team at Présence africaine. It featured the work of black priests, some of whom had studied in France or in Rome, had passed through the black Catholic intellectual circles around Diop, or had frequented the chaplaincy for colonial students in Paris. The topics of the contributions were wide-ranging: they included considerations of missionary strategy among peoples in the French Congo and Senegal's Casamance, of syncretic practices between Christianity and Haitian Vodou, and of parallels between Rwandan oral tradition and Hebrew psalms, among other subjects. Nonetheless, two themes emerge clearly from the collection. First of all, the authors, who were committed to showing that negritude and Catholicism were reconcilable, found points of resonance between African cultures and Catholic teachings and practices. Secondly, they simultaneously offered critiques, some of them scathing, of the status quo within the missionary church, and urged it to take a more positive and inclusive view of African culture.

An essay entitled "Propaganda and truth," by Father Sastre and Robert Dosseh, the Togolese priest who became the first African archbishop of Lomé in 1962, illustrates the collection's critical side. In it, the two clergymen attacked prevailing European views of Africa, which they characterized as negative, oversimplified, and born of a toxic combination of a superiority complex and a bad conscience. Catholic missionaries, through their writings and lectures, they argued, had played a key role in the development of disdainful European perceptions of Africa, and many of them continued to describe Africans as brutish, savage, bloodthirsty, and childish. This type of caricature, they complained, "is a source of ambiguity and misunderstanding, obscures real problems, and distances the young African elite from anything having to do with missions." They felt that European missionaries who could not or would not admire and value African culture were "quartermasters of a civilization and no longer the purveyors of the message of Christ, which should be incarnate in all civilizations. The missionary's task is not to resolve the African's problems for him, but to equip him to resolve them himself."[129] Africans should therefore become Catholics by remaining African, not by renouncing their culture and embracing a flawed European civilization that was not their own, while European missionaries should facilitate this process rather than obstruct it. Otherwise, Dosseh and Sastre contended, missionaries injured Africa as a whole, as well as their own endeavor.[130]

Father Joseph Thiam's contribution entitled "From tribal clan to Christian community" specifically addressed how African priests could find correlations and points of contact between their faith and their cultures. Thiam argued that the "black mentality adapts easily to a catholic Christianity—one that makes itself African in Africa." Thiam, who worked among Joola populations in Senegal's Casamance, felt that "the dispositions observed in the black soul are in fact providential preparation for the message of revelation." It was not hard, he claimed, to draw parallels between African beliefs about ancestors and the concept of a sin transmitted through generations, or a "big brother" who died to expiate the sins of all. Practices involving sacred food translated easily into the ritual of the Eucharist. He observed that in their celebration of patriarchy and familial solidarity, African mentalities approached those of the Hebrews of the Bible.[131]

Thiam's message, therefore, was that conversion to Christianity did not involve a radical renunciation of the African self; instead, it channeled and elevated existing impulses, provided it was presented in the proper way. In his view, the best people to make such presentations were clergy who understood Africa and Africans—Africans themselves. "We cannot ask a European priest, as great as his goodwill and his knowledge of mission work may be, to think and feel his faith outside of Western categories; i.e., to instruct in ways that he was never instructed in," Thiam asserted. He advised African priests to incorporate indigenous art and music into church structures and ceremonies, to make the liturgy livelier, and to encourage more exteriorization of prayer, in keeping with what he deemed to be African tendencies. "Christianity's ability to adapt," he argued, "is in fact the bedrock of its universality."[132]

Some European missionaries embraced such proposals for adapting Catholicism to African culture, but many others rejected them. One of the most remarkable things about *Des prêtres noirs* is that Monsignor Lefebvre, the archconservative in matters of doctrine who bitterly opposed the reforms of Vatican II, authored the preface, though in hindsight he seems particularly ill-suited to introduce a book arguing for Catholic accommodation to African culture. Many years later, Father Bissainthe recalled that he approached Lefebvre over the objections of leftist French Dominicans at Cerf, the Catholic press which copublished the book with Présence africaine. Yet, Bissainthe remembered, revealing his commitment to changing the church from the inside, "I did not want the book to be an act of dissidence, but a work of the church, and the 'chief' of the church in francophone Africa then was Monsignor Lefebvre." In the end, though Lefebvre raised questions about the message of the book, Bissainthe felt that the archbishop's participation sanctioned the endeavor in European Catholic circles.[133]

In his preface, Lefebvre acknowledged that there was a place for local culture in certain aspects of Catholic practice and celebration. In song, painting, and sculpture, he allowed, he had seen "happy adaptations" in various regions of francophone Africa. In a tone that showcased his persistent paternalism, he observed, "In Madagascar, in particular among the Betsileo people, there are wood sculptors who are genuine artists."[134] Yet Lefebvre also made it clear that some innovations were not acceptable: he urged caution in the case of dance, warning of the "danger of falling into the 'negro spiritual'" which, he asserted, had become "the only ceremony of pagan-Christian sects like Harrisism."[135] African dance could have a place, he felt, in ceremonies such as funeral processions, as long as it was stripped of any "lascivious" content, but he felt it was probably not appropriate for religious processions organized by the church. In addition, he felt that "animist or superstitious" ceremonies regarding stages of life such as birth, adolescence, marriage, and death had to be closely studied before they could be incorporated into Catholic celebrations. Unsurprisingly, he urged conservatism: the church should not change its ceremonies lightly, and only after careful deliberation and with the certainty that "spiritual outcomes would be better." Promoting order and hierarchy, he stressed that no innovations could or should be undertaken without the assent of the church hierarchy. "The church is beautiful," he wrote, "because she possesses the splendor of order, and order is unity within diversity. It is not uniformity, nor is it anarchy."[136]

Lefebvre's surprising participation in the *Des prêtres noirs* project may have been born of an impulse to try to corral or mute the message of black clergy, or, alternatively, of a desire to fulfill the Vatican's explicit instructions to develop and promote African priests. For all his conservatism and reactionary behavior, Lefebvre took his responsibilities to the Vatican very seriously. It is likewise important to consider and remember that not all African priests aligned themselves with leftist European clergy, nor supported innovations or adaptations in church practices and ceremony, even after Vatican II. For example, in a 1967 letter to Lefebvre, Monsignor Thiandoum emphasized his own distaste for liturgical reform. "I hope that, particularly in the case of the liturgy, African bishops will be prudent enough to avoid embarking on particular deleterious experiments. Personally, I am *opposed* to the idea that we immediately adopt a mass that is not *Latin* in our countries. I know that many *European* priests do not share my point of view, but we African bishops are better positioned than anyone else to decide what will best nourish the faith of our believers," he observed.[137] Thiandoum, who was quite critical of Lefebvre's hostility to Islam (explored later on), nonetheless agreed with the Frenchman on safeguarding the Latin mass. And Thiandoum did so while asserting, like Sastre, Thiam, Dosseh, and others, that Africans, and not Europeans, should be shaping Catholicism in Africa.

African priests' contention that they understood what was best for Africa has remained salient in the ensuing decades, as European and African political and social concerns have diverged in many domains. In fact, many African prelates have been far more doctrinally conservative than their European counterparts since Vatican II, especially on social questions such as women's roles in the church and homosexuality. For example, Robert Cardinal Sarah, Tchidimbo's successor as archbishop of Conakry whose own education and career were also marked by Sékou Touré's attacks on the church, has been a vocal leader of African prelates who fear their European counterparts are too tolerant of what Africans perceive as dire threats to the Catholic family, including divorce, homosexuality, and abortion.[138] Thus while some African clergymen at midcentury were radicals when it came to combating racial prejudice in the church, promoting Catholic adaptation to African culture, or advocating dialogue with Islam, it is a mistake to assume that African priests were (and are) always in the "radical" wing of the church on every issue. Indeed, their visions of Catholicism in Africa have often defied reigning European categories of radicalism or conservatism.

Though their numbers were small at midcentury, African clergy in French sub-Saharan Africa were not a homogeneous corps. Some were ambitious public intellectuals who engaged in the cultural politics of the day; others were shy, retiring men who preferred rural ministry or the monastery. Some of them traveled to Europe and pursued their education in France and Rome, but most attended seminary in Africa and became the apprentices of the European missionaries in their home territories. Most became secular clergy, but some sought to join the congregations that had trained them. Some deferred meekly to their missionary superiors, while others challenged French clergy's authority.

Nonetheless, some broader patterns can be discerned in their experience between 1945 and 1962. Up until, and indeed well beyond independence in many places, African priests worked in contexts where European clergy outnumbered them greatly. In that regard, they were pioneers within the church, embodying the transition from the European missions of the past to the African church of the future, that prospect that so terrified François Méjan. They often occupied a delicate position between the Vatican, which was pushing for the "indigenization" of the clergy, French missionary personnel who could be reluctant to comply, and, in some cases, radical African politicians who were skeptical of a faith they identified with colonialism. Many of them weathered the patronizing attitudes of French missionaries who thought Africans were inferior, or who resented their congregations' loss of territory, authority, and prestige. Some, especially Raymond-Marie Tchidimbo, suffered far worse than that.

Nonetheless, despite instances of virulent racism and a broader culture of condescension, it is important to remember that relations between many African priests and their French missionary mentors were close and strong. After all, Africans who took the path to the priesthood spent their formative years under the guidance of French men whom they respected and desired to emulate. Genuine bonds of affection linked them together in spite of the stresses of political and ecclesiastical transition. When Togo was still reeling after the 1963 assassination of its first president, the Catholic Sylvanus Olympio, Togolese Father Patrice Alou, a secular priest trained by the SMA mission, wrote to a French mentor, "In spite of all of the difficulties and painful instability of the moment, in fraternal prayer and charity, hand in hand, we will collaborate in the field of the Lord in Africa and in particular in Togo, which owes so much to its missionaries. Dear Father, I speak to you quite simply as a son . . . I am faithful to you in my prayers."[139] Similarly, it bears noting that when Monsignor Lefebvre eventually broke with the Vatican over its reforms, Monsignor Thiandoum tried his best to effect a reconciliation. Even though Thiandoum disapproved of Lefebvre's disobedience, he felt warmth for and personal loyalty to his mentor, later describing the situation as his "greatest sorrow."[140] Faith could be a powerful glue between men of God on either side of racial, colonial, and national divides.

faith as glue

6

FOE OR FRIEND?

Catholics and Islam on the Eve of
Independence in French Africa

AS FRENCH CATHOLIC MISSIONARIES, African clergy, and African lay Catholics traversed the political and social changes in postwar Africa, the question of Catholics' current and future relations with Muslims loomed large, particularly in territories such as Senegal and Sudan, where influential Catholic minorities lived among Muslim majorities. The issue was thrown into sharp relief shortly before Christmas 1959, just as France's sub-Saharan African colonies were moving swiftly toward full independence, when a provocative article on the future of Africa by Monsignor Marcel Lefebvre appeared in *La France catholique,* a conservative French Catholic daily. Lefebvre had just stepped down from eleven years of service as the apostolic delegate to French Africa, but he remained the archbishop of Dakar and was easily the most visible and powerful French prelate in Africa. As a result, his voice carried beyond Catholic circles to broader audiences, including French colonial authorities, African politicians, and the colonial and metropolitan publics.

Lefebvre entitled his piece "Where is Africa going? Are the Christian states going to hand Africa over to the Star?" By the "star" Lefebvre meant communism, and he discerned its rapid advance on all sides: in municipal elections in Madagascar, in the activities of the Union of the Peoples of Cameroon, under Sékou Touré's Guinean regime, and also, crucially, in French Sudan. "With each day that passes, the Russian and Chinese grip on Africa is becoming a reality!" he exclaimed. Then Lefebvre made a remarkable assertion, which proved to be the most incendiary aspect of the controversial article, and which sent shock waves through Catholic and Muslim circles in francophone sub-Saharan Africa and in France. "To the surprise of those who do not really understand Islam," he wrote, "the regions of Africa that are majority Muslim are the ones who are detaching themselves the most rapidly from the West and are turning to communism." Lefebvre argued that there was a great similarity between communism and Islam, claiming that they both relied on "fanaticism, collectivism, and enslavement of the weak."[1] Thus, in his view, Islam had laid a base that communism was ideally positioned to exploit as France's African colonies transitioned to independence.

To combat the spread of communism, Lefebvre called on the "Christian countries" of Europe to support the emerging African states with more than just technical assistance and financial aid. With a note of the bitterness of French Catholic missionaries who felt that the French colonial administration had long underestimated their worth as "civilizers" in the African colonies, he cautioned these "Christian countries" not to neglect culture and religion, which were their best ambassadors. "Coming with only a check in hand would be a great error," he lectured; "others will promise more." Essentially, Lefebvre felt that European powers such as France should deploy Christianity, and Catholicism in particular, as an ideological antidote to communism. "Though men of state, even most Catholic ones, would not yet dare to speak of it openly," he wrote, "they will have to choose between the Star and the Cross, between hell on earth and preparation for Heaven." The choice was already before them in Africa, he warned.[2]

Lefebvre's negative view of Islam and his fundamental belief in a European Catholic civilizing mission in Africa were enduring themes in French Catholic missionary discourse in France's sub-Saharan African colonies. His words echoed those of one of his predecessors, Monsignor Magloire Barthet, who served as the Spiritan apostolic vicar of Dakar from 1889 until 1898. Barthet, who, like Lefebvre, had a flair for the dramatic, frequently criticized the French colonial administration for what he perceived as favoritism toward Muslims, and he particularly resented the administration's use of Muslim chiefs to govern predominantly animist populations that missionaries wanted to convert to Catholicism. "Only the Christian populations [of Africa] will gradually adopt our ideas, our customs, our language and become deeply attached to France, while Muslims will always be our most implacable enemies," he wrote in a letter denouncing the administration of Senegal to legislator Charles Le Myre de Vilers in 1890.[3] In another letter to the legitimist deputy Albert de Mun, Barthet elaborated, "Muslims, however, will always be anti-European and therefore anti-French, because their goal is to dominate Africa in order to exploit it; as long as they see themselves as weaker than us, they will flatter us to win our favor so that they can participate more fully in the exploitation of the country, but the day they think it is possible to get rid of us, they will not hesitate to try . . . The forces we are obliged to keep in Algeria, after sixty years of occupation, are, I believe, a convincing proof of this."[4] Barthet's hostile attitude toward Islam at a time when France was actively extending its influence in sub-Saharan Africa through military and administrative expansion thus mirrors key aspects of Lefebvre's stance as France contemplated withdrawal sixty years later.[5]

It would be incorrect to conclude, however, that Lefebvre's words represented a broad, static, longstanding Catholic consensus on Islam in sub-Saharan Africa. Opinions even differed among French Catholic missionaries, who, given their evangelical aims, were perhaps more likely than African Catholic clergy or French and African lay believers to see Islam as a competitor or an enemy. Looking backward, one can find instances of Spiritans in coastal Senegal celebrating collaborations and relations with Muslims in the face of Freemasonry, atheism, or administrative anticlericalism, such as in electoral campaigns in the Four Communes in the 1880s, or on the occasion of the consecration of the cathedral of Dakar in 1936.[6]

Moreover, the White Fathers cultivated a more deliberate and respectful approach to Islam than the Spiritans, though they still considered it an inferior faith. In the words of priest-historian Aylward Shorter, "habitual criticism of Islam was not the right method to follow." Henri Marchal, a veteran of missions in the Sahara and Kabylia, who served as assistant head of the White Fathers between 1913 and 1947, was a key exponent of this doctrine. Marchal instructed missionaries not to talk about the errors of Islam or criticize Mohammed, but rather to understand and develop respect for Muslim beliefs and ways. Marchal believed that there were "salvific truths" in the Koran, and "Muslims could be saved through these truths if they were understood in the light of supernatural faith." He thus expounded a vision in which Muslims could "become Christians without knowing it."[7] Marchal played a central role in promoting the deep study of Islamic religion, law, history, and Arabic language among the White Fathers, helping to found the Institut des belles lettres arabes, an ancestor of the current Pontifical Institute for Arabic and Islamic Studies in Rome, which promotes itself today as a beacon of interfaith dialogue between Islam and Christianity.[8]

Lefebvre's article is thus best understood as an intervention in fascinating and complex dialogues about Islam that unfolded within the Franco-African Catholic world in the 1950s and early 1960s. The possibility of African independence from France and the perception that communism was gaining ground in sub-Saharan Africa were important contexts for these discussions, as was a widespread sense among Catholic missionary leaders that the window of opportunity to convert large numbers of Africans was closing. Over the course of the decade, priests and laypeople, both French and African, contemplated Catholicism's future on the continent with new urgency. One key aspect of that future would be Catholicism's ability to survive, let alone thrive, in regions that were predominantly Muslim, and its ability to reach remaining animist populations before Islam did (no one assumed that animism would resist one or the other monotheist creed). Lefebvre spoke for some Catholics when he equated Islam with vice, but a subset of them found the tone of his pronouncements counterproductive. And still others rejected his views completely, associating him with a dated colonial mentality, and / or arguing that the way forward was for Catholics to embrace Muslims and build bridges of understanding through faith. Finally, many prominent Catholic and Muslim Africans found the timing of his 1959 article extremely poor, as it complicated the politics of transition at independence, undermined public harmony, and had the unintended consequence of making Catholics in Africa feel even more vulnerable.

Catholic conversations about Islam in francophone sub-Saharan Africa on the eve of independence were thus significant in three key ways. First, they reveal a remarkable diversity of opinion about Islam within the broader Franco-African Catholic community that belied the strident pronouncements of one of its most prominent leaders. Second, these conversations had real consequences for Catholics and Muslims who were living side by side through the political transformations of independence. And finally, they developed competing threads of Catholic thinking that would come to a head at Vatican II in the wake of decolonization. Prominent figures in Catholic debates over Islam and relations with Muslims in French sub-Saharan Africa, including Lefebvre, missionaries who opposed him, and newly minted African prelates, carried their differences to Rome and shaped the church's deliberations about how to approach believers in other faiths. In that context, Lefebvre lost out to those who called for a more open and tolerant Catholicism that encouraged dialogue with Islam. The conversations about Islam in francophone sub-Saharan Africa on the eve of independence thus shed new light on the twentieth-century reformation of the Catholic Church.

CATHOLIC MISSIONARY VIEWS OF ISLAM IN THE 1950S

Missionary writings and correspondence from the regions of French sub-Saharan Africa with significant or growing Muslim populations reveal a broad range of Catholic opinions on Islam and Muslim/Christian relations in the 1950s. Lefebvre's alarmist view certainly had numerous adherents, who thought of Islam as a "peril," a menace, and a fierce competitor in an apocalyptic struggle for souls. Many of the senior French prelates in sub-Saharan Africa shared his negative opinion of Islam and were, like him, pessimistic about what kind of future African political self-determination might create. They tended to be older men who, like Lefebvre, had begun their missionary careers in the interwar years. As prelates, they were also responsible to their missionary superiors and to Rome for the numbers of conversions in their respective districts. Their reports and correspondence from the 1950s reveal a deep concern, and in some cases veritable paranoia, about the spread of Islam. Yet it is important to note that there were also notable voices on the Catholic left who saw Islam in very negative terms, including Emmanuel Mounier. In the course of his visit to West Africa, he observed, "One must reckon, finally, with the great obstacle that Islam presents to African emancipation. Everywhere it penetrates, it stifles initiative, energy, and creativity. In maintaining women in a position of systematic inferiority, it paralyzes the flowering of a more radiant civilization."[9] Crusty, conservative missionary veterans were thus not the only ones who viewed Islam with a jaundiced eye.

On the other hand, there were a growing number of French missionaries who rejected the hardline views of Archbishop Lefebvre. Whether influenced by interactions with Muslim communities on the ground, or by leftist Catholic ferment in France during and after the war, there were moderates who believed in harmonious coexistence as well as radical missionary activists who sought to strengthen connections and dialogues with Muslims. These missionaries tended to be younger—those who began their first missions in Africa after 1945 were more likely to have sympathy for African self-determination and interfaith dialogue than the "old colonials" who dominated the Catholic hierarchy on the continent. Institutional culture could also make a difference, though views were not uniform across congregations. For example, the White Fathers' emphasis on sophisticated study of Islam and a measure of respect for Muslims (with the caveat that Muslims lived in religious error) made it more likely, though by no means certain, that their priests cultivated moderate to progressive views on Islam. In general, individual missionaries harbored views of Islam along a spectrum that ranged from aggressively negative to very sympathetic, depending on their age, the nature and location of their deployment in Africa, and the culture of the organization they belonged to.

The idea that a decisive hour was at hand, when Africa's remaining animists would either be saved for the church or lost to Islam, was a key component of the alarmist and pessimistic Catholic point of view in the decade before independence. Even though the French state provided unprecedented financial support to missions in Africa via the FIDES after 1946, many Catholic executives still felt they were losing a battle against Islam. In a 1953 article entitled "The progress of Islam in Upper Volta" for the missionary periodical *Union missionnaire du clergé de France,* Monsignor Jean Lesourd, a White Father and apostolic vicar of Nouna, wrote of a "new era" in which missionaries "must, through intense and rapid action, get ahead of this dangerous threat [of Islam]. We are living in a time of choice for hearts and minds," he worried, "which has great implications for the future." Invoking older missionary arguments of administrative preference for Islam in terms similar to Lefebvre's, Lesourd denounced "European policy which, by either laicism or supposed neutrality, favors Muslims, who are supple and docile (at least by appearances) subjects, against protective actions by Catholic missionaries in favor of their believers." For his missionary readers, Lesourd painted a vivid and disturbing picture of Islamicization as a stealthy force which, like a stain, would spread out from multiple points of impact and eventually reach all the villages in the region.[10]

Even in the southern reaches of West Africa, where Islam was less entrenched, prelates sounded alarm bells in the 1950s. In his five-year report to the Vatican on his vicariate in 1955, Jean-Baptiste Boivin, SMA bishop of Abidjan, observed, "another great peril, which is extending further and further, even in Lower Côte d'Ivoire, is the Muslim peril." Like Lesourd and Lefebvre, Boivin faulted the French administration for "protecting" Muslims and allowing them to establish themselves as village chiefs. He complained of Muslim "peddlers" who traveled selling *gris-gris* (talismans) and spreading Islam in rural areas. He also noted that many educated Muslims sought to marry Christian women, and that missionaries were trying to put such young women on their guard, as their parents were usually happy if they married a teacher, lawyer, or doctor, regardless of his religion.[11] In Bouaké, a city in central Côte d'Ivoire, SMA Bishop André-Pierre Duirat also warned of Muslim "peril" and suggested that a turning point was coming. "One senses that the population is playing a waiting game, searching for its path," he wrote in a report. "Will it move toward the Christian side or will it turn to Islam? . . . We sense that the choice will be made in the near future." He begged for personnel, "if we do not want to be 'too late.' With the rapid rhythm of the evolution of the country, there is not a minute to lose."[12]

In the apostolic prefecture of Sokodé, in central Togo, Monsignor Jérome-Théodore Lingenheim, also an SMA missionary, employed an even more hysterical tone to describe an immediate and critical Catholic struggle with Islam. Lingenheim laced his correspondence with pronouncements in capital letters, to emphasize his points. In a report to SMA headquarters, he observed: "ISLAM IS ON THE MOVE," claiming that mosques and Koranic schools were popping up everywhere, even in areas where Islam had never been established before. "ISLAM IS THE MOST SERIOUS AND MOST IMMEDIATE MENACE of all the threats we face," he shouted on the page.[13] In another letter to his SMA superior, Lingenheim twice observed, in capital letters, "MASCULINE YOUTH ARE LITERALLY CONSTANTLY SOLICITED BY FOLLOWERS OF ISLAM."[14] Lingenheim's, Duirat's, and Boivin's anxiety regarding Islam is palpable, even if they exaggerated somewhat in hopes of getting more men and money from their superiors.

This elevated level of concern among missionary bishops prompted Monsignor Lefebvre to convene a special meeting of the hierarchy of French West Africa and of Chad to "exchange views" on Islam in April of 1955. Their conference produced a twenty-two-page printed report, which appears to have been for internal church use only. Two things stand out in the document. First is the urgency the hierarchy felt about the spread of Islam in sub-Saharan Africa. The report observed that there were few other places in the world where the church could hope for mass conversions. Yet, the report claimed, in the previous twenty years, conversions to Islam in sub-Saharan Africa had more than doubled the number of conversions to Catholicism.[15]

The second noteworthy point is that this group of church executives, doubtless influenced by their chairman Lefebvre, did not see Islam as a fellow religious bulwark against communism, but instead as a conduit *to* communism (and vice versa). The report drew parallels between the position of the individual man in Islam and in communism, in order to argue that African Muslims' beliefs made them susceptible to communist teachings. For example, "The Muslim man, deprived of both liberty and responsibility, and fully subject to the inescapable divine omnipotence, [joins] the Marxist man, who is fully subject to the law of historical determinism. On both sides, a blind and arbitrary force, divine for the Muslim and human for the Marxist, underlies the inexorable destiny of man." Moreover, the report argued, the "patriarchal organization in the family, in which everything is crushed under the absolute authority of the chief, means that Islam creates [atomized] individuals, rather than persons." This, in conjunction with the rapid social and economic changes taking place in Africa, created favorable conditions for the development of a mass proletariat, which would be easily seduced by Marxist ideology.[16] Catholic evangelists would have to make great efforts to counteract these dynamics.

From this perspective, Catholicism's two great bogeymen in sub-Saharan Africa—Islam and communism—actually nourished one another. In 1956, Monsignor François Couespel du Mesnil, director of the Antislavery Society of France, which raised funds to support missionary endeavors in Africa, argued that "expanding Islam wins battles for the Soviets" in Africa.[17] Lefebvre took the same position in his provocative article of 1959. And in 1961 Monsignor Joseph Bretault, a White Father with over thirty years of missionary experience in Upper Volta, complained of what he termed "the rapid invasion of communism, allied with Islam" in sub-Saharan Africa.[18]

The supposed linkage between Islam and communism was a fracture point, however, within Catholic dialogues about Islam in the 1950s. More moderate Catholic missionaries, even those who were critical of Islam, did not necessarily agree with the hierarchy that Islam was a path to communism. Indeed, some suggested the opposite in the 1950s—that Islam was an ally in a struggle against "atheistic materialism." In their eyes, moreover, Lefebvre's bull-in-a-china-shop approach to Christian-Muslim relations was counterproductive and potentially damaging to Catholic interests. This point of view is most clearly illustrated in a series of clashes between Lefebvre and the small contingent of White Fathers who worked within his episcopal jurisdiction in Dakar as the editors of *Afrique nouvelle,* the weekly Catholic newspaper of francophone Africa.[19] Founded in 1947 as a key part of the broader Catholic postwar push in French Africa, *Afrique nouvelle* developed into a widely read paper, which enjoyed a reputation as an insightful counterpoint to the official media in the colonies, and was consulted by Christian and Muslim African elites alike.[20]

Indeed, the story of Lefebvre's famous article entitled "Where is Africa going?" actually does not begin in 1959, when it appeared in *La France catholique,* but in 1950, when he tried to publish a nearly identical text in *Afrique nouvelle.* When Lefebvre approached the White Fathers' team with a version of it in September of that year, he put them in an awkward position. In keeping with their congregation's policy of sincere engagement with Islam, they felt that the paper, while explicitly Catholic, also had an apostolic mission to reach into Muslim milieus. Their formal strategy, as outlined by editor-in-chief Father Robert Rummelhardt in a 1954 memo to his superiors in Rome, was to avoid shocking Muslim sensibilities through direct attacks on Islamic doctrine, but rather to focus critiques on "social facts that ensued from Islam," including "tyranny that victimized African women" and the exportation of black slaves to Mecca, in hopes of "opening the eyes of the black Muslim elite and thereby attracting it to Christianity."[21] As White Father and archbishop of Bamako Pierre Leclerc later explained, his mission chiefs conceived of their work not as an effort to convert Muslim individuals, but more as "a general action *in the social arena,* to make people aware of and lead them toward the adoption of Catholic social teachings over Marxism, which could be the way to total Christianity."[22] These White Fathers did not fully embrace Islam as a religion of equivalent value to Catholicism, and they harbored vague hopes of subverting it in the long run, but they were anxious to reach out to Muslims and make common cause with them against the threat of communism.

Moreover, beginning in the spring of 1950, *Afrique nouvelle* had been openly advocating a "Muslim-Christian entente" to combat what the editors saw as a "Marxist invasion" in certain parts of French West Africa. In April, Rummelhardt had published an article entitled "Muslim-Christian coalition against atheistic communism," which he claimed had been inspired by encouragement from Rome. According to Rummelhardt, this article resulted in dialogues between himself and marabouts in Dakar, as well as an agreement with Abdel Kader Diagne, the president of the Muslim Fraternity of French West Africa, to cooperate informally.[23]

As a result, Rummelhardt felt that it was an inopportune time for *Afrique nouvelle* to publish Lefebvre's piece, because of what he termed the article's "overly sharp positions on Islam." He felt it was not a moment to clash "head-on" with Muslims. Moreover, Lefebvre had asked the White Fathers to insert the article into the paper unsigned, which would make it look like the work of the editors. These priests, who worked in Lefebvre's jurisdiction and depended on him for funding, told him they would publish the article if he signed it and formally ordered its insertion, but he did not insist.[24] Lefebvre was clearly itching to get his point of view into print, however, which resulted in the text's appearance in *Ecclésia* magazine, a Catholic periodical in the metropole, in 1953. It seems that Lefebvre did not expect that Muslims in West Africa would ever get wind of an article in a Catholic metropolitan journal. They did, however, aided gleefully by Albert Bayet, a notable Freemason and rationalist, who was a sociologist at the Sorbonne, president of the National Press Association and of the Ligue de l'enseignement, an organization committed to the defense and promotion of secular education.

Like François Méjan, Bayet was a fierce defender of French *laïcité*, and he saw Lefebvre's article as a means to attack the church at home and to sow division between Muslim and Catholic "clericalisms" in Africa.[25] For metropolitan audiences, he penned a retort to Lefebvre's piece in *La Manche laïque* entitled "Un document stupéfiant!" in which he told his readers, "Lefebvre declares war on Islam!"—in spite of the distinguished service of Muslim soldiers in France's armies. "You read it correctly, don't rub your eyes," he told readers, after quoting Lefebvre on how, without the proper aid, Africa would lose its way amid its endemic plagues of polygamy, domination of the weak, and superstition, and give itself over to Islam. "According to Mgr Lefebvre . . ." he observed, "Muslim beliefs are superstitions, and Mohammed taught them the route to vice." Bayet positioned himself and his fellow activists as defenders of religious tolerance and freedom of opinion. "We the secularists say, 'French brothers of Africa, do not think, when a Frenchman insults your religious beliefs, that it is France talking. France, because she is *laïque,* loves all of her children the same, whatever the color of their skin; she is the world leader of the essential fight for liberty and fraternity, she will win it by you, for you, with you," he declared.[26]

Bayet also took his message to African audiences in person. He traveled to Senegal in 1954, in an apparent attempt to develop the local

Masonic lodges, and prepared for his voyage by sending the text of Lefebvre's article, together with his own biting commentary on it, to all of the African schoolteachers in the French West African federation. Once on the ground, he spoke to schoolteachers in Dakar and Saint-Louis, again denouncing Lefebvre. The African teachers' unions in the Muslim territories of Senegal, Sudan, and Guinea responded by drafting a motion demanding the cessation of government subsidies to Catholic schools.[27]

The White Fathers at *Afrique nouvelle* could not contain their dismay. A year later, Rummelhardt reported to his superior general that Muslims in the federation were still incensed over the article, and marabouts were ordering their followers not to vote for Christian candidates such as Léopold Senghor. According to Rummelhardt, the colonial administration's Muslim affairs department "judged [the article] severely as a supremely awkward political gaffe by the most senior ecclesiastical figure in French Black Africa." Rummelhardt told a colleague (though he would later deny this), "the day the Apostolic Delegate wrote that article, he proved himself to be an imbecile."[28] In the view of moderates like Rummelhardt, Lefebvre was a dangerous extremist who was undercutting a practical approach to Muslims and the threat of communism in the federation. Clearly, however, the archbishop learned nothing from this uproar in 1953 that prevented him from inciting a subsequent firestorm in 1959.

Even as debates swirled between more extreme and less strident Catholic critics of Islam in sub-Saharan Africa in the 1950s, there were other missionary voices that advocated brotherly regard for Islam and Muslims without any overt instrumental or evangelical underpinnings. Even as the most prominent Spiritan in Africa was denouncing Islam, for example, there were some Spiritans who evinced much different attitudes toward Muslims. This was particularly the case in the apostolic prefecture of Kankan in "Upper" or northeastern Guinea, the heavily Muslim region where Raymond-Marie Tchidimbo took up his first post in 1952. Evidence from both Spiritan and African sources attests to a high level of mutual respect between Catholic missionaries and Muslims of Kankan. In the mid-1950s, there were 7,500 Catholics out of 670,000 inhabitants in the entire prefecture, spread across an area a fifth the size of metropolitan France. There were twenty-one missionary priests, eight nuns, six religious brothers and five lay missionaries—a total of forty Catholics to minister to this vast area.[29]

The fact that they were greatly outnumbered likely contributed to the Spiritans' development of strong relations with local Muslims and their leaders. For example, the Spiritan Catholic school in the town of Kankan proper taught many Muslim students. When it looked in 1950 as though the Spiritan leadership was going to remove two beloved French priests from the parish, Muslim members of the public rose to their defense. In an extraordinary letter to Spiritan superior general Louis Le Hunsec, prominent Muslim trader and local notable Papa Konaré, himself a veteran of Catholic education in Senegal, beseeched Le Hunsec not to allow the change. "I dare to hope, Monsignor," he wrote, "that YOU WILL LEAVE US THESE TWO PRIESTS WHO CONSTITUTE THE ONLY ELEMENT OF COMPREHENSION BETWEEN BLACKS AND WHITES HERE." He went on to plead on behalf of the Muslim families served by the school, who had approached him for help: "I ASK YOU, MOREOVER, MONSIGNOR, IN THE NAME OF THE FATHERS OF THE TWO HUNDRED MUSLIM STUDENTS WHO ATTEND THE CATHOLIC SCHOOL."[30] Konaré believed that angry Europeans in the Guinean capital of Conakry were campaigning against the priests in Kankan because one of them had said in a sermon that Christ himself did not differentiate between white and black men. Konaré hoped that Le Hunsec, because he had presided over the appointments of the African apostolic prefect Joseph Faye and métis apostolic Prefect Prosper Dodds in Senegal, would support, rather than punish this inclusive stance.[31]

Konaré was a highly assimilated, French-educated Muslim with prior experience of the Catholic Church, but the Spiritans in Kankan also got along very well with Sheikh Mohammad Sharif (1874–1955) or, as the missionaries called him, "the religious chief of the Muslims of Kankan." In the April 1954 issue of the Spiritan monthly magazine *Annales spiritaines,* which featured a series of articles on Kankan, apostolic prefect Maurice Le Mailloux devoted a page-long section of a lengthy article on his mission to the sharif. Le Mailloux respectfully described his ancestry and authority and noted the "sincere friendship" the sharif had

developed with Monsignor Lerouge, the former Spiritan bishop of Conakry who had died in 1949.[32] Describing an exchange of gifts between
the two, Le Mailloux noted the sharif's pronouncement that "our two
religions are parallel paths to God and that Christians and Muslims are
half-brothers 'of the same father, but not the same mother.'" Le Mailloux then related a gesture by the sharif that "profoundly touched" his
missionary community in 1952. The Spiritans told the sharif that they
planned to bless their new chapel on August 15, the celebration of the
assumption of the Virgin Mary, and that they would pray for him on
the occasion. The sharif decided to attend the ceremony in person and,
without any pomp or display, he took a seat on their benches and prayed
with them. A photographer captured the bishop and the sharif together
the moment the ceremony was over, which became the headlining illus-
tration of the entire piece. The caption clearly meant to emphasize Le
Mailloux's amity with the sharif, as two French officials also in the picture were not named.[33]

Nowhere in these magazine pages is there the hysteria about a Muslim
"peril" that peppered many missionary discourses on Islam. And this
picture of comity was not merely posturing for the metropolitan magazine's audience, as the mission's daily log reveals. On the occasion of the
sharif's death in September 1955, the Spiritans seemed genuinely moved.
Though journal entries were often laconic, the ones pertaining to the
sharif's death were somewhat more detailed. The diarist included a quote
from a European doctor who had tended the sharif to the end, "'One
could look in vain throughout all of [French West Africa] for a man of
this value." The mission superior immediately went to express his con-
dolences to the sharif's son, and the Spiritan priests and their bishop
were invited to attend the burial and went to pay their respects the following day. The diarist commented, "R.I.P. Will this be a place of pilgrimage? Without a doubt—everyone agrees that he was an upright, sincere soul. One could think that he was of 'the heart of the Church.'"[34]
The affection was evidently sincere, even if it was also the case that the
mission's local fortunes depended to a degree on the sharif's good will.
There was, therefore, room in the Spiritan imagination to see Muslims
in a much more positive light than Lefebvre's words would suggest.

Perhaps the most striking example of a progressive Catholic attitude
toward Islam in sub-Saharan Africa arrived in Dakar in the mid-1950s

Warm interfaith relations on the Feast of the Assumption of Mary: Monsignor Maurice Le Mailloux, prefect of Kankan, with Sheikh Mohammad Sharif, Kankan, August 15, 1952. Courtesy of ACSSp.

in the person of Father Luc Moreau, a Dominican friar from the congregation's Lyon province. Lefebvre, chronically short on personnel, had called on the Dominicans to run Catholic radio broadcasts in French West Africa and, subsequently, to serve as chaplains to Catholic students at the new University of Dakar. As noted, Lefebvre wanted to make sure that the church closely monitored and supported the faith of elite African students who would serve as the continent's future leaders. He soon regretted his invitation to the Dominicans, however. It was not long before he was complaining vociferously about the friars, faulting them for offenses that ranged from what they wore on their trips to Dakar's beaches to Father Moreau's views on Islam.

Moreau, who had spent two years studying in Cairo, styled himself a scholarly expert on Islam who preached mutual understanding and respect between the faiths, with an anticommunist slant.[35] He advocated for a dialogue of faith that went well beyond the moderate stance outlined above, in which Father Rummelhardt and his staff at *Afrique nouvelle* tried to build a Muslim following, yet simultaneously attacked Islam from a "social" point of view in the mid-1950s. Moreau outlined his approach in an article he published in *Afrique nouvelle* in May of 1959 entitled, "A call for a spiritual encounter" which carried the subheading "In a new Africa: Christians and Muslims." Its prominent placement on the first page suggested that the White Fathers' editorial team, which was then headed by the more radical Father Joseph-Roger de Benoist, supported Moreau's call for "collaboration in mutual respect" between Christians and Muslims as Africa moved toward political independence.[36]

In the article, Moreau argued that religious communities should not leave it to social or political "technicians" to shape Africa's future. "The faithful, in their capacity as believers, have an indispensable role, and a grave responsibility in the harmonious blossoming of the African community," he argued. Moreau acknowledged that a "courageous" open dialogue between Christians and Muslims would be challenging, and require "well-prepared interlocutors." Yet, he pointed out, Africa was a good place to try it: there was no history of violence between the Christian and Muslim communities; many families included both Muslims and Christians, children of both faiths were often classmates in school, and there was already much cooperation in civic life between Muslims and Christians. He hoped that dialogue between Muslims and Christians, which he characterized as a "prayer and a hope," would preserve a place for religion in the emerging African countries and in the rising African generations, particularly a young elite seduced by materialism and atheism. In an aside that may well have referred to Lefebvre, Moreau observed that this position on dialogue provoked the "objections of certain unenlightened Christians who see these conversations as a betrayal of missionary work, or, by contrast, of distrustful Muslims who consider them as more subtle attempts at conversion."[37]

Thus, while Moreau also positioned the faiths together against "atheistic materialism," he had a much more positive and sympathetic view of Islam than some of his Catholic brethren, and, apparently, less immediate desire to persuade Muslims to convert. Moreau reported with evident satisfaction to a Dominican colleague in June 1959 that a "Sudanese marabout" had written him a warm letter in reaction to the article. Moreau also reported that he had given a talk on "Malian" Islam to the clergy of Dakar, which he had distributed as a text to students at the university. "We will establish ourselves little by little," he wrote, "without beating a big drum."[38] He looked forward to a day when his conception of interfaith relations became the dominant point of view among Catholics in Africa.

Thus, on the eve of Monsignor Lefebvre's jarring article of December 1959, Catholic clergy in francophone sub-Saharan Africa harbored a wide range of views on Islam, which they aired both publicly and behind closed doors. There were stark differences of opinion within Catholic ranks on Islam's affinity with communism and its value as a fellow spiritual bulwark against "atheistic materialism." Moreover, attitudes on whether Islam was a foe or potential ally in the struggle with communism fueled debates on how best to approach Muslims in order to safeguard Catholic interests. Deep anxiety about Islam's rapid spread in the region proliferated alongside examples of profound respect for Muslim individuals and Islam. A variety of factors shaped clerical stances toward Islam, which were not necessarily consistent within congregations. Individuals' views depended, to a certain degree, on local circumstances and personalities, as the case of the Spiritans and the sharif of Kankan makes clear. Age often mattered: younger French missionaries who had come to Africa after World War II tended to be more likely to see Muslims in a positive light than the older generation of missionary prelates, who also had to report and justify the loss of potential converts to Islam to the Vatican. All in all, a healthy distrust and fear of Islam coexisted with a willingness to view Muslims as allies and fellow believers, especially when confronting atheism and militant secularism.

FALLOUT FROM THE "L. BOMB"

Lefebvre's article appeared in *La France catholique* at a moment of high political drama in francophone sub-Saharan Africa, only a few days after Charles de Gaulle had traveled to Senegal in December 1959 and signaled that France was open to further measures of independence for its African colonies. The archbishop's explicit linking of Islam to communism and his concurrent call for European states to use Christianity against a communist threat in Africa suggested to readers that he was calling for a Catholic crusade against Islam in tandem with the preservation of French rule in Africa. It was a superbly ill-timed intervention that risked creating antagonism between Muslims and Catholics, and between Africans and the French, as delicate negotiations about Africa's future were underway. Archbishop of Bamako Leclerc took to calling the article "the L. Bomb" and even compared it to the nuclear tests the French were then conducting in Reggane, Algeria.[39] Maurice Voisin, the caustic editor of the Dakar-based satirical weekly *Échos d'Afrique noire,* also referred to Lefebvre's article as "a veritable bomb."[40] The archbishop's stance angered African statesmen and prominent Muslims, and worried French officials. But many of his most vocal critics were Catholics, both French and African. Aghast at Lefebvre's insensitivity to the political climate, they scrambled to refute and defuse his toxic message in order to safeguard a Catholic future in independent Africa.

Lefebvre's piece had acute repercussions in Senegal and Sudan in particular, because he was headquartered in Dakar, because both states' populations were predominantly Muslim, and because of their rapidly evolving relationship with the metropole and with each other. In January of 1959, the two territories had joined together to form the Mali Federation. African proponents of federation had initially hoped to combine all of French West Africa into an entity that could marshal more economic and political resources than individual former colonies would have on their own, but ultimately only those two participated.[41] It was not initially clear how the existence of the Mali Federation would impact Senegal and Sudan's membership in the French Community, which had succeeded the French Union in 1958. That issue was front and center when the executive council of the Community met with de Gaulle in Saint-Louis, Senegal on December 11 and 12, 1959. One of the key items on the agenda was the federation's request, filed in September, that France "transfer competences" to Mali. This was essentially a demand for full independence, but presented in terms that emphasized that Mali's leaders, the Senegalese statesmen Mamadou Dia and Léopold Senghor, as well as Sudan's Modibo Keita, did not want to reject the French Community, as Sékou Touré's Guinea had in 1958. Instead, they hoped to remain part of the Community while independent. France, rather than balk at this change, signaled its willingness to play along, in order to keep the Community intact.[42] De Gaulle responded that the transfer of competences could occur without "rupture" and on December 13 he addressed the Federal Assembly of Mali and assured its members of France's support of the federation's new direction. He finished his speech with "Vive le Mali! Vive le Sénégal! Vive le Soudan! Vive la France!", telegraphing that independence would not destroy close relations between France and her former colonies.[43]

Lefebvre's pessimistic article, which appeared on December 18, and its assertion that "the regions of Africa that are majority Muslim are the ones that are detaching themselves the most rapidly from the West and are turning to Communism" appeared to be a direct riposte to these developments, though he had first written it in early November, and, as noted, had been reiterating some of its main points for years.[44] From the perspective of Senegalese and Sudanese political actors who were negotiating the evolution of Africa's relationship to France, Lefebvre's piece contradicted Charles de Gaulle's conciliatory message. Some of them also read it as an effort to sow dissension between the Catholic Senghor and the Muslim Keita.[45] His intervention was unfortunate, in their eyes, because it complicated their hopes of securing autonomy while staying in the French Community and maintaining links to the metropole. Lefebvre represented a supercilious, colonialist France that they did not want to engage with, but he had spoken to the public at large and thus they needed to refute him.

Tidjani Traoré, Sudan's minister of information and security, went on Radio-Mali to denounce Lefebvre as someone who "thinks colonialism continues, that paternalism is not dead, and that [the French] can still divide and rule in Africa." Contrasting Lefebvre with de Gaulle, whom he placed in the "camp of love, fraternity, and friendly collaboration," Traoré observed with irony, "We were not aware that Islam led to independence and to communism, we did not know that Islam was incompatible with Western civilization. We evidently did not know that Sudan was communist, and that, in certain places, French authority needed to be bolstered to keep Africans, those childish catechumens who want to say the mass before they are ready, on the right path."[46] Traoré spoke for a government that wanted to marginalize a powerful, discordant French voice that threatened to complicate the delicate political transitions that were taking place.

Unsurprisingly, Muslim religious leaders were also angered by Lefebvre's impolitic declarations. El Hadj Ibrahima Niasse, a Tidjani notable in Senegal who was widely revered as a holy teacher across West Africa, publicly attacked Lefebvre's article.[47] Like Traoré, he framed his written response of January 5, 1960, entitled "Africa for the Africans," as a rejection of continued colonialism, but as a Sufi leader he also defended Islam, and insisted on the error of equating Islam and communism. He denounced Lefebvre's piece as an attack on Islam in sub-Saharan Africa and exalted African nationalism, proclaiming that its triumph was inevitable, despite the "antiprogressive maneuvers" of its adversaries. "The time of foreign domination is over," he wrote, "and will not return." Niasse refuted Lefebvre's argument linking Islam and communism by pointing out that communism came to Africa from Europe. Noting that Lefebvre had either not thought through his argument, or else was completely ignorant of the nature of Islam, Niasse advised, "The truth is that Islam and communism are two completely distinct and clearly opposed doctrines." Moreover, he argued, Islam had been present in Africa for centuries before the arrival of Christianity or communism, which were both European imports. In his view, Africa was less likely to become communist if Europeans withdrew.[48]

Niasse also took special care to overturn Lefebvre's argument that Islam enslaved the weak, using domineering Europe as his foil. As a prominent Sufi surrounded by acolytes and *talibés,* it is possible that he worried that the archbishop's accusations of Muslim domination might strike close to home. "I would like to know," he asked rhetorically, "if it was the Muslims who enslaved the Europeans, conquerors of Africa, who subjected people to colonization for centuries, or if it is the Europeans who subjugated the Muslims." He then floated the idea that prominent Europeans (and Catholic leaders) enjoyed more power over their respective countrymen than African Muslims did. "If the few privileges that certain Muslims chiefs enjoy vis-à-vis their brothers constitute enslavement, I would be truly astonished, because in non-Muslim countries men enjoy the same sorts of privileges in much greater proportions. And there, these privileges are exercised more dangerously against workers and the poor, whether they are held by a political or a religious leader." Niasse then offered Lefebvre, who had evoked the French Revolution of 1789 in his article, a lesson in French history, by pointing out the vast wealth the church had amassed through its control of land and revenue under the Old Regime. He concluded this piece of the argument with the suggestion that Lefebvre had portrayed Islam in negative terms that actually more aptly described Catholicism.[49] The aggressive and defensive aspects of Niasse's response relay his deep indignation at the archbishop's approach to Islam, and also suggest that he worried that Lefebvre's message about Islam might prove persuasive to at least some African ears.

A chorus of lay defenders of Islam, both French and African, also publicly denounced Lefebvre's equation of communism and Islam. Vincent Monteil, a former French army officer who was conducting research on the Muslim world at the Institut fondamental de l'Afrique noire in Dakar between 1959 and 1967, gave a public talk on January 14, 1960, in which he assailed Lefebvre's connection of Islam and communism. Monteil, who converted to Islam later in life, was a close friend and eventual biographer of Louis Massignon, the French Catholic thinker who dedicated much of his life to promoting understanding between Muslims and Christians, and Monteil's talk reflected this impulse.[50] Like Niasse, Monteil refuted the idea that Islam and communism were particularly compatible by suggesting that Lefebvre's argument could easily be adapted to Christianity, citing examples of Christian fanaticism and violence such as the inquisition or slavery. He also included statements by Soviet leaders denouncing Islam as contrary to their aims. He concluded with a quote, initially employed by Catholic priest Henri Chambre in reference to Christianity, "'the Marxist project is *radically* opposed to the Muslim project . . . It is not the opposition of one lifestyle to another, but two conceptions of the world confronting one another.'"[51] In Monteil's mind, the fundamental materialism and atheism of communism divided it irrevocably from Christian or Muslim spiritualism.

In another sweeping denunciation of the archbishop that also enveloped the administration of Senegal's Catholic president Senghor, Ciré Ly, an activist Muslim medical student, attracted some 1,500 people to a talk entitled "From the seminary to the mosque" on January 24, 1960.

The crowd, which included prominent doctors, lawyers, professors and several elected deputies, packed the Le Mali movie house in Dakar to hear him, according to French diplomats who secretly reported on the gathering.[52] Ly, who had campaigned for improvements in conditions for students in the mid-1950s, was then pursuing a medical internship at the Le Dantec hospital in Dakar and writing up a doctoral thesis. According to French spies, Ly said that he considered Lefebvre's words a provocation to Islam and Muslims, who made up 90 percent of the population of Senegal, and he accused the archbishop of trying to sow discord between Sudan and Senegal. In the course of the talk, Ly also attacked Léopold Senghor's government for the high proportion of Catholics among its ministers, including the French-born minister of finances André Peytavin; François Dieng, minister of education and culture; Émile Badiane, minister of information; and the French Dominican priest Louis-Joseph Lebret, minister of general economy.[53] Finally, he expressed astonishment that Lefebvre's provocation had not resulted in a formal questioning or sanctioning of the Vatican's representative in a Muslim country.[54]

There is no doubt that Senghor was acutely aware of the politics of religion in his position as the Catholic president of a majority Muslim country, and he too refuted the vision of Islam put forth by Lefebvre, though not right away. In November of 1960, three months after Senegal and Sudan had abandoned the Mali Federation, Senghor authored a call for "Cooperation between Islam and Christianity" which was published by Senegal's Ministry of Information and reprinted in *Afrique nouvelle*. The president placed himself in the company of Muslim leaders such as Maḥmūd Shaltūt, the Grand Imam of Al Azhar in Cairo, who had already called for Christians and Muslims to unite against atheism, and of Abdelkader El Fassi, the Moroccan ambassador to West Germany, whom he quoted as saying, "'Christianity and Islam can and should get along, marry their efforts, and emphasize what they have in common to confront the gathering momentum of the enemies of God.'"[55] Like Rummelhardt, Moreau, and Niasse, Senghor felt Islam was opposed to, and not a conduit for, the dangers of atheistic materialism. He portrayed Christianity and Islam as natural allies, not enemies, in Africa.

Nonetheless, Ciré Ly's attacks on Senghor's cabinet highlighted how Lefebvre's words could be deployed against the church and Catholic individuals. This possibility was deeply troubling to many French and African Catholics in Africa, who found themselves on the defensive in the wake of the archbishop's clumsy pronouncements. The prospect of independence made them especially attuned to the fate of the Catholic Church in the majority Muslim states of Senegal and Sudan, and the prospects of harmony between Catholics and Muslims after French withdrawal. Lefebvre's avowed hostility to Islam put the French Catholic hierarchy on the ground in Mali in the awkward position of having to refute its most well-known prelate in an effort to safeguard positive relations with the Muslim majority and the emergent local governments. Moreover, individual African and French Catholics also strove to publicize their opposition to the archbishop's stance. Even some French Catholic priests and prelates who eyed Islam with suspicion saw the political need to reject Lefebvre's message. Thus Catholics, not all of whom were uniformly favorable to Islam, became some of Lefebvre's most fervent opponents, because they feared the backlash against him would endanger the future of Catholicism in newly independent Africa.

As Lefebvre had targeted Sudan in his piece, the Catholic hierarchy there was on the front lines of the effort to defuse the tensions he had stoked. Monsignor Pierre Leclerc, the White Father and archbishop of Bamako who coined the "L. Bomb" moniker, concurred with one of his mission superiors that Lefebvre's article was a "catastrophe," and complained that the country was still feeling the consequences in late January, and likely would for some time.[56] In mid-February, Leclerc huddled with the other prelates of Sudan as well as Monsignor Jean-Marie Lesourd of Nouna in Upper Volta, and Monsignor Jean-Marie Maury, who had succeeded Lefebvre as apostolic delegate in July of 1959. Maury was appalled by his predecessor's article, and had written to White Father superior general Father Léo Volker in late January that it had created a "grave" and "very delicate" situation in Dakar, which he feared would have "serious" consequences.[57] All of the men at the February meeting were European-born Frenchmen, as no African priests had yet been promoted to positions of leadership in Sudan. As noted above, Lesourd was quite hostile to Islam and Leclerc was a proponent of the

White Father's idea of trying to persuade Muslims to embrace Christianity through social action. Nonetheless, together with their colleagues, they launched a public relations campaign to disavow Lefebvre, focusing on Catholic support for independence and the ability of peoples of varied faiths to unite to bolster the young country. Maury called on the government in Bamako to calm the waters and was officially received by Modibo Keita and Minister of State Jean-Marie Koné.[58] During a mass at the cathedral in Bamako, the apostolic delegate spoke extemporaneously, affirming, "The church always witnesses with emotion the birth of a new state, which brings its own original genius and values to the human patrimony." He continued, "So that the church can bring its values to the world that is being constructed, you must engage yourselves entirely as Christians in temporal affairs."[59] Maury thus affirmed church support for independence, yet simultaneously staked a claim that Christianity should help to shape the new order.

The same week the French prelates of Sudan released a declaration which reiterated these themes. It said, in part,

> The bishops of Sudan salute with affection the young Sudanese Republic, whether considered on its own or as part of the original and fraternal association that is the Mali Federation. They are very pleased with the climate of peace, of mutual comprehension, and the concern for justice that presides in this delicate period of preparation for complete independence. In the name of the church, whose qualified representatives they are, without giving up their liberty and without involving themselves in political questions that are not in their domain, the bishops of Sudan declare themselves ready to bring all of their help to the construction of a spiritually elevated society that is worthy of humanity and which will be a source of true well-being by creating a social and economic order that better corresponds to eternal divine law and to human dignity. They invite all believers, regardless of which religious family they belong to, to maintain in modern Sudan the primacy of spiritual values, the only guarantee of peoples' true progress toward liberty, justice, and charity.

In this carefully crafted missive, the bishops distanced themselves from Lefebvre by claiming to be the genuine representatives of the church and affirming their support for Sudan's independence. They asserted their freedom of action, yet promised not to meddle in politics. Finally, they insisted on the importance of spirituality and reached out to "other religious families" (by which they meant Muslims), in a call to make sure spiritual values remained central in the emerging political and social order. This closing note was an attempt to bring Muslims into a joint effort to combat communism, which they feared would prove seductive to Modibo Keita and those around him. They thus rejected Lefebvre's idea that Islam was a conduit to communism, rather positing that it could be a fellow rampart against it if Catholics did not antagonize Muslims.[60]

This line was largely in keeping with ideas that Leclerc had developed over time. Leclerc was certainly wary of Islam, and particularly of the recent local appearance of Wahhabism, brought back by African students from Cairo's El Azhar University. Leclerc characterized Wahhabism as "purist, rigorous, modernist, and nationalist," but not communist in the least. Indeed, Leclerc connected Islam to communism only in a negative sense. In his view, the failures of Islam opened the door to communism—a very different claim than the one Lefebvre had made. Invoking the same idea of a "decisive moment" which obsessed many missionaries in 1950s West Africa, Leclerc felt that "traditional" West African Islam was unable to offer new answers to people who were impatiently seeking political and social progress in an "underdeveloped country." He believed that people in Sudan were thus turning either to Christianity or Marxism as possible ways forward, seduced by the apparent *"efficiency"* of Marxism, even if they did not fully comprehend what it meant in practice. Leclerc condemned the "tactlessness" and "spiteful anger" of Lefebvre's position, and favored making common cause with reformist Islam in the face of communism.[61] Also hailing Shaltūt's call for Christians and Muslims to unite against atheism, Leclerc observed, "It is serious and unjust to say Islam is similar to communism in its methods. Do we want to push it toward communism or do we want a 'holy war' at the very moment when Al Azhar is advocating for a union of spiritualists against communism?"[62] Leclerc observed to his superiors in Rome that Maury's speech and the bishops' declaration had laid out the "real" position of the church on the political changes in Mali. According to the archbishop, members of the government, as well as Catholics and Muslims, received both initiatives with great satisfaction, which helped to dissipate the uproar caused by Lefebvre's article.[63]

Meanwhile, as the Catholic hierarchy scrambled to clarify its stances on independence and Islam, public refutation of Lefebvre's piece also bubbled up from the faithful. Members of the young, French-educated West African Catholic elite were particularly appalled by the archbishop's screed, which, they protested, had placed them in an "untenable position" and "compromis[ed] the existence and the future of the Church in Africa." Some fifty African Catholic students signed an open letter to Lefebvre which was reproduced (without their individual names) in *L'Essor,* the newspaper of the Union soudanaise-Rassemblement démocratique africain, Sudan's dominant political party.[64]

Echoing the 1956 declaration of the Catholic African students in France, which had taken some French Catholics to task for melding their evangelical mission with the colonial system, these students emphasized the challenges of being African Catholics as Africa neared political independence from France.[65] "If," they wrote to Lefebvre, "as Christians, we follow the line of your article and, out of phobia of Communism, we sneer at Independence and Islam, we ipso facto cut ourselves off from our own people. And in rejecting us, our African brothers reject the Church." Their surprise and outrage at Lefebvre's ham-fisted disregard of the sensitive political context is palpable in the letter. "We are astonished," they wrote, "that you published this essentially political article as the archbishop of Dakar." It was especially galling to them because even though Lefebvre had given up his role as apostolic delegate, he was still, in their eyes, the "voice incarnate of the church for all of the Christians of the bush." They claimed that they took no pleasure in opposing Lefebvre, but felt "obligated," in their capacity as the Catholic African elite, to contest his statements.[66]

As they denounced Lefebvre's portrayals of Catholicism, Islam, and African independence, the students seized on alternative Catholic visions of Muslims and of Africa's future to show that the church was in fact supportive of African self-determination and rapprochement between religious communities on the ground. They contrasted his words with those of Maury, whom they quoted as saying, on the occasion of Cameroon's independence, "'The Catholic Church . . . does not meddle in [political] activities WHICH ARE NOT IN ITS DOMAIN.'" They accused Lefebvre of contradicting the "movement of History" and numerous episcopal and pontifical pronouncements in support of independence and African self-determination. Moreover, they asserted their solidarity with Muslims by objecting to Lefebvre's "denunciation" of Islam. They faulted him for displaying an "inadmissible intolerance vis-à-vis millions of our African brothers, alas, at the very moment when the collaboration of all, across religious affiliations, is already proving fruitful." They deployed Catholic universalism to parry Lefebvre's statement that Muslims were "detaching themselves from the West" by arguing that the church was above all nations and cultures, regardless of origin. Finally, they reminded him, as had Niasse and Monteil, that Christianity had its own unsavory history of "fanaticism" and "slavery" that Lefebvre identified with Islam.[67] While addressed to Lefebvre, the letter was primarily aimed at reassuring Sudan's predominantly Muslim elite that Catholics supported independence and favored alliances with the Muslim community.

Father Luc Moreau, Lefebvre's Dominican *bête noire* in Dakar, cited both the Catholic students and Ibrahima Niasse in a lengthy unsigned article entitled "Christians and Muslims are not enemies in black Africa" which summarized the issues at stake and denounced Lefebvre's point of view. It appeared in late February of 1960 in the left-leaning metropolitan Catholic weekly *Témoignage chrétien*.[68] A standard-bearer of the new left French Catholicism that had emerged in the crucible of German occupation, *Témoignage chrétien* was opposed politically to the conservative *La France catholique,* which had published Lefebvre's piece. The fact that this debate also played out in the metropolitan press illustrates again how the circuits of the Franco-African Catholic world crossed the boundaries of metropole and colony, and how French Catholic journalists (and presumably their audiences) took an interest in the fate of African missions they had long supported, and of their coreligionists in the soon to be ex-colonies.

Moreau took Lefebvre and other "foreign" spectators to task for not recognizing Africans' agency in their own destiny, and blindly repeating the idea that African Islam was a path to communism. Moreau, styling himself as a local expert vis-à-vis such foreigners and yet exuding a measure of all-knowing French missionary paternalism, argued that the African Muslim community was indeed under threat from communism, but not because Muslim values had some underlying affinity with it, as Lefebvre had suggested. Much like Bishop Leclerc, Moreau worried that the weakness of African Islam in the face of new societal pressures, such as the growth of a struggling proletariat in the continent's cities, would push African Muslims toward communism. The political situation was problematic too, he claimed. He argued that many African marabouts who had supported the "yes" vote for the French Community in 1958 (Niasse had been among them), and who enjoyed certain advantages under the colonial regime, were fearful of losing control of their followers at independence.[69] He asserted that African Islam lacked "thinkers" and "theologians" who could help the faithful wrestle with the issues and questions posed by Africa's social and political transformation. There were Muslim African intellectuals, he conceded, but they did not usually think in spiritual terms. He advocated for Islamic reform: "a return to a purer Islam, untangled from bastardized customs" to provide spiritual answers to modern dilemmas, and noted that a movement for the revival of Arabic was already underway. Acknowledging that many Christians feared that reform was a path to the "'fanaticism' of the Arab world," he argued that reformist efforts, such as plans to found an Institute of Islamic Study in Dakar, were advancing in a completely African spirit and framework.[70] Moreau thoroughly embraced the hope that a purified and reinvigorated African Islam could be a bulwark against communism.

Moreau's conclusion reiterated the thrust of his 1959 *Afrique nouvelle* article on the need for a genuine spiritual exchange between Muslims and Christians in Africa. This, he felt, was practically the only way forward for Christians who wanted to contribute to building the new Africa in their capacity as Christians. "Attached to the same God," he affirmed, "[Christians and Muslims] will mutually interrogate each other and confront our faith and our aspirations in his name." It was, in his view, the duty of religious leaders (such as Lefebvre and Muslim thinkers) to prepare the way for this dialogue, as only the path of spiritual encounter could "root the African soul in the world of God."[71] Moreau thus also wanted to combat "atheistic materialism" but felt the best way was by joining spiritual forces, not scapegoating Islam.

As he made this case to French Catholic audiences, Moreau practiced what he preached in Dakar. Between March and June 1960, he convened three local meetings of Badaliya, a prayer movement founded by Louis Massignon in Cairo in 1934 in which Christian adherents opened themselves to greater understanding of Catholicism and of Islam by praying with and for their Muslim neighbors.[72] Despite avowing "deep distress" at how closely Mohammed and his followers approached yet did not see the "mystery of Jesus" at the foundation of Islam, and acknowledging the weighty historical and spiritual consequences of this "failure," Moreau counseled his flock to move toward their Muslim brothers, not away from them.[73] It is not clear exactly who joined the Dakar group, but Moreau kept it a small and private experiment. The first meeting on March 28, 1960 coincided with the end of Ramadan, and about a dozen Christians gathered at the residence of an African congregation of nuns to, as Moreau put it, "join ourselves *as Christians* in the Muslim celebration of Korité."[74]

The group's extant circulars, almost certainly authored by Moreau, cast sincere prayer for Muslims as a supreme act of Christian charity and an emulation of Christ's example of sacrificing oneself for others—an act of "participating in his redemption of man."[75] Moreau emphasized that Badaliya's attitude to Muslims and their faith was "eminently Catholic."[76] He argued that the greatest way for Christians to demonstrate charity toward their Muslim brothers was to join their appeals to Christ with Muslim prayers, because Muslims did not recognize that Christ was the unique mediator of all prayer to God. Christians would thus provide the missing ingredient in Muslim prayers, ensuring God would receive them. There was no need, he asserted, to wait for the day when Muslims would come back to the fold—indeed, such prayer was the first step toward that day and the "most solid bond of reconciliation."[77] Moreau wanted Christians to understand Islam from a spiritual perspective, and though he believed Muslims to be living in error, he did not harbor a hankering to convert them en masse right away.

This was all too much for Monsignor Lefebvre. Enraged by Moreau's attitude, writings, and activities, the archbishop threatened to strip the priest of his ability to celebrate mass or speak publicly in the Archdiocese of Dakar. In a 1961 letter to Moreau's Dominican superior in France, Maurice Corvez, the archbishop wrote, "I do not doubt [Moreau's] goodwill or his zeal, but I question the influence of his conception of Islam and of Christian-Muslim relations, which I find very harmful and dangerous for the souls of our Senegalese Catholics."[78] Corvez, with the backing of the Dominican executive Michael Browne, pushed back very firmly, insisting that Lefebvre had misunderstood the situation and that Moreau would stay put, even if he could not celebrate mass.[79] Yet the archives reveal that the Dominican leadership also urged Moreau to be cautious, lest he endanger their other initiatives in Dakar through his defiance of Lefebvre.[80] Moreau remained in Dakar, but it appears that the nascent Badaliya did not survive the archbishop's wrath. Or, it may have fallen apart of its own accord. There are a few hints that its third meeting was riven by debate over the nature and purpose of the group—Moreau acknowledged disagreement in a subsequent circular and invited people to write to him over the summer vacation with continuing questions.[81] Either way, it seems Moreau kept a lower profile until Lefebvre departed Dakar in 1962, and then forged a positive relationship with his African successor, Archbishop Hyacinthe Thiandoum.[82]

It seems that Lefebvre may not have realized the depth of the uproar his article had caused. In mid-January of 1960, White Father Henri Étienne observed from Dakar that Muslims "were very unhappy with the article" but that Lefebvre "does not appear to grasp the gravity of the situation."[83] In March of that year, the archbishop addressed the controversy in *Horizons africains,* Senegal's Catholic magazine, in order to present "some details" which he claimed would "enlighten those who may not have fully understood the ideas of the article." He told readers that he had composed it in early November for a Canadian publication, and not as a reaction to de Gaulle's visit in mid-December, observing that "national sovereignty is an excellent thing," as long as it was exercised in a framework of loving God and one's neighbor. He also claimed that *La France catholique* had cut out some material. But he reiterated his initial claim that communism was a clear and present danger in

Africa, and that Islam was not a barrier to it.[84] In April, French diplomatic sources at the Vatican reported that Cardinal Sigismondi, the secretary of the Propaganda Fide, admitted that Lefebvre's great authority among Africans was shaken by the incident, though he also indicated that the Vatican had not considered moving Lefebvre to another post.[85] Perhaps Lefebvre had not fully absorbed the lesson of 1953, which was that whatever he said in the wider francophone press was likely to reach audiences in Africa. Given the archbishop's previous miscues, it is not unimaginable that he thought he could talk about Africa as though Africans themselves could not hear or read him, or as though their agency in their own futures mattered less than French maneuvers. This blindness, whether willful or not, undermined Lefebvre's stated purpose of safeguarding a Catholic future in Africa. His many critics, and particularly Catholic ones in both France and Africa, felt that his line of attack jeopardized that future instead.[86]

While fascinating in themselves, Catholic approaches to Muslims in French sub-Saharan Africa presaged and influenced dialogues about Islam that unfolded at Vatican II between 1962 and 1965 and beyond. Indeed, some of the key interlocutors from the Franco-African Catholic world, including Monsignor Lefebvre, Father Luc Moreau, and several newly appointed African bishops, attended the council and shared their views. Lefebvre, as is widely known, headed a bloc of conservative prelates who were skeptical of proposed innovations to church doctrine, including increased openness toward other faith communities. Yet Moreau and the West African bishops brought their more positive and conciliatory skeins of Catholic thought vis-à-vis Islam and Muslims to the very heart of the church itself.

African archbishops Hyacinthe Thiandoum and Luc Sangaré, who replaced Lefebvre and Leclerc in the heavily Muslim archdioceses of Dakar and Bamako respectively in 1962, made a point of emphasizing their appreciation for Islam both at home and in Rome. Sangaré was reportedly sought out by Malian Christians and Muslims alike as a man of God, and liked to refer to himself as an "imam" charged with "meditating on the word of the creator to his creatures."[87] Thiandoum, who counted Muslims among his close friends, mentors, and family members, wasted no time in affirming his commitment to solidarity with them, by according prominent marabouts and Muslim relatives places of honor at his 1962 consecration.[88] During that ceremony, in his first speech as archbishop, Thiandoum stated, "'The presence in this place of worship . . . of the highest representatives of our Protestant and Muslim brothers, united as witnesses to a solemn act which is a living picture of the reality to which an African statesman (Mamadou Dia, present at the ceremony) alluded when speaking of the Supreme head of the Catholic Church whom he called the Pope of "Dialogue," that is to say, the shared search by all men of goodwill for the beauty, the truth, the good that is God!"[89] Thiandoum thus enveloped the Muslim Dia, the pope, and their respective coreligionists in an all-encompassing embrace, emphasizing commonalities and shared values.

This was certainly a political move in the context of newly independent Senegal, but one that nonetheless reflected deeply held convictions. Throughout his career, Thiandoum advocated for dialogue between Christians and Muslims. In a lengthy interview for *Paris-Match* in 1969, he maintained that Africa's particular contribution to Christendom and the world at large was a model of dialogue and fraternity between those of different faiths.[90] This stance earned him outpourings of respect from Muslim leaders in Senegal upon his death in 2004. In the words of Bassirou Diagne, the leader (*Grand Serigne*) of the Muslim Lebu community in Dakar, Thiandoum had "brought about friendship, peace, and stability between the two religions."[91]

Thiandoum, Sangaré, and other Africans brought this sensibility to Vatican II, and it infused their work there. In addition, Father Moreau played a key role in the ascendancy of Louis Massignon's views of Islam at the council.[92] In a confidential diplomatic report on "Senegal and the Council," French ambassador to Senegal Jean de Lagarde reported that Thiandoum made the following intervention at the second session of the council: "'Why can our council not clarify, for pastoral purposes, the more intimate relations that the Catholic Church wishes to encourage with certain other great religious families? Among them, could we highlight Islam, because of its numerical importance on the black continent and in Asia; because, above all, of the place it reserves for the works of the Bible, and which, because of this, brings it close to Christianity in a particular way; and finally, after an experience of collaboration, which, in the social and cultural domain, has already proved its worth. It seems to me that such collaboration is completely aligned with the speech that Pope Paul VI gave inaugurating this second session of Vatican II.'" Lagarde then noted that before leaving for the third session Thiandoum wrote, "'Pope Paul VI has devoted special attention to the local [faiths] in the Third World. We have proof of this in passages of the encyclical *Ecclesiam suam* and the recent creation of a secretariat for non-Christian religions and the Mixed Commission for relations between the Catholic Church and Islam. Africa, for its part, hails with great satisfaction these types of initiatives from the supreme chief of the Catholic Church.'"[93] It is thus clear that cultivating respect for and dialogue with Islam and Muslims was at the heart of Thiandoum's vision of the council.

And this vision proved influential, prevailing over Lefebvre's approach. In October 1965, Paul VI proclaimed the declaration *Nostra aetate* on the relationship of the church to non-Christian religions. The declaration, which had been approved by the attending bishops by an overwhelming majority, listed the many similarities between Christianity and Islam and openly promoted dialogue between Christians and Muslims, stating, "Since in the course of centuries not a few quarrels and hostilities have arisen between Christians and Muslims, this sacred synod urges all to forget the past and to work sincerely for mutual understanding and to preserve as well as to promote together, for the benefit of all mankind, social justice and moral welfare, as well as peace and freedom."[94] Thus, Vatican II enshrined the open, welcoming, and respectful Catholic strains of thought about Islam, illustrating just one way in which ferment in the Franco-African Catholic world helped to shape the reorientation of the church as a whole at midcentury.

Meanwhile, for Lefebvre, the council's advocacy of dialogue with other religions and respect for religious freedom amounted to a relativism that suggested that Catholicism was not the one and true faith, something he could not accept.[95] Later in life, when hearkening back to his missionary days in Africa he observed, "The church in Africa was respected because it clearly told the truth. But Vatican II gave the impression that one truth could be as good as another. That has resulted in a general deterioration of moral values."[96] Lefebvre, unable to countenance the council's innovations regarding the liturgy, the structure of the Catholic Church, or its approach to the world, subsequently founded a fraternity of dissenting priests, the Society of Saint Pius X, which retained the Latin mass and adhered to preconciliar doctrine. In the 1970s and 1980s, he was in open conflict with the Vatican, styling himself as an apostle of the true church, a stance that culminated in his excommunication in 1988 for ordaining traditionalist bishops without Rome's permission. In a theatrical twist, the prefect for the Congregation of Bishops who signed the excommunication order was none other than Bernard in Cardinal Gantin, the first African archbishop of Cotonou whose elevation to the episcopate had so dismayed François Méjan in the 1950s.[97]

As noted, in the late 1970s, Thiandoum, by then also a cardinal, volunteered to mediate between the Vatican and Lefebvre, the man who had ordained him. Thiandoum saw Lefebvre as a spiritual father and someone who had done much for the growth of the Catholic Church in Senegal. Thiandoum met privately with his mentor and tried to coax Lefebvre back into the fold, to no avail. In a 1977 interview, Thiandoum reiterated his opinion that Africa's contribution to the "universal church" was "dialogue," which he defined as a profound "search for comprehension" between people.[98] Ultimately, however, he found that promoting dialogue and mutual respect between Muslims and Catholics in Senegal proved far easier than defusing Lefebvre's quarrel with the church.

7

SLAVERY AND CHARITY

Connecting French Catholics to Africa

WHILE FUTURE RELATIONS WITH Muslims were a particular concern for Catholics in Africa, one of the key questions confronting Catholic activists in France at midcentury was how to define French Catholics' relationship with their African coreligionists. They wanted to continue to interest French donors in church endeavors in Africa, even as the African colonies pulled away from the metropole politically. The ubiquitous French Catholic missions in Africa and the dioceses led by newly minted African prelates depended on the support of comparatively wealthy French Catholic parishioners, as African communities often did not have the funds to bankroll parish upkeep or the construction of churches and housing for clergy, let alone the costs of running Catholic schools and medical stations. Moreover, missions were constantly short of money as they tried to expand their audience or to found new initiatives and institutions.

Catholic fundraising for Africa in France necessarily involved public relations efforts that tried to attract metropolitan donors through particularly Catholic portrayals of Africa and its people. Missionary leaders and publicists communicated what they saw as Africans' most pressing needs and enlisted French donors with assurances that contributions would safeguard a Catholic future for the continent. These charitable efforts and their attendant public relations campaigns had first developed in the late nineteenth century when the preeminence of French civilization (including its Catholic heritage), as well as the benefits of French colonization in a "benighted" Africa, went largely unquestioned in France.[1] By the 1950s and 1960s, however, the place of Catholicism in the relationship between France and Africa was not so clear-cut. Those who "translated" and presented Africa and Africans to French Catholic donors wrestled with how to construct a persuasive narrative of continued connection between French and African Catholics in the context of African independence and pressures to repudiate Eurocentrism within the church itself. Old saws about superior French Catholic civilization saving a depraved Africa were by no means dead, but they did not fit the new circumstances easily.

French Catholics at midcentury learned about Catholic communities in Africa via missionary publications, through personal connections to missionaries, or in their home dioceses, especially if their parish clergy were especially interested in missions. In addition to sporadic fundraising efforts of individual French parishes and towns, which sometimes adopted a "twin" parish or town in Africa, a quartet of longstanding Vatican-sponsored "pontifical" organizations raised awareness and money for missionary endeavors on a nationwide scale.[2] These included the Œuvre Pontificale de la Propagation de la Foi, founded in 1822 to support the extension of the faith via missions, the Sainte-Enfance, founded in 1843 to support the care and instruction of children in the missions, the Œuvre de Saint-Pierre-Apôtre, founded in 1889 to support the development of indigenous clergy, and the Société antiesclavagiste de France (henceforth the Antislavery Society), founded in 1888 to "pursue the abolition of slavery in Africa, and particularly in territories under French influence or not claimed by any European power."[3] Of the four, the Antislavery Society was the only one focused solely on Africa. The society's efforts to define its purpose and goals in the 1950s and 1960s provide an instructive case study of how French Catholic fundraisers negotiated the shifting sands of the late colonial period and the early years of independence, while trying to keep Catholics in the metropole reaching in their pockets for Africans who desired independence from France.

In the early to mid-1950s, the Antislavery Society experienced a striking revival by highlighting the ongoing existence of slavery and slaving in Africa, a topic that was then garnering attention at the United Nations and in the wider French media. At the same time, the society wrestled with the definition of and the extent of African slavery. It seized upon the situations of African women and girls who could not choose their marriage partners as a means of widening the French public's conception of slavery and styled the missions it funded as forces for the liberation of oppressed African women. Its propaganda tended to demonize Muslims as slaveholders or slave traders, and often depicted French administrators as woefully ignorant or ineffectual in the face of enduring slavery. Its calls for donations in these years frequently portrayed Africa as a dark moral wilderness that desperately needed French Catholics' help for a better future. The society's appeals to donors reflected the hysteria about the closing window of opportunity in Africa that was so prevalent in missionary discourse at the time. Its stance was in many ways a forceful and panicked restatement of a Catholic version of the French civilizing mission, in which missionary activists claimed that they alone were in a position to effect necessary, meaningful, and lasting change in African societies.

Between the late 1950s and late 1960s, however, the society's approach to French donors underwent a gradual shift away from focusing on the "backward" aspects of African society, including slavery and the perceived subjection of women. By then it was facing an identity crisis of sorts, as its French Catholic interlocutors increasingly questioned the importance of antislavery activism, while some Africans found its emphasis on slavery demeaning or inappropriate against the backdrop of African political liberation. As African colonies became independent, the society muted its antislavery message and simply privileged its role in the dissemination of funds to missions, highlighting their needs without extended negative discourse on the societies they served. Africans, other than indigenous prelates asking for funds, thus receded from the French public's view, while French missionaries and their construction projects, schools, and dispensaries took center stage. Finally, in 1968, the society dropped the antislavery moniker altogether and changed its name, at Vatican urging, to Aide aux missions d'Afrique (Aid for the African Missions). While a degree of French Catholic paternalism and notes of bitterness about the end of the empire continued to surface in the organization's public relations campaigns, its tone had changed markedly from the twilight days of French Africa, reflecting the pivotal shifts that had taken place in the French Empire and within the Catholic Church in the late 1950s and the 1960s.

FRANCE, AFRICA, AND SLAVERY

Although African slavery became an increasingly unwieldy theme for French Catholic fundraisers in the mid-twentieth century, it had galvanized the metropolitan public in the late nineteenth century as France extended its rule over wide swaths of the continent. Though many people in France today are more aware of republican initiatives of abolition in the French colonies during the Revolution of 1789–1799 and again in 1848, the late nineteenth-century movement was a Catholic missionary endeavor, led by Charles-Martial Cardinal Lavigerie, archbishop of Algiers and founder of the White Fathers.[4] Lavigerie, who was firmly convinced that the key to ending slavery was the mobilization of European public opinion, was a master communicator and public relations expert who crisscrossed Europe in the late 1880s and early 1890s, building a transnational movement that claimed the allegiance of antislavery societies in France, Britain, Germany, and Italy.[5]

Lavigerie was most effective on his home turf. On July 1, 1888, he delivered an impassioned speech to a packed house at the church of Saint-Sulpice in Paris, denouncing the continuing plague of slavery in Africa.[6] He staged a spectacular mise-en-scène to motivate his French audience, as well as the wider European public, to comprehend and support antislavery efforts on the "dark continent." On the steps leading to the high altar sat African children who had been purchased and freed from slavery by French White Fathers. Their liberators, clad in white burnouses with red fezzes on their heads, stood on the choir steps as imposing soldiers of the antislavery crusade.[7] "This is the prayer that the slaves of Africa address to you today, through my voice: Christians of

Europe, cross the sea that separates us and come to our aid!" Lavigerie thundered at the end of his talk.[8] He inspired the foundation of the Antislavery Society of France that same year, and served as its first honorary president while traveling Europe to encourage similar groups. In the words of historian Seymour Drescher, the cardinal stimulated a pan-European movement that "minted antislavery as the gold standard of Western civilization."[9]

The Vatican supported Lavigerie's antislavery efforts from the outset with funding and publicity. Pope Leo XIII, eager to carve out a prominent place for Catholicism in an arena hitherto dominated by anglophone Protestants, called for the abolition of slavery in his 1888 encyclical *In plurimis*.[10] Though he addressed this document to the bishops of Brazil, where slavery remained legal at that date, he also mentioned African slavery, at Lavigerie's suggestion.[11] In November 1890, the pope went further by issuing the encyclical *Catholicae ecclesiae* on slavery in the missions, particularly in Africa, which designated Lavigerie as the representative of the cause vis-à-vis the various European powers. This directive outlined a Catholic conception of the civilizing mission in Africa that was to remain a touchstone for the Antislavery Society: "wherever Christian customs and laws are in force, wherever religion establishes that men serve justice and honor human dignity, wherever the spirit of brotherly love taught by Christ spreads itself, there neither slavery nor savage barbarism can exist." The pope closed the missive by decreeing that an annual collection would take place every year on the Epiphany in order to fund the missions in Africa and their fight against slavery. The significance of the Epiphany was that it was the day the "Son of God first revealed himself to the nations, when he showed Himself to the Magi" and thus embodied the idea of missionaries going forth among peoples who did not know Christianity.[12] Leo also made a handsome personal donation of 300,000 gold francs to the society.

The epiphany collection remained the cornerstone of the society's activity in France for decades to come, defining its fundraising rhythm. In its early years, the group channeled most of its money to support "freedom villages" of African slaves purchased by missionaries. The hope was that these would become model Christian communities that other Africans would emulate, but they had very mixed results and the effort was largely abandoned by 1914. Though it went through some inactive periods in the interwar years, the society never totally disintegrated.[13] Then, over sixty years after its founding and on the eve of the end of French sovereignty in Africa, it experienced a rapid resurgence under the leadership of Monsignor François Couespel du Mesnil, who took the helm in 1951.[14] He reinvigorated the nationwide collection on the Epiphany, amassing greater contributions year after year and building the society's campaigns into a key source of funding for French Catholic missions in Africa, as well as a thread connecting French parishioners to the missions and to their African coreligionists. Every year, the Vatican would apportion the fruits of the collection between the various apostolic prefectures, vicariates, and, after the institution of the Catholic hierarchy in 1955, the dioceses and archdioceses of French Africa. The papal delegate to French sub-Saharan Africa would then execute the transfer of funds from the society to each locale.

This midcentury renaissance of the Antislavery Society took place amid a heightened buzz in France about the persistence of slavery and slave trading in French sub-Saharan Africa, and the trafficking of Africans from French territories to buyers on the Arabian Peninsula in particular. Between 1952 and 1955, multiple articles in Catholic and mainstream media explored the topic, often taking a sensationalist approach. "There are still slave traders!" screamed a 1955 title in the popular illustrated weekly *Paris-Match,* headlining an article that detailed the odyssey of Awad El Djoud, an African citizen of French Sudan in a servile relationship to a Tuareg notable, who had taken him on the *hajj* and sold him into slavery while in Saudi Arabia.[15] Awad had managed to escape and return to Sudan, winding up in Bamako, where reporters for the White Fathers' Catholic weekly *Afrique nouvelle* had tracked him down in 1954.[16] In addition, articles on African slavery in a variety of popular venues such as *Noir et Blanc, France-Soir, Samedi-Soir,* and *Pourquoi pas?,* as well as more specialized organs such as the *Nouvelle revue française d'Outre-Mer, Afrique nouvelle,* and *La Croix* reached a wide audience of Catholics, people interested in the colonies, and general readers in the first half of the decade.[17]

Politics at the United Nations provided key context for this flurry of French interest in slavery and slave trading, as Charles Greenidge and his fellow British antislavery activists tried to get the international community to take slavery seriously as a contemporary problem. They succeeded in bringing about the establishment of an ad hoc UN committee, which met in 1950 and 1951 and undertook research on the persistence of slavery, serfdom, pawning, debt peonage, and forced marriage throughout the world. Jane Vialle, a woman of French and African parentage who was then representing Ubangi-Shari in the French Senate, was the token female on this five-member panel.[18] Its work ultimately led to the drafting of the Supplementary Convention on the Abolition of Slavery in 1956, which reinforced an international agreement signed thirty years before. Yet this UN undertaking was plagued from the start by fighting between colonial powers and successor states, between Cold War blocs, and between righteous European activists and representatives of countries where forms of servitude persisted, like the Persian Gulf states or Latin American nations whose Amerindian populations lived in debt peonage.[19]

Indeed, slavery became a bone of contention in the context of rising antagonism between France and the Arab world over French rule in North Africa in the early 1950s. Arab countries, some of which were implicated in the committee's findings on slavery and slave trading, were simultaneously denouncing France at the UN for oppressing its restive North African colonies, even before war broke out in Algeria in 1954. Indignant French apologists used slavery to retaliate. In 1952, *France-Soir,* one of France's leading dailies at the time, published an exposé by journalist Jacques Alain describing traffic in slaves from Western Africa to Saudi Arabia two years before Awad's story came to light. Entitled "From the Sahara to Arabia, I followed the convoys of slaves," it featured the provocative subheading: "Each month, African girls are sent to Asia and the rich territories of the oil magnates, where they are taught the art of pleasing their future masters."[20] In a boldfaced box just below the headline the editors pointedly denounced the Arab countries that complained of French policy in North Africa. "At the moment when twelve Arab countries are accusing France at the UN for utilizing 'methods contrary to development and civilization' in North Africa," they bridled, "the gripping testimony that *France-Soir* is publishing today, and which is also the subject of a report to the UN, demonstrates—as if it were necessary to do so—that the accusers themselves are the most backward countries."[21]

The tone of such arguments flags how slavery fit into strategic, patriotic narratives about the beneficial role France continued to play in its Overseas Territories. For example, Awad's case spurred the Protestant minister, politician, and activist Emmanuel La Gravière and Georges Le Brun Keris, the French president of the African Federation of the MRP from 1954 until 1960, to demand a legislative investigation, which La Gravière undertook in Africa and then published as an official report of the French Union in 1956.[22] La Gravière, who would applaud François Méjan's excoriation of the church for repudiating France and French civilization two years later, published an article in the *Nouvelle revue française d'Outre-Mer* summing up his findings, in which he noted the "paradox" of the Saudi Arabian delegate's denunciation of French policy in Tunisia at the UN, given that the Saudi regime was complicit in African slaving.[23]

The theme of Arab duplicity also nourished explicitly Catholic narratives about slaving in Africa. Father Robert Rummelhardt, the editor at *Afrique nouvelle* who published Awad's story in 1954, evoked the "monstrous hypocrisy of those in the Middle East today who pose as liberators of African peoples, yet who impose in their own countries the most degrading yoke possible on the necks of Africans, who are born, like all other men, for liberty and dignity."[24] Yet Rummelhardt was not simply a French patriot angered by Arab posturing, as the American consul in Dakar at the time believed, but rather had a primarily Catholic goal in bringing the story to light.[25] For him, the exposé on slavery was part and parcel of his strategy to persuade the African Muslim elite to renounce Islam and embrace Christianity by focusing on social questions that impacted Africans of both faiths, rather than doctrinal divisions.

French Catholic activists such as Rummelhardt and the champions of the Antislavery Society thus both contributed to and benefited from the buzz about slavery in the Francophone world at midcentury, though they had their own Catholic stakes in highlighting its persistence. The sensationalist exposés about Arabs buying Africans or African Muslims selling slaves to finance their pilgrimages to Mecca helped publicize the cause of slavery when Monsignor du Mesnil was trying to reinvigorate the society. Alain's account in particular evoked tropes dear to Catholic antislavery activists: brutal armed nighttime *razzias* carried out by rapacious traders, and young African girls as the innocent victims of cruel Muslim rapists. Lavigerie himself could not have conjured up more dramatic imagery to market his cause. Yet this brand of slavery ultimately proved to be peripheral to the society's fundraising strategy in France. While Alain had claimed in 1952 that five thousand African victims of slavery were transported across the Red Sea per month, La Gravière estimated in 1956 that the total was closer to a couple of hundred a year.[26] In point of fact, the Antislavery Society and the missions it supported began defining much more fundamental and widespread practices in African societies as slavery and targeting them for elimination. These French Catholics were actually not primarily interested in exposing a clandestine trade, but in bringing about a veritable revolution in African communities.

DEFINING SLAVERY TO DONORS

Broader media hype notwithstanding, Monsignor du Mesnil still found himself struggling to convince French clergy, who played a crucial role in publicizing and executing the Epiphany collection throughout the country, that slavery was indeed a social plague throughout French Africa in the 1950s. "How many times I have heard the exclamation 'What! There are still slaves . . . ?'" he observed to the society's officers in 1952.[27] This predicament reflected longstanding tensions within the society about whether its purview was narrowly confined to antislavery or encompassed broader support for Catholic missionaries who were engaging in a general "civilizing mission" in Africa. For example, doubt was present in an internal, unsigned 1926 memo, which argued that the society's social mission was no longer valid "because it was limited to the suppression of the slave trade, which is now an accomplished fact, and to the abolition of slavery, which is relegated now to sporadic and criminal practice." The author recommended that the society redefine its mission and change its statutes.[28] But another anonymous note, drafted three days later, responded that while the slave trade had died down, "it is nonetheless incontestable that there persist among the blacks of our French colonies practices and customs that are acts of slavery: it is important to bring these practices and customs to an end." Moreover, the author continued, a 1908 modification of the first article of the society's statutes, proposed by its president Georges Picot, specified that the society's goals included "the disappearance of abuses of which African populations are the victims" as well as to "take a most active interest in the fate of freed slaves and indigenous populations in general." According to this member, the society therefore did not have to redefine itself at all.[29]

In his energetic revival of the society in the early 1950s, du Mesnil embraced this more expansive definition of slavery and nurtured a broad conception of the society's social purpose, which, he argued, had always been intended in its statutes. Claiming that Lavigerie himself had foreseen the "evolution of modern times," du Mesnil quoted the cardinal at a 1952 meeting of the society that "'the question therefore of the suppression of the slave trade in central Africa is combined with another larger question, that of the moral and material amelioration of the indigenous populations.'" Catholic missions were the most important instruments of this betterment: as du Mesnil further cited Lavigerie, "'and since we are talking about a general overhaul of barbaric mores and ideas, one must consider the salutary influence of Christian missions as a major and necessary factor . . .'"[30] Du Mesnil thus wanted to insist on the importance of combating slavery, but also to make the case that the society's support of missionary efforts to civilize Africa more generally was in keeping with its original mission. His successor, Canon Marcel Leveque, initially took much the same line when he took over in 1957.

Du Mesnil's determination to highlight African slavery and the civilizing work of missions meant that the solicitation materials he put together every year for the Epiphany collection tended to portray Africa and Africans in a negative, often scathing, light. He actively sought the testimony of French missionaries at work in Africa, and relayed messages of doom and gloom that he thought were most likely to stimulate the French clergy and their parishioners to donate. He had a willing partner in Monsignor Lefebvre, who, in his capacity as the Vatican's delegate to sub-Saharan Africa, distributed the money the Antislavery Society raised in its campaigns to the missions. In a lengthy 1952 letter to du Mesnil, Lefebvre made the striking assertion (which du Mesnil subsequently quoted to Cardinal Fumasoni-Biondi, the secretary of the Propaganda Fide, and reproduced in the society's brochures) that, "Only those who do not know Africa can think it is liberated; those who affirm that slavery has disappeared and that money to free its prisoners is not useful have only studied the continent's problems in a superficial way." Here the archbishop assumed the pose of the veteran missionary who knew the ground better than government officials or media experts, quashing the idea that France's African colonies were making progress on his register of civilization. He argued that "actual slavery" continued to exist, citing the persistence of nomadic slavers in the Sahara and slaveholding Muslim "chiefs" in French West Africa, as well as "harems of fetishist polygamist chiefs." Moreover, Lefebvre asserted that many African women were bought and sold into marriages against their will, which he categorized as a form of slavery.[31]

Lefebvre's views on slavery and his pessimism about the general state of African society were shared by other missionaries on the ground, particularly those of an older generation, many of whom had attained positions in the church hierarchy. The themes of widespread persistent slavery in Muslim and animist African communities, as well as the subjugation of African women, surfaced over and over in the missionary testimony the society deployed in its public relations campaigns in France in the early 1950s. For example, with his 1952 Epiphany appeal to the French Catholic hierarchy, Monsignor du Mesnil enclosed a report by Father Charles Tisserant, a Spiritan missionary and renowned botanist who had worked in Ubangi-Shari in French Equatorial Africa since 1911.[32] Tisserant, it should be noted, was also the brother of one of the most high-ranking French prelates of the day. His brother, Eugène Cardinal Tisserant, had become dean of the College of Cardinals in 1951, and the family name would have resonated in the ecclesiastical circles du Mesnil was trying to rouse to action. The report, entitled "Note on the current state of slavery in French black Africa," argued that although the "spectacular" slave raids of Lavigerie's day had largely disappeared, slavery persisted in Africa's animist societies. Moreover, like Lefebvre, it asserted that the status of women in sub-Saharan Africa was essentially akin to slavery.[33]

Tisserant painted a portrait of African society that was diametrically opposed to European Catholic values. Drawing on his experience in Central Africa, he described slavery as an "ethnic fact" in animist societies, which, he claimed, "is linked to the basic organization of society in clans or patriarchal families: groups of people who have or believe they have a common origin."[34] The clan, he explained to his French readers, was "the negation of the family as we conceive of it in our civilized societies: the father, the mother, and their children." His explanation of slavery hinged on the importance of the clan and its well-being in the eyes of its members. He described a ubiquitous belief among "primitive Africans" that every person was born with a "protective spirit" that "in a manner of speaking, lives within him." If the protective spirit was a strong one, the individual would be favored in life, enjoy freedom and wealth, and possess useful skills. On the other hand, if the spirit was weak, or became weak, the person in question would suffer hardships such as poverty, illness, or enslaved or short-lived parents. In this understanding of the world, Tisserant claimed, any misfortune in the life of an individual was taken as a sign of a weak protective spirit, which was seen as dangerous to the clan as a whole as it could escape at night and "sow death and sickness around it." The unfortunate "owner" of such a spirit was sometimes kept as a subjugated worker in his clan, sometimes poisoned, and most often exiled and / or sold into slavery, sometimes to nefarious Muslims such as Arabs from the Nile basin or Hausas, who, according to Tisserant, were constantly crisscrossing central Africa, smuggling goods and slaves on rural paths far from the main roads. If questioned by the French authorities, these Muslims would claim their slaves were free and willing domestic employees.[35]

For Tisserant and many like-minded missionaries, therefore, slavery was a cultural problem that required a cultural solution, which only the church could provide. By contrast, secular or governmental efforts to curb it were futile. He claimed that a League of Nations census in the early 1930s failed to detect slavery in Africa because local populations manipulated or deceived the census takers. Furthermore, he added, the colonial state's decrees that outlawed slavery and tried to alleviate the subjection of African women were ineffective, and, in many cases, not applied. Essentially, Tisserant advocated for a thorough-going assault on African culture and values. "Only education, and Christian education at that, can modify the mentality of these races and make the ethnic cause of slavery disappear in the long run," he wrote. Moreover, he reiterated, only Christian education could "give the African woman the place she should occupy in black society." Hence, he asserted to prospective donors, the Antislavery Society was a "precious auxiliary" of the Catholic missions in Africa that were attacking slavery at its source.[36]

Tisserant's report made waves in France. It was reproduced in nearly all the *"semaines religieuses"* or weekly diocesan bulletins across the country and major press outlets echoed its message.[37] Monsignor du Mesnil commented, "This report has been extremely precious for me and has enabled me to better communicate the importance of our work."[38] Indeed, it was such a success that the society decided to publish a longer, book-length version, which appeared with Plon in 1955.[39] Entitled *Ce que j'ai connu de l'esclavage en Oubangui-Chari* (What I saw of slavery in Ubangi-Shari), it also became a key instrument of propaganda for the Antislavery Society. Du Mesnil reserved four hundred copies and sent some of them as gifts to powerful patrons within the church, including Marc-Armand Lallier, bishop of Nancy and Toul, Jules-Géraud Cardinal Saliège, archbishop of Toulouse, Joseph-Marie Martin, archbishop of Rouen, Henri Varin de la Brunelière, bishop of Fort-de-France, Martinique, Georges Cardinal Grente, archbishop of Mans, and Pierre-Marie Cardinal Gerlier, archbishop of Lyon.[40] In his accompanying letters to these elite clergymen, du Mesnil referred to how the "articles that have recently appeared in the papers and the report that was lodged with the office of the Assembly of the French Union show the importance of the problem [of slavery], which French Catholics cannot lose interest in."[41] Apparently the book found an audience—in early 1956, he corresponded with Plon about another printing.[42]

Tisserant's book amplified and expanded many of the themes present in his shorter report, presenting a damning picture of African attitudes and customs, and arguing that Christian missions were the only effective way of combating them. He struck a possessive, all-knowing, and paternal tone—consistently referring to "our Africans" in the course of his discussion.[43] In reference to African warfare, he evoked cannibalism, the ultimate marker of African barbarity in the French public imagination. And describing how some slaveholders would count their slaves as family members in order to claim French government family allocations, while also benefiting from the unremunerated labor of the slave, he observed, "[This practice] is perfectly in keeping with the mentality of our people [Africans]!"[44] Tisserant's pessimistic paternalism was also evident in his private correspondence—after a stay in Europe he observed upon his return to the mission at Boukoko that "my Christians" had not appeared to "have improved themselves in the six months they were left by themselves."[45] Like Lefebvre, he regarded African society with a jaundiced eye.

AN "APOSTOLATE OF LIBERATION" FOR AFRICAN WOMEN

Nowhere was this kind of negative missionary view more in evidence than in prevailing French Catholic propaganda about the status of women in sub-Saharan Africa. Lefebvre, Tisserant, and many French missionary leaders described women in both Muslim and animist African communities as veritable slaves of their fathers, uncles, husbands, and clans. For Catholic activists, the status of women in African societies was a conspicuous marker of the relative advance of "civilization" on the continent, and they envisioned women as the change agents of a new social order. As Monsignor Jean Lesourd, prelate of Nouna in Upper Volta, wrote to Monsignor du Mesnil, "With our 'subversive' ideas of Christian liberties, we are leading a veritable revolution in the eyes of the African family patriarchs."[46] Yet missionary efforts to bring an "apostolate of liberation" to African women took center stage in the Antislavery Society's fundraising campaigns in a 1950s French Catholic milieu that was itself still very patriarchal.[47] Indeed, the missionary model of a "liberated" Christian wife and mother was a woman who was a partner, rather than a slave, of her spouse, yet remained firmly in the domestic sphere. Their program, while truly revolutionary in many African communities, thus also reflected the social conservatism of many of their French donors. This juxtaposition highlights the church's profoundly different standing in French and African societies in the period: long a bastion of social conservatism in France, it was often a radical social force in Africa.

Of course, the theme of saving oppressed African women was not new—indeed the status of women in indigenous societies around the globe had long been fodder for a variety of European civilizing impulses in the colonial era.[48] For decades, French Catholic missionaries in Africa had decried women's subordinate roles and tried to utilize women to Christianize African communities, reasoning that stable Christian families rested on Christian wives and mothers who would raise children in the church.[49] According to du Mesnil, Lavigerie himself had identified the "problem of the black woman." The director quoted the cardinal in a 1952 report to the Antislavery Society's general assembly: "'Throughout Africa, the woman is the slave of the man: only she works, the man holds the power of life or death over her, she has fallen into such an abject state that she has trouble comprehending what our missionaries tell her . . .'"[50] Yet, despite these antecedents, the society's emphasis on women in the 1950s was nonetheless quite remarkable. Oppressed African women turned out to be the ideal vehicles for widening the French public's definition of slavery and proving its continued existence, as well as constructing a picture of African depravity that would motivate donors to support missionary efforts.

The "slavery" of African women was everywhere in the propaganda materials and correspondence of the society in the 1950s. A 1953 booster article in *La Croix* argued that women were essentially up for auction in Africa and that "rather than having lost its *raison d'être,* the Antislavery Society is more necessary than ever" because of the increasing commercial value of women, which condemned them to servitude.[51] In the 1952 letter that appeared in the society's brochures, Monsignor Lefebvre excoriated what he called the "the slavery of the so-called dowry," which he defined as the "buying and selling of women and girls"—a veritable bondage that, he argued, was much more common and, in certain areas, even worse than traditional slavery.[52] Father Tisserant, who published two separate articles on marriage and dowry practices in Ubangi-Shari, also devoted significant space in his report to the society to the "emancipation of the black woman" whose situation he likened to "the status of the slave."[53]

Implicitly and explicitly invoking the values he assumed French readers would harbor, Tisserant conjured visions of helpless women at the mercy of their extended relations. A girl in an animist community in Central Africa, he asserted, was not under the control of her father but of the council of the clan, who would designate her older brother or an uncle to contract the marriage and receive the dowry. Needless to say, girls themselves were rarely consulted about their fate. The rapid inflation of dowry prices in the recent past meant that bidding wars ensued where girls were shuttled from one bidder to another, depending on who produced the highest final price. Even after marriage, a girl remained a member of her clan, which could still use her as a means of extracting gifts from her husband, or, in extreme cases, take her back and demand a higher dowry, and which would, in Tisserant's words, "not hesitate at all to put her in the arms of another man until the original husband paid the difference." Girls were often married to polygamists much older than themselves, or, if they were Christian, to "inveterate pagans."[54] Tisserant thus proffered a spectacle of women being shuttled between multiple sexual partners while greedy male relatives played the role of pimp, a tableau of African society that was meant to shock French Catholic donors into giving.

Missionaries across French sub-Saharan Africa who corresponded with the Antislavery Society echoed Tisserant's claims. They welcomed funds from the society to combat unwanted marriages by intervening in dowry negotiations and feeding, clothing, and instructing women who fled their communities. Spiritan Monsignor Michel Bernard wrote from Conakry, Guinea in 1954, "I do not think it is exaggeration to say that the status of women in the Muslim and polygamist society we have here in Guinea is similar to slavery."[55] His successor, Monsignor Gérard de Milleville, told du Mesnil that "your aid will help us above all to form liberated, Christian women in boarding dormitories where we prepare them for marriage and for their lives as heads of households, while we keep an eye on dowry negotiations to make sure the marriage does not appear to be a purchase and to assure the liberty of consent . . ."[56] In a 1957 thank you letter, White Father Monsignor Joseph Bretault, bishop of Koudougou, wrote: "While the brutal and public slavery of yore has disappeared little by little from black Africa, slavery still exists, alas, in our regions of Upper Volta among young women and girls, who are still, according to custom, promised in marriage to old polygamists who already have five or six or more wives."[57] Bretault used the society's money to assist some 478 girls who rebelled against their families in 1954–1955.[58]

Similarly, in 1958, Monsignor Dieudonné Yougbaré, who had become the first Burkinabé bishop in 1956, thanked the society ardently for its annual funding to his diocese of Koupéla, Upper Volta. "We are thinking of using this money primarily for the upkeep of the numerous girls who take refuge with the nuns to escape from their selfish relatives, who want to dispose of them in an arbitrary manner," he reported.[59] In Bouaké, Côte d'Ivoire, SMA bishop André-Pierre Duirat wrote to Monsignor du Mesnil in 1954 that he would use the society's donation to found a project "for the education of young girls to prepare them for marriage and to thus deliver them from the hold of pagan custom which awards them so easily to the highest bidder."[60] Dozens more examples reveal that these initiatives vis-à-vis African women, funded by the Antislavery Society, were at the heart of the missionary project across French Africa. The society proudly reproduced missionary testimony of their efforts to eradicate female subjection in its brochures and mailings to clergy and parishioners.

Yet what did the "liberation" of African women mean exactly to French Catholic missionaries and to the Antislavery Society? It had a very different valence in Africa than it was beginning to have in European milieus at midcentury, though in both cases it signaled an overthrow of dominant mores. In his Epiphany appeal in December of 1954, du Mesnil characterized the "liberation of the black woman" as a "complex and very delicate problem." He then quoted Monsignor Joseph Cucherousset, the Spiritan bishop of Bangui (Ubangi-Shari), that "women must not 'pass from slavery to debauchery.'"[61] For these Catholic activists, what they termed "the advancement of women" did not point to sexual freedom, but to what Monsignor Yougbaré in Upper Volta called "marriage conforming to the liberty of Christ."[62] Indeed, they had a very specific kind of liberation in mind.

Missionaries and their activist partners at the Antislavery Society saw two routes out of "slavery" for African women—becoming a Christian wife or becoming a nun. Both, of course, required a heavy dose of Catholic discipline. Monsignor Lefebvre was a particularly enthusiastic booster of congregations of African nuns as a means of liberation for women. To his mind, encouraging such congregations was the "most effective way to fight against the slavery and debasement of women," and he called upon the Antislavery Society to support them. In the 1952 letter that du Mesnil used for publicity, Lefebvre, employing the language of Catholic personalism, wrote, "To facilitate the liberation and the moral recovery of women, apart from decrees and administrative measures, there is a way that only the Catholic Church has carried out in black Africa: the constitution of congregations of indigenous nuns. They are admirable examples of the liberation of woman and the dignity of her person."[63] Monsignor Lesourd in Upper Volta also believed that "the advancement of the African woman culminates in the training of African nuns."[64] Thus, in missionary eyes, not only did the congregations of African nuns benefit the individual women who joined them; they set an example of empowerment to their countrywomen.[65]

Indeed, missionaries across French Africa found nuns, and African nuns in particular, to be precious auxiliaries in their efforts vis-à-vis African women. In a 1958 letter to the society, Lesourd observed, "There is nothing better to reach [women] than the apostolic action of our African nuns. They have an astonishing savoir-faire and innate psychological sense for how to approach these pagan women. They acquire an unmistakable influence on women and girls. As a result, we put all the work with women and girls in our stations in their hands."[66] Nuns, both African and European, worked with African women in so-called *sixas* or *centres ménagers* across the colonies. These mission installations, which often housed women fleeing their Muslim or animist communities and / or preparing for Christian marriage, provided both spiritual and practical education.[67] Often funded at least in part by the Antislavery Society, they were a central initiative for the missions to realize a Catholic vision of marriage and family in Africa.

Exact curricula at different *sixas* varied, but the overall thrust was the same: the liberation of African women meant educating them to be

Catholic wives and mothers. Female liberation was inextricably twinned with a Catholic moral education. This involved instruction in Catholic doctrine as well as "conjugal morality," and, at the better-equipped missions, training in domestic arts. Women often lived at the *sixa,* on the mission's dime, for a period of several months while completing a *stage,* which translates loosely to an "internship" or training course. As Lesourd described it to the society, "under the guidance of European or African nuns, they [African women] receive instruction about religion, about their future duties as wives and mothers. They learn to run their future household, to knit, to sew, and to better their cooking. Your allocation is very precious for the upkeep of this work."[68] In Conakry, Monsignor Bernard similarly extolled the work of the European and African nuns who educated young girls for Christian marriage and homemaking in the region he oversaw. "I am convinced this is the surest way to reveal to women their dignity and to prepare them for true and sound / healthy emancipation," he wrote.[69] In the eyes of the missionaries, African women needed careful guidance to accede to the right kind of freedom.

The Antislavery Society and the missionaries it funded stressed how they were promoting a model of Christian marriage where the partners willingly came together as equals on the basis of mutual love and common faith to found a family. They contrasted this with their view of African marriage as the purchase of a woman, irrespective of her feelings, as if she were a piece of livestock.[70] In these narratives, non-Christian women often came across, implicitly or explicitly, as victims who lacked the agency and wherewithal to contest the supremacy of their male relatives. Tellingly, however, this monolithic image of subjugated women sometimes fractured when it came to imposing Catholic mores. One of the most vocal champions of the *sixas,* Monsignor Lesourd, painted quite a different picture of "enslaved" African women while explaining his missions' efforts to educate women to Canon Leveque, du Mesnil's successor at the Antislavery Society: "In our regions, women are very independent and in the home they often follow their whims. Once married, they conserve this desire for liberty and husbands often have a lot of trouble obtaining a little submission from them in the interests of the home / family. The discipline of the *Centre ménager* educates them gently and teaches them to control themselves."[71] Here, the problem was not that the women Lesourd referred to were enslaved; rather, they were too fractious and unruly to supervise a proper Christian household.

This tension between liberation and control in missionary Catholic discourse on African women also surfaced in the work of Sister Marie-André du Sacré-Cœur, a scholarly member of Lavigerie's White Sisters congregation who attended the Antislavery Society's general assembly in May of 1953 with Monsignor Lefebvre.[72] Trained as a jurist, but harboring an anthropological bent, Marie-André wrote several books on society and the family in West Africa between 1930 and 1960, some of which were translated into English and Italian. Her 1939 book, *La femme noire en Afrique occidentale,* established her as an expert on the situation of women in both Muslim and animist African communities. In it she touted the Christian ideal "of the family and of marriage, based on the Christian principles of individual liberty and equality before moral law." She argued that with respect to the contraction of marriage and the duties it imposed, such as fidelity, spouses were "perfectly equal." She also asserted that both parents exercised "paternal" authority over children, who were to honor both parents, according to the commandments. She portrayed Christian African brides as becoming the "companions" of their husbands, sharing work and taking charge when their spouses were away—something unthinkable, she claimed, in "pagan" households. "The wife's servile fear is giving way to a frank and cordial union, with common interests, pains and joys," she wrote. Yet African women's liberation in the context of Christian marriage had its limits: "But this equality does not destroy the necessary hierarchy," she pointed out. "In Christian households, the man has primacy and the woman must remain submissive to him, like the church is submissive to Christ."[73] Indeed, here lay the "delicate" aspect of women's Christian liberation in Africa—missionaries were trying to provoke a veritable revolution yet keep it within prescribed boundaries.

Sister Marie-André's work on African women also veered between scathing condemnation and tepid embrace of African societies and cultures. Staunch Catholic that she was, she harshly condemned African Islam and animism in personalist terms as having "no respect for human life, nor for the personhood of women nor children. . . . They do not inspire pity for the weak and suffering, nor respect for those afflicted with misfortune, because they do not know how to love."[74] Yet as early as 1939 she was also suggesting that the evangelization of Africa was not at all linked to its "Europeanization." Citing seventeenth-century directives from the Propaganda Fide, she argued that the church had always taught that indigenous cultures and rites should remain intact, except when contrary to "the inalienable rights of the human person," thus intimating that elements of African culture and society could be preserved alongside women's Christian liberation.[75]

Similar thinking in her 1953 book, *La condition humaine en Afrique noire,* inspired Father Tisserant to pen a critique of it to Monsignor du Mesnil at the Antislavery Society.[76] While Tisserant claimed that he approved of the book overall, he saw Marie-André as too "optimistic." He felt that she harbored an impossible desire: the "humanization and Christianization" of African clan systems that he had identified as the basis of slavery. In his mind, Christianity would have to destroy the clan, as it had among the Romans and the Franks.[77] It may be that Tisserant just wanted to safeguard his standing as an expert on the subject of African slavery or harbored the disdain for nuns who moved beyond the domestic sphere that was common among priests of his generation. Yet his response to her book reflected a deep impulse in missionary circles, shared by the activists at the Antislavery Society in the early 1950s, to describe Africa as a land of overwhelming immorality, depravity, and downright wickedness that needed the balm of Christian charity immediately. That emphasis on the negative would begin to evolve at the end of the decade as the political climate shifted in French Africa and new currents of Catholic thought, some of them espoused by Catholic Africans, became ascendant within the church.

MANAGING THE MESSAGE IN A TIME OF TRANSITION

While the Antislavery Society did not wade into the details of colonial politics in the 1950s, the rapidly shifting political landscape in Africa lurked in the background of the correspondence of its leaders and the missionaries they funded. Indeed, the society echoed missionary hysteria about the church's future in Africa, calling on French Catholics to donate before it was too late to "save" the continent. Missionaries worried about losing Africans to communism or Islam, or the extent to which social and political upheaval would drown out their evangelical message. Though they often critiqued French administrators for tolerating slavery or turning a blind eye to "barbaric" African customs, there was also an unspoken sense that a French departure from Africa would be detrimental to the missions. In 1957 Father Isidore Perraud, the secretary of the Apostolic Delegation of Dakar, spoke for many when he wrote to the Antislavery Society that "Africa awaits missionaries and catechists: it is the 'last quarter hour.'"[78]

This mounting anxiety is evident in Monsignor du Mesnil's solicitation letters to French clergy in the 1950s. Striking a paternalist note, he repeatedly stressed the responsibility incumbent on French Catholics to assist Africans. In 1954, for example, he opened his annual letter to the French clergy with the assertion that Catholicism must make rapid headway in a swiftly changing Africa. "Events in Africa show the urgency of religious penetration in the territories of the French Union," he began. "The mentality of our black brothers is rapidly evolving. We must Christianize. It is an absolute necessity for peace and for civilization."[79] After the Algerian War had begun, du Mesnil evoked the conflict there obliquely in his annual letter to the French episcopate in December of 1955. "For a year now," he wrote, "the events taking place in Africa show the gravity of the missionary appeals that I echoed to you in December of 1954. Should not the church intensify its proselytism at the moment when the old structures of these countries are undergoing profound disruptions? In this new world, with its familial and social evolution, one can only expect disorder if Christianity is absent. What a threat to peace." He also evoked the social work of the missions "in the face of a growing Islam, which we must reckon with more than ever."[80] In sum, his fundraising letters betray a clear sense of fear that the opportunity to Christianize Africa was slipping away, with possibly disastrous consequences.

The Vatican of Pope Pius XII, heavily influenced by Monsignor Lefebvre, embraced this view as well. At Easter 1957, less than a year after the *loi-cadre* devolved more autonomy to the territories of the French Union, the pope issued the encyclical *Fidei donum,* which was subtitled "On the Present Condition of the Catholic Missions, Especially in Africa."[81] To Catholics in Europe he wrote, "We deem it fitting at the present moment to direct your serious attention to Africa—the Africa that is at long last reaching out toward the higher civilization of our times and aspiring to civic maturity; the Africa that is involved in such grave upheavals as perhaps have never before been recorded in her ancient annals." He went on to evoke the rapid political and social change on the continent, and the dangers of communism and "technological" society to the implantation of Catholicism in "'darkest' Africa." Calling upon Catholics to aid the African missions, he warned,

> Any delay or hesitation is full of danger. For the people of Africa have made as much progress toward civilization during the past few decades as required many centuries among the nations of Western Europe. Thus, they are more easily unsettled and confused by the introduction of theoretical and applied scientific methods, with the result that they tend to be unduly inclined to a materialistic outlook on life. Hence a condition of affairs is sometimes brought about that is difficult to correct and in the course of time may prove to be a great obstacle to the growth of faith, whether in individuals or in society at large. For this reason, it is imperative that help should be given now to the shepherds of the Lord's flock in order that their apostolic labors may correspond to the ever-growing needs of the times.[82]

The panic of the church leadership about the future of Africa was thus abundantly clear, as was its tone of condescension and paternalism toward Africans. The Vatican wanted to see a monumental effort from more established European Catholic communities to win the continent for Christ at a decisive historical moment.

Fidei donum galvanized the Antislavery Society, though dramatic shifts within the church and the French Union would soon eclipse the pope's message. Canon Leveque, who took over as director general of the society when du Mesnil died in February 1957, made it a central part of his fundraising appeal for the Epiphany collection of 1958. He wrote to the clergy of France and to the editors of Catholic periodicals that the encyclical "rang out like a cry of alarm." He urged the French clergy to "eloquently recommend" the collection in light of the encyclical and asked the press to publish testimonials and articles on their readers' "personal responses to the call of Pius XII" for Africa.[83] Yet by the fall of 1958, Pius would be dead, the French Union would become the French Community, and Guinea would be fully independent. The canon, still new to the job, found himself trying to reach French Catholic donors in very different circumstances than his predecessor.

In the years that followed, Leveque increasingly shifted the tone of the society's propaganda to emphasize to the French Catholic public that French missionaries in Africa, rather than enslaved Africans, were the recipients of its charity. This likely reflected his belief that conservative French Catholics might be resentful of Africans who were rejecting French rule, as well as a sense that insisting on African depravity was less palatable (and compelling) to Catholics on the left side of the political spectrum. In 1959, he launched what he thought might become a quarterly periodical, *Aide aux missions françaises d'Afrique,* to relay the experiences and needs of French missionaries in Africa to the French Catholic public.[84] While the first article of that first issue was entitled "The liberation of the African woman," Leveque nonetheless harbored some measure of doubt about the society's close identification with antislavery.[85] That same year, he admitted to Monsignor Maury, Lefebvre's replacement as apostolic delegate for francophone Africa, that the name of the Antislavery Society seemed "timeworn" and suggested that "adjustments" were possible, though he ultimately concluded that its evocation of Lavigerie's persistent prestige was a boon.[86] Yet it is telling that the title of the new periodical emphasized the society's role as a benefactor to the French missions rather than its antislavery work.[87] And in 1965, Leveque changed its title to *Aide aux missionnaires français d'Afrique* from *Aide aux missions françaises d'Afrique.* Claiming that "missions françaises" provoked umbrage in Africa, he nonetheless continued to insist on keeping the word "French" in the title, to remind his reading public of their "permanent duty" to

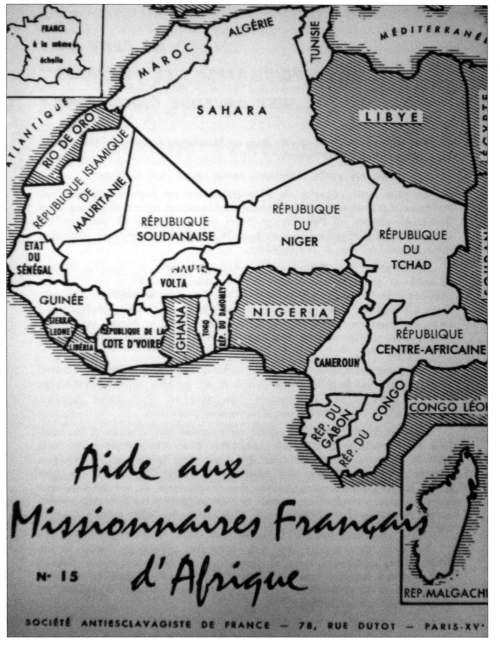

Aide aux missionnaires français d'Afrique, publication of the French Antislavery Society.
Courtesy of AEA and of MAfr.

those Catholics from their own communities who served the missions.[88] This statement reflected a significant shift—the society was no longer insisting as shrilly on a paternalist French Catholic duty to Africans, but appealing to its public on behalf of their own compatriots abroad.

Indeed, after independence, slavery became an increasingly difficult subject for African prelates too. In a fascinating 1962 letter to Leveque that he insisted remain secret, Monsignor Paul Zoungrana, the White Father who became the first African archbishop of Ouagadougou and then went on to be the first African cardinal from a former French colony in 1965, testified to the persistence of slavery and the subjugation of women in Africa. He wrote, "We sometimes hear that the Antislavery Society does not make sense anymore, because slavery is suppressed everywhere. That is not correct, however, because slavery is far from being suppressed! In our black Africa for example, and in particular in our Upper Volta, young women are still slaves in the context of marriage, and that is why the archbishop of Ouagadougou extends his hand to you, in all confidentiality." Zoungrana claimed that teenage girls were often married to men of seventy or to lepers and that if they fled such marriages they ran afoul of customary justice and often fell victim to poisoning and even murder at the hands of their families. He also evoked slave traffic in the context of the *hajj*: "When certain pilgrims depart for Mecca, they bring many young women and sell them in the course of the journey to pay for the trip. This is unworthy of our twentieth-century democracy, it is incompatible with our Christian conception of the person as the child of God, and how can our recent independence, carefully forged by France, survive with this kind of cancer?" Referring to a forthcoming law to protect young women, that he "hoped would be beneficial," he observed that laws were no good without morals.[89] Yet Zoungrana was not comfortable publishing this blistering indictment of his own society. It seems likely that he did not want his words to detract from African aspirations and the new independence of his country, or to invite political reprisals against the church in Maurice Yaméogo's increasingly restrictive state.[90]

The society's final move away from identifying itself with antislavery and attendant African depravity occurred in the wake of Vatican II, which encouraged and embraced new currents within the church. In 1968, Canon Leveque wrote to Gregorio Cardinal Agagianian, the prefect of the Sacred Congregation for the Evangelization of Peoples (the new, updated name of the Propaganda Fide) that many of his interlocutors had suggested that the Antislavery Society change its name as well. These included Monsignor Giovanni Mariani, the new apostolic delegate in Dakar, as well as bishops' councils and parish priests in France. Indeed, in a 1968 letter Mariani observed, "in these young countries who are proud of their independence and their liberty, the reminder of past trials and tribulations is a very delicate thing and often leads to difficulty and misunderstandings."[91] Yet a few weeks later, he seemed to move away from this idea, writing, "if I suggested a name change for your society it was not that I heard recriminations about it in Africa, but more, as you sense yourself, because of the mentality in Europe."[92] Mariani felt the name recalled a history that Africans preferred to forget, whereas French clergy said that antislavery seemed outdated and antique to their parishioners. Leveque agreed: while the antislavery name evoked Lavigerie, who still enjoyed widespread name recognition in France, the canon felt that it would be better for the society to "present itself" as an organization for missionary aid. This was, he asserted, "what Lavigerie's foundation had always been, in fact, from the beginning" and claimed that "our episcopate would be happy to see this update of our name."[93] He thus repurposed the argument made by several of his predecessors that antislavery was not the sole goal of the society; rather it had a broader social mission.

Leveque proposed changing the name of the society to the title that the organization had been using on its periodical: Aide aux missionaires français d'Afrique, or, more simply, Aide aux missionnaires d'Afrique. Though Leveque liked the idea of connecting French parishioners to "their" missionaries, he knew that by 1968 the Vatican would prefer to deemphasize French national ties in the African context. Regardless, however, Leveque insisted that it was necessary to keep the word missionary in the title of the society, because he felt it "touched the heart of the faithful" and reminded them that they had a "concrete obligation" to the priests, nuns, and laypeople from their own parishes and dioceses who had gone to work in Africa.[94] He still felt that the best way to motivate French Catholics to donate was to prod them to identify with the French Catholic activists they could imagine as like themselves, as opposed to evoking the barbarity of Africans, or national obligations to people who had not lived under French rule for nearly a decade.

The Vatican did not entirely approve of Leveque's proposed name change, and Agagianian's reasoning reveals some dissonance between the goals and perspectives of the church hierarchy and French Catholic activists. He agreed that it was time to drop the antislavery moniker, but suggested "Aide aux missions d'Afrique" instead of "Aide aux missionnaires d'Afrique." He felt that the term "missionaries" excluded the indigenous clergy, whose development and promotion had long been a Vatican priority and, at times, a source of conflict between church executives and French missions. Agagianian asserted that it was precisely the indigenous clergy who needed the most support, because most of them could not rely on a European missionary congregation for funding. Moreover, he wrote, "you well know that more and more ecclesiastical districts are being entrusted to local clergy, which makes the pontifical collection 'pro Afris' even more apt."[95] Clearly, Agagianian's mind was not on the ability of French Catholics to identify and relate to the missionaries they sent to Africa, but on developing and supporting the African clergy. This reflected the more inclusive view of the church developed at Vatican II, as well as a sense that the future of the church increasingly lay outside its "old" dioceses of Western Europe, where vocations and professions of belief were dropping precipitously.

In the second issue of *Aide aux missions françaises d'Afrique*, which came out just after the bulk of France's sub-Saharan African colonies became independent in 1960, Canon Leveque opened with a plea to French Catholics not to cease their support for the evangelization of Africa. He quoted the newly appointed African archbishop of Abidjan, Monsignor Bernard Yago, on the continued importance of French Catholic activism on the continent: "'Christian Frenchmen who are listening to me, I speak to you in the name of our common faith. The good work that France has already done is not complete . . . That is why your attitude should not be that of a man consumed by pique, who withdraws sniggering at the catastrophes he predicted and wished for, but rather that of the disciple of Christ, conscious of his constant duty of social and international charity.'"[96] Leveque himself was not immune to occasional expressions of bitterness. Echoing the sentiments of François Méjan and some frustrated French missionaries, in 1961 he chafed against "reverse racism" that made it more difficult for white Frenchmen to evangelize in an independent Africa and in 1965 he complained, "It is a fact that a perverse and outdated racism penetrates the minds of certain Africans."[97] Yet he hoped that political independence would not prove to be an estrangement between French and African Catholics, and that charity would continue to flow to the French missions that still dominated the church infrastructure in the former colonies.

Analysis of fundraising data indicates that his wishes were gratified. The society's evolving rationales and emphases in these turbulent decades appear to have been successful, or, at the very least, not overly detrimental to its solicitation goals. In the wake of the Epiphany collection of January 1961, the first one after independence, Leveque reported to Rome that the society had raised 804,500 "new francs" in its annual drive, an increase of 12 percent over the previous year (the new franc, introduced in 1960, was valued at a hundred old francs.)[98] Moreover, this was a 63 percent increase over the previous five years, a time period that witnessed the promulgation of the *loi-cadre* in 1956, the ongoing war in Algeria, the advent of the Fifth Republic, and Guinea's rejection of the French Community, amid widespread debate over France's continued role in Africa.[99] Using old francs, he noted that the collection had nearly "quadrupled" in the ten previous years from 23,590,948 francs in 1951 to 80,450,000 francs in 1961.[100] In 1964, the society celebrated the collection of the equivalent of over a hundred million old francs, "100 times" what it had collected at the end of World War II.[101] Even accounting for inflation, rising French disposable income, and a more professional approach to fundraising, this increase is significant. Moreover, the reborn society had staying power—it is noteworthy that the organization persists today and still conducts the Epiphany collection in France to benefit the Catholic Church in Africa.[102]

It appears, therefore, that despite a drastic decline in French vocations in the course of the 1950s and the upheavals of decolonization, the former Antislavery Society succeeded in maintaining French Catholic support for missions in Africa.[103] The society's trajectory through the 1950s and 1960s highlights both continuities and ruptures. It shows that the Franco-African Catholic world long outlasted the French Empire in Africa, though it evolved dramatically. In the early 1950s, though missionary discourse often criticized the French administration for not doing enough to "civilize" Africans, its focus on the "backwardness" of African society, as exemplified by slavery and the subjection of women, meshed well with a paternalistic French colonial mindset. Yet this approach became increasingly outmoded as African colonies moved toward independence and the Vatican promoted Africans to positions of leadership within the church. An emphasis on African vice did not fit the spirit of the newly minted African states, nor, more importantly, of the Catholic Church after Vatican II. By the late 1960s, therefore, antislavery was definitively sidelined.

CONCLUSION

Decolonization and Vatican II

ON OCTOBER 11, 1962, Pope John XXIII convened the highly anticipated Second Vatican Council in Saint Peter's Basilica. Vatican II is an
endpoint of sorts for this story, but of course it was also a new beginning, one whose consequences are still unwinding in the church today.
It followed close on the heels of the liquidation of the French Empire,
two years after the great wave of political independence across the former
colonies of West and Central Africa, and a mere eight months after the
Évian Accords ended the war in Algeria. Vatican II is difficult to characterize in simplistic terms because it was a mammoth and revolutionary
undertaking that touched on a vast number of matters ranging from minutiae to central tenets of the church. Debates still rage about the council's legacy, and whether its innovations helped to anchor the church in
the modern world, or hastened a decline in Catholic faith in the church's
European strongholds.

Yet there is no question that decolonization helped to precipitate Vatican II and shaped its outcome. Questions that fueled tense conversations and fiery debates in the postwar Franco-African Catholic world
took center stage at the council. These included whether the Catholic

Church was first and foremost a European church or a universal church, whether Catholicism was a conservative pillar of order or a force to liberate the world's subjugated and exploited populations, whether the church was unwaveringly bound to tradition or would change with the times, and how Catholics should relate to adherents of other religions.

Many of the individuals whose paths are explored in this book either participated in or closely observed Vatican II. Former or current French missionary prelates in Africa, including Marcel Lefebvre, were among the council fathers. So was Luc Moreau, Lefebvre's radical Dominican challenger in Dakar, who helped to communicate Louis Massignon's tolerant views on Islam at the council. Most of the new francophone African bishops who had been appointed in the late 1950s and early 1960s attended, including Bernardin Gantin, archbishop of Cotonou; Raymond-Marie Tchidimbo, archbishop of Conakry; Hyacinthe Thiandoum, archbishop of Dakar; Bernard Yago, archbishop of Abidjan; Dieudonné Yougbaré, bishop of Koupéla; and Paul Zoungrana, archbishop of Ouagadougou.[1] Thiandoum, as we have seen, used the council as an opportunity to communicate an African point of view on Catholic relations with Islam. In the wings of the council, African Catholic intellectuals of the African Society of Culture, organized by Alioune Diop, lobbied for their vision of a universal church. Meanwhile, the members of the Association of Catholic African Students in France published a special preconciliar issue of *Tam-Tam* and carefully watched developments in Rome. For nearly all of these denizens of the Franco-African Catholic world, the council's meaning, along with their visions of Catholicism and its future, were bound up with their interpretations of the changing postwar relationship between France and Africa.

In his opening speech, which he composed himself, Pope John conveyed a message of hope about the work of the council and humanity in general, rejecting the pessimism of "prophets of doom" who saw only "calamity and disaster in the present state of the world" and who were "always forecasting worse disasters, as though the end of the world were at hand."[2] One could imagine that John might put embittered French colonial apologists in that category. The pope felt that the church should lead by explanation rather than harsh condemnation, claiming that people were seeing the "lethal fruits" of disregard for God and his laws

African prelates at Vatican II, 1962. From left to right: Monsignor Hyacinthe Thiandoum, archbishop of Dakar; Monsignor Robert-Casimir Dosseh-Anyron, archbishop of Lomé; Monsignor Bernardin Gantin, archbishop of Cotonou. From *Horizons africains*, no. 145 (December 1962): 3.

for themselves. Invoking personalism, he stated, "people are ever more deeply convinced of the dignity of the human person." What is especially important, he argued, is that "experience has taught men that violence inflicted on others, the might of arms, and political domination are of no help at all in finding a happy solution to the grave problems which afflict them."[3] He also spoke of the church reaching out beatifically to all men, a reference to Christians not in communion with the Roman Church and peoples of other faiths.

John's optimism, his message of inclusion, and his condemnation of oppression resonated with African Catholic intellectuals and priests, as well as young, progressive European clergy. Adrian Hastings, who as a youthful White Father transmitted the teachings of Vatican II via newsletter to parishes across anglophone Africa, noted in his reminiscences about the council: "The conciliar themes of localization and pluralism, of the recognition of the positive values of different cultures and even other religious traditions, the new use of the vernacular in the liturgy, ecumenical *rapprochement,* all this conformed with the general early 1960s stress on African political and cultural values, on decolonializa- tion [sic], on the social necessity of cooperation and unity across the di- visions of tribe, race, and religion."[4] Indeed, many of the council's cen- tral concerns and accomplishments corresponded closely to what the members of the militant African Catholic intellectual elite had been calling for since the late 1940s.

John's words and the council itself also meshed particularly well with Africa's new political independence. Father Robert Sastre's contribution to Alioune Diop's conciliar collection on *Personnalité africaine et catholi- cisme* entitled "Un Concile à l'heure de l'Afrique," as well as the special preconciliar issue of *Tam-Tam* on "L'Église à l'heure de l'Afrique," both evoke this convergence between Catholic and African renewal in the early 1960s.[5] As Hastings observed, "probably in no other conti- nent did the Vatican Council coincide quite so neatly and sympatheti- cally with a major process of secular change as in Africa." There seemed to be, he observed, "a natural harmony" and a shared sense of hopeful- ness for rejuvenation of the church and for the birth of independent African states. If the council had happened ten years earlier, he speculated, this resonance would not have existed.[6] Indeed, a lot had changed in the African church between Léopold Senghor's complaints of missionary racism in Dakar in 1947 and the heady days of Vatican II. As Sastre put it, "Once could say that all of the schemas in which Europe wanted to lock black humanity have burst apart, one after another, revealing to Europe its own limits and opening up a new conception of man."[7]

Indeed, the stunning wave of decolonization on the African continent clearly influenced Pope John's thinking about the role of the church in the world as he prepared for the council. As the nuncio to France be- tween 1944 and 1953, and the Vatican's liaison to UNESCO in the 1950s, he witnessed firsthand the rapid postwar developments in the Franco- African Catholic world.[8] Subsequently, during his pontificate, he pre- sided over key steps in the transition from a missionary church in a French colonial context to an indigenous church in sovereign African states by promoting most of the francophone African bishops, and is- suing speeches and letters of congratulation on the occasion of the independence of nearly every former French African colony.[9] On September 11, 1962, exactly one month before the start of Vatican II, he delivered a radio address to the faithful "of all the world" in which he delighted in the fact that, "for the first time in history, the fathers at the council will truly come from all nations" and would bring their varied "intelligence and experience" to "heal the scars" of the two world wars. In this talk, he also insisted on "the fundamental equality of all peoples in the exercise of rights and duties amid the family of peoples," a refutation of racism and European colonial domination. Finally, he inserted an idea that was not in earlier drafts prepared by his European theologians: "Vis-à-vis the underdeveloped countries," he instructed, "the church presents itself as it is and as it wants to be: the church of all, and especially the church of the poor."[10] These ideas represented his determination to steer the church in a new direction and eschew its exclusive identification with the rich, the dominant, and Europe.

Moreover, John said himself that he was thinking of Africa as he formulated his guidance on the eve of the council. On October 4, he visited the Catholic shrines at Assisi and Loreto, marking the first trip a pontiff had taken outside of Rome in an official capacity (other than to the papal retreat at Castel Gandolfo) since 1870. Though it was a closely guarded secret, he had received a diagnosis of terminal stomach cancer less than two weeks before, and the surprising journey was both a personal pilgrimage and a political move to set the tone for the council that he knew would outlast him. In his sermon at Assisi, home of Saint Francis, patron saint of the poor, John reiterated the idea that the council was to focus on "'the church of the poor.'"[11] The very next day, just a week before the opening of the council, John warmly received Léopold Senghor, now president of independent Senegal, at the Vatican. The pontiff noted with delight that majority-Muslim Senegal was the first independent African state to establish diplomatic relations with the Vatican, and offered his blessings to "all of young, strong, and much-beloved Africa." He told Senghor that "yesterday, during Our voyage to the sanctuaries of Loreto and Assisi, your country, and Africa as a whole, was particularly on Our mind, in Our prayers and in the fervent wishes We expressed for all of the nations of the earth."[12] John also said that his visit with Senghor would always be linked to his memories of his day of pilgrimage and the delight it brought to the faithful worldwide, thus tying together his thoughts about Africa and his vision for the future of the church.

It is also possible to discern the influence of Alioune Diop, Senghor's fellow Senegalese Catholic, in the pontiff's words about the council. In 1962, Diop and the African Society of Culture convened a symposium of some forty African priests and lay Catholics in Rome to prepare for the council.[13] Their goal was to define what Africa desired from Vatican II, as well as what it could bring to the council's work on spiritual, theological, liturgical, and social questions. In an interview on Vatican Radio during this preparatory symposium, Diop laid out his vision of African expectations of and possible contributions to the council in terms strikingly similar to those John would employ in some of his pronouncements later that year. Diop claimed that the "peoples of the Third World" and African men of culture, regardless of religion, had "enormous" expectations of the church because of its "profoundly catholic vocation" and its "immense patrimony of charity and reflection amassed over centuries." This was because, he argued, the problems of Africa were not merely political and economic, but moral and spiritual. "What peoples of color complain of, and those from black Africa in particular, is that their dignity has never been recognized," he said.[14] For Diop, as he put it elsewhere, the church, which acknowledged that dignity, could serve as a sort of "moral guarantor" for emerging Africa by advocating for the continent's poor of all faiths both at home and on the world stage.[15]

As far as what Africa could bring to the council, Diop cited "a certain sense of community life, a spirit of tolerance vis-à-vis all human groups, a profound intuition, ill-expressed but deeply felt, of the spiritual unity of the world." He believed that exchanges between Europeans and Africans at the council could showcase "virtues" that Europe had turned away from, but could still be found in Africa. "In the domains of thought, of moral life, artistic life, relations between different communities, Africa can contribute to the making of a world of peace, a world where each person will feel respected, recognized, and loved," he told Vatican Radio.[16] It appears that John XXIII agreed wholeheartedly: at his meeting with Senghor, he applauded the people of Senegal as "very attached to their noble traditions of community life, enamored of ancestral wisdom and sensitive to art." He went on to say, "your country is a land of liberty, a great place to live, where the church develops freely among the other spiritual families."[17] These themes of community, artistic sensibility, respect across confessional lines, and the validity of black culture so dear to Diop and his black Catholic intellectual collaborators had thus made it to the very center of the Catholic Church.

Of course, John's thoughts, though they set the tone for the initial proceedings and for how many Catholics would later interpret Vatican II, did not define the totality of a council of over two thousand church fathers, who continued their work for three additional sessions after his death in 1963. If the public spirit of the council seemed to align more closely with the postwar visions of Catholicism championed by Alioune Diop, Joseph Ki-Zerbo, Robert Sastre, Joseph Michel, and Luc Moreau, Vatican II also prominently featured a strong and resentful echo of the conservative side of the Franco-African Catholic world. Monsignor Lefebvre, by far the most prominent prelate in postwar French Africa, did not like what he saw in Rome.[18] Lefebvre, who was deeply pessimistic about the future of Africa in the 1950s, and who had stirred up controversy by expressing ongoing support for colonial rule and equating Islam with communism on the very eve of independence, was completely at sea in the open and optimistic era fostered by John XXIII. John, Lefebvre subsequently noted, "did not value me as Pope Pius XII had."[19]

The simultaneous end of French rule in Africa and the advent of the new pope shifted the ground dramatically beneath Lefebvre's feet, dealing a blow to his lofty personal ambitions. Years later, he remained angry and bewildered at how the world had changed around him in the late 1950s and early 1960s. "I continued to do what I had always done until the council—what had earned me nominations as archbishop, apostolic delegate, Spiritan superior general, assistant to the pontifical throne, and to be received every year by Pope Pius XII, who, if he had lived, might have made me a cardinal," he later wrote.[20] He complained of the "fall of my star," marveling at how someone as competent and esteemed as himself could suddenly be manifestly "in the wrong" without changing his views. There was no question that he seethed with frustration at the church's eagerness to change with the times in Africa. In the 1980s, he criticized the church for what he perceived as a heedless race to Africanize its personnel. "I sometimes urged prudence," he wrote. "If there were only two African priests in a particular place, the Vatican wanted one of them to be the bishop but should have nonetheless made sure that he had the requisite qualities! Moreover, before making them into archbishops, they could have made them auxiliaries, as had been done before. But de Gaulle rushed all of the independences, the Americans did a bit of pushing, and so the church had to follow!" he concluded bitterly.[21] This point of view, complete with its anti-American component, aligned with the ideas of French patriots like François Méjan and conservative Catholics like François Charles-Roux, who had believed wholeheartedly in a French civilizing mission, and resented the forces in the church that appeared to be undermining French dominance in Africa.

At Vatican II, Lefebvre became one of the most extreme members of a minority faction of bishops known as the International Group of Fathers, or just the Group, that staunchly opposed the council's innovations on almost all fronts.[22] Clinging to a vision of one, true, hierarchical church, Lefebvre rejected the idea that Catholicism should adapt to the times, eschewing changes in the liturgy and the conciliar proclamation of freedom of religion, which implied to him that the church was adopting a relativist position and conceding the validity of other faiths. In the third session, for example, in keeping with the negative view of Islam that he had expressed during his posting in Dakar, he argued, "One cannot affirm the liberty of all religious communities in human society without also according moral liberty to these communities: morality and religion are intimately linked, for example polygamy and the Islamic religion."[23] After the council, which he described as a "betrayal" and "self-destruction of the church," he founded the Society of Saint Pius X, an ultra-traditionalist group that used the preconciliar Latin mass.[24] As noted, his successor in Dakar, Monsignor Hyacinthe Thiandoum, tried unsuccessfully to coax him back into the fold, but Lefebvre flouted a direct papal order in 1988 when he consecrated four traditionalist bishops. The Beninese cardinal Bernardin Gantin signed the ensuing order to excommunicate the man who had been the most powerful Roman Catholic prelate in Africa in the 1950s, when Gantin had been ordained and promoted to his first leadership post as auxiliary bishop of Cotonou. It was, indeed, a dramatic conclusion to Lefebvre's once promising career.

As for Thiandoum, Gantin, and their fellow African prelates, Vatican II was a momentous occasion because it was the first time Africa was truly represented by black Africans in a church council, though European missionary bishops also traveled to Rome on behalf of many African dioceses. In March of 1963, *Horizons africains,* the magazine of the Archdiocese of Dakar, lauded the valuable expertise that African bishops had already brought to discussions of liturgy, social customs, and ways the church could render its message more comprehensible to populations in the developing world. Yet, it went on to say, the symbolic value of African participation was perhaps more significant than any concrete policy recommendation: "already the most important effect of the presence of African bishops at the council is being felt beyond its meeting halls: it is the growing awareness of all of the blacks of Africa and America—common people and leaders alike—that they are 'somebody' in the church . . . that the Catholic Church is 'their church.'"[25] Alongside the political changes on the African continent, this conciliar participation affirmed that Africans were charting a new, independent course in the Catholic Church and in the world at large.

The handful of historians who have examined the African bishops' participation in the council tend to agree with this assessment.[26] The African prelates were a tiny minority in the council: at the opening of the first session there were sixty-one of them, out of over two thousand men present.[27] Of these, sixteen hailed from former French sub-Saharan Africa, including Madagascar. Because a number of these francophone African prelates had studied in Rome, they were actually more at home at the council than many of the European missionary bishops who attended.[28] In general, they tended to be moderates that leaned toward innovation. As Archbishop Gantin put it in a report on the first session of the council, "Not having a glorious Christian past, we looked more easily to the future. Thus while representatives of European Catholics spoke of liturgical 'revival,' us others thought more readily of assimilation and adaptation."[29] As Thiandoum did in the case of Catholic relations with Islam, African prelates pushed for change in domains they felt particularly passionately about. Yet, at times, their desire to prove that Africans were ready to be full-fledged members of the church took them into conservative territory. Most of them opposed doing away with clerical celibacy, for example, because they did not want their European peers to think that Africans could not handle the discipline of the church in this regard.[30]

Many observers testified that although their numbers were small, the African bishops were remarkably well organized and unified. Realizing they would have to cooperate to be heard in the council, they put in place a general secretariat that coordinated their stances on particular issues and drew up candidates for various conciliar commissions. The post of secretary general was held by Laurean Rugambwa from Tanganyika, the first black African cardinal, whom John XXIII had elevated in 1960.[31] In the words of French theologian Yves Congar, the unity of the African delegation was "'one of the revelations of the council.'"[32] Marie-Dominique Chenu, the French theologian who attended the council as an expert assistant to the French missionary bishop of Antsirabe, Madagascar, echoed this assessment, noting in an article for *Tam-Tam* that every time a bishop from Africa or Madagascar intervened, he spoke for his colleagues. Chenu also noted that the council prompted African bishops to converse across formerly rigid linguistic and political boundaries.[33]

The reaction in France and in African Catholic intellectual circles was that the solidarity and poise of the African delegation at Vatican II was proof positive that the African church had reached "maturity."[34] Pope Paul VI, who succeeded John XXIII in 1963, endorsed this view and staged dramatic papal affirmations of Africa's full membership in the church during the latter sessions of the council. In 1964, he finally canonized the Catholic martyrs of Uganda. Beatified by Benedict XV in 1920, their status had become a cause célèbre for Alioune Diop and other African Catholic activists who demanded Africans be included in the ranks of Catholic saints. In early 1965, Paul VI made another highly symbolic move when he elevated Archbishop of Ouagadougou Paul Zoungrana to the cardinalate, making him the first black prince of the church from formerly French Africa.

Zoungrana's meteoric rise from priest to archbishop to cardinal unfolded during, and was intimately connected to, the simultaneous

sweeping changes in French Africa and in the church. Born in Ouagadougou in 1917, Zoungrana was baptized by Monsignor Joanny Thévenoud, the French White Father who laid much of the Catholic Church's
foundation there between 1903 and 1949. Ordained by Thévenoud in 1942
as one of colonial Upper Volta's first three priests, he served as vicar at
Ouagadougou's cathedral before joining the White Fathers himself in
1948 and then pursuing a doctorate in Rome. His time in Rome exposed
Zoungrana to the interior workings of the Vatican and gave him the tools
to talk with his European counterparts in academic terms. He then returned to Upper Volta and taught canon law at the White Fathers' senior seminary at Koumi between 1954 and 1958, before taking up the task
of organizing the church's social work in the territory. In 1960, he personified the church's drive to "Africanize" its leadership on the continent in advance of political decolonization, when John XXIII consecrated him archbishop in a lavish ceremony in Saint Peter's Basilica,
just three months before Upper Volta became independent from France.[35]
Five years later, with his eloquence, expertise in canon law, and varied
experience in Rome and Africa, Zoungrana was again the ideal man to
embody the Vatican's ongoing promotion of the African church at
the council. At the council's close, as a newly minted cardinal, he was
one of a handful of church leaders selected to read one of its final
messages.[36]

Taken together, the trajectories of Zoungrana and not-to-be cardinal
Marcel Lefebvre illustrate the remarkable transformations within the
Franco-African Catholic world in the postwar era. In hindsight, the
rapid pace of developments between the late 1940s and early 1960s is
breathtaking. The militancy of African Catholic students, clergy, and intellectuals, together with progressive European missionaries, had
pushed the church to favor African independence and promote Africans
in its ranks, and embrace a Catholic, personalist strand of negritude. The
Vatican, which had a more clear-eyed view of the possibility of decolonization than many of the Europeans who were engaged in colonial Africa, played a role in this reorientation. Popes had set the stage for it
between the wars, but it was only in the postwar era that the Vatican
began to force the issue and overcome Europeans' resistance. A striking
process of generational change in the French missionary clergy, as well

Paul Zoungrana as a new cardinal, 1965. Courtesy of AGMAfr.

as the emergence of a robust French Catholic left after World War II, facilitated this transformation.

Yet there were also important continuities in the Franco-African Catholic world that were masked by these dramatic changes. Money and personnel for Catholic endeavors still flowed freely from France to Africa, as the trajectory of the Antislavery Society attests. French prelates still held the majority of episcopal seats in former French Africa for years to come, even if they had stepped away from the most important and visible posts. French priests, nuns, and laity remained thick on the ground, and the church in Africa depended on them. This was thrown into relief when Sékou Touré abruptly expelled all of the French clergy from Guinea in 1967. A total of seventy-six French priests, ten French religious brothers and approximately sixty French nuns departed, leaving a skeleton crew of Africans behind. Priests from neighboring African countries rushed to try to fill the void, depleting their own thin ranks in the process.[37]

In addition to the persistence of French religious personnel across Africa, the French state, which had discovered the usefulness of Catholic missions for its new emphasis on African development at the close of World War II, remained heavily involved in promoting Catholic education in its former colonies. Tepid and inconsistent support for missions across French Africa in the interwar period gave way to the FIDES program in 1946. A veritable bonanza for the missions, the FIDES channeled millions of francs to Catholic schools and healthcare initiatives across postwar French Africa. After losing formal political control, France continued to provide extensive material support to its successor African states through a mutation of the FIDES program known as *Coopération*. Thousands of young French men and women traveled to Africa as *coopérants,* teaching in schools and providing a variety of technical assistance in healthcare and infrastructure improvements. Though not all of the *coopérants* were Catholic, most of the sponsored schools were. Cash-strapped African governments tended to welcome this aid, especially since the African elite were largely the products of French education. For French officials, *Coopération's* support of Catholic schools furthered dearly held goals of cementing the use of the French language and maintaining French cultural influence on the African continent.[38] Any Méjan-style bitterness about a Vatican "betrayal" of France in Africa thus did not impede further investment in French Catholic endeavors on the continent for years to come.

Indeed, the Franco-African Catholic world described in this book continues to exist today, despite ruptures and new dynamics. Linguistic affinity, circuits of education, an entangled past, and, above all, a shared faith have maintained it over time. It nonetheless reflects the broader state of Christianity as a whole, which is undergoing one of the most dramatic transformations in its history. While Christian observance and priestly vocations have plummeted in Europe in the past several decades, they have exploded in Africa, Asia, and Latin America. In 2050, Africa will have over a billion Christians and two hundred million of them will be Catholic—many more than Europe.[39] Meanwhile, in 2007, fewer than half the people in France considered themselves even vaguely Catholic, and only 8 percent of the population actively practiced Catholicism.[40] According to official church statistics, in the course of 2012 the number of priests in Europe decreased by 1,375, part of a consistent decline over time. By contrast, the developing world saw the greatest increases in clergy, with 1,076 and 1,364 new priests in Africa and Asia respectively that year.[41] This trend has helped shift the locus of Catholic conservatism from Europe to Africa, where prelates are more likely to be traditionalist on social questions.

In the Franco-African Catholic world, the flow of clergy between the two continents has reversed in extraordinary fashion. France, which had led Europe in sending astonishing numbers of Catholic missionaries around the globe at the turn of the twentieth century, could not produce enough priests for its own parishes by the dawn of the twenty-first.[42] The rarity of vocations among French youth have led the French episcopate to rely increasingly on elderly French clergy and foreign-born priests, a majority of them African, to fill its ranks. This practice, along with the steep decline in Catholic observance in France, was thrown into sharp relief on the occasion of the widely publicized murder of Father Jacques Hamel while he was celebrating mass for a diminutive audience of three nuns and two parishioners in Saint-Étienne-du-Rouvray on a Tuesday morning in July 2016.[43] Hamel, a local son aged eighty-five who had been ordained in 1958, was filling in for the African parish priest, Father Auguste Moanda-Phuati, who was on vacation visiting family in the Democratic Republic of the Congo. Moanda-Phuati noted of Hamel, "he could have retired at seventy-five years old, but seeing how few priests were around he decided to stay and work, to continue to be of service to people."[44] By March of 2015, there were 1,689 foreign-born priests working in the Catholic Church of France, of which 1,048 hailed from francophone Africa, including the former Belgian colonies of the Democratic Republic of the Congo, Rwanda, and Burundi.[45] Moreover, Africans have come to dominate some of the many missionary groups founded in France to evangelize abroad. In 2016, for example, 1,279 of the 2,604 members of the Spiritan congregation hailed from the African continent, while 873 were from Europe. France, home to 260 of these, still furnished the most of any European country, but its preeminence within the organization has eroded dramatically since midcentury.[46] This represents a truly remarkable change in the space of just two generations.

Pope Pius XII and Pope John XXIII, who presided over the postwar, preconciliar church, both grasped on some level that the future of Catholicism lay in its mission fields outside of Europe and North America, though they would likely have been shocked by the scale of the shift that took place in the succeeding fifty years. Under Pius, the Vatican began a more concentrated push for the indigenization of clergy in African missions, but those missions simultaneously tied themselves more closely to the French colonial state and Pius trod awkwardly between lauding French rule and affirming African self-determination. Under John, the Vatican expressed open enthusiasm for African independence and adopted the language of Catholic negritude honed by Alioune Diop and his collaborators. Yet the Vatican itself was still a European preserve, and remained so even as non-European Catholic populations exploded in the years after the council. At the papal election of 2013, for example, twenty-eight of the 115 voting cardinals were Italian, and sixty of them hailed from somewhere in Europe.[47] These men recognized, however, that it was time for a non-European pope. Though excited rumors of an African appointee swirled during the conclave, the assembly chose its first pontiff from Latin America, Argentine Jorge Bergoglio, a Jesuit who took the name Francis I. Influenced by the dire poverty rampant on his home continent and the example of John XXIII, Francis has aggressively showcased his personal humility and reasserted the church's role as the comforter and defender of the world's poor and weak.[48] Though the pendulum may swing yet again, it appears that Europe's stranglehold on the church hierarchy may soon be a relic of the past.

ABBREVIATIONS

NOTES

ARCHIVES AND KEY PERIODICALS

ACKNOWLEDGMENTS

INDEX

ABBREVIATIONS

AAD	Archives de l'Archidiocèse de Dakar
AAEA	Archives Aide aux Églises d'Afrique (formerly la Société antiesclavagiste de France)
ACSSp	Archives de la Congrégation du Saint-Esprit (Spiritans)
ADN	Archives diplomatiques, Nantes
ADPF	Archives dominicaines de la Province de France
ADPL	Archives dominicaines de la Province de Lyon
AEF	Afrique équatoriale française / French Equatorial Africa
AGMAfr	Archives générales de la Société des missionnaires d'Afrique (White Fathers)
AMEP	Archives des Missions étrangères de Paris
ANF	Archives nationales de France
ANOM	Archives nationales d'Outre-Mer
ANS	Archives nationales du Sénégal
AOF	Afrique occidentale française / French West Africa
APPP	Archives de la Préfecture de Police de Paris
ASMA	Archives de la Société des missions africaines
BDIC	Bibliothèque de documentation internationale contemporaine
CNAEF	Centre national des archives de l'Église de France
CSSp	Congrégation du Saint-Esprit (Spiritains) / Fathers of the Holy Spirit (Spiritans)
ENFOM	École nationale de la France d'Outre-Mer
FEANF	Fédération des étudiants d'Afrique noire en France / Federation of Black African Students in France

FIDES	Fonds d'investissement pour développement économique et social
IDEO	Institut dominicain d'études orientales
JEC	Jeunesse étudiante chrétienne
MAfr	Missionnaires d'Afrique (Pères Blancs) / Missionaries of Africa (White Fathers)
MEP	Missions étrangères de Paris / Foreign Missions of Paris
MLN	Mouvement africain de libération nationale / African National Liberation Movement
MRP	Mouvement républicain populaire
OURS	Office universitaire de recherche socialiste
PDG	Parti démocratique de Guinée / Democratic Party of Guinea
SAC	Société africaine de culture / African Society of Culture
SEC	Société européenne de culture / European Society of Culture
SJ	Society of Jesus (Jesuits)
SMA	Société des missions africaines / Society of African Missions
TRP	Très Révérend Père / Most Reverend Father (or Superior General)
UN	United Nations
UNESCO	United Nations Educational, Scientific and Cultural Organization

NOTES

Introduction: Catholic Conversations at the End of Empire

1. Guinea's vote was 95 percent in favor of no, while the yes votes in the other French African territories were similarly skewed. Frederick Cooper, *Citizenship between Empire and Nation: Remaking France and French Africa, 1945–1960* (Princeton, NJ: Princeton University Press, 2014), 317.
2. Elizabeth Schmidt, *Cold War and Decolonization in Guinea, 1946–1958* (Athens, OH: Ohio University Press, 2007), 171–172, 178, 182.
3. Délégation apostolique de Dakar, *Statistiques annuelles des missions catholiques en Afrique française, année 1957–1958* (Dakar: Imprimerie Mission Catholique), ACSSp 2F 1.3 a5.
4. In French, FIDES stood for Fonds d'investissement pour développement économique et social.
5. See "Subventions du FIDES aux établissements scolaires," Chapitre 1072 in ANOM 1FIDES 71 / 552.
6. Touré's tenure as head of state was marked by a number of *"complots,"* which resulted in the exile, imprisonment, or death of perceived opponents. For an exhaustive study of Touré, albeit by a French diplomat active in Franco-Guinean relations, see André Lewin, *Ahmed Sékou Touré (1922–1984): Président de la Guinée,* 8 vols. (Paris: l'Harmattan, 2009–2011).
7. Mgr de Milleville, "Comment l'Église de Guinée a défendu ses écoles," confidential. ACSSp 6I 1.6 b4.
8. For Tchidimbo's memories of this time, see Raymond-Marie Tchidimbo, *Noviciat d'un evêque: huit ans et huit mois de captivité sous Sékou Touré*

(Paris: Fayard, 1987). For a detailed account of the Catholic Church under Touré by a former missionary, see Gérard Vieira, *L'Église catholique en Guinée à l'épreuve de Sékou Touré (1958–1984)* (Paris: Karthala, 2005).

9. François Méjan, "L'Église catholique et la France d'Outre-Mer," *L'année politique et économique*, no. 133–134 (Nov.–Dec. 1956): 401–556. At this time Méjan was the president of the Administrative Tribunal of Lille.

10. François Méjan, *Le Vatican contre la France d'Outre-Mer?* (Paris: Librairie Fischbacher, 1957). Méjan's father, Louis Méjan, had been director of *Cultes* at the Ministry of the Interior when the separation of church and state became law in 1905, and François became involved in ongoing negotiations regarding separation between France and the Vatican in the 1950s. See William Guéraiche, "François Méjan, Maurice Deixonne: une amitié entre nécessité politique et tentation d'histoire," *Recherche socialiste*, no. 3 (June 1998): 63–78.

11. Here Méjan was quoting François Mitterrand. See Méjan, *Le Vatican*, 137; François Mitterrand, "Immobilisme en Afrique noire?" *L'Express*, June 4, 1955, 4.

12. Méjan, *Le Vatican*, 15. For a parallel attack on the church for being anti-French, see Edmond Paris, *Le Vatican contre la France* (Paris: Librairie Fischbacher, 1957). Paris focused most closely on Vatican policy in Algeria, the Middle East, and Europe.

13. Méjan, *Le Vatican*, 73, 75.

14. Ibid., 17.

15. Ibid., 31–33.

16. Ibid., 199.

17. Ibid., 18 (emphasis in original).

18. *Der Spiegel*, Jan. 1, 1958, 28–29; "Black Bishops," *Time* 70, no. 26 (Dec. 23, 1957): 26–27. For numerous reviews, see OURS 71 APO 16.

19. For lists, see Méjan's notes and Fischbacher's sheet, OURS 71 APO 15.

20. See these cards and letters among others in OURS 71 APO 17.

21. W. d'Ormesson to F. Méjan, Neuilly-sur-Seine, Jan. 14, 1957, OURS 71 APO 17 (ellipsis in original).

22. In English it is often translated as the "framework law." Under the *loi-cadre*, each individual French African Overseas Territory gained control over its internal budget and civil service, though France remained sovereign in the realms of defense, foreign policy, and in cases where initiatives or structures crossed territorial boundaries. These concessions were prompted by fear of violence in sub-Saharan Africa. One lasting consequence was the so-called "balkanization" of French Africa into its constituent territories, a development bemoaned by African federalists. Frederick Cooper, *Decol-*

onization and African Society: The Labor Question in French and British Africa (Cambridge: Cambridge University Press, 1996), 413, 424–431; Cooper, *Citizenship between Empire and Nation,* 252–256.

23. See Tony Chafer, *End of Empire in French West Africa: France's Successful Decolonization?* (Oxford: Berg, 2002), 163–221.

24. On political polarization in postwar France, see Robert Gildea, *France since 1945,* 2nd ed. (Oxford: Oxford University Press, 2002), 35–64.

25. On French Christians and the Algerian War, see Darcie Fontaine, *Decolonizing Christianity: Religion and the End of Empire in France and Algeria* (Cambridge: Cambridge University Press, 2016).

26. Examples include MRP founders and former *résistants* Georges Bidault and Joseph Hours. See also the book by MRP secretary and president of its wing in French sub-Saharan Africa Georges Le Brun Keris, *Mort des colonies? Colonialisme, anticolonialisme et colonisation* (Paris: Centurion, 1953). On MRP colonial policy, see R. E. M. Irving, *Christian Democracy in France* (London: George Allen & Unwin, 1973), 199–230. For a recent rethinking of the roots of Christian Democracy in postwar France, Germany, and Austria, see James Chappel, *Catholic Modern: The Challenge of Totalitarianism and the Remaking of the Church* (Cambridge, MA: Harvard University Press), especially 144–181.

27. Liberation theology was a constellation of grassroots and top-down initiatives across Latin America between the late 1950s and the 1980s. See David Tombs, *Latin American Liberation Theology* (Boston: Brill, 2002); Jennifer S. Hughes, "The Catholic Church and Social Revolutionaries," in *Religion and Society in Latin America: Interpretive Essays from Conquest to Present,* ed. Lee M. Penyak and Walter J. Petry (Maryknoll, NY: Orbis Books, 2009). For the important influence of French theologians on liberation theology, see Gerd-Rainer Horn, *Western European Liberation Theology: The First Wave (1924–1959)* (Oxford: Oxford University Press, 2008), 291–301. One of the movement's central figures, Peruvian Gustavo Gutiérrez, is a Dominican who studied in France in the 1950s.

28. Jean Vinatier, *Les prêtres ouvriers, le Cardinal Liénart et Rome: histoire d'une crise, 1944–1967* (Paris: Éditions ouvrières, 1985); Charles Suaud and Nathalie Viet-Depaule, *Prêtres et ouvriers: une double fidelité mise à l'épreuve, 1944–1969* (Paris: Karthala, 2004).

29. Cooper, *Citizenship between Empire and Nation*; Gregory Mann, *From Empires to NGOs in the West African Sahel: The Road to Nongovernmentality* (Cambridge: Cambridge University Press, 2015); Gary Wilder, *Freedom Time: Negritude, Decolonization, and the Future of the World* (Durham, NC: Duke University Press, 2015).

30. On imagining decolonization beyond the strictly political, see Farina Mir, "The Archives of Decolonization: Introduction," *American Historical Review* 120 (2015): 844–845 and the accompanying *AHR* roundtable. On how another institution with both French and African constituencies negotiated this period, see Ruth Ginio, *The French Army and Its African Soldiers: The Years of Decolonization* (Lincoln: University of Nebraska Press, 2017).

31. Joseph-Roger de Benoist, *Église et pouvoir colonial au Soudan français: administrateurs et missionnaires dans la Boucle du Niger (1885–1945)* (Paris: Karthala, 1987); Patrick J. N. Tuck, *French Catholic Missionaries and the Politics of Imperialism in Vietnam, 1857–1914: A Documentary Survey* (Liverpool: Liverpool University Press, 1987); Gérard Vieira, *Sous le signe du laïcat: documents pour l'histoire de l'Église catholique en Guinée* (Dakar: Presses de l'Imprimerie Saint-Paul, 1992); J. P. Daughton, *An Empire Divided: Religion, Republicanism, and the Making of French Colonialism, 1880–1914* (Oxford: Oxford University Press, 2006); Aylward Shorter, *Cross and Flag in Africa: The "White Fathers" during the Colonial Scramble* (Maryknoll, NY: Orbis Books, 2006); Charles Keith, *Catholic Vietnam: A Church from Empire to Nation* (Berkeley: University of California Press, 2012); Elizabeth A. Foster, *Faith in Empire: Religion, Politics, and Colonial Rule in French Senegal, 1880–1940* (Stanford, CA: Stanford University Press, 2013). De Benoist, Vieira, and Shorter are or were Catholic missionaries.

32. Notable exceptions in the French sphere include Keith, *Catholic Vietnam* and Fontaine, *Decolonizing Christianity*. Fontaine deals mostly with European Christians, as converts were few in Algeria. See also Brian Stanley, ed., *Missions, Nationalism, and the End of Empire* (Grand Rapids, MI: William B. Eerdmans, 2003).

33. In the French African context, scholarship on decolonization and religion has largely focused on Islam as a means of resistance to French rule, as well as on interactions between Muslims and the French state in the metropole. On the former, see Omar Carlier, *Entre nation et djihad: histoire sociale des radicalismes algériens* (Paris: Presses de la Fondation nationale des sciences politiques, 1995); James McDougall, *History and the Culture of Nationalism in Algeria* (Cambridge: Cambridge University Press, 2008). On the latter, see Joan Wallach Scott, *The Politics of the Veil* (Princeton, NJ: Princeton University Press, 2010); Naomi Davidson, *Only Muslim: Embodying Islam in Twentieth Century France* (Ithaca, NY: Cornell University Press, 2012); Mayanthi Fernando, *The Republic Unsettled: Muslim French and the Contradictions of Secularism* (Durham, NC: Duke University Press, 2014). See also Sarah Abrevaya Stein, *Saharan Jews and the Fate of French Algeria* (Chicago: University of Chicago Press, 2014) and the special issue on

"Decolonization and Religion in the French Empire" of *French Politics, Culture & Society* 33, no. 2 (2015), ed. Giuliana Chamedes and Elizabeth A. Foster.

34. Barbara Cooper, *Evangelical Christians in the Muslim Sahel* (Bloomington: Indiana University Press, 2006), 14–15. Other exceptions include Phyllis Martin, *Catholic Women of Congo-Brazzaville: Mothers and Sisters in Troubled Times* (Bloomington: Indiana University Press, 2009); Charlotte Walker-Said, *Faith, Power and Family: Christianity and Social Change in French Cameroon* (Oxford: James Currey, 2018).

35. Frederick Cooper, "Conflict and Connection: Rethinking African History," *American Historical Review* 99 (1994): 1516–1545.

36. Gary Wilder mentions Christian intellectual influences on Senghor but does not delve into them deeply. Gary Wilder, *The French Imperial Nation-State: Negritude and Colonial Humanism between the Two World Wars* (Chicago: University of Chicago Press, 2005), 244–245; Wilder, *Freedom Time*, 231–235.

37. Tony Judt, *Postwar: A History of Europe since 1945* (New York: Penguin, 2005), 228–229.

38. John W. O'Malley, *What Happened at Vatican II?* (Cambridge, MA: Harvard University Press, 2008), 17.

39. Pope Pius XII, *Evangelii praecones,* June 2, 1951, http://w2.vatican.va/content/pius-xii/en/encyclicals/documents/hf_p-xii_enc_02061951_evangelii-praecones.html.

40. Pius XII, "Christmas Radio Message," Dec. 24, 1955, in *Catholic Documents: Containing Recent Pronouncements and Decisions of His Holiness Pope Pius XII*, XX (1956), 45.

41. Pius XII, *Fidei donum,* April 21, 1957, http://w2.vatican.va/content/pius-xii/en/encyclicals/documents/hf_p-xii_enc_21041957_fidei-donum.html.

42. G. Wesley Johnson, *The Emergence of Black Politics in Senegal: The Struggle for Power in the Four Communes, 1900–1920* (Stanford, CA: Stanford University Press, 1971). The citizens of the Four Communes were also unique in that they were able to maintain their personal status under Islamic law, which had major consequences in the domains of marriage and inheritance. Otherwise, prior to 1946, there was an extremely narrow path to French citizenship for Africans, which involved renouncing their personal status in favor of the French Civil Code and demonstrating assimilation to French ways. Not many applied, and most applications were rejected. Cooper, *Citizenship between Empire and Nation,* 6.

43. Cooper, *Citizenship between Empire and Nation,* 20.

44. Ibid., 8, 88–89, 124–164.
45. J. Bouchard, "Les missions d'Afrique (1402–1789)," in *Histoire universelle des missions catholiques, Tome II: Les missions modernes,* ed. Simon Delacroix (Paris: Grund, 1957), 227–245.
46. The Spiritans (CSSp) and the White Fathers (MAfr) were congregations, whose members took extra vows and lived by particular rules, whereas the Society of African Missions (SMA) was a society of apostolic life whose members did not take supplementary vows, but nonetheless lived and worked communally according to constitutions drawn up in service of their stated mission of evangelizing Africa. General histories of these missionary groups have mostly been written by their members. On the Spiritans, see Henry J. Koren, *To the Ends of the Earth: A General History of the Congregation of the Holy Ghost* (Pittsburgh: Duquesne University Press, 1983). On the White Fathers, see Jean-Claude Ceillier, *History of the Missionaries of Africa (White Fathers): From the Beginning of Their Foundation by Msgr Lavigerie until his Death (1868–1892),* trans. Aylward Shorter (Nairobi: Paulines Publications Africa, 2011); Shorter, *Cross and Flag in Africa.* On the SMA, see John Murray Todd, *African Mission: A Historical Study of the Society of African Missions Whose Priests Have Worked on the Coast of West Africa and Inland, in Liberia, the Ivory Coast, Ghana, Togoland, Dahomey, and Nigeria, and in Egypt, since 1856* (London: Burns & Oates, 1962); Patrick Gantly, *Histoire de la Société des missions africaines (SMA): de la fondation par Mgr de Marion Brésillac (1856) à la mort du Père Planque (1907),* 2 vols. (Paris: Karthala, 2009–2010).
47. On access to nuns' archives, see Sarah A. Curtis, "Writing the Lives of Saints: Archives and the Ownership of History," *French Historical Studies* 40, no. 2 (2017): 241–266.
48. Nuns, both French and African, were more numerous than priests on the ground. See Geneviève Lecuir-Nemo, "Femmes et vocation missionnaire: permanence des congrégations féminines au Sénégal de 1819 à 1960: adaptation ou mutations? Impact et insertion" (doctoral thesis, Université de Paris I, 1994–1995); Sœur Marie Sidonie Oyembo Vandji, *Les Sœurs de l'Immaculée Conception de Castres: 150 ans de présence missionnaire au Gabon* (Libreville: CERGEP, 1999); Phyllis Martin, "Life and Death, Power and Vulnerability: Everyday Contradictions at the Loango Mission, 1883–1904," *Journal of African Cultural Studies* 15 (2002): 61–78; Chantal Paisant, ed., *La mission au féminine: témoignages de religieuses missionnaires au fil d'un siècle (XIXe–début XXe)* (Turnhout: Brepols, 2009); Sarah A. Curtis, *Civilizing Habits: Women Missionaries and the Revival of French Empire* (Oxford: Oxford University Press, 2010), 177–208; Elizabeth A. Foster, "'En mission il faut se faire à tout': les Sœurs de la Conception Immaculée de

Castres au Sénégal, 1880–1900," trans. François Proulx, *Histoire et missions chrétiennes* 16 (2010): 73–108.

49. Délégation apostolique de Dakar, *Statistiques annuelles des missions catholiques en Afrique française, année 1954–1955* (Dakar: Imprimerie Mission Catholique), ACSSp 2F 1.3 a5.

1. Postwar Winds of Change: Church and State in French Africa

1. Senghor served as a deputy from Senegal-Mauritania to the first and second National Constituent Assemblies in 1945–1946, and then as a deputy from Senegal to the National Assembly of the Fourth Republic from 1946 until 1958 and of the Fifth Republic from late 1958 until mid-1959. http://www2 .assemblee-nationale.fr/sycomore/fiche/(num_dept)/6385.

2. Though Senghor went on to a secular secondary school, the Spiritans watched his progress and felt his success there reflected well on them. P. Lalouse to TRP Le Hunsec, Dakar, Mar. 24, 1927; Mgr Grimault to TRP Le Hunsec, Dakar, July 13, 1927, ACSSp 3I 1.17 a3. On his education and thoughts of the priesthood, see Janet G. Vaillant, *Black, French, and African: A Life of Léopold Sédar Senghor* (Cambridge, MA: Harvard University Press, 1990), 21–33.

3. Joseph-Roger de Benoist, *Histoire de l'Église catholique au Sénégal: du milieu du XVe siècle à l'aube du troisième millénaire* (Dakar / Paris: Clairafrique / Karthala, 2008), 388–389. This was a significant position: Catlin appeared on an administrative list of AOF notables in 1943. Directeur général des Affaires politiques, administratives et sociales to M. le Directeur du Cabinet, May 5, 1943, ANS AOF O 692 (31).

4. Léopold Sédar Senghor to Mgr Le Hunsec, Paris, Jan. 21, 1947, ACSSp 3I 1.18 b10.

5. Senghor quoted in Jean Rous, *Léopold Sédar Senghor: la vie d'un président de l'Afrique nouvelle* (Paris: John Didier, 1967), 16.

6. Deputy Léopold Sédar Senghor to Mgr Le Hunsec, Paris, Mar. 20, 1947, ACSSp 3I 1.18 b10 (capitalization in the original). Senghor's personal experience as a prisoner of war between 1940 and 1942 reshaped his own thinking about politics, race, and culture. Gary Wilder, *Freedom Time: Negritude, Decolonization, and the Future of the World* (Durham, NC: Duke University Press, 2008), 52–59.

7. Senghor was so influential in the drafting of this constitution that the first version was known as "La constitution Senghor." Frederick Cooper, *Citizenship between Empire and Nation: Remaking France and French Africa* (Princeton, NJ: Princeton University Press, 2014), 69–81, 95–120.

8. Senghor to Le Hunsec, Mar. 20, 1947. The Spiritan community in Dakar prominently displayed portraits of Pétain, and, according to French authorities, clergy manifested support for him after 1942. P. Cournarie, "Rapport sur l'activité de Mgr Grimaud [sic], Evêque de Dakar, depuis 1940," Dakar, Sept. 9, 1944, ANOM AP 2286/14.

9. On Africans' experiences as prisoners of war, see Armelle Mabon, *Prisonniers de guerre "indigènes": visages oubliés de la France occupée* (Paris: La Découverte, 2010); Raffael Scheck, *French Colonial Soldiers in German Captivity during World War Two* (Cambridge: Cambridge University Press, 2014).

10. Dozens were killed and hundreds wounded. Differences over casualties and the degree to which the violent French response was premeditated have spawned a legal dispute between historians Armelle Mabon and Julien Fargettas. See Mabon, *Prisonniers de guerre "indigènes,"* 193–211, and Julien Fargettas, *Les tirailleurs sénégalais: les soldats noirs entre légendes et réalités, 1939–1945* (Paris: Tallandier, 2012), 283–294. See also Myron Echenberg, "Tragedy at Thiaroye: The Senegalese Soldiers' Uprising of 1944," in *African Labor History*, ed. Peter C. Gutkind, Robin Cohen, and Jean Copans (Beverly Hills: Sage, 1978), 109–128. For Senghor's reaction, see his poem "Thiaroye" in Léopold Sédar Senghor, *The Collected Poetry*, trans. Melvin Dixon (Charlottesville: University Press of Virginia, 1991), 68.

11. Rapport de l'enquête sur les missions religieuses, 81, ANOM AP 3349/5.

12. See list of attendees in ACSSp 3I 1.18 a4.

13. On Faye's unhappy tenure as prefect, see Elizabeth A. Foster, "A Mission in Transition: Race, Politics, and the Decolonization of the Catholic Church in Senegal," in *In God's Empire: French Missionaries and the Modern World*, ed. Owen White and J. P. Daughton (Oxford: Oxford University Press, 2012), 257–277.

14. "Réunion des Ordinaires de l'Afrique occidentale française à Bobo-Dioulasso du 26 novembre au 1 décembre 1945," 8–10, ACSSp 3I 1.18 a4.

15. Mgr Le Hunsec to Mgr Thévenoud, Paris, Jan. 12, 1946, ACSSp 3I 1.18 a4.

16. "Réunion des Ordinaires," 3–4.

17. "Irregularités et empêchements d'ordinations" to Très Saint Père, Bobo Dioulasso, Dec. 2, 1945, ACSSp 3I 1.18 a4.

18. Mgr Grimault to Mgr Le Hunsec, Dakar, Jan. 18, 1946, ACSSp 3I 1.18 a4.

19. Mgr Le Hunsec to Mgr Thévenoud (copy), undated but responds to Thévenoud's letter of Sept. 12, 1946; Mgr Le Hunsec to "Excellence" [Thévenoud], Paris, Jan. 12, 1946, ACSSp 3I 1.18 a4.

20. Mgr Grimault to Eminentissime Seigneur et Père, Dakar, Jan. 22, 1946, ACSSp 3I 1.18 a4.

21. Mgr Thévenoud to Mgr Le Hunsec, Ouagadougou, Sept. 12, 1946, ACSSp 3I 1.18 a4.
22. Publications from these meetings are in ACSSp 2F 1.3 a1.
23. Pope Benedict XV, *Maximum illud,* Nov. 30, 1919, in *Selected Papal Encyc-licals and Letters,* vol. 1, new and enlarged ed. (London: Catholic Truth Society, 1941), 12–13.
24. Pius XI, *Rerum ecclesiae,* Feb. 28, 1926, in *Selected Papal Encyclicals and Letters,* 17–18.
25. Ibid., 18.
26. Elizabeth A. Foster, *Faith in Empire: Religion, Politics, and Colonial Rule in French Senegal, 1880–1940* (Stanford, CA: Stanford University Press, 2013), 117–139.
27. Prouvost's status as a representative of the Pope caused great excitement in some African Catholic communities. See P. Prouvost, "Au hasard des rencontres en Afrique," *Echos missionnaires,* no. 34 (Nov.–Dec. 1947): 179. The Vatican had considered Prouvost for the new diplomatic post of papal delegate to all of French Africa in 1940 but tabled the idea during the war. In 1945–1946 Prouvost knew that the Vatican was considering making him its permanent representative to French Africa, and he wanted no part of it.
28. On his biography, see "Prouvost, Henri (1895–1983)," in Archives des Missions étrangères de Paris, http://archives.mepasie.org/fr/notices/notices-biographiques/prouvost, and Guy Pannier, "Visiteur apostolique ou inquisiteur? Le père Henri Prouvost des Missions étrangères de Paris envoyé par Rome en Afrique après la seconde guerre mondiale," *Histoire et missions chrétiennes,* no. 14 (June 2010): 166.
29. The current MEP archivist says there is no report there now. In 1986, Paule Brasseur reported that the MEP archivist had indicated "remarks of a po-litical nature" by Prouvost that were still confidential, but it is unclear if these amounted to a report. Paule Brasseur, "L'Église catholique et la dé-colonisation en Afrique noire," in *Les chemins de la décolonisation de l'empire colonial français: colloque organisé par l'I.H.T.P. les 4 et 5 octobre 1984,* ed. Charles Robert Ageron (Paris: CNRS, 1986), 57, n. 5.
30. A letter from Prouvost to Monsignor Faye intercepted by the French au-thorities sheds light on the Vatican's expectations for the mission. See AOF Commission DEA no. 2233 Lettre du R. P. Henry [*sic*] Prouvost à Mgr Jo-seph Faye interceptée 23 août 1945, ANS AOF O 692 (31). Ruth Ginio notes that wartime postal surveillance in French West Africa usually did not reproduce entire letters, except when they thought them particularly impor-tant, an indication that the state was watching the missions carefully.

Ruth Ginio, *French Colonialism Unmasked: The Vichy Years in French West Africa* (Lincoln: University of Nebraska Press, 2017), 110.

31. P. Prouvost to [P. Cuenot], Madagascar, Oct. 23, 1945, MEP DP 100.1.

32. P. Prouvost, "Au Congo sur les deux rives du fleuve," *Echos missionnaires,* no. 27 (Oct. 1946): 184.

33. Prouvost, "Au hasard des rencontres en Afrique," 181–182.

34. These tropes may also reflect Prouvost's opinion of his French audience, and Cuenot's editing, as they are less visible, though not absent, in Prouvost's letters. Prouvost was wary of allowing Cuenot to publish any material outside of the MEP's own magazine out of fear of offending the Vatican. P. Prouvost to P. Cuenot, Nkongsamba [Cameroon], Jan. 23, 1946, MEP DP 100.1.

35. Prouvost, "Au hasard des rencontres en Afrique," 179–181. Prouvost identifies this as a village served by the White Fathers, so it was either in Upper Volta, French Sudan, or the apostolic vicariate of Nzérékoré in Guinea.

36. P. Prouvost to P. Cuenot, Ambanja, Nov. 18, 1945, MEP DP 100.1.

37. P. Prouvost to P. Cuenot, Douala, Jan. 28, 1946, MEP DP 100.1.

38. P. Prouvost to P. Cuenot, Rome, Nov. 22, 1946; P. Prouvost to P. Cuenot, Sinematiali [Côte d'Ivoire], May 14, 1946, MEP DP 100.1.

39. Spiritan memoirists tell of an imperious and impatient Prouvost, who insulted the bishop, devalued their work, and did not comprehend travel difficulties in Lower Congo. Friteau resigned several weeks later. See Pannier, "Visiteur apostolique ou inquisiteur?" 180–183, and Jean Ernoult, "Les Spiritains au Congo: de 1865 à nos jours," *Mémoire spiritaine: études et documents* 3 (1995): 57. Ernoult discounts rumors that Friteau was a Pétainist.

40. P. Prouvost to P. Cuenot, Abidjan, May 29, 1946, MEP DP 100.1. See also Mgr Grimault to TRP, Thiès, Aug. 18, 1946; Mgr Grimault to TRP, Dakar, Sept. 3, 1946, ACSSp 3I 1.18 b9, and the administration's dossier on Grimault's obstinacy, ANOM AP 2286/14. According to Grimault, Prouvost advised him to resign for health reasons in France, but not immediately, so it would not seem like a consequence of the visit.

41. P. Prouvost to P. Cuenot, Maison Carrée [Algeria], Sept. 4, 1946, MEP DP 100.1.

42. For more, see "Encore des hécatombes!" *Echos missionnaires,* no. 24 (May 1946): 75. See also P. Cuenot to P. Prouvost, Paris, Mar. 6, 1946, MEP DP 100.1.

43. P. Cuenot to P. Prouvost, Paris, Dec. 28, 1945, MEP DP 100.1. Tenaud was not killed in 1945, but was murdered in Laos in the early 1960s.

44. P. Cuenot to P. Prouvost, Paris, Mar. 6, 1946.

45. P. Prouvost to P. Cuenot, Cotonou, Mar. 29, 1946, MEP DP 100.1.
46. P. Prouvost to P. Cuenot, Abidjan, May 29, 1946.
47. P. Prouvost to P. Cuenot, Brazzaville, Feb. 23, 1946, MEP DP 100.1.
48. P. Prouvost to P. Cuenot, Nkongsamba, Jan. 23, 1946.
49. P. Prouvost, "Le malaise actuel à Madagascar," *Echoes missionnaires* 5, no. 26 (Aug.–Sept. 1946): 154–155.
50. Ministre des Affaires étrangères to M. l'Ambassadeur de France à Rome Vatican, Paris, June 15, 1946, ADN 576PO/1/1217.
51. On Bidault's tenure as foreign minister, see Jean-Rémy Bezias, *Georges Bidault et la politique étrangère de la France (Europe, États-Unis, Proche-Orient) 1944–1948* (Paris: L'Harmattan, 2006).
52. Eric Jennings, *Free French Africa in World War II: The African Resistance* (New York: Cambridge University Press, 2015), 5, 49–50.
53. Directeur des Affaires politiques, Note sur les rapports de l'administration colonial avec l'Église catholique, confidential, Algiers, Aug. 9, 1944, ADN 576PO/1/1191.
54. The administration in French West Africa decreed on October 7, 1943 to subsidize religious schools based on students' examination results and the number of qualified teachers at each institution. This was nearly two years after Éboué outlined his policy of cooperation. M. Cauet, Inspecteur général des Colonies, Directeur général des Finances, Note pour le Directeur général des Affaires politiques, administratives et sociales, Dakar, May 19, 1947, ANS AOF O 717 (31).
55. See W. D. Halls, *Politics, Society and Christianity in Vichy France* (Oxford: Berg, 1995).
56. On Éboué's Freemasonry, see Jennings, *Free French Africa*, 25.
57. Brian Weinstein, *Éboué* (New York: Oxford, 1972), 120–121, 160.
58. Père Augustin Berger, "Le Gouverneur général Felix Éboué, la franc-maçonnerie et les missions catholiques," ACSSp 3J3.29 b2.
59. See Table I.1 in the Introduction.
60. Martin Shipway, "Thinking like an Empire: Governor Henri Laurentie and Postwar Plans for the Late Colonial French 'Empire-State,'" in *The French Colonial Mind, Volume 1: Mental Maps of Empire and Colonial Encounters,* ed. Martin Thomas (Lincoln: University of Nebraska Press, 2011), 225; Weinstein, *Éboué*, 229.
61. Weinstein, *Éboué*, 226.
62. Shipway, "Thinking like an Empire," 219, 225.
63. Jeremy Rich, "Marcel Lefebvre in Gabon: Revival, Missionaries, and the Colonial Roots of Catholic Traditionalism," in *Views from the Margins: Creating Identities in Modern France,* ed. Kevin J. Callahan and Sarah Curtis

(Lincoln: University of Nebraska Press, 2008), 68; Jennings, *Free French Africa,* 41–44; Weinstein, *Éboué,* 248.

64. Rich, "Marcel Lefebvre in Gabon," 68–69.
65. Ernoult, "Les Spiritains au Congo," 110–111.
66. Directeur des Affaires politiques, Note sur les rapports de l'administration colonial avec l'Église catholique. On Protestant complaints, see Barbara Cooper, *Evangelical Christians in the Muslim Sahel* (Bloomington: Indiana University Press, 2006), 248–249. On Brazzaville, see Institut Charles de Gaulle, *Brazzaville: Janvier–Février 1944: aux sources de la décolonisation* (Paris: Plon, 1988).
67. On Pleven being devout, see Geoffrey Adams, *Political Ecumenism: Protestants, Jews and Catholics in de Gaulle's Free France, 1940–1945* (Montreal: McGill-Queen's University Press, 2006), 220.
68. Henri Laurentie to Mgr Biéchy, Algiers, May 11, 1944, ACSSp 3J3.29 b3.
69. Participants included the governors of the constituent colonies, the five missionary bishops of Loango (Monsignor Friteau), Libreville (Monsignor Tardy), Bangui (Monsignor Marcel-Auguste-Marie Grandin, a Spiritan), Brazzaville (Monsignor Biéchy), and Berbérati (Monsignor Pierre Sintas, a Capucin), as well as Pastor Jean-Elie Bourelly, director of the French Protestant missions, the presidents of the Chambers of Commerce, senior administrators, and businessmen representing forestry and mining concerns. "Avant-propos," in "Politique indigène de l'Afrique equatoriale française" (Brazzaville: Imprimerie officielle de l'A.E.F.), I-II. ANS AOF O 171 (31).
70. Martin Shipway, *The Road to War: France and Vietnam, 1944–1947* (Providence: Berghahn Books, 1996), 24.
71. "Politique indigène de l'Afrique equatoriale française," 23.
72. Gouverneur Général Brévié to lieutenants gouverneurs and Administrateur de la Circonscription de Dakar, confidential, Dakar, Feb. 6, 1933, ANS, AOF 17G 73 (17).
73. "Politique indigène de l'Afrique equatoriale française," 23–24.
74. Henri Laurentie, Lecture at ENFOM, Feb. 19, 1945, ANF 72AJ / 535.
75. "Politique indigène de l'Afrique equatoriale française," 26.
76. Ministre des Colonies to Gouverneur général de l'AOF, Paris, Aug. 28, 1936, ANS AOF O 717 (31).
77. Foster, *Faith in Empire,* 141–167.
78. Untitled report, deuxième partie: "Valeur juridique et politique de la convention de Saint-Germain-en-Laye," 9–10, ANOM AP 3349 / 4.
79. On postwar French policy toward African Muslims, see Gregory Mann and Baz Lecocq, "Between Empire, *Umma,* and the Muslim Third World: The French Union and African Pilgrims to Mecca, 1946–1958," *Comparative Studies of South Asia, Africa and the Middle East* 27 (2007): 367–383.

80. Laurentie shared a view common among French Catholic missionaries that African Islam was unsophisticated. In contrast to Christianity, he told his ENFOM students, "which permits adherents to attain a higher responsibility and does not restrain its catechumens once they are on its path," Islam "tends to impede the very progress that it provokes and to the extent it stimulates progress, it is not aimed at the spiritual development of the *indigène*." Henri Laurentie, Lecture at ENFOM, Feb. 19, 1945, ANF 72AJ / 535.

81. Ministre des Affaires étrangères to M. l'Ambassadeur de France à Rome Vatican, Paris, June 15, 1946.

82. Mgr P. Biéchy to M. le Ministre des Colonies, Paris, Aug. 17, 1945, ADN 576PO/1/1217.

83. See Étienne de Burin de Roziers to Gouverneur Laurentie, Paris, Nov. 6, 1945; Directeur des Affaires politiques Laurentie to M. Burin des Rosiers [sic], Cabinet du Général de Gaulle, Nov. 27, 1945; Gouverneur du Tchad, "Note sur l'envoi de missions catholiques au Tchad," Fort-Lamy, Oct. 24, 1945, ANOM AP 2190 / 5. On the history of French Catholic missions in Chad in this period see Jean Luc Enyegue, "The Creation of the Jesuit Vice-Province of West Africa and the Challenges of Africanization, 1946–1978" (PhD diss., Boston University, 2018), 18–103.

84. Ministre des Affaires étrangères to M. l'Ambassadeur de France à Rome Vatican, Paris, June 15, 1946. The French Catholic intellectual Emmanuel Mounier expressed similar fears during a two-month visit to the continent in the spring of 1947, described in Chapter 2. In Liberia he observed, "The enormous port of Monrovia is not built for its small republic, nor are the roads that American genius is throwing down in all directions. The little republic that Europeans still consider to be a 'blank' in the array of known colonies, rather than a reality worthy of interest, could tomorrow become, through American will, the jumping off point for the invasion of Africa of manufactured products that impoverished Europe can no longer supply . . ." Emmanuel Mounier, "La route noire (fin)," *Esprit*, N.S. no. 137 (Sept. 1947): 332–333. On Mounier's anti-Americanism, see Seth D. Armus, *French Anti-Americanism 1930–1948* (Lanham, MD: Lexington Books, 2007), 57–90.

85. Ministre des Affaires étrangères to M. l'Ambassadeur de France à Rome Vatican, Paris, June 15, 1946.

86. Ministre des Affaires étrangères to M. L'Ambassadeur de la France à Washington, Sept. 27, 1947, ANOM AP 2286 / 9. The articles, written by Louis Aujoulat, are in this file.

87. Gouverneur général p. i. to M. le Commissaire aux Colonies, Secret, Dakar, July 26, 1944, ANOM AP 2192 / 10.

88. On Laurentie's role, see Brasseur, "L'Église catholique," 57.

89. Ministre des Colonies to MM les Gouverneurs généraux et Gouverneurs des colonies, Secret, Paris, Nov. 7, 1946, ANOM AP 3349 / 4.

90. Rapport de l'enquête sur les missions religieuses, 83. A forthcoming work by Matthew Sutton will explore how, during World War II, the Office of Strategic Services (a predecessor of the Central Intelligence Agency) in the United States recruited American missionaries around the world as intelligence agents and he has evidence that this took place in French West Africa in the early years of the war. I thank him for sharing his unpublished research with me. On French responses to United Nations public health initiatives in Africa, see Jessica Pearson-Patel, "Promoting Health, Protecting Empire: Inter-Colonial Medical Cooperation in Postwar Africa," *Monde(s)*, no. 7 (2015): 213–230.

91. Rapport de l'enquête sur les missions religieuses, 58.

92. P. Prouvost to P. Cuenot, Cotonou, Mar. 29, 1946.

93. Marcel J. Brun to M. Dennery, Direction d'Amérique, Ministère des Affaires étrangères, July 25, 1946, ANOM AP 2190 / 1. On Dennery, an early Gaullist, see Louis Joxe, "Étienne Dennery," *Politique étrangère* 45, no. 1 (1980): 7–8.

94. On Brun, see Cooper, *Evangelical Christians*, 248–249, and "France," *The Living Church*, Feb. 28, 1943, 8.

95. *Convention Revising the General Act of Berlin, February 26, 1885, and the General Act and Declaration of Brussels, July 2, 1890: Signed at Saint-Germain-en-Laye, September 10, 1919*, Treaty Series 1919, No. 18, Cmd. 477 (London: His Majesty's Stationery Office, 1919), 97–112.

96. A 1922 decree regulating private education and religious observance in French West Africa tried to stave off this perceived threat. Decree, Paris, Feb. 4, 1922; Decree, Dakar, Mar. 26, 1922, ANS AOF O 93 (31). These regulations were difficult for many French Catholic missions to fulfill, but colonial officials often deliberately ignored their violations. See report by Gouverneur général to Ministre des Colonies, Dakar, [Feb?] 18, 1927, ANS AOF O 67 (31); Gouverneur du Sénégal to Gouverneur général, Saint-Louis, Sept. [16?], 1922; Gouverneur général p. i. to Gouverneur du Sénégal, Oct. 31, 1933, ANS AOF O 321 (31).

97. Undated handwritten note, ANOM AP 3349 / 4.

98. Rapport de l'enquête sur les missions religieuses, 75.

99. Ibid., 55–57.

100. Undated, handwritten "Conclusion générale (à écrire)," ANOM AP 3349 / 4.

101. In a 1948 response to objections to subsidies for missionaries in New Caledonia by the secretary general of the militantly secular French League for

the Defense of the Rights of Man and Citizen, Minister of Overseas France Paul Coste-Floret pointed out that such subsidies were by then common policy across France's Overseas Territories. Coste-Floret, who became a leader of the MRP, was yet another example of an influential Catholic in the postwar French colonial milieu. Ministre Coste-Floret to Monsieur le Secretaire général de la Ligue française pour la défense des droits de l'homme et du citoyen, June 10, 1948, ANOM AP 3349 / 4.

102. P. Prouvost to P. Cuenot, Brazzaville, Feb. 23, 1946.

103. Frederick Cooper, *Decolonization and African Society: The Labor Question in French and British Africa* (Cambridge: Cambridge University Press, 1996), 404.

104. Circulaire à MM les Hauts Commissaires de la République et à MM les Gouverneurs chefs de territoire, May 27, 1948, ANOM AP 3349 / 1. On state education of new African citizens after the war, see Harry Gamble, *Contesting French West Africa: Battles over Schools and the Colonial Order, 1900–1950* (Lincoln: University of Nebraska Press, 2017), 211–241.

105. Cooper, *Decolonization*, 176.

106. Demandes de subventions présentées par des établissements d'enseignement privé, Rapport présentée au comité directeur du FIDES, ANOM 1FIDES 15 / 93.

107. On Aujoulat, see Étienne Thévenin, "Louis-Paul Aujoulat (1910–1973): un médecin chrétien au service de l'Afrique," in *Églises et santé dans le tiers monde*, ed. Jean Pirotte and Henri Derroitte (Leiden: Brill, 1991), 57–76.

108. AOF Fiche de présentation no. 9, Préfecture apostolique de Ziguinchor, ANOM 1FIDES 15 / 93.

109. AOF Fiche de présentation no. 10, Vicariat apostolique de Ouagadougou, ANOM 1FIDES 15 / 93.

110. To compare, see Demandes de subventions présentées par des établissements d'enseignement privé, Rapport présentée au comité directeur du FIDES, ANOM 1FIDES 15 / 93, and Rapport au comité directeur du FIDES, Objet: Section générale (2ième partie) Chapitres 1071 et 1072, 3–5, ANOM 1FIDES 43 / 321.

111. Rapport au comité directeur du FIDES, 1. Protestants were more present in the domain of public health, which was tiny compared to education, especially in French Equatorial Africa.

112. Rapport au comité directeur du FIDES, 3–5.

113. "Chapitre 1072—Enseignement," ANOM 1FIDES 43 / 321.

114. Rapport au comité directeur du FIDES, 3–5. In Cameroon, 28 out of 40 requests received 199,800,000 francs of support.

115. "Chapitre 1072—Enseignement," ANOM 1FIDES 43 / 321.

116. Direction des Affaires politiques, Note pour le Directeur du Personnel, Diffusion restreinte, ANOM AP 3349 / 7.

117. Pierre Jean Marie Delteil, Directeur-Adjoint des Affaires politiques, Note pour Monsieur le Directeur du Personnel, Dec. 24, 1952, ANOM AP 3349 / 7. On Delteil's career, see Richard Bradshaw and Juan Fandos-Rius, *Historical Dictionary of the Central African Republic,* new ed. (London: Rowman & Littlefield, 2016), 213.

118. Delteil, Note pour M. le Directeur du Personnel.

119. État numérique des missionnaires français (Pères et Frères) dans les missions confiées aux Pères Blancs, Archiviste Lemière, July 19, 1951; Père M. Taris to M. le Comte Vladimir d'Ormesson, Rome, July 27, 1951, ADN 576PO/1/1254.

120. See chart in *Aide aux Missions françaises d'Afrique,* no. 12 (1965): inside front cover.

121. D'Ormesson telegram to Diplomatie Paris, Rome, Dec. 13, 1951, ADN 576PO/1/1254.

122. F. Mitterrand, Ministre de la France d'Outre-Mer to M. le Ministre des Affaires étrangères, confidentiel, Paris, Dec. 2, 1950, ADN 576PO/1/1254.

123. Mgr Lefebvre to Ministre de la France d'Outre-Mer, Dakar, May 11, 1951, ADN 576PO/1/1254.

124. F. Mitterrand to M. le Ministre des Affaires étrangères, confidential, Paris, Dec. 2, 1950. On the 1921 agreement, see Harry W. Paul, *The Second Ralliement: The Rapprochement between Church and State in France in the Twentieth Century* (Washington, DC: Catholic University of America Press, 1967), 55.

125. M. Wladimir d'Ormesson Ambassadeur de France près le Saint-Siège to M. Robert Schuman Ministre des Affaires étrangères, Rome, June 22, 1951, ADN 576PO/1/1254.

126. Annexe à la dépêche de l'Ambassade de France près le Saint-Siège en date du 22 juin 1951, ADN 576PO/1/1254.

127. D'Ormesson telegram, Rome, July 9, 1951, ADN 576PO/1/1254.

128. Coded Telegram 280 Diplomatie to Ambassadeur, Paris, July 21, 1951, ADN 576PO/1/1254.

129. M. Christian de Margerie to M. Robert Schuman Ministre des Affaires étrangères, Rome, Aug. 24, 1951, ADN 576PO/1/1254.

130. De Benoist, *Histoire de l'Église catholique,* 366, 387–388.

131. Cited in ibid., 368.

132. When he left Dakar in 1962, Lefebvre was hailed as a "great builder of churches, a creator of parishes, missions, posts, and even dioceses, which grew from 44 to 65 during his time as Apostolic delegate in French Africa."

In Dakar itself, the church grew from three churches in 1947 to thirteen churches serving nine parishes in 1962. *Horizons africains,* no. 137 (Mar. 1962): 8–9, 16. In 1960, Spiritan inspector Father Neyrand noted Lefebvre's "amazing material accomplishments" in the Archdiocese of Dakar. H. Neyrand, "Rapport sur l'archidiocèse de Dakar (1960)," May 1960, ACSSp 3I 1.19 a8.

133. De Benoist, *Histoire de l'Église catholique,* 389.

134. There was significant student violence in former French territories, including Senegal and Tunisia, alongside 1968 demonstrations in Paris. Burleigh Hendrickson, "Imperial Fragments and Transnational Activism: 1968(s) in Tunisia, France and Senegal" (PhD diss., Northeastern University, 2013).

135. Léopold Sédar Senghor to Mgr Giovanni Mariani, June 26, 1968; M. René Brouillet, Ambassadeur de France près le Saint-Siège to M. Michel Debré, Ministre des Affaires étrangères, confidential, Rome, Aug. 21, 1968, ADN 184PO/1/661.

2. A Truly Universal Church: Alioune Diop and Catholic Negritude

1. Damas, in particular, is a popular subject of late. Recent titles include Kathleen Gyssels, *Black-Label, ou, les déboires de Léon-Gontran Damas* (Caen: Passages, 2016); Hanétha Vété-Congolo, ed., *Léon-Gontran Damas: une négritude entière* (Paris: l'Harmattan, 2015); Carrie Noland, *Voices of Negritude in Modernist Print: Aesthetic Subjectivity, Diaspora and the Lyric Rhyme* (New York: Columbia University Press, 2015); Reiland Rabaka, *The Negritude Movement: W. E. B. Du Bois, Léon Damas, Aimé Césaire, Léopold Senghor, Frantz Fanon, and the Evolution of an Insurgent Idea* (Lanham, MD: Lexington Books, 2015); Gary Wilder, *Freedom Time: Negritude, Decolonization, and the Future of the World* (Durham, NC: Duke University Press, 2015); F. Bart Miller, *Rethinking Négritude through Léon-Gontran Damas* (Amsterdam: Rodopi, 2014).

2. There is barely any scholarship on Diop, and he is often merely mentioned in passing in studies of Senghor, Césaire, Damas, and others. At present there are only two book-length studies available: Frédéric Grah Mel, *Alioune Diop: le bâtisseur inconnu du monde noir* (Adibjan: Presses universitaires de Côte d'Ivoire, 1995), and Philippe Verdin, *Alioune Diop, le Socrate noir* (Paris: Lethielleux, 2010). See also tributes offered on the thirtieth anniversary of *Présence africaine* in *Hommage à Alioune*

Diop (Rome: Éditions des amis italiens de Présence africaine, 1977) and in the special issue of *Présence africaine* in honor of the hundredth anniversary of his birth: *Présence africaine,* no. 181–182 (2010). See also Geoffrey Coats, "From Whence We Come: Alioune Diop and Saint-Louis, Senegal," *Research in African Literatures* 28, no. 4 (1997): 206–219; Christopher L. Miller, "Alioune Diop and the Unfinished Temple of Knowledge," in *The Surreptitious Speech: Présence Africaine and the Politics of Otherness 1947–1987,* ed. V. Y. Mudimbe (Chicago: University of Chicago Press, 1992), 427–434.

3. Grah Mel, *Alioune Diop.*

4. Sarah Frioux-Salgas, "Entretien avec le poète, romancier et essayiste Daniel Maximin," *Gradhiva* 10 (2009): 158.

5. Condetto Nenekhaly Camara, "Conscience nationale et poésie négro-africaine d'expression française," in *Les étudiants africains et la literature négro-africaine d'expression française,* ed. Amady Aly Dieng (Oxford: African Books Collective, 2009), 12. Also known as Néné Khaly, Khaly Nene, Condetto Nénékhaly-Camara, and Ibrahima Basil Nénékhaly-Condetto Camara (1930–1972), he was a Guinean playwright, poet, ethnographer, archaeologist, and minister in Sékou Touré's government who studied in Dahomey, Paris, and Dakar in the 1950s. See "Nenekhaly-Camara, Condetto" and "Pastoria" in *Historical Dictionary of Guinea,* by Thomas O'Toole and Janice Baker, 4th ed. (Lanham, MD: Scarecrow Press, 2005), 150, 156, and Djamilah Nénékhaly, "Qui est Ibrahima Basil Nénékhaly-Condetto Camara, poète et dramaturge?" Guinée Culture, July 21, 2014, http://guineeculture.org/Qui-est-Ibrahima-Basil-Nenekhaly.html.

6. French police concluded in 1955 that the political orientation of *Présence africaine* was getting closer to that of Communist publications. APPP 77W4047 / 413099. In 1969, Marxist historian and activist Jean Suret-Canale reflected that at the outset *"Présence africaine*'s stated intention to be open to everyone worried us more than reassured us." Marxists were concerned that this "bourgeois initiative" with famous names on the masthead might be a "colonial project of mystification." Yet he ultimately lauded the magazine's insistence on the value of African culture. J. Suret-Canale quoted in "Temoignages" in *Mélanges: réflexions d'hommes de culture* (Paris: Présence africaine, 1969), 27–28.

7. For Diop's letter applying to join the SEC, see "Lettre de M. Alioune Diop à M. Campagnolo," Paris, June 20, 1952, *Comprendre,* no. 9 (Sept. 1953): 69.

8. *Hommage à Alioune Diop.*

9. Verdin, *Alioune Diop,* 117. Georges Balandier observed that in this role Diop "was not at all what the [colonial regime] was certainly hoping he would

be—a black official [installed merely] to keep up appearances." Georges Balandier, *Conjugaisons* (Paris: Fayard, 1997), 234. Barthes was a "liberal" in colonial administrative circles—he argued for the suppression of the *indigènat* and forced labor, though he vehemently opposed the 1947 African railway strike. See Tony Chafer, *The End of Empire in French West Africa: France's Successful Decolonization?* (Oxford: Berg, 2002), 67, and Frederick Cooper, *Citizenship between Empire and Nation: Remaking France and French Africa* (Princeton, NJ: Princeton University Press, 2014), 95, 133–134, 179.

10. Verdin, *Alioune Diop,* 127. On the SFIO in Senegal and its relationship to Senegalese political parties, see Ruth Schachter Morgenthau, *Political Parties in French-Speaking West Africa* (Oxford: Oxford University Press, 1964), 136–165.

11. Balandier uses elegance, *Civilisés, dit-on* (Paris: Presses universitaires de France, 2003), 74; Balandier, *Conjugaisons,* 234.

12. Balandier, *Civilisés, dit-on,* 46.

13. Balandier, *Conjugaisons,* 235–236.

14. Alioune Diop to R. Père Supérieur des Pères du Saint-Esprit, Paris, July 16, 1947; Alioune Diop to TRP, Paris, Aug. 4, 1947; Alioune Diop to TRP, Paris, Aug. 5, 1947, ACSSp 3I 1.18 b10.

15. On Catholic culture in colonial Saint-Louis, see Elizabeth A. Foster, *Faith in Empire: Religion, Politics, and Colonial Rule in French Senegal, 1880–1940* (Stanford, CA: Stanford University Press, 2013), 21–42; Hilary Jones, *The Métis of Senegal: Urban Life and Politics in French West Africa* (Bloomington: University of Indiana Press, 2013).

16. Verdin, *Alioune Diop,* 40.

17. Valentin Mathurin was a veteran of World War I who returned to France in the 1920s and became a clerk and an activist. He was an early leader of the Ligue de défense de la race nègre and wrote for its publication *Race nègre.* He was also an officer of Senegal-Amicale. He participated in the demonstrations of Feb. 6, 1934. J. S. Spiegler, "Aspects of Nationalist Thought among French-Speaking West Africans 1921–1939" (PhD diss., Nuffield College, Oxford University, 1968), 162, 163, 206–209, 289.

18. Coats, "From Whence We Come," 207.

19. Alioune Diop, "History of a Black Schoolboy (by Himself)," originally published 1931, trans. Geoffrey Coats, *Research in African Literatures* 28, no. 4 (1997): 217.

20. Coats, "From Whence We Come," 207, 209.

21. Verdin, *Alioune Diop,* 42–7.

22. Janet G. Vaillant, *Black, French, and African: A Life of Léopold Sédar Senghor* (Cambridge, MA: Harvard University Press, 1990), 213. On Eyoum Moudio,

see Iwiyé Kala-Lobé, "Lorsque l'enfant paraît," in *Mélanges*, 74–75. Iwiyé Kala-Lobé, also known as Ernest Iwiyé Kala-Lobé, was Diop's brother-in-law, worked at *Présence africaine*, and was secretary of the SAC in the 1960s.

23. Grah Mel, *Alioune Diop*, 52; Verdin, *Alioune Diop*, 61.

24. John Hellman, *The Communitarian Third Way: Alexandre Marc's Ordre Nouveau, 1930–2000* (Montreal: McGill-Queen's University Press, 2002), 114.

25. "Le R. P. Maydieu est mort," *Présence africaine* N.S. 1/2 (Apr.–June 1955): 3. Iwiyé Kala-Lobé later remarked: "I have rarely met anyone as human, as tolerant, as seductive, as eclectic as Father Maydieu!" Kala-Lobé, "Lorsque l'enfant paraît," 77.

26. Alioune Diop, "Niam n'goura ou les raisons d'être de *Présence africaine*," *Présence africaine* 1 (Nov.–Dec. 1947): 8.

27. Grah Mel, *Alioune Diop*, 54–55.

28. Jacques Louis Hymans, *Léopold Sédar Senghor: An Intellectual Biography* (Edinburgh: Edinburgh University Press, 1971), 114.

29. Frioux-Salgas, "Entretien avec le poète," 156.

30. Alioune Diop to Marguerite Marteau, Oct. 31, 1943, quoted in Verdin, *Alioune Diop*, 100.

31. Grah Mel, *Alioune Diop*, 54–5; Verdin, *Alioune Diop*, 92.

32. Verdin, *Alioune Diop*, 95.

33. Alioune Diop to Marguerite Marteau, Oct. 31, 1943, in Verdin, *Alioune Diop*, 98.

34. Ibid., 100.

35. Ibid., 98–100.

36. On the lack of paper, see Kala-Lobé, "Lorsque l'enfant paraît," 74.

37. Diop, "Niam n'goura," 7.

38. Ibid., 13.

39. Alioune Diop, "L'Europe vue par un africain," *Comprendre* 9 (Sept. 1953): 90.

40. Alioune Diop, "On ne fabrique pas un peuple," *Présence africaine* 14 (1953): 14.

41. Verdin, *Alioune Diop*, 122. Mounier once wrote, "*Esprit* was myself and my personal history." Much the same could be said for Diop and *Présence africaine*. Mounier quoted in R. William Rauch, *Politics and Belief in Contemporary France: Emmanuel Mounier and Christian Democracy, 1932–1950* (The Hague: Martinus Nijhoff, 1972), 58.

42. Vaillant, *Black, French, and African*, 126, 213.

43. Grah Mel, *Alioune Diop*, 59.

44. On the lecture, see Hymans, *Léopold Sédar Senghor*, 114.

45. Samuel Moyn, "Personalism, Community, and the Origins of Human Rights," in *Human Rights in the Twentieth Century*, ed. Stefan-Ludwig

Hoffmann (Cambridge: Cambridge University Press, 2011), 89. Mounier's early death undoubtedly contributed to the fact that he is less well known among anglophones than his fellow personalist Jacques Maritain. James Chappel has pointed out that the language of personalism was more widespread in the interwar church than Moyn suggests. The frequent use of the language of personalism among French Catholic missionaries confirms this. James Chappel, "All Churches Have Heretics: On Catholicism, Human Rights, and the Advantages of History for Life," The Immanent Frame, June 5, 2015, https://tif.ssrc.org/2015/06/05/all-churches-have-heretics-on -catholicism-human-rights-and-the-advantages-of-history-for-life.

46. Emmanuel Mounier, *Le personnalisme,* in *Œuvres, Tome III: 1944–1950* (Paris: Seuil, 1962), 429–430.

47. Rauch, *Politics and Belief,* 83. For Mounier's use of the term, see the special issue of *Esprit* on "Confrontation: rupture entre l'ordre chrétien et le désordre établi," *Esprit* 1, no. 6 (Mar. 1, 1933). Mounier maintained that there could be atheistic or other personalisms, though his was Christian. Mounier, *Le personnalisme,* 430.

48. Moyn, "Personalism, Community," 88.

49. Philippe Pétain, "L'éducation nationale," *Revue des deux mondes,* Aug. 15, 1940, quoted in John Hellman, *Emmanuel Mounier and the New Catholic Left 1930–1950* (Toronto: University of Toronto Press, 1981), 167–168.

50. Father Maydieu also became a personalist in the interwar period, and, like Mounier, taught for a time at Vichy's elite training school at Uriage before opposing the regime. Hellman, *Mounier and the New Catholic Left,* 164–183. In 1944, Maydieu was arrested, tortured, and imprisoned for resistance activities. Nancy Jachec, *Europe's Intellectuals and the Cold War: The European Society of Culture, Post-War Politics and International Relations* (London: I. B. Tauris, 2015), 248 n. 46. For more on Maydieu, see David Gaillardon, ed., *Jean-Augustin Maydieu (1900–1955): Actes des colloques Bordeaux, 23–25 novembre 1995, Paris, 15 janvier 1996* (Paris: Cerf, 1998).

51. Moyn, "Personalism, Community," 87–88; Hellman, *Mounier and the New Catholic Left,* 4–5, 8–9. Both Hellman and Moyn note that many people have incorrectly characterized Mounier as a consistent man of the left.

52. Moyn and Marco Duranti have shown that the European recognition of human rights was not a triumph of secular liberalism, but rather had Christian roots. Moyn, "Personalism, Community," 85–86. See also Samuel Moyn, *Christian Human Rights* (Philadelphia: University of Pennsylvania Press, 2015), and Marco Duranti, *The Conservative Human Rights Revolution: European Identity, Transnational Politics, and the Origins of the European Convention* (New York: Oxford University Press, 2017).

53. On Vietnam, see Phi Vân Nguyen, "The Vietnamization of Personalism: The Role of Missionaries in the Spread of Personalism in Vietnam, 1930–1961," *French Colonial History* 17 (2017): 103–134. Ngo Dinh Diem, the leader of South Vietnam between 1954 and 1963, utilized a somewhat idiosyncratic personalism, which he attributed directly to Mounier, as the guiding philosophy of his domestic and foreign policy. Edward Miller, "The Diplomacy of Personalism: Civilization, Culture, and the Cold War in the Foreign Policy of Ngo Dinh Diem," in *Connecting Histories: Decolonization and the Cold War in Southeast Asia, 1945–1962,* ed. Christopher E. Goscha and Christian F. Ostermann (Washington, DC: Woodrow Wilson Center Press, 2009), 376–402. In the case of Québec, Mounier's personalism influenced Gaston Miron, the emblematic poet of the Quiet Revolution. David Palmieri, "From Personalism to Decolonization: Gaston Miron between French Canada and Québec," *Québec Studies* 60 (2015): 125–152.

54. Exceptions include Nadia Yala Kisukidi, "L'influence vivante du personnalisme de Mounier sur la philosophie esthétique et la poésie de Léopold Sédar Senghor," *COnTEXTES* 12 (2012), https://journals.openedition.org/contextes/5592; Michael Kelly, "Emmanuel Mounier and the Awakening of Black Africa," *French Cultural Studies* 17, no. 2 (2006): 207–222, but Kelly deals only with Mounier's travel in and perceptions of Africa, not his impact on African Catholic intellectuals and clergy.

55. Vaillant, *Black, French, and African,* 177, 261; Kisukidi, "L'influence vivante," 1. Though the French Catholic thinkers Jacques Maritain and Pierre Teilhard de Chardin were also important for Senghor, they belonged to an older generation, born about twenty-five years before. He and Mounier were just a year apart in age.

56. Verdin, *Alioune Diop,* 123. On government sponsorship, see Kelly, "Emmanuel Mounier," 211.

57. He wrote, "In that little capital, I'm not sure I could have found twenty whites of the quality of the twenty Africans with whom I spent the afternoon of Easter." Mounier, "Lettre à un ami africain," *Présence africaine* 1 (Nov.–Dec. 1947): 37.

58. Camus was editor in chief of *Combat* between August 1944 and June 1947. On his tenure see Albert Camus, *Camus at Combat: Writing 1944–1947,* ed. Jacqueline Lévi-Valensi, trans. Arthur Goldhammer (Princeton, NJ: Princeton University Press, 2006). For citations of the *Combat* articles, see Emmanuel Mounier, *Œuvres, Tome IV: Recueils posthumes, correspondance* (Paris: Seuil, 1963), 866–867.

59. Emmanuel Mounier, *L'éveil de l'Afrique noire* (Paris: Seuil, 1948).

60. Mounier, "Lettre à un ami africain," 37.
61. Emmanuel Mounier, "La route noire," *Esprit* N.S. no. 135 (July 1947): 69.
62. Ibid., 68–70, and Emmanuel Mounier, "La route noire (fin)," *Esprit* N.S. no. 137 (Sept. 1947): 323.
63. Mounier, "La route noire (fin)," 336–340.
64. On Southeast Asia, see Andrée Viollis, "Quelques notes sur l'Indochine," *Esprit* 2, no. 3 (Dec. 1, 1933): 401–448, and pieces in a special issue on colonization, *Esprit* 3, no. 39 (Dec. 1, 1935). On Tunisia, see Emmanuel Mounier, "Chronique interraciale: la Tunisie a la fièvre? Oui, d'un mal blanc," *Esprit* 5, no. 56 (May 1937): 343–344.
65. On *colons* in Africa, see Emmanuel Mounier, "L'Afrique devient-elle majeure?" in *Œuvres, Tome III: 1944–1950*, 308, and Mounier, "La route noire (fin)," 309, 326, 328.
66. Mounier, "La route noire (fin)," 340. On this same theme in Togo, see ibid., 328.
67. Mounier, "La route noire," 67, 77.
68. On colonial Dakar, see Liora Bigon, *French Colonial Dakar: The Morphogenesis of an African Regional Capital* (Manchester: Manchester University Press, 2016).
69. He referred to the Medina as Médina-la-désolée. Mounier, "La route noire," 72–74.
70. Ibid., 71.
71. Ibid., 82; Mounier, "La route noire (fin)," 314, 331, 334.
72. Mounier, "La route noire," 76.
73. Mounier, "L'Afrique devient-elle majeure?" 309.
74. Mounier, "La route noire (fin)," 316.
75. Mounier, "L'Afrique devient-elle majeure?" 309. See also Mounier, "La route noire (fin)," 315. Note that he quotes one of Diop's friends (maybe Diop himself) on African aversion to work in Mounier, "La route noire," 69.
76. Mounier, "L'Afrique devient-elle majeure?" 308.
77. See, for example, Mounier, "La route noire," 85; Mounier, "L'Afrique devient-elle majeure?" 310.
78. Mounier, "Lettre à un ami africain," 37.
79. Ibid., 38, 42–43.
80. Kala-Lobé, "Lorsque l'enfant paraît," 71, 74. Thomas Diop became Senegal's permanent delegate to UNESCO and a member of the executive committee of the SAC. See "Nouvelles de la Société africaine de culture," *Présence africaine* N.S. 41 (2e trimestre, 1962): 190. Diop is a common surname in Senegal—I have no indication that he was related to Alioune Diop.

81. See frontispiece and "Sommaire" in *Présence africaine* 1 (Nov.–Dec. 1947) and Salah D. Hassan, "The Cultural Politics of the Early *Présence Africaine* 1947–1955," *Research in African Literatures* 30, no. 2 (1999): 206–207.

82. The lack of tribute to Mounier may also be because he passed away in March 1950, just as issue 8/9, directed not by Diop but by Theodore Monod, was published, and the next issue did not come out until the following year. See "Le R. P. Maydieu est mort!"

83. Raymond-Marie Tchidimbo, *L'homme noir dans l'Église* (Paris: Présence africaine, 1963), 13.

84. Raymond Tchidimbo, "L'étudiant africain face à la culture latine," *Présence Africaine* 14 (1953): 55–64.

85. Tchidimbo, *L'homme noir*, 45, 70. For more on Tchidimbo, see the Introduction and Chapter 5. Mounier remains influential among some African clergy. See, for example, Abbé Roger Rubuguzo Mpongo, *Repenser les relations Europe-Afrique avec Marc Saignier et Emmanuel Mounier: au delà des polémiques coloniales* (Paris: L'Harmattan, 2012).

86. Joseph Ki-Zerbo, "Génération sacrifiée?" *Tam-Tam*, Jan. 1955, 7–9. For more on Ki-Zerbo and *Tam-Tam*, see Chapter 4.

87. Verdin, *Alioune Diop*, 123.

88. See the frontmatter of *Présence africaine* N.S. 1/2 (Apr.–Jul. 1955), but note that it also contained "Le R. P. Maydieu est mort!" On the shift at *Présence africaine*, see also Jacques Howlett, "Esquisse d'une histoire de la politique culturelle de *Présence africaine*," in *Mélanges*, 43, and Hassan, "The Cultural Politics," 204.

89. Howlett, "Esquisse d'une histoire," 43.

90. Report, July 1956, APPP 77W4047/413099. In 1958, the police raided the Présence africaine publishing house looking, unsuccessfully, for copies of a lengthy pamphlet sponsored by the Federation of Black African Students in France (FEANF) denouncing French use of torture in Algeria: Khar N'Dofene Diouf et al., *Le sang de Bandoëng* (Paris: Présence africaine, 1958). "Perquisitions opérées," Oct. 9, 1958, APPP 77W4047/413099.

91. On Campagnolo, see Nancy Jachec, *Europe's Intellectuals*.

92. Présence africaine, "Peut-on dresser le Vatican contre les peuples de couleur?" *Présence africaine* N.S. 16 (Oct.–Nov. 1957): 4.

93. Lists of members are available in the back pages of *Comprendre*.

94. "Lettre de M. Alioune Diop à M. Campagnolo," 69. See also Campagnolo's preface to the letters at the top of the page.

95. Nancy Jachec, *Europe's Intellectuals*, 72.

96. Umberto Campagnolo, "Responsabilités européennes," *Comprendre*, no. 9 (Sept. 1953): 78–83. Campagnolo also rehashed these ideas in his

talk "Europe in the world and the politics of culture" at the general meeting of the SEC that same year.

97. The Christian Berber Algerian writer Jean Amrouche agreed with Diop, as did Maydieu, Jacques Havet, Claude Aveline, Jacques Madaule, Norberto Bobbio, Jean-Jacques Mayoux, Pierre de Lanux. See Jachec, *Europe's Intellectuals,* 79, 84. Many French critics of Campagnolo had been active in the resistance.

98. Jachec, *Europe's Intellectuals,* 73. In the preface to a 1988 tribute volume, Senghor wrote that Albert Tévoédjrè "incarnates, at the same time, the African man of culture and the humanist of the twentieth century. I clarify: that of the *civilization of the universal* that Pierre Teilhard de Chardin announced to us." Léopold Sédar Senghor, "Préface" to René Coste et al., *Albert Tévoédjrè, compagnon d'aventure* (Paris: Berger-Levrault, 1988), 7.

99. Campagnolo, "Responsabilités européennes," 79–81.

100. Ibid.

101. Ibid., 79, 82.

102. For more detail, see Chapter 4.

103. Alioune Diop, "Colonialisme et nationalisme culturels," *Présence africaine* N.S. 4 (Oct.–Nov. 1955): 8, 11–12.

104. Présence africaine, "Liminaire: en retard," *Présence africaine* N.S. 3 (Aug.–Sept. 1955): 3.

105. Alioune Diop, "L'Occident chrétien et nous," *Présence africaine* N.S. 6 (Feb.–Mar. 1956): 146.

106. Ibid., 143.

107. Alioune Diop, "Colonialisme et nationalisme culturels," 7.

108. Alioune Diop, "L'Occident chrétien et nous," 146.

109. Ibid., 143–144, 146.

110. Alioune Diop, "Colonialisme et nationalisme culturels," 8, n. 1.

111. They were canonized in 1964 by Paul VI during Vatican II. Paul VI was the first pontiff to visit Africa (in 1969), and he went to Namugongo, site of the killings. In 1953, Diop mentioned them in "On ne fabrique pas un people," 13, n. 1. And in 1959, Diop published a letter of Louis Massignon in *Présence africaine* in which Massignon, doing exactly what Diop hoped European Catholics would, reflected on his own pilgrimage to the place where Karoli (Charles) Lwanga had been burned in Uganda, stating, "I think that Karoli Lwanga and his fellow martyrs are the Latter Day Saints, and that they greatly outshine the miserable tactical use they are put to by the missionaries of my catholic church [sic]. I think they are the Sign of the Judgment, the Supreme Beauty, Virile Heroic Adolescence, which jumps into the fire rather than allow the violation of Sacred

Hospitality, and the Right of Asylum / Shelter, which my miserable country violates in Algeria all day long." Louis Massignon, "Message à M. Alioune Diop," *Présence africaine* N.S. 27 / 28 (Aug.–Nov. 1959): 363.

112. Pope Benedict XV, *Maximum illud*, Nov. 30, 1919, in *Selected Papal Encyclicals and Letters*, vol. 1, new and enlarged ed. (London: Catholic Truth Society, 1941), 12–13.

113. Diop, "L'Occident chrétien et nous," 143–144. Bonnichon, a Jesuit father who served as dean of Aurore University in Shanghai and used personalism in writing about international law, had been imprisoned by the Chinese regime and had written of his experience in *Études* the year before. See A. Bonnichon, "Un homme décrié: le missionnaire," *Études* (Dec. 1955): 330–343 and "La cellule 23," *Études* (Sept. 1954): 161–200. See also his "Il rispetto della persona umana nell'applicazione des diritto penale," *Quaderni di iustitia* 9 (1957). Lebbé, who died in 1940 soon after being captured, held, and released by Chinese Communist forces, was known as a Sinophile missionary who advanced the cause of Chinese clergy at the Vatican. The debate over his legacy revolved around European missionary methods and the promotion of indigenous clergy and culture within the church.

114. Présence africaine, "Peut-on dresser le Vatican?" 7.

115. Ibid., 5–6.

116. On the Présence africaine publishing house, see Ruth Bush, *Publishing Africa in French: Literary Institutions and Decolonization, 1945–1967* (Liverpool: Liverpool University Press, 2016), 71–91.

117. Alioune Diop, "Préface" to François Houang, *Âme chinoise et christianisme* (Tournai: Casterman, 1957), 9.

118. Principal congregations active in China included the Lazarists, the Jesuits, and the MEP. In 1885, the majority of the six hundred foreign missionaries in China were French. See J. Weber and F. de Sesmaisons, eds., *La France en Chine 1843–1943* (Paris: L'Harmattan, 2013), 11.

119. Houang was also in the French resistance and then taught at the École normale supérieure. Jachec, *Europe's Intellectuals*, 249–250 n. 85.

120. In the late 1970s, Houang authored a book on Mgr Lefebvre and Vatican II: *Les réalités de Vatican II et les désirs de Monseigneur Lefebvre* (Paris: Fayard, 1978).

121. Diop, "Préface" to Houang, *Âme chinoise*, 9. Houang had invoked the rose window motif at the SEC's 1953 General Assembly. Jachec, *Europe's Intellectuals*, 85–86.

122. Later in life, Tévoédjrè became an SMA brother.

123. Alioune Diop, "Préface" to Albert Tévoédjrè, *L'Afrique révoltée* (Paris: Présence africaine, 1958), 9.

124. See Chapter 4 for more on the MLN.

125. Diop, "Préface" to Tévoédjrè, *L'Afrique révoltée,* 11.

126. Ibid. Sheen had argued that the Russians had shouldered the cross without Christ and that Americans had adopted Christ without the cross. Notably, Sheen served as a co-consecrator when Pope John XXIII promoted Africans Bernard Yago and Paul Zoungrana in a joint ceremony in Saint Peter's basilica on May 8, 1960. On Sheen, see Kathleen Riley, *Fulton J. Sheen: An American Catholic Response to the Twentieth Century* (Staten Island, NY: St. Pauls / Alba House, 2004); Christopher Lynch, *Selling Catholicism: Bishop Sheen and the Power of Television* (Lexington: University Press of Kentucky, 1998).

127. Diop, "Préface" to Tévoédjrè, *L'Afrique révoltée,* 11–12 (emphasis in the original).

128. Tévoédjrè, *L'Afrique révoltée,* 123.

129. Ibid., 113.

130. Ibid., 111 (emphasis in the original).

131. Ibid., 128.

132. Alioune Diop, "Impressions de voyage," *Présence africaine* N.S. 29 (Dec. 1959–Jan. 1960): 5.

133. "Résolutions de la rencontre des étudiants catholiques africains à Rome (17–24 avril 1957)," *Tam-Tam,* June–July 1957, 36.

134. "Discours de M. Ki-Zerbo au nom des étudiants," *Tam-Tam,* June–July 1957, 8.

135. "Discours de Son Exc. Mgr Sigismondi," *Tam-Tam,* June–July 1957, 10–13.

136. See "La voix du Pape," *Tam-Tam,* June–July 1957, 1–2.

137. The congress took place between March 26 and April 1, 1959. In 1959, Good Friday was March 27 and Easter Sunday was March 29. For more on the SAC and the 1959 congress, see Grah Mel, *Alioune Diop,* 169–197.

138. John W. O'Malley, *What Happened at Vatican II?* (Cambridge, MA: Harvard University Press, 2008), 17.

139. Father Robert Sastre, "Théologie et culture africaine," *Présence africaine* N.S. 24 / 25 (Feb.–May 1959): 132. On the selection of Rome as the venue, see Alioune Diop, "Le sens de ce Congrès (Discours d'ouverture)," *Présence africaine* N.S. 24 / 25 (Feb.–May 1959): 40.

140. Alioune Diop, "Le sens de ce Congrès," 40, 42, 44, 45.

141. "Synthèse de la sous-commission de théologie," *Présence africaine* N.S. 24 / 25 (Feb.–May 1959): 407–408 (emphases in the original).

142. "S. S. Jean XXIII reçoit les écrivains et artistes noirs," *Présence africaine* N.S. 24 / 25 (Feb.–May 1959): 427.

143. Thomas Cahill, *Pope John XXIII* (New York: Viking, 2002), 151; Peter Hebblethwaite, *Pope John XXIII* (Garden City, NY: Doubleday, 1985), 231.

144. The French ambassador to the Vatican sent a copy of the pope's speech to Paris, emphasizing that John spoke in French. M. Roland de Margerie, Ambassadeur de France près le Saint-Siège to M. Couve de Murville, Ministre des Affaires étrangères, Rome, Apr. 2, 1959, ADN 576PO/1/1389.
145. "S. S. Jean XXIII reçoit les écrivains et artistes noirs," 427.
146. Ibid., 427–428.
147. After John XXIII died in 1963, Alioune Diop and Georges Ngango, then a student, traveled to Rome to present the new Pope Paul VI with a memo summing up African hopes and expectations for Vatican II. Jean-Paul Messina, *Evêques africains au Concile Vatican II, 1959–1965: le cas du Cameroun* (Paris: Karthala, 2000), 43. See also Georges Ngango, "L'Occident chrétien face à l'éveil des non-occidentaux," *Présence africaine* N.S. 45 (1e trimestre, 1963): 205–211.
148. See "Résumé des questions discutées au course des deux journées d'études à Rome (26 et 27 mai 1962) sur la présence et l'expression de la personnalité africaine dans la vie catholique," *Présence africaine* N.S. 44 (4e trimestre, 1962): 249–254.
149. Copies of these letters are published as appendices in *Présence africaine* N.S. 44 (4e trimestre, 1962): 245–248. For more on this effort, see P. Meinrad Hegba, SJ, "Un malaise grave," in *Personnalité africaine et catholicisme* (Paris: Présence africaine, 1963), 14–15.
150. Quoted in "Lettre aux Catholiques africains," reproduced in *Présence africaine* N.S. 44 (4e trimestre, 1962): 245.
151. Verdin, *Alioune Diop,* 222–223.
152. Marilyn J. Matelski, *Vatican Radio: Propagation by the Airwaves* (Westport, CT: Praeger, 1995), xix, 101.
153. Guy de la Tournelle, Ambassadeur de France près le Saint-Siège to M. Couve de Murville, Ministre des Affaires étrangères, Rome, Mar. 6, 1963, ADN 576PO/1/1449.
154. "Causerie de M. Alioune Diop à Radio-Vatican (Résumé de sa conférence du 5 mars)," ADN 576PO/1/1449.
155. "Causerie de M. Alioune Diop."

3. Theologies of Colonization: Debating the Legitimacy of Empire

1. Joseph Michel, "Mon entretien avec le Père Gabel," ACSSp SF 27.2.
2. Vitoria was born around 1483 and died in 1546. The Spanish conquest of the Aztec Empire took place between 1519 and 1521, and Spanish forays against the Inca Empire began in the late 1520s. The most relevant of

Vitoria's writings here are "De Indis" and "De Indis relectio posterior, sive de iure belli." For English translations, see Francisco de Vitoria, *Political Writings,* ed. Anthony Pagden and Jeremy Lawrance (Cambridge: Cambridge University Press, 1991), 231–327.

3. The only article to treat aspects of this controversy in detail is Michel Legrain, "La querelle du *Devoir de décolonisation* autour du P. Joseph Michel et de l'aumônerie des étudiants d'Outre-Mer (1954)," *Histoire et missions chrétiennes,* no. 10 (2009): 95–117.

4. For more on Catholics and the Algerian War, see Darcie Fontaine, *Decolonizing Christianity: Religion and the End of Empire in France and Algeria* (Cambridge: Cambridge University Press, 2016).

5. Joseph Michel, "Le devoir de décolonisation," Reproduced in *Mémoire spiritaine,* no. 4 (1996): 135–139.

6. Joseph-Vincent Ducattillon, "Théologie de la colonisation," *Revue de l'Action populaire,* no. 90 (July–Aug. 1955): 769.

7. Ibid., 770. Both authors were apparently unaware of, or perhaps unable to read, Catholic thought on colonization and slavery that emerged from the Portuguese context. See Richard Gray, "The Papacy and the Atlantic Slave Trade: Lourenço da Silva, the Capuchins, and the Decisions of the Holy Office," *Past and Present* 115 (1987): 52–68; Luiz Felipe de Alencastro, "Portuguese Missionaries and Early Modern Antislavery and Proslavery Thought," in *Slavery and Antislavery in Spain's Atlantic Empire,* ed. Josep M. Fradera and Christopher Schmidt-Nowara (New York: Berghahn Books, 2013), 43–73.

8. Jean Ernoult and Paul Coulon, "Histoire d'un historien spiritain: le Père Joseph Michel (1912–1996)," *Mémoire spiritaine,* no. 4 (1996): 51–55.

9. Ibid., 64–65.

10. At that time, priests from Martinique and Madagascar assisted Michel. Secrétariat de l'Épiscopat, "Colonialisme et décolonisation (première note)," Nov. 15, 1954, 4. ACSSp SF 26.3.

11. The office also published *Alizés,* the monthly bulletin of Catholic students from the French Antilles, and *Fehim-Pihavanana,* the monthly bulletin of Catholic Malagasy students, but these were not as widely known as *Tam-Tam.* Initially, *Tam-Tam* was typed and copied on plain white paper, but beginning in 1955, it was printed and bound in a professional manner. It came out between four and eight times a year in the 1950s.

12. Sébastien Abessolo, "Théologie et colonialisme," *Tam-Tam,* Nov.–Dec. 1952, 8–9.

13. Michel, "Le devoir de décolonisation," 137–139.

14. "Hierarchie catholique et morale coloniale," special issue of *Tam-Tam,* Nov. 1954.

15. See, for example, P. Michel to M. l'Abbé, Paris, Sept. 12, 1951, ACSSp SF 27.1.
16. On a French Catholic civilizing mission, see J. P. Daughton, *An Empire Divided: Religion, Republicanism, and the Making of French Colonialism, 1880–1914* (Oxford: Oxford University Press, 2006), and Elizabeth A. Foster, *Faith in Empire: Religion, Politics, and Colonial Rule in French Senegal, 1880–1940* (Stanford, CA: Stanford University Press, 2013). On a French republican civilizing mission, see Alice L. Conklin, *A Mission to Civilize: The Republican Idea of Empire in France and West Africa, 1895–1930* (Stanford, CA: Stanford University Press, 1997).
17. Joseph Michel, "Le devoir de décolonisation," supplement to *Alizés,* Apr.–May 1954; *Fehim-Pihavanana,* May 1954; *Tam-Tam,* Mar.–Apr. 1954; Joseph Michel, "Le devoir chrétien de décolonisation," *Actualité religieuse dans le monde,* Dec. 1, 1954, 3–4. Pax Christi, an international Catholic association that promoted peace through education, was founded in France in 1944. Cardinal Feltin was its international president from 1950 until 1964. Sabine Rousseau, *La colombe et le napalm: des chrétiens français contre les guerres d'Indochine et du Vietnam, 1945–1975* (Paris: CNRS, 2002), 117.
18. Joseph Michel, "Le devoir de décolonisation," 139–140, 143.
19. Ibid., 146.
20. Ibid., 152. Folliet was a prominent orator, journalist, sociologist, and, eventually, a priest, with an abiding interest in colonial questions. Antoine Deléry, *Joseph Folliet (1903–1972): parcours d'un militant catholique* (Paris: Cerf, 2003).
21. Michel, "Le devoir de décolonisation," 153.
22. Rousseau, *La colombe et le napalm,* 113–114. Rousseau points to the spring of 1954 as a turning point within the church on colonial questions. Prior to that, Catholic protest against the war in Indochina had come from militants on the margins of French Catholicism. Ibid., 131–134.
23. "Souvenirs inédits du Père J. Michel sur 'Le devoir de décolonisation,'" *Mémoire Spiritaine* no. 4 (1996): 132. Pius XII named Bressolles to direct the Sainte-Enfance in 1947. Prior to that, Bressolles had been vice-rector of the University of Paris and the chaplain of the French Navy.
24. Mgr Lefebvre to R. Père, Dakar, Apr. 17, 1954, ACSSp 3I 1.19 a10.
25. François Charles-Roux was the scion of a wealthy Marseillais merchant family and his father, Jules Charles-Roux, who had advocated tirelessly for colonial commercial interests as a legislator, had been one of the founding members of the Union coloniale, the ancestor of the Comité. On Jules, see Stuart M. Persell, *The French Colonial Lobby 1889–1938* (Stanford, CA: Hoover Institution Press, 1983), 120–125. François was also a member of the Institut de France and the Académie des Sciences coloniales. See Adrien

Dansette, *Notice sur la vie et les travaux de François Charles-Roux (1879–1961)* (Paris: Firmin Didot, 1963). For a study on commercial interests at the time of decolonization that relies heavily on the Comité's records, see Jacques Marseille, *Empire colonial et capitalisme français: histoire d'un divorce* (Paris: Albin Michel, 1984).

26. For summary and chronology, see Secrétariat de l'Épiscopat, "Colonialisme et décolonisation (première note)," 1–3. The first articles in the series were François Charles-Roux, "Le problème chrétien devant la conscience coloniale," *Nouvelle revue française d'Outre-Mer* (Sept. 1953): 223–227; "Expansion coloniale et Christianisme" (Oct. 1953): 255–260; "De quelques reproches adressés à la colonisation française moderne" (Nov. 1953): 287–292; "Lyautey, Gallieni, Brazza et la colonisation" (Dec. 1953): 331–335; "L'expansion coloniale française et l'indigène" (Jan. 1954): 3–8.

27. François Charles-Roux, "Existe-t-il un 'peché de colonialisme' et un 'devoir chrétien de décolonisation'?" *Nouvelle revue française d'Outre-Mer* (June 1954): 239–242. For follow up articles, see Charles-Roux, "Evêques français de jadis et expansion coloniale" (July–Aug. 1954): 298–304; "Colonisation française et institutions, coutumes, traditions et civilisations indigènes" (Oct. 1954): 423–429.

28. Charles-Roux, "Existe-t-il," 241. On Samory, see A. S. Kanya-Forstner, *Conquest of the Western Sudan: A Study in French Military Imperialism* (London: Cambridge University Press, 1969); on Rabah, see Michael M. Horowitz, "Ba Karin: An Account of Rabeh's Wars," *African Historical Studies* 3, no. 2 (1970): 391–402.

29. Villot went on to become a cardinal and Vatican secretary of state. Antoine Wenger, *Le cardinal Jean Villot (1905–1979): Secrétaire d'État de trois papes* (Paris: Desclée de Brouwer, 1989).

30. Secrétariat de l'Épiscopat, "Colonialisme et décolonisation (première note)"; Secrétariat de l'Épiscopat "Colonialisme et décolonisation (deuxième note)," Nov. 19 1954, ACSSp SF 26.3.

31. Villot asked the bishop of Angers Monsignor Henri Chappoulie to compose the circulars. Chappoulie in turn designated Father Jean Blanc, an editor of the missionary periodical *Union missionaire du clergé de France,* to write them. See the notes appended to Michel's (apparently illicit) copies of the circulars in ACSSp SF 26.3. Chappoulie shared many of Michel's sentiments. See Henri Chappoulie, "Le problème colonial et les catholiques français d'aujourd'hui," in *Colonisation et conscience chrétienne,* by Chappoulie et al. (Paris: Fayard, 1953), 9–12. This book helped to provoke Charles-Roux's aforementioned editorial campaign.

32. Ducattillon, "Théologie de la colonisation." This periodical, founded just after the turn of the century, focused on social issues and Catholic Action. A survey by Jean-Yves Calvez shows that a variety of positions on colonial questions appeared in its pages in the early 1950s. "L'Action populaire dans une de ses revues," annex to Jean-Yves Calvez, *Chrétiens penseurs du social: l'après guerre (1945–1967)* (Paris: Cerf, 2006), 196–201.

33. Examples include the Radical Pierre Mendès-France and the Socialist Guy Mollet, both prime ministers in the mid-1950s. Todd Shepard, *The Invention of Decolonization: The Algerian War and the Remaking of France* (Ithaca, NY: Cornell University Press, 2006), 63–64.

34. Ducattillon's argument using Vitoria was similar to that made by Georges Le Brun Keris in *Mort des colonies? Colonialisme, anticolonialisme et colonisation* (Paris: Centurion, 1953). Le Brun Keris was the president of the African Federation of the MRP from 1954 until 1960.

35. Ducattillon, "Théologie de la colonisation," 771.

36. Fiche chronologique du Frère Joseph-Vincent Ducattillon, ADPF.

37. The 1901 law was the first in a series of three anticlerical measures that emerged from the Dreyfus Affair. A 1904 law banned congregations from teaching in France and a 1905 law separated church and state. On the expulsion of congregations, see Patrick Cabanel and Jean-Dominique Durand, eds., *Le grand exil des congrégations religieuses françaises, 1901–1914: colloque international de Lyon, Université Jean Moulin Lyon III, 12–13 juin 2003* (Paris: Cerf, 2005).

38. Auguste Viatte, *D'un monde à un autre: journal d'un intellectuel jurassien à Québec, 1939–1949*, vol 1: *1939–1942*, ed. Claude Hauser (Saint-Nicolas, Canada: Communication Jurassienne et Européenne, 2001), 62, n. 188.

39. Joseph-Vincent Ducattillon, *Le vrai et le faux patriotisme* (Paris: Spes, 1933).

40. Fiche chronologique du Frère Joseph-Vincent Ducattillon. These speeches are in Joseph-Vincent Ducattillon, *Une renaissance française: ses conditions spirituelles* (Paris: Plon, 1939).

41. Viatte, *D'un monde à un autre*, 62, n. 188.

42. Joseph-Vincent Ducattillon, *La guerre, cette revolution (le sort de la civilisation chrétienne)* (New York: Maison française, 1941), 16, 53.

43. See Martin Evans's interviews with Bernard Boudouresque, Robert Davezies, Jacques Berthelet, and Daniel Campiano in *The Memory of Resistance: French Opposition to the Algerian War (1954–1962)* (Oxford: Berg, 1997), 84–87, 101–105, 125–129, 148–149.

44. Ducattillon's elevation to superior and his subsequent reappointment were accomplished by the circumvention of normal Dominican elective proce-

dures. François Leprieur, *Quand Rome condamne: Dominicains et prêtres-ouvriers* (Paris: Plon / Cerf, 1989), 446.

45. The Dominican leaders at the time were Spain's Emmanuel Suarez and, after 1955, Ireland's Michael Browne. Leprieur, *Quand Rome condamne,* 476. Leprieur suggests that Ducattillon may have been trying to head off further sanctions, yet he faults him for perpetuating flaws that were later repudiated by Vatican II.

46. "Le T. R. P. Ducattillon, 1898–1957," *Cahiers religieux d'Afrique du Nord* (Oct.–Dec. 1957): 173–174.

47. Ducattillon, "Théologie de la colonisation," 771, 777.

48. Ibid., 777–779.

49. Ibid., 778–781.

50. Ibid., 782.

51. Michel suggested that Ducattillon was unwilling to meet. P. Michel to Cardinal Feltin, Paris, June 12, 1956, ACSSp SF 27.2.

52. P. Perbal to P. Michel, Paris, July 30, 1955, ACSSp SF 27.2. On Perbal's career, see Willi Henkel, "Albert Perbal," in *Biographical Dictionary of Christian Missions,* ed. Gerald H. Anderson (Grand Rapids, MI: William B. Eerdmans, 1999), 526–527.

53. See, for example, P. Perbal to P. Michel, Rome, Mar. 23, 1956, ACSSp SF 27.2.

54. Ibid.

55. P. Perbal to P. Michel, Paris, July 30, 1955.

56. On this incident, see Alistair Horne, *A Savage War of Peace: Algeria 1954–1962* (New York: New York Review of Books, 2006), 147–152.

57. See "Une importante déclaration des étudiants catholiques africains en France," *Le Monde,* Apr. 13, 1956, 5; "Le devoir de décolonisation en Algérie," *Témoignage chrétien,* Apr. 13, 1956, 4; "Déclaration des étudiants catholiques d'Afrique noire en France," *Afrique Nouvelle,* Apr. 24, 1956, 6; "Déclaration des étudiants catholiques d'Afrique noire en France," *Tam-Tam,* Apr.–May 1956, 4–6.

58. "Déclaration des étudiants catholiques d'Afrique noire en France," ACSSp SF 27.2.

59. Joseph-Vincent Ducattillon, "Actualité du patriotisme," *La Croix,* May 29, 1956, 5. On *La Croix,* see Yves Pitette, *Biographie d'un journal: La Croix* (Paris: Perrin, 2011).

60. Ducattillon, "Actualité du patriotisme," 5.

61. Ibid.

62. Editorial board, "L'actualité du patriotisme," *La Croix,* June 12, 1956, 5.

63. Ibid. (emphasis in the original). On Buttin, see Roger le Tourneau, "Confluent, dernier numéro, avril 1967, Hommage à Paul Buttin," *Revue de*

l'Occident musulman et de la Méditerranée, no. 4 (1967): 197–199; Paul Buttin, *Le drame du Maroc* (Paris: Cerf, 1955).

64. Editorial board, "L'actualité du patriotisme."

65. Émile Gabel, "Le drame algérien I. Perspectives politiques," *La Croix*, May 17, 1956, 1.

66. Émile Gabel, "Le drame algérien II. Construire par l'amitié," *La Croix*, May 18, 1956, 1, 6.

67. Émile Gabel, "Le drame algérien III. Le devoir des Français," *La Croix*, May 20–21, 1956, 1, 6.

68. Marie-José de Saint-Marc and Jean-Louis Monzat to R. P. Ducattillon, Paris, June 4, 1956, ACSSp SF 27.2.

69. Mgr Chappoulie apparently asked Perbal to write a refutation of "Actualité du patriotisme," but it was never published. P. Perbal to P. Michel, Rome, June 8, 1956, and P. Michel, "Les choses bougent," ACSSp SF 27.2. For Perbal's analysis of Ducattillon's argument, see P. Perbal to P. Michel, Rome, June 5, 1956, ACSSp SF 27.2.

70. "Un article du R. P. Ducattillon sur 'l'actualité du patriotisme,'" *Le Monde*, May 30, 1956, 3; "A propos de l'article du R. P. Ducattillon sur les problèmes coloniaux," *Le Monde*, June 3–4, 1956, 5.

71. "Texte envoyé à *La Croix*, au *Monde*, au Cardinal Feltin," ACSSp SF 27.2. A reprint of this text, without Perbal's letter attached, can be found in "'Traitres' ou 'patriotes'?" *Informations catholiques internationales*, June 15, 1956, 27–28. Michel's decision to disseminate Perbal's letter critiquing Ducattillon's "Théologie de la colonisation" in *Revue de l'Action populaire* angered the editors of that magazine, who resented being tarred in the conflict. See [P. Bigo?] to P. Michel, Vanves, June 6, 1956, ACSSp SF 27.2.

72. "Texte envoyé à *La Croix*, au *Monde*, au Cardinal Feltin."

73. Mgr Lefebvre to P. Michel, Dakar, June 5, 1956, ACSSp SF 27.2. In an ironic twist on the Ducattillon / Michel antagonism, Lefebvre, a Spiritan, clashed frequently with the Dominican chaplains at the University of Dakar, characterizing them as radicals. See Marcel Lefebvre, "Evangélisateur et grand organisateur de l'Église en Afrique," *Fideliter*, Sept.–Oct. 1987, 25–26, and Chapter 6.

74. "Orientations d'Église: S. Em. Le Cardinal Feltin rappelle et précise les principes," *La Croix*, Apr. 26, 1956, 4.

75. P. Michel to Cardinal Feltin, Paris, June 12, 1956.

76. The Malagasy priests are not named in the sources. Bosc (b. 1909) directed the "Routes internationales des jeunes" in France and North Africa for Pax Christi in 1952. He later traveled to over fifty countries, wrote several books, and taught international relations. Daniélou (b. 1905) edited the Catholic

magazine *Études* and then acceded to the chair in Christian origins at the Institut Catholique. He participated as an expert at Vatican II and drafted several conciliar documents. He became cardinal in 1969 and a member of the Académie française in 1972. De Lestapis (b. 1903) became an expert on questions of family, population, and demographics. He taught at the Institut Catholique and authored numerous books on marriage, women in the workplace, and family planning. Jean-Marie Mayeur and Yves-Marie Hilaire, eds., *Dictionnaire du monde religieux dans la France contemporaine,* vol. 1, *Les jésuites,* ed. Paul Duclos (Paris: Beauchesne, 1985), 48, 83–84, 182–183. De Soras, also a Jesuit, wrote on religious and political questions, including colonialism.

77. Michel, "Mon entretien avec le Père Gabel." This line appears in the conclusion to "De Indis." Vitoria, *Political Writings,* 291–292.

78. Michel, "Mon entretien avec le Père Gabel."

79. Joseph-Vincent Ducattillon, *Patriotisme et colonisation* (Tournai: Desclée, 1957).

80. The French title was "Sens chrétien de la vocation militaire." Quoted in Michel, "Mon entretien avec le Père Gabel."

81. On leftist Catholics in postwar France, see Denis Pelletier and Jean-Louis Schlegel, eds., *À la gauche du Christ: les chrétiens de gauche en France de 1945 à nos jours* (Paris: Seuil, 2012).

82. Ducattillon, "Actualité du patriotisme," 5.

4. Entirely Christian and Entirely African: African Catholic Students in Postwar France

1. This meeting took place April 6–7, 1956 in a Franciscan monastery. Students from Paris, Toulouse, Bordeaux, and Montpellier attended. Jean Pliya, "L'Association des étudiants catholiques en France: historique et activités," in *L'Afrique chrétienne II & III,* ed. Abravanel Haïm (Lezay (Deux-Sèvres): Chopin, 1960–1961), 220. The group was also known as the Union of Catholic African Students (UECA).

2. "Déclaration des étudiants catholiques d'Afrique noire en France," ACSSp SF 27.2 and *Tam-Tam,* Apr.–May 1956, 4–6. For press, see "Une importante déclaration des étudiants catholiques africains en France," *Le Monde,* Apr. 13, 1956, 5; "Le devoir de décolonisation en Algérie," *Témoignage chrétien,* Apr. 13, 1956, 4; "Déclaration des étudiants catholiques d'Afrique noire en France," *Afrique nouvelle,* Apr. 24, 1956, 6.

3. "Déclaration des étudiants catholiques d'Afrique noire en France."

4. Ibid.

5. According to Jean Pliya, there were about twenty students at the conference in Pau, though the attendees represented larger constituencies. Two hundred students participated in the 1957 pilgrimage to Rome. Pliya, "L'Association," 220.

6. On African students in France, see Jean-Pierre Ndiaye, *Enquête sur les étudiants noirs en France* (Paris: Réalités africaines, 1962); Sékou Traoré, *La Fédération des étudiants d'Afrique noire en France (F.E.A.N.F.)* (Paris: L'Harmattan, 1985); Charles Diané, *La FEANF et les grandes heures du mouvement syndical étudiant noir* (Paris: Chaka, 1990); Fabienne Guimont, *Les étudiants africains en France, 1950–1965* (Paris: L'Harmattan, 1997); Michel Sot, ed., *Étudiants africains en France 1951–2001: cinquante ans de relations France-Afrique, quel avenir?* (Paris: Karthala, 2002); Amady Aly Dieng, *Les premiers pas de la Fédération des étudiants d'Afrique noire en France (FEANF) (1950–1955) (de l'Union française à Bandoung)* (Paris: L'Harmattan, 2003); Amady Aly Dieng, *Les grands combats de la FEANF: de Bandung aux indépendances 1955–1960* (Paris: L'Harmattan 2009); Amady Aly Dieng, *Histoire des organisations d'étudiants africains en France (1900–1950)* (Dakar: L'Harmattan, 2011); Thierno Bah, "Les étudiants d'Afrique noire et la marche vers l'indépendance," in *L'Afrique noire française: l'heure des indépendances,* ed. Charles-Robert Ageron and Marc Michel (Paris: CNRS, 1992), 41–56; Tony Chafer, "'Students and Nationalism': The Role of Students in the Nationalist Movement in Afrique occidentale française (AOF), 1946–1960," in *AOF: réalités et héritages: societies ouest-africaines et ordre colonial, 1895–1960,* vol. 1, ed. Charles Becker et al. (Dakar: Direction des Archives du Sénégal, 1997), 388–407; Louisa Rice, "Between Empire and Nation: Francophone West African Students and Decolonization," *Atlantic Studies: Global Currents* 10, no. 1 (2013): 131–147; Françoise Blum, "L'indépendance sera révolutionnaire ou ne sera pas: étudiants africains en France contre l'ordre colonial," *Cahiers d'histoire: revue d'histoire critique* 126 (2015): 119–138; Félix Germain, *Decolonizing the Republic: African and Caribbean Migrants in Postwar Paris, 1946–1974* (East Lansing: Michigan State University Press, 2016), 1–20. A few of them mention Catholic students in passing.

7. "Tam-Tam et la presse," *Tam-Tam,* Dec. 1955, 26–33.

8. Charles-Edouard Harang, *Quand les jeunes catholiques découvrent le monde: les mouvements catholiques de jeunesse de la colonisation à la coopération 1920–1991* (Paris: Cerf, 2010), 112.

9. N. Bancel and J. Devisse, "La presse étudiante noire en France de 1943 à 1960," in *Le rôle des mouvements d'étudiants africains* (Paris: UNESCO / L'Harmattan, 1993), 205–206.

10. Aly Dieng, *Les premiers pas*, 237–238; Diané, *La FEANF*, 94. The only exception is Valérie Marie Ngongo-Mbede, "Joseph Ki-Zerbo, militant chrétien, africaniste et féministe," in *Hommage au Professeur Joseph Ki-Zerbo: Actes du colloque international sur l'histoire du Burkina Faso, Ouagadougou, le 26 novembre 2008*, ed. Moussa Willy Bantenga et al. (Ouagadougou: L'Harmattan Burkina, 2010), 155–177.

11. It may also result from a conflation of African Catholic students with their senior coreligionists such as Léopold Senghor and Félix Houphouët-Boigny, who had long worked within the French colonial framework. Students faulted them for supporting de Gaulle's proposal for a French Community and the failure to preserve African unity afterwards.

12. On the FEANF statement, see Tony Chafer, *The End of Empire in French West Africa: France's Successful Decolonization?* (Oxford: Berg, 2002), 130.

13. Aly Dieng, *Histoire des organisations*, 65–67.

14. "A. S. de 'L'Association des étudiants ouest-africains' qui a été fondé récemment," May 12, 1939, APPP Associations 3541 P-1.

15. Fabienne Guimont, "Les étudiants africains en France et leur organisation: la FEANF (1950–65)," in *Étudiants africains en France*, ed. Sot, 119.

16. See "Tableaux comparatifs" attached to M. Galy, Administrateur en chef de la France d'Outre-Mer to M. le Haut-Commissaire gouverneur général de l'Afrique occidentale française, Paris, Apr. 10, 1953, ANS O 668 (31).

17. "Adresses des étudiants togolais qui sont embarqués pour la France," ASMA Strasbourg 50 / 2.

18. On the 50 percent, see Gérard Cholvy and Yves-Marie Hilaire, eds., *La France religieuse: reconstruction et crises, 1945–1975* (Toulouse: Privat, 2002), 73. For the numbers in Africa, see Délégation apostolique de Dakar, *Statistiques annuelles des missions catholiques en Afrique française, année 1951–1952* (Dakar: Imprimerie Mission Catholique), ACSSp 2F 1.3 a5. Note that clergy estimated that 30 percent of the African students at the University of Dakar in 1958 were Catholic—striking given the predominance of Islam in the region. Rapport, Assemblée des archevêques d'A.O.F. à Dakar, Apr. 16, 17, 18, 1958, 15. AGMAfr Volker 669 / 1.

19. Jean Capelle, *L'éducation en Afrique noire à la veille des indépendances* (Paris: Karthala, 1990), 181.

20. Haut-Commissaire Cornut-Gentille to Gouverneur du Sénégal, de la Mauritanie, du Soudan, etc., Apr. 17, 1954, ANS O 666 (31).

21. In academic year 1951–1952 there were 763 state scholarship students and 377 students not on state scholarships from French West Africa. In 1952–1953, there were 898 state scholarship students and 503 not on state scholarships. The numbers of students not on scholarship are likely deflated as they were harder to track. See "Tableaux comparatifs."

22. Mgr Strebler to R. P. Kern, Lomé, Aug. 12, 1951, ASMA Strasbourg 55 / 61.

23. Abbas Guèye, Député du Sénégal to M. le Haut-Commissaire, Paris, Jan. 3, 1952, ANS O 669 (31).

24. ? to M. l'Aumônier, Mar. 19, 1951, ACSSp SF 27.1.

25. P. de Benoist to P. Gelot, Dakar, Apr. 22, 1954, AGMAfr Durrieu 462 / 5.

26. See, for example, P. de Benoist to P. Lanfry, Dakar, July 21, 1958, AGMAfr Volker 669 / 3.

27. Lefebvre's was not the first such effort, but it became the most important one. In August 1943, Monsignor Louis Le Hunsec, then the Spiritan superior general, in partnership with the Archdiocese of Paris, nominated Father Joseph Borteyrou to serve as a "colonial" chaplain to Catholics from the empire in the capital. Borteyrou's successor, Father Le Dortz, took over in 1947 and took part in a meeting involving a number of French student groups organized by Ad Lucem. The meeting resolved on the creation of the Office of Overseas Students (Office des étudiants d'Outre-Mer), which would be open to all colonial students, but would be an essentially Catholic institution. Yet according to Father Michel, the office went from being Catholic, to Christian, to spiritualist, to neutral in orientation. P. Joseph Michel, Aumônier général des étudiants d'Outre-Mer to Mgr Bertin, Président des Œuvres pontificales missionnaires, Paris, Apr. 22, 1951, ACSSp SF 27.1.

28. Pius XII, *Fidei donum,* Apr. 21, 1957, http://w2.vatican.va/content/pius-xii /en/encyclicals/documents/hf_p-xii_enc_21041957_fidei-donum.html.

29. Mgr Joseph Strebler, "Rapport annuel du Vicariat apostolique de Lomé, Togo 1948," Lomé, Oct. 9, 1948, 9. ASMA Rome 2D 21. For more on the Collège Saint Joseph see Koffi N. Tsigbé, "Evangélisation et alphabetization au Togo sous domination colonial (1884–1960)," *Cahiers de la recherche sur l'éducation et les savoirs* 12 (2013): 105–106.

30. Mgr Strebler, "Rapport annuel du Vicariat apostolique de Lomé, Togo 1948," 9.

31. Mgr Strebler to R. P. Kern, Lomé, Aug. 12, 1951, ASMA Strasbourg 55 / 61.

32. Mgr Strebler to R. P. Kern, Lomé, July 14, 1951, ASMA Strasbourg 55 / 61.

33. Mgr Strebler to R. P. Kern, Lomé, Aug. 12, 1951.

34. P. Michel to M. l'Abbé, Paris, Sept. 12, 1951, ACSSp SF 27.1. This copy of the letter is unsigned, but specific references within denote Michel as the author.

35. Victor Tenneroni to Mgr [Strebler], Gap, June 25, 1948, ASMA Strasbourg 50 / 2. *Mia Holo* means "Our friend" in Ewe. The paper, Togo's first, was founded in 1911 by German Catholic missionaries. Kodjona Kadanga, "La presse et la naissance de l'opinion publique," in *Histoire des Togolais des*

origines aux années 1960, Tome 4: Le refus de l'ordre colonial, ed. Nicoué Gayibor (Lomé: Karthala-Presses de l'Université de Lomé, 2011), 207.

36. On weight loss, see Clovis Olympio to R. P., Mulhouse, Mar. 7, 1952, ASMA Strasbourg 50 / 2. On Koudry's health, see Gabriel Koudry to R. P., Paris, Aug. 22, 1954; Gabriel Koudry to R. P., Paris, Oct. 3, 1954, ASMA Strasbourg 50 / 3.

37. Fadior, "Entre nous africaines," *Tam-Tam,* Apr. 1953, 18–21.

38. Vincent Gbikpi to R. P., Huos, Apr. 25, 1947, ASMA Strasbourg 50 / 2.

39. "Les étudiants d'Outre-Mer en France—Document no. 1," Service presse-information, JEC, Paris, Oct. 8, 1954, ACSSp SF 27.1. This was an excerpt from a published article: Joseph Ki-Zerbo, "Le sourire de la concierge," *Tam-Tam,* Mar.–Apr. 1954, 4–6.

40. David and Couthon, "Réponses aux questions posées à la page 25 du no. 1 de *Tam-Tam,*" Saumur, Feb. 26, 1952, ACSSp SF 27.1.

41. Toutane, "La vie dans les facultés," *Tam-Tam,* May 1953, 14.

42. Gabriel Koudry to R. P., Paris, Jan. 7, 1954, ASMA Strasbourg, 50 / 3.

43. Alcione M. Amos, "Afro-Brazilians in Togo: The Case of the Olympio Family, 1882–1945," *Cahiers d'études africaines* 41 (2001): 294–296.

44. On the Christianity and Europhile culture of Togo's great trading families, including the Olympios, see N'Buéké Goeh-Akue and Badjow Tcham, "Facteurs d'homogénéité, facteurs de différenciation sociale," in *Histoire des Togolais, Tome 4,* ed. Gayibor, 252.

45. An album featuring the architecture of colonial Lomé notes that a notable home in rue de la Gare that belonged to a Patrick Seddoh was too disfigured to be included in its pages. Yves Marguerat and Lucien Roux, *Trésors cachés du vieux Lomé: l'architecture populaire ancienne de la capitale du Togo,* 2nd ed. (Lomé: HAHO, 1993), 13, n. 3. On pages 14–15 there is a 1905 photo with a Seddoh home in it. See also photos of an Olympio compound, 38–40.

46. A. K. Patrick Seddoh to Mgr Strebler, Aug. 12, 1950, ASMA Strasbourg 50 / 2.

47. Vincent Gbikpi to R. P., Toulouse, Jan. 2, 1948, ASMA Strasbourg 50 / 2.

48. Many students lost their funding that year. Alex Dosseh to R. P., Paris, Feb. 21, 1953, ASMA Strasbourg 50 / 2.

49. Mgr Strebler to Gabriel Koudry, Hagenau, Aug. 29, 1952, ASMA Strasbourg 55 / 62.

50. Alex Dosseh to R. P., Paris, Feb. 21, 1953. The song is "Terre de nos aïeux," which Alex composed with his brother and future archbishop of Lomé, Robert Dosseh. Adimado M. Aduayom, Ayélé G. Ekué, and Badjow K. Tcham, "La lutte pour l'indépendence: de la République autonome de Togo

à la République togolaise (1856–1960)," in *Histoire des Togolais, Tome 4*, ed. Gayibor, 676, n. 3.

51. Alex Dosseh to R. P., Paris, Feb. 21, 1953.

52. Gabriel Koudry to P., Paris, Feb. 19, 1956, ASMA Strasbourg 50/3.

53. See "Renseignement étudiants africains de Paris" in ANS O 669 (31).

54. "Les étudiants d'Outre-Mer en France—Document no. 4," Service presse-information, JEC, Paris, Oct. 8, 1954, ACSSp SF 27.1. See documents pertaining to the state of the *maison* in 1953 in ANS O 668 (31).

55. "Les étudiants d'Outre-Mer en France—Document no. 3," Service presse-information, JEC, Paris, Oct. 8, 1954, ACSSp SF 27.1.

56. Gabriel Koudry to R. P., Paris, Jan. 7, 1954.

57. Profile of Joseph Ki-Zerbo dated Sept. 1958 in APPP 77W5173/650096. For detailed information on Ki-Zerbo's student career, see ANS O718/627 (31). His wife, née Jacqueline Coulibaly, has her own file: ANS O718/628 (31).

58. Fadior, "Entre nous africaines," 18.

59. Of these 202, 74 had state scholarships. The tables note that the numbers of non-scholarship students are likely too low. See "Tableaux comparatifs."

60. "Rapport général sur la situation des étudiants Sénégalais en France," ANS O 666 (31).

61. Fadior, "Entre nous africaines," 19.

62. One could also find rooms or beds for less money at foyers which did not provide food or offered meals à la carte.

63. Fadior, "Entre nous africaines," 21.

64. "Les étudiants d'Outre-Mer en France—Document no. 2," Service presse-information, JEC, Paris, Oct. 8, 1954, ACSSp SF 27.1.

65. "Rapport général sur la situation des étudiants Sénégalais."

66. On the JEC, see G. Cholvy, *Histoire des organisations et mouvements chrétiens de jeunesse en France (XIXe-XXe siècle)* (Paris: Cerf, 1999), 223–228.

67. "Les étudiants d'Outre-Mer en France—Document no. 2."

68. Ibid.

69. Joseph Ki-Zerbo, "Témoignage d'un étudiant catholique," *Présence africaine* 14 (1953): 69–70.

70. P. Michel to M. l'Abbé, Paris, Sept. 12, 1951.

71. Quirin Feliho was rated seventy-third out of 220 students from Lomé who received their Primary School Certificate in 1947 (Gabriel Koudry was third). *Journal officiel du territoire du Togo*, Dec. 1, 1947, 1073.

72. Canon Aberer to P. Kern, Séminaire de Zillisheim, July 23, 1948, ASMA Strasbourg 50/2. Aberer wanted Feliho out of his establishment, but the boy's father told Mgr Strebler that he wanted his son to try to spend another two to three years in France to further his education, perhaps at a

school in Nancy. By October 1948, Quirin had left the school for Paris, where his father had arranged for a delegate from the Togolese Assembly to look after him. Strebler instructed the mission not to give Quirin "a penny." See Vincent Feliho to Mgr Strebler, Lomé, Sept. 15, 1948; Mgr Strebler to P., Lomé, Oct. 31, 1948, ASMA Strasbourg 50 / 2.

73. Canon Aberer to TRP Provincial, Séminaire de Zillisheim, Nov. 9, 1947, ASMA Strasbourg 50 / 2. Folly may have referred to Louis Folly, a Togolese student who went to France in 1947 to study at the "École Eyrolles"—the precursor to today's École spéciale des travaux publics—or to Dominique Folly, who went to the lycée de Gap in 1947 to prepare for a career in education. See "Adresses des étudiants togolais qui sont embarqués pour la France," ASMA Strasbourg 50 / 2.

74. Canon Aberer to P. Kern, Séminaire de Zillisheim, July 23, 1948.

75. Canon Aberer to TRP Provincial, Séminaire de Zillisheim, Nov. 9, 1947.

76. P. Kern to M. le Directeur du Collège St. André, Nov. 2, 1950, ASMA Strasbourg 50 / 2.

77. P. to M. Christiano Olympio, Sept. 4, 1950, ASMA Strasbourg 50 / 2.

78. Basile Mensah, "Editorial," *Tam-Tam,* Mar.–Apr. 1954, 3. Mensah served in the army from 1943 until 1950, becoming a radio operator. See "Extrait du livret individuel d'homme de troupe et de sous-officier: Basile Mensah classe 1942" in ANS O718 / 740 (31). This file also contains paperwork on Mensah's scholarships and student career.

79. David and Couthon, "Réponses aux questions posées."

80. P. Michel to M. l'Abbé, Paris, Sept. 12, 1951.

81. Ki-Zerbo, "Témoignage d'un étudiant catholique," 67.

82. L. [Ambra?] to R. P., Bordeaux, Apr. 22, 1947, ASMA Strasbourg 50 / 2.

83. P. Michel to M. l'Abbé, Paris, Sept. 12, 1951.

84. Ki-Zerbo, "Témoignage d'un étudiant catholique," 68.

85. Ibid., 70.

86. See *Hommage au Professeur Joseph Ki-Zerbo,* ed. Bantenga et al.; Florian Pajot, *Joseph Ki-Zerbo: itinéraire d'un intellectual africain au XXe siècle* (Paris: L'Harmattan, 2007).

87. Pliya, "L'Association," 222. Pliya's student records and scholarship solicitations are in ANS O718 / 835 (31). See Toufic's presidential speech opening the 1959 annual meeting, ACSSp SF 26.2. In the 1960s, Toufic worked for the Organisation de coopération et de coordination pour la lutte contre les grandes endémies. Nicolas Toufic, "L'onchocercose oculaire en Afrique de l'Ouest d'expression française," *Ophthalmalogica* 159 (1969): 11–23.

88. On Codjia, see "Historique du CNHU-HKM", 2012, 6, http://www.cnhu -hkm.org/IMG/pdf/HISTORIQUE_DU_CNHU-HKM-2.pdf. On Johnson,

see Samuel Decalo, "Raymond Messanvi Johnson," in *Historical Dictionary of Togo,* 3rd ed. (Lanham, MD: Scarecrow Press, 1996), 169.

89. For an interview with Joachim, see Bennetta Jules-Rosette, *Black Paris: The African Writers' Landscape* (Urbana: University of Illinois Press, 1998), 79–83.

90. Mensah attended the École coloniale and his thesis entitled "La préparation aux fonctions publiques supérieures d'Outre-Mer (1958 / 1959)" is in ANOM 123COL 148/3. On later political difficulties, see Basile Mensah "La raison fondamentale de nos échecs politiques" in ADN 176PO/1/1. On Kaya, see Rémy Bazenguissa-Ganga, *Les voies du politique au Congo: essai de sociologie historique* (Paris: Karthala, 1997), 433. Kaya also has a slim police file: APPP 77W5103 / 645908. Dogbeh appears on a list entitled "Africains en France 1956–1957" in BDIC Fonds JEC F delta1980 / 104. On Olory-Togbe, who is listed as director of publication in *Tam-Tam*'s 1956 issues, see http://copainsdavant.linternaute.com/p/emmanuel-olory-togbe-3523826.

91. Diop is referred to as "notre ainé" in "*Tam-Tam* et la presse," *Tam-Tam,* Dec. 1955, 36.

92. For more on Lastel, see Madeleine [Lastel] Cartier, "La rue Thibaud," *Mémoire spiritaine* (1996): 105, and Andrew Daily, "Race, Citizenship, and Antillean Student Activism in Postwar France 1946–1968," *French Historical Studies* 37, no. 2 (2014): 339–341. Frantz Fanon did not contribute to *Tam-Tam,* as Aly Dieng suggests, but published his own unrelated magazine called *Tam-Tam* while he was a student. Aly Dieng, *Les grands combats,* 179; David Macey, *Frantz Fanon: A Biography,* 2nd ed. (London: Verso, 2012), 126.

93. Maddy Lastel, "Antillais et Africains se comprennent-ils?" *Tam-Tam,* Feb. 1955, 12.

94. Pajot, *Joseph Ki-Zerbo,* 39.

95. Joseph Ki-Zerbo, "Discours adressé au Cardinal Feltin au nom des étudiants catholiques d'Outre-Mer" *Tam-Tam,* Dec. 1954, 15.

96. Ibid., 15–16.

97. "Discours de Son Eminence Cardinal Feltin aux étudiants d'Outre-Mer" *Tam-Tam,* Dec. 1954, 18–19.

98. Ki-Zerbo, "Discours adressé au Cardinal Feltin," 14.

99. "Resolutions de la rencontre des étudiants catholiques africains à Rome (17–24 avril 1957)," *Tam-Tam,* June–July 1957, 33–36.

100. Ibid., 36.

101. "Discours de M. Ki-Zerbo au nom des étudiants," *Tam-Tam,* June–July 1957, 8.

102. "Discours de Son Exc. Mgr Sigismondi," *Tam-Tam,* June–July 1957, 10–13.

103. Pius XII sent them a signed statement of welcome, exhorting them to "prepare themselves seriously and courageously" for their "future professional, social, and political roles," and to seek inspiration in church teachings, all while obeying their bishops. "La voix du Pape," *Tam-Tam,* June–July 1957, 1–2.

104. B. Duclos to P. Kaya, May 6, 1977, quoted in Sylvaine Guinle-Lorinet, "Un temps pour la guerre et un temps pour la paix. Itinéraire franciscain de la seconde moitié du XXe siècle: Bertrand Duclos (1917–1995)," *Annales du Midi: revue archéologique, historique et philologique de la France méridionale* 118, no. 256 (2006): 564 (ellipsis in original).

105. Ibid., 558.

106. Salah D. Hassan, "Inaugural Issues: The Cultural Politics of the Early 'Présence Africaine' 1947–1955," *Research in African Literatures* 30, no. 2 (1999): 195, 201; Germain, *Decolonizing the Republic,* 7.

107. Chafer, *End of Empire,* 175, 179.

108. Charles De Gaulle, *Memoirs of Hope: Renewal and Endeavor,* trans. Terence Kilmartin (New York: Simon & Schuster, 1971), 53–58.

109. Pajot, *Joseph Ki-Zerbo,* 50–51; On Dicko, see Joseph Ki-Zerbo, preface to Ahmadou Dicko, *Journal d'une défaite autour du Référendum du 28 septembre 1958 en Afrique noire* (Paris: L'Harmattan, 1992), x. Senegal's Cheikh Hamidou Kane, Abdoulaye Wade, and Christian Valantin, among others, were in the MLN. Amady Aly Dieng, *Mémoires d'un étudiant africain, Tome 1: De l'École régionale de Diourbel à l'Université de Paris (1945–1960)* (Dakar: CODESRIA, 2011), 91.

110. See, for example, "l'ASPECT FONCTIONNEL DE LA PERSONNE HUMAINE EST CELUI QUI A ÉTÉ LE PLUS EXALTÉ DANS LE 'PERSONNALISME' AFRICAIN" in "Manifeste du Mouvement africain de libération nationale," 12. APPP 77W5173 / 650096 (emphasis in the original).

111. Ki-Zerbo, preface to Dicko, *Journal d'une défaite,* xv, xxiii, xxxii–xxxiii.

112. Alexis Codjia and his fellow Beninese physician Martin Edouard Goudoté were among the fourteen signers of the manifesto.

113. Ki-Zerbo, preface to Dicko, *Journal d'une défaite,* xv.

114. Ibid., xxix–xxxi; Dicko, *Journal d'une défaite,* 125.

5. Men of Transition: African Clergy in Postwar French Africa

1. François Méjan, *Le Vatican contre la France d'Outre-Mer* (Paris: Librairie Fischbacher, 1957), 57–63.

2. Ibid., 73, 75.

3. Alioune Diop, "Peut-on dresser le Vatican contre les peuples de couleur?" *Témoignage chrétien*, Dec. 20, 1957, 13.

4. Présence africaine, "Peut-on dresser le Vatican contre les peuples de couleur?" *Présence africaine* N.S. 16 (Oct.–Nov. 1957): 3–4.

5. Secular clergy denotes priests who did not join a congregation or order with a set of rules. Those who did were called "regular" clergy. Some African priests and prelates did become White Fathers or Spiritans, but they were a tiny minority at midcentury.

6. Supérieur général Louis Durrieu to Ordinaires d'AOF, Maison-Carrée, Algeria, June 21, 1948, AGMAfr Durrieu 459 / 3.

7. "Extrait du compte-rendu de la réunion des chefs de mission," Séminaire régional de Kacabere, Oct. 12, 1948, AGMAfr Durrieu 458 / 4.

8. "Instructions de la S. C. de la Propagande à Son Excellence Monseigneur Lefebvre en date du 22 novembre 1948," in "Première 'Conférence plenière' des Ordinaires des Missions de l'Afrique occidentale française," Dakar, Apr. 25–30, 1949, 41, ACSSp 2F 1.3 a1.

9. Délégation apostolique de Dakar, *Statistiques annuelles des missions catholiques en Afrique française, année 1951–1952* (Dakar: Imprimerie Mission Catholique), ACSSp 2F 1.3 a5. On Cameroon's unique missionary history, see Kenneth Orosz, *Religious Conflict and Language Policy in German and French Cameroon, 1885–1939* (New York: Peter Lang, 2008), and Charlotte Walker-Said, *Faith, Power and Family: Christianity and Social Change in French Cameroon* (Oxford: James Currey, 2018).

10. Supérieur général Durrieu to confrères, Maison-Carrée, Algeria, Apr. 25, 1952, AGMAfr Durrieu 458 / 3.

11. See "Alumni seminarii majoris rubyensis sacerdotio aucti," July 17, 1951; "Prêtres indigènes: état nominal par vicariate et par séminaire" for Tanganyika Territory, Rhodesia and Nyassaland [sic], Afrique Belge, AGMAfr Durrieu 458 / 3. See also Méthode Gahungu, *Former les prêtres en Afrique: le rôle des Pères Blancs (1879–1936)* (Paris: L'Harmattan, 2007), and *La formation dans les séminaires en Afrique: pédagogie des Pères Blancs* (Paris: L'Harmattan, 2008).

12. P. Cormy, "Prêtres sortis du Grand Séminaire de Koumi A.O.F.," Koumi, June 12, 1952, AGMAfr Durrieu 458 / 3. Most of the graduates were from Upper Volta—largely Ouagadougou—but there were a few from Sudan and Senegal. Sixteen were serving as vicars or parish priests in the field and one was teaching at the junior seminary at Pabré, Upper Volta. One of them, future cardinal Paul Zoungrana, had joined the White Fathers congregation. Several were still at Koumi, two were studying in Rome, one was ill, and one had joined a monastery. Father Cormy also noted that two

other African priests had started at Koumi but finished their studies elsewhere.

13. Délégation apostolique de Dakar, *Statistiques annuelles, 1951–1952.*
14. P. J. Hébert to Mgr, Naso [sic], Aug. 20, 1947, AGMAfr Durrieu 459 / 3. For a time, Joseph Ki-Zerbo taught alongside Hébert at the Nasso seminary. http://lefaso.net/spip.php?page=impression&id_article=8960.
15. Supérieur général Louis Durrieu to Ordinaires d'AOF, Maison-Carrée, June 21, 1948.
16. "Extraite de la lettre circulaire #2 de Mgr Durrieu du 8 Dec. 1947," AGMAfr Durrieu 458 / 4.
17. P. Savary to Mgr Durrieu, Pabre, Dec. 26, 1949, AGMAfr Durrieu 459 / 3.
18. Mgr Durrieu to P. Savary, Jan. 31, 1950, AGMAfr Durrieu 459 / 3.
19. Supérieur général Louis Durrieu to Ordinaires d'AOF, Maison-Carrée, June 21, 1948.
20. Vicariat apostolique de Lomé, Rapport quinquennal, 1950, 90–92. ASMA Rome 2D 24.
21. The Spiritan junior seminary in Senegal dated from 1847. Henry J. Koren, *To the Ends of the Earth: A General History of the Congregation of the Holy Ghost* (Pittsburgh: Duquesne University Press, 1983), 464; "Notice historique sur le Séminaire indigène de la Sénégambie," ACSSp 3I 2.b.
22. Mgr Lefebvre to R. P., Dakar, Feb. 18, 1952; Mgr Lefebvre to TRP, Ambanja, Madagascar, Sept. 7, 1951, ACSSp 3I 1.19 a10.
23. Mgr Lefebvre to R. P., Dakar, Feb. 18, 1952.
24. Mgr Lefebvre to R. P., Mar. 10, 1952, ACSSp 3I 1.19 a10. On the accusations, see Chapter 1.
25. P. [?] to R. P., Dakar, Feb. 10, 1952, ACSSp 3I 1.19 a10.
26. Mgr Lefebvre to R. P., Mar. 10, 1952.
27. Vicariat apostolique de Dakar, Rapport quinquennal à la Sacrée Congrégation de la Propagande 1951–1955, 25. ACSSp 3I 1.19 a6.
28. Koren, *Ends of the Earth*, 461–65; "Notice historique," ACSSp 3I 2.b.
29. Adrian Hastings, *The Church in Africa, 1450–1950* (Oxford: Clarendon Press, 1994), 555–556. The same was largely true for Protestants. Yoruba Samuel Adjai Crowther served as an Anglican bishop in Sierra Leone between 1843 and 1891, but no other African became a diocesan Anglican bishop until after 1950.
30. Elizabeth A. Foster, "A Mission in Transition: Race, Politics, and the Decolonization of the Catholic Church in Senegal," in *In God's Empire: French Missionaries and the Modern World*, ed. Owen White and J. P. Daughton (Oxford: Oxford University Press, 2012), 257–277.
31. Vicariate apostolique de Dakar, Rapport quinquennal, 1951–1955, 16 (emphasis in the original).

32. There were always exceptions: in 1955 the Spiritan religious superior in Senegal reported that young Father Henri Venet "could not get along with his fellow Spiritans nor with the Blacks, on whom he was very hard." P. Bourgoing to TRP, Thiès, Mar. 16, 1955, ACSSp 3I 1.19 a10.

33. P. Wouters to Mgr Durrieu, Rome, June 24, 1948, AGMAfr Durrieu 458 / 4.

34. "Extrait du compte-rendu de la réunion des chefs de missions."

35. He also felt that Africans suffered too many health problems in Rome.

36. "Extrait d'une lettre de Mgr le Supérieur général à P. Wouters," Maison-Carrée, Algeria, June 14, 1948, AGMAfr Durrieu 458 / 4.

37. Vicariat apostolique de Lomé, Rapport quinquennal, 1950, 95.

38. Ibid., 95–97. Gbikpi had written a thesis on training in African junior seminaries and had apparently put the White Fathers' establishments in a category labeled "those who use bad methods." P. Wouters to Mgr Durrieu, Rome, May 17, 1952, AGMAfr Durrieu 458 / 4.

39. P. Prouvost to P. Cuenot, Nkongsamba [Cameroon], Jan. 23, 1946, MEP DP 100.1.

40. In 1951, Spiritans noted that the Vatican asked that African priests accrue five years of experience before joining a congregation, but this does not seem to have been observed in all cases. "Réunion des Ordinaires Spiritains de l'Afrique occidentale française à Dakar," Mar. 30 and Apr. 2, 1951, ACSSp 3I 1.19 a5.

41. Mgr Durrieu to Mgr Dupont, [Bobo-Dioulasso?] Dec. 11, 1950, AGMAfr Durrieu 459 / 3.

42. Chefs de mission Pères Blancs et al. to Mgr Durrieu, Koumi, Nov. 26, 1952, AGMAfr Durrieu 459 / 3.

43. Mgr Durrieu, "Note du Conseil de la Société," Rome, Dec. 11, 1952, AGMAfr Durrieu 459 / 3.

44. [P. Neyrand?] to R. P. Supérieur principal du District du Sénégal, Paris, July 3, 1956, ACSSp 3I 1.19 a11. In cases where there was not a Spiritan community but a single Spiritan Father living and working alongside a secular African priest, the congregation asked that the African priest attend communal prayers to keep the rhythm of Spiritan religious life.

45. P. Bourgoing to TRP, Thiès, July 21, 1956, ACSSp 3I 1.19 a11.

46. P. Neyrand to P. Bourgoing, Paris, June 29, 1957, ACSSp 3I 1.19 a11.

47. "Visite aux abbés indigènes" du P. Cormy, Koumi, Oct. 15, 1951, AGMAfr Durrieu 459 / 3.

48. P. Groell to P. Quénet, Brin, May 5, 1953, ACSSp 3I 1.19 a10. "Le P. Gandner me dit qu'il voit tout 'en noir.'"

49. Claude Goure, "Conversation avec Raymond-Marie Tchidimbo: ne rougissez pas de votre passé!" *Panorama aujourd'hui* 142 (Oct. 1980): 19.

50. Journal de communauté de Faranah, Oct. 11, 1952, ACSSp 6I 2.5a.

51. Journal de communauté de Faranah, Dec. 7, 1952.

52. P. Cousart to TRP, Mamou, Nov. 4, 1952, ACSSp 6I 1.4.5. On Cousart's career, see Gérard Vieira, *Sous le signe du laïcat: l'Église catholique en Guinée, Tome II: Les temps des prémices* (Dakar: Imprimerie Saint-Paul, 1998), 27.

53. P. Cousart to TRP, Mamou, Nov. 4, 1952.

54. [?] to R. P., Paris, Nov. 12, 1952, ACSSp 6I 1.4.5.

55. P. Neyrand, Visite de la communauté de Faranah, Feb. 20–21, 1954, ACSSp 6I 1.3 a5.

56. See, for example, the acrimony between Tchidimbo, then archbishop of Conakry, and Father Nicolas Moysan, the head of the Spiritan Province of France, over the disposition of personnel in Guinea in 1962. Mgr Tchidimbo to R. P. Moysan, Rome, Oct. 27, 1962; R. P. Moysan to Mgr Tchidimbo, Paris, Oct. 30, 1962; Mgr Tchidimbo to R. P. Moysan, Rome, Nov. 2, 1962, ACSSp 6I 1.3 a8.

57. P. Morvan to TRP, Sébikotane, Feb. 4, 1954, ACSSp 3I 1.19 a10.

58. P. Delisse to Mgr Durrieu, Garango, Jan. 3, 1952, AGMAfr Durrieu 459 / 3.

59. Ibid.

60. Mgr Durrieu to P. Delisse, Maison-Carrée, Algeria, Jan. 24, 1952, AGMAfr Durrieu 459 / 3.

61. Supérieur général Durrieu to confrères, Maison-Carrée, Algeria, Apr. 25, 1952.

62. Ibid.

63. P. Bourgoing to TRP, Sonzay, Oct. 11, 1958, ACSSp 3I 1.19 a11 (emphasis in the original).

64. P. Bourgoing to TRP, Dakar, Dec. 1. 1958, ACSSp 3I 1.19 a11.

65. Délégation apostolique de Dakar, *Statistiques annuelles des missions catholiques en Afrique française, année 1957–1958* (Dakar: Imprimerie Mission Catholique), ACSSp 2F 1.3 a5. Refer also to Table 5.1.

66. In addition, a son of Senegal's métis elite, Monsignor Prosper Dodds, born in Saint-Louis in 1915, presided over the diocese of Ziguinchor in Senegal's remote Casamance. It appears that the Vatican intended to nominate Father Jean Tabi to a leadership post in Cameroon, but he died accidentally in 1951. Jean-Paul Messina and Jaap van Slageren, *Histoire du Christianisme au Cameroun: des origines à nos jours: approche œcuménique* (Paris: Karthala, 2005), 182–183.

67. Etoga found Graffin to be so disrespectful and difficult that he welcomed a Vatican proposition to leave Yaoundé and found a new diocese at Mbalmayo in 1961. Messina and van Slageren, *Histoire du Christianisme*, 183.

68. François Méjan, "Nouvelles précisions sur l'attitude de l'Église catholique dans les territoires d'Outre-Mer français" *L'année politique et économique,* no. 135 (Jan.–Feb. 1957): 75–76 (emphasis in the original).
69. On Gantin's nomination and consecration, see documentation in ASMA Rome 2K 1.
70. Mgr Maury to TRP Volker, Dakar, Feb. 27, 1960, AGMAfr Volker 669/1 (emphasis in the original). Unlike Lefebvre, Maury was only responsible for West Africa, as Pope John XXIII divided French Africa into several territories, each with its own delegate.
71. Ibid.
72. Ibid. On Yago's nomination and consecration see documentation in ASMA Rome 2K 4.
73. The American cardinal Fulton Sheen was a co-consecrator.
74. Mgr Maury to TRP Volker, Dakar, Feb. 27, 1960.
75. Mgr Maury to Père Lanfry, Dakar, Feb. 4, 1961, AGMAfr Volker 669/1.
76. For varying interpretations regarding whether Touré favored federation over independence and whether the no vote was Touré's top-down imposition or the result of a grassroots push from the left, see Frederick Cooper, *Citizenship between Empire and Nation: Remaking France and French Africa, 1945–1960* (Princeton, NJ: Princeton University Press, 2014), 314–317, and Elizabeth Schmidt, *Cold War and Decolonization in Guinea* (Athens: Ohio University Press, 2007), 144–146.
77. Schmidt, *Cold War and Decolonization,* 171–172.
78. Ibid., 157–158.
79. Délégation apostolique de Dakar, *Statistiques annuelles, 1957–1958.*
80. Mgr de Milleville to TRP, Conakry, Dec. 9, 1960, ACSSp 6I 1.3 a7.
81. P. Kerloc'h to TRP, Kindia, Aug. 23, 1961, ACSSp 6I 1.3 a7. See also Mgr de Milleville, "Comment l'Église de Guinée a défendu ses écoles," confidential. ACSSp 6I 1.6 b4.
82. Mgr de Milleville, "Comment l'Eglise de Guinée a défendu ses écoles."
83. Quoted in P. Kerloc'h to TRP, Kindia, Aug. 23, 1961.
84. P. Kerloc'h to TRP, Kindia, Aug. 23, 1961.
85. Mgr de Milleville, "Comment l'Église de Guinée a défendu ses écoles."
86. Extract from *Horoya* (the PDG's newspaper), Conakry, Sept. 2, 1961, in ACSSp 6I 1.6 b4.
87. Raymond-Marie Tchidimbo, *Noviciat d'un evêque: huit ans et huit mois de captivité sous Sékou Touré* (Paris: Fayard, 1987), 118.
88. Mgr de Milleville to TRP, Conakry, Sept. 22, 1960, ACSSp 6I 1.3 a7.
89. Mgr de Milleville to TRP, Dakar, Mar. 2, 1961, ACSSp 6I 1.3 a7. De Milleville already had praise for Tchidimbo in 1958: Mgr Milleville to TRP, Conakry, Feb. 5, 1958, ACSSp 6I 1.4.6.

90. Mgr de Milleville to P. Tchidimbo, Rome, Sept. 13, 1961, ACSSp 6I 1.6 b4.

91. Mgr Le Mailloux to TRP, Jan. 8, 1958, ACSSp 6I 1.5 a6.

92. Vieira, *Sous le signe du laïcat*, 406. Le Mailloux had invested heavily in rapidly increasing the schools in the prefecture. On his watch, the prefecture had also served as a bank for Guinean soldiers serving elsewhere in the French Union but had spent the money so that had they all come back to claim their due, it would have been unable to pay. See ACSSp 6I 1.5 a6. Le Mailloux eventually went back to work as a missionary priest in central Africa.

93. Mgr Lefebvre to TRP Griffin, Dakar, Sept. 17, 1958, ACSSp 6I 1.5 a1.

94. TRP Francis Griffin to Cardinal Préfet de la Propagande, Paris, Oct. 20, 1958, ACSSp 6I 1.5 a1. In the council's vote, Tchidimbo came in third behind two French candidates. See results, Oct. 18, 1958, ACSSp 6I 1.5 a1.

95. P. Neyrand, Visite de la communauté de Faranah, Feb. 20–21, 1954.

96. P. Neyrand, Prefecture de Kankan, Visite de l'Annexe de Bardou, July 5, 1960, ACSSp 6I 1.3 a5. On Kankan, see P. van Nies to Mgr. Kankan, June 8, 1957, ACSSp 6I 1.5 a6.

97. P. Neyrand, Rapport sur le Préfecture de Kankan, 1960, ACSSp 6I 1.3 a5.

98. P. Neyrand, Préfecture de Kankan, Visite de l'Annexe de Bardou; P. Neyrand to P. Kerloc'h, Paris, Dec. 22, 1961, ACSSp 6I 1.3 a7. See also P. Neyrand to Mgr de Milleville, Paris, Feb. 13, 1958, ACSSp 6I 1.4.6.

99. P. Kerloc'h to TRP, Kindia, Apr. 16, 1959, ACSSp 6I 1.4.6.

100. Agence France Presse dispatch, Conakry, Aug. 28, 1961, ACSSp 6I 1.6 b4.

101. Mgr de Milleville to P. Tchidimbo, Rome, Sept. 13, 1961.

102. Maury was particularly worried about the future of the church in Mali, which was friendly with Touré's regime. Mgr Maury to TRP Volker, Dakar, Mar. 7, 1962, AGMAfr Volker 669/1.

103. Cardinal Agagianian to TRP François [sic] Griffin, Rome, Jan. 19, 1962, ACSSp 3I 1.19 a9.

104. Mgr Maury to Mgr de Milleville, Dakar, Dec. 2, 1961, ACSSp 6I 1.6 b4.

105. Mgr Maury, "Note sur l'arrestation des Pères de Nzérékoré (Guinée)," Dakar, Apr. 7, 1962, AGMAfr Volker 669/1.

106. Mgr Maury to TRP Volker, Dakar, Feb. 5, 1962; Mgr Maury to TRP Volker, Dakar, Feb. 22, 1962, AGMAfr Volker 669/1.

107. Mgr Maury to TRP Volker, Dakar, Feb. 5, 1962.

108. Mgr Maury to TRP Volker, Dakar, Feb. 22, 1962.

109. Mgr Maury, "Note sur l'arrestation des Pères."

110. On Dosseh's nomination and consecration, see ASMA Rome 2K 6 and *Afrique Nouvelle*, June 27–July 3, 1962.

111. "Quatre nouveaux archevêques africains," *La Croix*, Apr. 5, 1962, 1.

112. TRP Griffin to Eminence Réverendissime, Paris, Jan. 30, 1962, ACSSp 6I 1.3 a8.

113. TRP Griffin to Eminence Réverendissime, Paris, Jan. 30, 1962, ACSSp 3I 1.19 a9.

114. "Sacre de LL. EE. NN. SS. H. Thiandoum, archevêque de Dakar, et R. Tchidimbo, CSSp, archevêque de Conakry," ACSSp 6I 1.3 a8.

115. P. Bourgoing to TRP Griffin, Rufisque, June 5, 1962, ACSSp 6I 1.3 a8.

116. "Lettre ouverte à l'Archevêque de Conakry," extract from *Horoya*, Aug. 1961, ACSSp 6I 1.6 b4.

117. "Sacre de LL. EE. NN. SS. H. Thiandoum et R. Tchidimbo."

118. P. Bourgoing to TRP Griffin, Rufisque, June 5, 1962. This quote was printed as a headline in *Horoya*, June 2, 1962, 1.

119. Gérard Vieira, *L'Église catholique en Guinée à l'épreuve de Sékou Touré (1958–1984)* (Paris: Karthala, 2005), 119.

120. On Sastre's career, see Raymond Messanvi Johnson, *Un exemple de vie: Mgr Robert Sastre (1926–2000)* (Lomé: Saint-Augustin Afrique, 2012). Johnson, a Togolese who became that country's first psychiatrist, met Sastre in 1956 at the Catholic chaplaincy in the rue Thibaud and considered him a "brother and a friend."

121. Robert Sastre, "Théologie et culture africaine," *Présence africaine* N.S. 24/25 (Feb.–May 1959): 132–133.

122. Raymond Tchidimbo, "L'étudiant africain face à la culture latine," *Présence Africaine* 14 (1953): 55–64. In 1954, skeptical student journalists at *Tam-Tam* commented, "One sees that even with continual reference to a guide such as Mounier, one can still arrive at cogitations that are, at the very least, hazardous." *Tam-Tam*, Jan.–Feb. 1954, 18. Tchidimbo had planned to release his book in 1960 but as he got pulled into the struggles between the church and Touré's regime, he feared that it would appear to be a plug for his personal promotion and delayed its publication. Raymond-Marie Tchidimbo, *L'homme noir dans l'Église* (Paris: Présence Africaine, 1963), 70–75, 12. For more on Mounier, see Chapter 2.

123. Tchidimbo, *L'homme noir*, 45.

124. Ibid., 70.

125. Ibid., 36–39.

126. Ibid., 43.

127. "Débats: 20 Sep. à 21 h.," *Présence africaine* N.S. 8/10 (June–Nov. 1956): 208–209 (emphasis and capitalization in the original).

128. The book was published by the Catholic press Cerf, but "under the direction of Présence africaine." See title page of A. Abblé et al., *Des prêtres noirs s'intérrogent* (Paris: Cerf, 1956).

129. Robert Dosseh and Robert Sastre, "Propagande et vérité," in *Des prêtres noirs*," 147–149.

130. Ibid., 140–141.

131. Joseph Thiam, "Du clan tribal à la communauté chrétienne," in *Des prêtres noirs*, 49–51.

132. Ibid., 53–55.

133. Léonard Kinkupu, Gérard Bissainthe, and Meinrad Hebga, *Des prêtres noirs s'intérrogent: cinquante ans après . . .* (Paris: Karthala, 2006), 287.

134. Marcel Lefebvre, "Lettre-Préface," in *Des prêtres noirs*, 12.

135. Harrisism was an evangelical movement launched by William Wadé Harris across Liberia, Côte d'Ivoire, and Ghana between 1913 and the mid-1920s. Harris attacked indigenous religion, but he also approved of polygamy and other practices that did not sit well with European missionaries. See David A. Shank, *Prophet Harris: The "Black Elijah" of West Africa* (Leiden: Brill, 1994).

136. Lefebvre, "Lettre-Préface," 12–13.

137. Mgr Thiandoum to Mgr Lefebvre, Dakar, May 1, 1967, ACSSp 3I 3.1 a2 (emphasis in the original).

138. Sarah was a student at the Spiritan junior seminary at Dixinn before the PDG forced its closure in 1961, and later finished his training in France, Rome, and Senegal. Ordained in 1969, he assumed the mantle of archbishop of Conakry after Tchidimbo was released from prison and resigned the post in 1979. On his views, see Molly Jackson, "African Bishops Criticize Vatican's Priorities as 'Eurocentric,'" *Christian Science Monitor,* Oct. 25, 2015, https://www.csmonitor.com/World/Global-News/2015 /1025/African-bishops-criticize-Vatican-s-priorities-as-Eurocentric, and "Cardinal Sarah Says the Christian Family Counters Both Islamic, Western Extremism," Catholic News Agency, Oct. 14, 2015, https://www .catholicnewsagency.com/news/cardinal-sarah-says-the-christian -family-counters-both-islamic-western-extremism-26500.

139. Patrice Alou to TRP Provincial, Bourg-en-Bresse, July 24, 1964, ASMA Strasbourg 50 / 6.

140. J. Pires, "L'affaire Mgr Lefebvre: 'ma plus grande peine,'" *Le Soleil,* Apr. 16, 1999. Clipping in ANS, Centre de Documentation, Dossier Hyacinthe Thiandoum.

6. Foe or Friend? Catholics and Islam on the Eve of Independence in French Africa

1. Marcel Lefebvre, "Où va l'Afrique? Les états chrétiens vont-ils livrer l'Afrique noire à l'Étoile?" *La France catholique,* Dec. 18, 1959, 4.
2. Ibid.
3. Mgr Barthet to Député Lemyre de Villiers [sic], Saint-Louis, Sept. 12, 1890, ACSSp 3I 1.14 b1.
4. Mgr Barthet to Comte de Mun, Dakar, June 22, 1892, ACSSp 3I 1.14 b2.
5. On French expansion in the region and relations with Muslims in this period, see A. S. Kanya-Forstner, *The Conquest of the Western Sudan: A Study in French Military Imperialism* (London: Cambridge University Press, 1969); David Robinson, *Paths of Accommodation: Muslim Societies and French Colonial Authorities in Senegal and Mauritania, 1880–1920* (Athens: Ohio University Press, 2000).
6. Elizabeth A. Foster, *Faith in Empire: Religion, Politics, and Colonial Rule in French Senegal, 1880–1940* (Stanford, CA: Stanford University Press, 2013), 33–34; 130–132.
7. Aylward Shorter, *Cross and Flag in Africa: The "White Fathers" during the Colonial Scramble (1892–1914)* (Maryknoll, NY: Orbis Books, 2006), 146, 151.
8. Pontificio Istituto di Studi Arabi e d'Islamistica, "About us," http://en.pisai .it/the-pisai/about-us/.
9. Emmanuel Mounier, *L'éveil de l'Afrique noire* (Paris: Seuil, 1948), 123.
10. Mgr Jean Lesourd, "Progrès de l'Islam dans la Haute Volta," *Union missionnaire du clergé de France: édition documentaire,* no. 3 (1953): xv–xvi.
11. Mgr Boivin, Rapport quinquennal 1955, Vicariat apostolique d'Abidjan, Abidjan, Oct. 12, 1955, ASMA Rome 2D 40.
12. Mgr Duirat, Rapport quinquennal 1955, Préfecture apostolique de Bouaké, Bouaké, Sept. 1955, ASMA Rome 2D 47.
13. Mgr Lingenheim, Rapport sur la visite de Son Excellence Mgr le Délégué Apostolique to TRP, Sokodé, Mar. 25, 1953, ASMA Strasbourg, 56 / 16 (emphasis in the original).
14. Mgr Lingenheim to TRP Provincial, Sokodé, May 1, 1953, ASMA Strasbourg, 56 / 16 (emphasis in the original).
15. "Notes sur l'Islam: échanges de vues entre les ordinaires de l'A.O.F.-Tchad les 25–26 avril 1955" (Dakar: Imprimerie de la Mission Catholique), 9, 13, ACSSp SD C13.9.
16. Ibid., 7–8.
17. Mgr F. du Mesnil to Excellence Révérendissime, Paris, Dec. 8, 1956, AAEA Box 5 / Animation 1951–1969. For more on the society, see Chapter 7. Please

note that the AEA archives have moved to the CNAEF and have been reorganized since this research was conducted.

18. Mgr Joseph Bretault to Chanoine Leveque, Koudougou, Dec. 30, 1961, AAEA Burkina II. Bretault, born in Nantes, had first come to Upper Volta as a missionary in 1930. He became the first apostolic prefect of Ouahigouya in 1947 and then the first apostolic vicar of the same district in 1954, when its seat transferred to Koudougou. Joseph-Roger de Benoist, *Église et pouvoir colonial au Soudan français: administrateurs et missionnaires dans la boucle du Niger (1885–1945)* (Paris: Karthala, 1987), 400.

19. Rapport de Mgr Durrieu, Supérieur des Pères Blancs à S.E. le Cardinal Fumasoni-Biondi sur le comportement de la Maison généralice des Pères Blancs dans ses relations avec S. E. Mgr Lefebvre, ordinaire de Dakar, au sujet de l'hebdomadaire *Afrique Nouvelle*, Rome, Dec. 11, 1954, AGMAfr Durrieu 464.

20. On the paper's history, see Annie Lenoble-Bart, *Afrique nouvelle: un hebdomadaire catholique dans l'histoire 1947–1987* (Talence: Maison des sciences et de l'homme d'Aquitaine, 1996).

21. Rapport "L'affaire Islam," AGMAfr Durrieu 464. On Rummelhardt's reporting on slavery, see Chapter 7 and R. R., "La route des esclaves noirs commence à Villa Cisneros et aboutit à la Mecque," *Afrique nouvelle,* Aug. 4, 1954, 1, 4; R. R. "Trafiquants et marchés," *Afrique nouvelle,* Aug. 11, 1954, 1, 4; R. R., "Le Tibesti, gare de triage," *Afrique nouvelle,* Aug. 18, 1954, 1, 4.

22. Mgr Leclerc to P. Lanfry, Bamako, Oct. 20, 1957, AGMAfr Volker 675/1 (emphasis in the original).

23. Rapport "L'affaire Islam."

24. Rapport "L'affaire Islam."

25. Both Bayet and Méjan contributed to an edited collection put out by the Institut d'études juridiques de Nice, Centre de sciences politiques: *La laïcité* (Paris: Presses universitaires de France, 1960).

26. Albert Bayet, "Un document stupéfiant!" *La Manche laïque,* Jan. 1954, AGMAfr Durrieu 464.

27. Rapport "L'affaire Islam;" Bayet, "Un document stupéfiant!"

28. P. Rummelhardt to Mgr Durrieu, Dakar, Sept. 7, 1954, AGMAfr Durrieu 462/5. By contrast, Lefebvre's admiring disciple Bernard Tissier de Mallerais quotes Bernard Cornut-Gentille, high commissioner of French West Africa between 1951 and 1956, as saying, "'Mgr Lefebvre is the most intelligent man I have met in Africa. So when he comes to see me I pay close attention to what I say to him and I listen carefully to what he tells me.'" Bernard Tissier de Mallerais, *Marcel Lefebvre* (Condé-sur-Noireau, France: Clovis, 2002), 248.

29. Mgr Le Mailloux, "La Préfecture apostolique de Kankan," *Annales spirit-aines* 64, no. 3 (Apr. 1954): 35.
30. Papa Konaré to Mgr Le Hunsec, Kankan, Feb. 14, 1950, ACSSp 6I 1.5 a4 (emphasis in the original). Konare's hand-typed letterhead listed him as Agent de Commerce, Conseiller privé du Gouvernement de la Guinée, Chevalier de la Légion d'Honneur, Chevalier du mérite commercial, Titulaire de la médaille d'honneur du travail. On Muslims attending Catholic school in Senegal, see Denise Bouche, "L'école française et les musulmans au Sénégal de 1850 à 1920," *Revue française d'histoire d'Outre-Mer* 61, no. 223 (1974): 218–235.
31. Joseph Yamine, a Lebanese Christian merchant in Kankan, also wrote to Le Hunsec in defense of the priests, Fathers Jean-Marie Dronval (b. 1910, ordained 1937) and Paul Dambach (b. 1922, ordained 1948), crediting them for reawakening him to religion and mentioning that Christians and Muslims alike supported them. Joseph Yamine to Mgr. Kankan, Feb. 13, 1950, ACSSp 6I 1.5 a4. It seems there was more to the controversy than a dispute over a sermon—see additional documents in ACSSp 6I 1.5 a4. On Fathers Dronval and Dambach, see Gérard Vieira, *Sous le signe du laïcat: l'Église catholique en Guinée, Tome II: Le temps des prémices 1925–1958* (Dakar: Imprimerie Saint-Paul, 1998), 375–376; 409.
32. On this friendship, see Lansiné Kaba, *Cheikh Mouhammad Chérif et son temps: ou Islam et société à Kankan en Guinée, 1874–1955* (Paris: Présence africaine, 2004), 214–217.
33. M. L. M. (Maurice Le Mailloux), "Nos missions malinkées," *Annales spiritaines* 64, no. 3 (Apr. 1954): 36, 39.
34. Journal de communauté de Kankan-Kouroussa, Sept. 8, 1955, ACSSp 6I 2.4.
35. In 1953 the Dominicans founded the Institut dominicain d'études orientales (IDEO) in Cairo with the encouragement of Eugène Cardinal Tisserant, who worked with Father Marie-Dominique Chenu on the idea. Tisserant's goal was to "prove to Muslim elites that Christian clergy could take a great interest in Muslim religion and culture without trying to convert them." Yet Tisserant held negative views of Islam, similar to Lefebvre's, and also felt it was preparing the way for communism. Étienne Fouilloux, *Eugène, cardinal Tisserant, 1884–1972: une biographie* (Paris: Desclée de Brouwer, 2011), 435–436, 441. On the IDEO, see also Régis Morelon, "L'IDEO du Caire et ses intuitions fondatrices sur la relation à l'Islam," in *Mémoire dominicaine 15: Les dominicains et les mondes musulmans* (Paris: Cerf, 2001), 137–216.
36. Luc Moreau, "Pour une rencontre spirituelle," *Afrique nouvelle*, May 29, 1959, 1. Later, while teaching at the Institut catholique de l'Afrique de l'Ouest

in Abidjan, he published René Luc Moreau, *Africains musulmans: des communautés en mouvement* (Paris: Présence africaine, 1982).

37. Moreau, "Pour une rencontre spirituelle," 1–2.

38. Fr. Luc Moreau to Fr. Augstin [sic], Dakar, June 3, 1959, ADPL B1356 / BA2.

39. Archbishop of Bamako to Père Lanfry, Bamako, Jan. 25, 1960; Archbishop of Bamako to Père Lanfry, Feb. 24, 1960, AGMAfr Volker 675 / 1. Indeed, the hierarchy's declaration in response to the article shared the front page of the February 24 issue of *Afrique nouvelle* with coverage of the "first French A-bomb." *Afrique nouvelle* steered clear of editorializing on the situation, though it printed Lefebvre's "New Year's wishes" on an interior page of the January 1, 1960 issue. In this piece, Lefebvre, trying to tamp down the furor, wrote of how people of all backgrounds and faiths were "passengers together on the ship of Senegal and Mali," and addressing himself to "those who do not share our faith," he affirmed "our profound affection for their persons, their families, and we assure them of our devotion: schools, dispensaries, nurseries, are open wide to them, and may they understand that we want to do even more so that they can live in peace." M. Lefebvre, "Vœux du Nouvel An," *Afrique nouvelle,* Jan. 1, 1960, 4.

40. Maurice Voisin, "Mais que veut exactement Son Excellence Monseigneur Lefebvre?" *Echos d'Afrique noire,* Jan. 9, 1960, 1, 6.

41. Frederick Cooper, *Citizenship between Empire and Nation: Remaking France and French Africa* (Princeton, NJ: Princeton University Press, 2014), 332–336. Dahomey and Upper Volta were party to the initial talks but pulled out. Côte d'Ivoire, under the leadership of Félix Houphouët-Boigny, was vigorously opposed to federation, as it feared it would end up subsidizing poorer members.

42. They thus bypassed the provision in the 1958 constitution that equated a state's vote for independence with leaving the Community. As Frederick Cooper observes, "It was a measure of the nearly desperate desire of the French government to hold together something that resembled the Community created the year before that it was willing to consider such an option." Cooper, *Citizenship between Empire and Nation,* 342–343.

43. Quoted in Cooper, *Citizenship between Empire and Nation,* 368.

44. Tissier de Mallerais, *Marcel Lefebvre,* 256–257. Father Henri Étienne's correspondence confirms that Lefebvre had written this earlier for the Canadian daily *Le Devoir.* P. Henri Étienne to [P. Volker?], Jan. 12, 1960, AGMAfr Volker 669 / 4.

45. Senghor and Dia were frustrated by Lefebvre's article. Mouradian, Chargé d'affaires de France ad interim to M. le Ministre des Affaires étrangères, Dakar, Feb. 22, 1962, ADN 184PO/1/319.

46. "Declaration de M. Tidiani Traoré, Ministre de l'Information et de la sé-curité du Mali à propos de l'article de Monseigneur Lefebvre, archevêque de Dakar, paru dans *La France catholique* du 18 décembre 1959," ANS Fonds Fédération Mali 00013. Copies are also in ANS Fonds Fédération Mali 00510; ACSSp 3I 1.19 b4. The broadcast aired on Saturday, De-cember 26 and on Sunday, December 27, 1959. See "De Gaulle et les autres," *Paris-Dakar*, Dec. 30, 1959, 1. An annotated copy of this article in the White Fathers' archives (AGMAfr Volker 669/4) lists both dates, and Father Étienne reported that Traoré had "openly attacked Monsignor [Lefebvre] two times on the radio and in *Paris-Dakar*." P. Henri Étienne to [P. Volker?], Jan. 12, 1960.

47. Moreau claimed Niasse did so somewhat reluctantly, because he felt had to. See XXX [pseud.], "En Afrique noire, chrétiens et musulmans ne sont pas des chiens de faïence," *Témoignage chrétien*, Feb. 26, 1960. On Niasse, see Mervyn Hiskett, "The 'Community of Grace' and Its Opponents, the 'Rejecters': A Debate about Theology and Mysticism in Muslim West Africa with Special Reference to Its Hausa expression," *African Lan-guage Studies* 17 (1980): 99–140; Rüdiger Seesemann, *The Divine Flood: Ibrahim Niasse and the Roots of a Twentieth-Century Sufi Revival* (Oxford: Oxford University Press, 2011).

48. This text, *Ifriqiyya li-l-Ifriqiyyin*, is elusive. I am relying on a French trans-lation marked "confidential" in the AGMAfr. El Hadj Ibrahima Niasse, "L'Afrique va aux Africains," unknown trans., Kaolack, Jan. 5, 1960, AG-MAfr Volker 669/4.

49. Ibid.

50. On Massignon and Islam, see Louis Massignon, *Testimonies and Reflec-tions: Essays of Louis Massignon*, ed. Herbert Mason (Notre Dame, IN: University of Notre Dame Press, 1989); Pierre Rocalve, *Louis Massignon et l'Islam* (Damascus: Institut français de Damas, 1993); Jerrold Siegel, "The Islamic Catholicism of Louis Massignon," in *Between Cultures: Europe and Its Others in Five Exemplary Lives* (Philadelphia: University of Pennsylvania Press, 2016), 115–151.

51. Vincent Monteil, "Conférence donnée à Dakar le 14 Jan. 1960: Islam et Marxisme," AGMAfr Volker 669/7.

52. Rapport secret, Senegal, Dakar, Feb. 1, 1960, ADN 184PO/1/369. Note that the top of the document is also dated January 24, 1960. The text of this talk is not in a published collection of Ly's student writings. Ciré Ly, *Où va l'Afrique?* (Dakar: NIS, 198?).

53. Peytavin, active in the MRP, was known as "le Nègre-Blanc" and opted for Senegalese citizenship in 1960.

54. Rapport secret, Senegal, Dakar, Feb. 1, 1960.

55. Léopold Senghor, "Pour une cooperation entre l'Islam et le Christianisme," *Afrique nouvelle,* Nov. 16, 1959, 8. On Shaltūt and socialism, see Kate Zebiri, *Maḥmūd Shaltūt and Islamic Modernism* (Oxford: Oxford University Press, 1993), 55–57.

56. Archbishop of Bamako to Père Lanfry, Bamako, Jan. 25, 1960, AGMAfr Volker 675 / 1.

57. Mgr Maury to TRP Volker, Dakar, Jan. 20, 1960, AGMAfr Volker 669 / 1.

58. Mgr Maury to TRP Volker, Dakar, Feb. 6, 1960; Communiqué de l'A.F.P. Feb. 20, 1960, AGMAfr Volker 669 / 1.

59. Quoted in Communiqué de l'A.F.P. Feb. 20, 1960.

60. Mgr Pierre Leclerc (archevêque de Bamako), Mgr Didier de Montclos (préfet apostolique de Sikasso), Mgr Étienne Courtois (préfet apostolique de Kayes), Mgr René Landru (préfet apostolique de Gao), "Déclaration de l'Épiscopat du Soudan, Feb. 20, 1960, AGMAfr Volker 669 / 7.

61. Mgr Leclerc to P. Lanfry, Bamako, Oct. 20, 1957 (emphasis in the original).

62. "Communisme au Soudan?" Circulaire de l'Archevêque Leclerc, Bamako, Jan. 6, 1960, AGMAfr Volker 675 / 5.

63. Archbishop of Bamako to Père Lanfry, Bamako, Feb. 24, 1960.

64. "Lettre ouverte d'un groupe d'étudiants catholiques africains à l'archevêque de Dakar," *L'Essor hebdomadaire: organe de l'Union soudanaise-R.D.A.,* Feb. 5, 1960, 3. Modibo Keita was the chief of the Union soudanaise-Rassemblement démocratique africain, which, after the elections of March 1959, held all eighty seats in the legislature. On Keita, see Modibo Diagouraga, *Modibo Keita: un destin* (Paris: l'Harmattan, 1992).

65. See also Chapter 4. "Déclaration des étudiants catholiques d'Afrique noire en France," *Tam-Tam,* Apr.–May 1956, 4–6.

66. "Lettre ouverte d'un groupe d'étudiants."

67. Ibid. (emphasis in the original).

68. XXX [pseud.], "En Afrique noire, chrétiens et musulmans."

69. On Niasse's stance in 1958, see Leonardo Villalón, *Islamic Society and State Power in Senegal: Disciples and Citizens in Fatick* (Cambridge: Cambridge University Press, 1995), 206–207. Niasse endorsed de Gaulle's Community plan in 1958 alongside Falilou Mbacké and Tidiane Sy, but then protested the new constitution of the Mali Federation. He and Sy founded the Parti de la solidarité sénégalaise to challenge Senghor's Union progressiste sénégalaise, but did not win much support.

70. XXX [pseud.], "En Afrique noire, chrétiens et musulmans," 11.

71. Ibid., 12.

72. Louis Massignon, *Badaliya: au nom de l'autre (1947–1962)*, ed. Maurice Borrmans and Françoise Jacquin (Paris: Cerf, 2011).

73. Badaliya de Dakar Lettre no. 2, Dakar, May 8, 1960, ADPL B1350/1960.

74. Badaliya de Dakar Lettre no. 1, Dakar, Apr. 8, 1960, ADPL B1350/1960 (emphasis in the original).

75. Badaliya de Dakar Lettre no. 2. On charity, see Badaliya de Dakar Lettre no. 1. Moreau is listed as the contact person in Badaliya de Dakar Lettre no. 3, June 17, 1960, ADPL B1350/1960.

76. Badaliya de Dakar Lettre no. 2.

77. Badaliya de Dakar Lettre no. 1.

78. Mgr Lefebvre to R. P. Provincial des PP. Dominicains, Dakar, Sept. 16, 1961, ADPL B1350/1961.

79. P. Maurice Corvez to Mgr Lefebvre, Sept. 28, 1961, ADPL B1350/1961.

80. P. Gobert to P. Moreau, Rome, Oct. 3, 1961, ADPL B1350/1961.

81. Badaliya de Dakar, Lettre no. 3.

82. When Moreau was named a Dominican provincial superior in 1971, Thiandoum sent him a warm congratulatory letter, signed, "your friend forever in Jesus Christ." Mgr Thiandoum to P. Moreau, Dakar, Dec. 31, 1971, ADPL B1350/Dakar 1957–1971.

83. P. Étienne to P. [Volker ?], Dakar, Jan. 12, 1960.

84. Marcel Lefebvre, "Le message de notre Archevêque," *Horizons africains*, no. 118 (Mar. 1960), 1.

85. Guy de la Tournelle, Ambassadeur de France près le Saint-Siège to Couve de Murville, Ministre des Affaires étrangères, Rome, Apr. 13, 1960, ADN 576 PO/1/1467.

86. Claude Hettier de Boislambert, the French diplomatic representative to the Mali Federation and then ambassador to Senegal between 1960 and 1962, remarked in his memoirs that Lefebvre "is certainly a great Christian. I believe he is a wise theologian. As a diplomat, he is more questionable." Claude Hettier de Boislambert, *Les fers de l'espoir* (Paris: Plon, 1978), 540–541.

87. Daniel Konaté, *Monseigneur Luc Auguste Sangaré, archevêque de Bamako: le pasteur et le citoyen* (Bamako: Jamana, 2000), 44–45. For more on Sangaré and the church in Mali, see Pierre Diarra, *Cent ans de catholicisme au Mali: approche anthropologique et théologique d'une rencontre (1888–1988)* (Paris: Karthala, 2009).

88. For extensive coverage of Thiandoum's consecration, including numerous photographs, see *Horizons africains*, no. 140 (June 1962). See also Chérif Elvalid Sèye, *Mgr Hyacinthe Thiandoum: à force de foi* (Paris: L'Harmattan, 2007), 75–76. According to the French ambassador in Dakar in 1962, Thiandoum was "someone highly esteemed in Dakar, in both European and African circles, and by non-Christians as well." Claude Hettier de

Boislambert, Ambassadeur to Ministre des Affaires étrangères, Dakar, Apr. 10, 1962, ADN 576PO/1/1449. On Thiandoum's family, see Sidy Diop, "La famille du Cardinal: un arbre à deux branches," *Le Soleil* (Dakar), Apr. 16, 1999, 13; Charles Faye, "Le cursus d'un ecclésiaste peu ordinaire," *L'Info7,* May 19–20, 2004, 3, in ANS, Centre de Documentation, Dossier Hyacinthe Thiandoum.

89. Quoted in Le chargé d'affaires de France, a.i. Le Mire to Ministre d'Affaires étrangères, Dakar, May 26, 1962, ADN 576PO/1/1449.

90. Robert Serrou, "Dieu est blanc avec les blancs, nègre avec les nègres," *Paris-Match,* no. 1033, Feb. 22, 1969, 40.

91. "Témoignage: Grand Serigne de Dakar, Bassirou Diagne 'Un exemple à méditer,'" *Le Quotidien,* May 24, 2004, 3. See also Mamadou Biaye, "Disparition de Hyacinthe, Cardinal Thiandoum: le dialogue islamo-chrétien perd un allié," *Le Quotidien,* no. 419, May 18, 2004, in ANS, Centre de Documentation, Dossier Hyacinthe Thiandoum.

92. Christian S. Krokus, "Louis Massignon's Influence on the Teaching of Vatican II on Muslims and Islam," *Islam and Christian-Muslim Relations* 23, no. 3 (July 2012): 329–345. The French ambassador to Senegal noted regarding Islam at Vatican II, "It is possible that the Dominicans will prove to be more audacious in this matter than the White Fathers, who would doubtless have liked to have had a monopoly of the subject." Ambassadeur Jean de Lagarde to Ministre des Affaires étrangères Maurice Couve de Murville, Dakar, Sept. 29, 1964, confidential, ADN 576PO/1/1449.

93. Ambassadeur Jean de Lagarde to Ministre des Affaires étrangères Maurice Couve de Murville, Dakar, Sept. 29, 1964.

94. "Declaration on the Relation of the Church to Non-Christian Religions *Nostra aetate* proclaimed by His Holiness Pope Paul VI on October 28, 1965," http://www.vatican.va/archive/hist_councils/ii_vatican_council/documents/vat-ii_decl_19651028_nostra-aetate_en.html.

95. Marcel Lefebvre, *Un évêque parle: Mgr Marcel Lefebvre écrits et allocutions, 1963–1974* (Niort: Dominique Martin Morin, 1974); Marcel Lefebvre, *J'accuse le Concile!* 2nd ed. (Martigny: Saint-Gabriel, 1976).

96. Steven Greenhouse, "Archbishop Lefebvre, 85, Dies; Traditionalist Defied the Vatican," *New York Times,* Mar. 26, 1991, http://www.nytimes.com/1991/03/26/obituaries/archbishop-lefebvre-85-dies-traditionalist-defied-the-vatican.html.

97. Peter Stanford, "Cardinal Bernardin Gantin," *The Guardian,* May 14, 2008, https://www.theguardian.com/world/2008/may/15/catholicism.religion.

98. Ousmane Seck, "Le Cardinal Thiandoum à la presse: le dialogue principal apport de l'Afrique à l'Église universelle," *Le Soleil,* Feb. 7, 1977 in ANS, Centre de Documentation, Dossier Hyacinthe Thiandoum.

7. Slavery and Charity: Connecting French Catholics to Africa

1. On missionary PR in the late nineteenth century, see J. P. Daughton, *An Empire Divided: Religion, Republicanism and the Making of French Colonialism 1880–1914* (Oxford: Oxford University Press, 2006), 227–259.
2. See brochure "Quête de l'Épiphanie 1961," AAEA Box 6 / Correspondance. Lyon adopted the diocese of Koupéla in Upper Volta in 1958, Viviers adopted Laghouat in the Algerian Sahara, and Lille adopted Cameroon as a whole. Please note that the AAEA archives have moved to the CNAEF and have been reorganized since this research was conducted.
3. Société antiesclavagiste de France, Règlement général, 1. AAEA Box 6 / Administration. The Œuvre Pontificale de la Propagation de la Foi is not to be confused with the Propaganda Fide, the branch of the Roman Curia dedicated to evangelism, which was founded in the seventeenth century. The Œuvre Pontificale's work served the Propaganda Fide's mission, however.
4. On the 1794 abolition of slavery, see Miranda F. Spieler, "The Legal Structure of Colonial Rule during the French Revolution," *William and Mary Quarterly* 66 (2009): 365–408. On 1848 in Africa, see Martin Klein, *Slavery and Colonial Rule in French West Africa* (Cambridge: Cambridge University Press, 1998), 19–36. The measures in 1794 and 1848 were aimed primarily at white slave owners in the French colonies. A 1905 law prohibited enslavement and slave trading by subjects in France's West African holdings, though it did not abolish slavery outright. See Richard Roberts, "The End of Slavery in the French Soudan, 1905–1914," in *The End of Slavery in Africa*, ed. Suzanne Miers and Richard Roberts (Madison: University of Wisconsin Press, 1988), 282–307.
5. François Renault, *Lavigerie, l'esclavage africain et l'Europe 1868–1892, Tome II: Campagne antiesclavagiste* (Paris: E. de Bocard, 1971), 87–110, 116–117; William Mulligan, "The Anti-Slave Trade Campaign in Europe, 1888–1890," in *A Global History of Anti-Slavery Politics in the Nineteenth Century,* ed. William Mulligan and Maurice Bric (Basingstoke, UK: Palgrave Macmillan, 2013), 149–170.
6. "Conférence sur l'esclavage africain, faite à Saint-Sulpice, le 1er juillet 1888, par S. Em. Le Cardinal Lavigerie," in *Documents sur la Fondation de l'Œuvre antiesclavagiste,* by Charles Cardinal Lavigerie (Saint-Cloud: Vve Eugène Belin et fils, 1889), 45–73.
7. "Procès-verbal de l'Assemblée générale de la Société antiesclavagiste de France," Apr. 28, 1938, AAEA Box 6 / Administration. Lavigerie went so far as to found a separate (short-lived) armed brotherhood of religious, based

in Algeria, to combat slavery. Bertrand Taithe, "Missionary Militarism? The Armed Brothers of the Sahara and Léopold Joubert in the Congo," in *In God's Empire: French Missionaries and the Modern World,* ed. Owen White and J. P. Daughton (Oxford: Oxford University Press), 135–137.

8. Lavigerie, "Conférence sur l'esclavage," 73.

9. Seymour Drescher, *Abolition: A History of Slavery and Antislavery* (Cambridge: Cambridge University Press, 2009), 385.

10. On overlooked Catholic antislavery activism, see Amalia Ribi Forclaz, *Humanitarian Imperialism: The Politics of Anti-Slavery Activism, 1880–1940* (Oxford: Oxford University Press, 2015), 2–7, 17.

11. Pope Leo XIII, *In plurimis,* Rome, May 5, 1888, http://w2.vatican.va/content /leo-xiii/en/encyclicals/documents/hf_l-xiii_enc_05051888_in-plurimis .html. On Lavigerie's influence, see Renault, *Lavigerie, l'esclavage africain,* 74.

12. Pope Leo XIII, *Catholicae ecclesiae,* Rome, Nov. 20, 1890, http://w2.vatican .va/content/leo-xiii/en/encyclicals/documents/hf_l-xiii_enc_20111890 _catholicae-ecclesiae.html.

13. Forclaz claims that the society completely ceased to exist after 1918, which is not the case, though it went through extended inactive periods between 1924 and 1938 and again during World War II. See Forclaz, *Humanitarian Imperialism,* 1, 42. See also Denise Bouche, *Les villages de liberté en Afrique noire française 1887–1910* (Paris: Mouton, 1968), 251.

14. The executive directors have to be distinguished from the honorary presidents, of whom Lavigerie was the first. Former honorary presidents included prelates such as Monsignor Alexandre Le Roy, Spiritan superior general; distinguished Catholics with colonial interests such as Georges Picot or Charles Le Myre de Vilers, a governor of Cochinchina and resident-general of Madagascar; and military men such as Vice-Admiral Henri Joubert and Vice-Admiral Jules Le Bigot.

15. Georges de Caunes, "Il y a encore des marchands d'esclaves," *Paris-Match,* June 25, 1955, 94–98. Facing the title page is a full-page photograph of Awad el Djoud speaking with Father David Traoré, an African White Father. The caption reads, "This priest was Awad's first ally in Bamako, even though Awad is Muslim."

16. See also Chapter 6 and R. R., "La route des esclaves noirs commence à Villa Cisneros et aboutit à la Mecque," *Afrique nouvelle,* Aug. 4, 1954, 1, 4; R. R. "Trafiquants et marchés," *Afrique nouvelle,* Aug. 11, 1954, 1, 4; R. R., "Le Tibesti, gare de triage," *Afrique nouvelle,* Aug. 18, 1954, 1, 4. On the case in recent scholarship, see Bruce S. Hall, "Bellah Histories of Decolonization, Iklan Paths to Freedom: The Meanings of Race and Slavery in the

Late-Colonial Niger Bend (Mali), 1944–1960," *International Journal of African Historical Studies* 44 (2011): 79–84; Baz Lecocq, *Disputed Desert: Decolonisation, Competing Nationalisms and Tuareg Rebellions in Northern Mali* (Leiden: Brill, 2010), 116–127, and "Awad El Djouh and the Dynamics of Post-Slavery," *International Journal of African Historical Studies* 48 (2015): 193–208; Gregory Mann, *From Empires to NGOs in the West African Sahel: The Road to Nongovernmentality* (New York: Cambridge University Press, 2015), 112. Hailing from Goundam, not far from Timbuktu, Awad El Djoud was a *bellah,* or servile person, in Tuareg society. For more, see Baz Lecocq, "The Bellah Question: Slave Emancipation, Race, and Social Categories in Late Twentieth-Century Northern Mali," *Canadian Journal of African Studies* 39 (2005): 42–68.

17. Not cited elsewhere in the chapter are "L'esclavage en Afrique noire," *Samedi-Soir,* Jan. 8, 1953, 4, 10; G. Normand, "À travers l'Afrique, sur la route des esclaves," *Noir et Blanc,* Apr. 29, 1953, 278–279; Jean Welle, "Oui, il y a encore des marchands d'esclaves," *Pourquoi pas?,* Mar. 27, 1953, 39–40.

18. For more on Vialle, a journalist, *résistante,* activist, and politician, who was killed in a 1953 plane crash, see Jacques Serre, "Jane Vialle," in *Hommes et destins: dictionnaire biographique d'Outre-Mer,* vol. 9: *Afrique noire* (Paris: Académie des sciences d'Outre-Mer, 1989), 759–769.

19. Suzanne Miers, *Slavery in the Twentieth Century: The Evolution of a Global Pattern* (Walnut Creek, CA: AltaMira Press, 2003), 323–332.

20. Jacques Alain, "Du Sahara à l'Arabie, j'ai suivi les derniers convois d'esclaves," *France-Soir,* Dec. 4, 1952, 6.

21. Editorial, *France-Soir,* Dec. 4, 1952, 6.

22. Emmanuel La Gravière, "Rapport," Assemblée de l'Union française, Session de 1955–1956, no. 75. On La Gravière, see his French senate profile at https://www.senat.fr/senateur-4eme-republique/la_graviere_emmanuel0539r4.html# 1940–1958.

23. On Méjan and La Gravière's relationship, see their correspondence from 1957 and 1958 in OURS 71 APO 17. Emmanuel La Gravière, "L'affaire du trafic d'esclaves noirs," *Nouvelle revue française d'Outre-Mer* 48, no. 1 (Jan. 1956): 4.

24. R. R., "Le Tibesti," 4. Rummelhardt also alleged that remnants of Rommel's Afrika Korps in Libya served as middlemen by selling arms to slavers from Western Africa that ultimately made their way into the hands of "insurgents" in French North Africa. He relied heavily on Alain and Dr. M. G. Schenk, *Er zijn nog slaven* (Amsterdam: IVIO, 1953).

25. On the American consul, see Miers, *Slavery in the Twentieth Century,* 348.

26. Alain, "Du Sahara à l'Arabie," 6; La Gravière, "L'affaire du traffic," 3–4.

27. Unsigned, undated report post Sept. 1952, 1. AAEA Box 6 / Administration.

28. Unsigned document, Paris, Jan. 8, 1926, AAEA Box 6 / Administration.

29. Note, Paris, Jan. 11, 1926, AAEA Box 6 / Administration.

30. "Assemblée de la Société antiesclavagiste," Apr. 30, 1952, 2, AAEA Box 6 / Administration.

31. Mgr Marcel Lefebvre to Mgr François du Mesnil, Dakar, Sept. 16, 1952, AAEA Box 5 / Société. This letter was reproduced in diocesan bulletins. See for example *La semaine religieuse du diocèse de Saint-Brieuc et Tréguier*, Dec. 25, 1953, 821–822.

32. Charles Tisserant, *Catalogue de la flore de l'Oubangui-Chari* (Toulouse: P. Julia, 1950). He also authored a Banda / French dictionary and a Banda grammar book.

33. Charles Tisserant, "Note sur l'état actuel de l'esclavage en Afrique noire française," Paris, Aug. 28, 1952, AAEA Box 6 / Correspondance.

34. Tisserant, "Note sur l'état actuel," 1. See Alice L. Conklin, *In the Museum of Man: Race, Anthropology, and Empire in France, 1850–1950* (Ithaca, NY: Cornell University Press, 2013), 180 on the meaning of *ethnie.*

35. Tisserant, "Note sur l'état actuel," 1–2.

36. Ibid., 1–3.

37. Mgr du Mesnil to P. Tisserant, Jan. 20, 1953, AAEA Box 5 / Société. For echoes, see J. P., "Il y a encore des esclaves en Afrique," *La Croix*, Dec. 18, 1952, 3; as well as the articles in *France-Soir, Noir et Blanc, Pourquoi pas?* and *Samedi-Soir* cited above.

38. Mgr du Mesnil to P. Tisserant, May 6, 1953, AAEA Box 5 / Société.

39. Maurice Bourdel to Mgr du Mesnil, Paris, Apr. 28, 1955, AAEA Box 5 / Société. The first printing comprised 1,000 copies.

40. All of the relevant correspondence is in AAEA Box 5 / Société.

41. Mgr du Mesnil to Cardinal Liénart, July 5, 1955, AAEA Box 5 / Société.

42. Charles Orengo to Mgr du Mesnil, Paris, Feb. 2, 1956, AAEA Box 5 / Société.

43. Charles Tisserant, *Ce que j'ai connu de l'esclavage en Oubangui-Chari* (Paris: Société antiesclavagiste de France, 1955), 1, 55, 56, 64, 66.

44. Ibid., 48, 64. On the establishment of family allocations in postwar French Africa, see Frederick Cooper, *Decolonization and African Society: The Labor Question in French and British Africa* (Cambridge: Cambridge University Press, 1996), 300–303, 314–321.

45. P. Charles Tisserant to Monsignor, Boukoko, Jan. 10, 1953, AAEA Box 5 / Société.

46. Mgr Jean Lesourd to Mgr, Nouna, 1953, AAEA Burkina III.

47. "Apostolate of liberation" is used as a section heading in Jean Pélissier, "L'esclavage sévit encore en Afrique . . ." *La Croix*, Jan. 7, 1954, 3.

48. See, among many others, Gregory Massell, *The Surrogate Proletariat: Moslem Women and Revolutionary Strategies in Soviet Central Asia, 1919–1929* (Princeton, NJ: Princeton University Press, 1974); Susan Pedersen, "National Bodies, Unspeakable Acts: The Sexual Politics of Colonial Policy-Making," *Journal of Modern History* 63 (1991): 647–680; Lata Mani, *Contentious Traditions: The Debate on Sati in Colonial India* (Berkeley: University of California Press, 1998).

49. Missionaries in interwar Senegal complained that the administration deferred to indigenous customs that subordinated women: see Elizabeth A. Foster, *Faith in Empire: Religion, Politics, and Colonial Rule in French Senegal* (Stanford, CA: Stanford University Press, 2013), 141–167. On the other hand, some administrators in Cameroon "criminalized" African marriage practices. Charlotte Walker, "Legislating the Trafficking and Slavery of Women and Girls: The Criminalization of Marriage, Tradition, and Gender Norms in French Colonial Cameroon, 1914–1945," in *Sex Trafficking, Human Rights, and Social Justice*, ed. Tiantian Zheng (London: Routledge, 2010), 150–169. The French set a minimum age of consent for marriage at fourteen for girls and sixteen for boys in the Mandel Decree of June 15, 1939. In 1951, the Jacquinot Decree stated that women who reached the age of twenty-one could marry freely, without the consent of or financial obligations to their parents, but missions complained it was hard to enforce. In 1961, Bishop Jean Lesourd observed that legislation against forced marriage in independent Upper Volta had no effect in rural areas. Mgr Jean Lesourd to M. le Chanoine, Nouna, Sept. 20, 1961, AAEA Burkina III.

50. "Assemblée de la Société antiesclavagiste," Apr. 30, 1952, p. 3.

51. Pélissier, "L'esclavage sévit encore en Afrique," 3.

52. Mgr Lefebvre to Mgr du Mesnil, Sept. 16, 1952.

53. Tisserant, "Note sur l'état actuel," 2. See also Charles Tisserant, "Le mariage dans l'Oubangui-Chari," *Bulletin de l'Institut d'études centrafricaines* N.S., no. 2 (1951): 73–102, and "Quelques remarques au sujet de la dot," *Bulletin de l'Institut d'études centrafricaines* N.S., no. 3 (1952): 187–200.

54. Tisserant, "Note sur l'état actuel," 2.

55. Mgr Bernard to Mgr, Conakry, Feb. 4, 1954, AAEA Conakry.

56. Mgr de Milleville to Mgr, Conakry, Jan. 19, 1956, AAEA Conakry.

57. Mgr Joseph Bretault to Directeur général, Koudougou, Aug. 19, 1957, AAEA Burkina II. Bretault also claimed that the French administration supported slavery.

58. See "Œuvre de la liberation de l'esclavage et du paganisme 1954–1955" attached to Mgr Joseph Bretault to Mgr, Koudougou, Sept. 24, 1955. For the

previous year, see "État de nos œuvres de libération au 30 juin 1953," attached to Mgr Joseph Bretault to Mgr, Koudougou, Aug. 28, 1953, AAEA Burkina II.

59. Mgr D. Yougbaré to Mgr, Koupéla, Jan. 2, 1958, AAEA Burkina II.
60. Mgr A. Duirat to Mgr du Mesnil, Bouaké, Sept. 13, 1954, AAEA Côte d'Ivoire II.
61. Mgr François du Mesnil to Excellence révérendissime, Paris, Dec. 8, 1954, AAEA Box 7 / Personnel.
62. Mgr D. Yougbaré to Mgr, Koupéla, Jan. 2, 1958.
63. Mgr Lefebvre to Mgr du Mesnil, Sept. 16, 1952.
64. Mgr Jean Lesourd to M. le Chanoine, Nouna, July 21, 1960, AAEA Burkina III.
65. Becoming a missionary nun was a way for French women to escape rigid gender roles somewhat. See Elizabeth A. Foster, "'En mission il faut se faire à tout': les Sœurs de la Conception Immaculée de Castres au Sénégal, 1880–1900," trans. François Proulx, in *Femmes missionnaires: l'autre visage de la mission,* ed. Sarah A. Curtis, *Histoire et missions chrétiennes* 16 (2010): 73–108; Sarah A. Curtis, *Civilizing Habits: Women Missionaries and the Revival of French Empire* (Oxford: Oxford University Press, 2010).
66. Mgr Jean Lesourd to M. le Chanoine, Nouna, June 15, 1958, AAEA Burkina III.
67. Kenneth Orosz traces the term *sixa* to the pidgin English word for "sister," noting that these institutions were first created under German colonial rule in Cameroon. Kenneth J. Orosz, "The 'Affaire des Sixas' and Catholic Education of Women in French Colonial Cameroon, 1915–1939," *French Colonial History* 1, no. 1 (2002): 46, n. 23.
68. Mgr Jean Lesourd to M. le Chanoine, Nouna, July 21, 1960.
69. Mgr Michel Bernard to Mgr, Conakry, Feb. 4, 1954.
70. Many African women in Cameroon, both Protestant and Catholic, thoroughly embraced this model. Charlotte Walker-Said, "Christian Marriage between Tradition and Modernity: Catholic and Protestant Women and Marriage Education in Late Colonial Cameroon, 1939–1960," *Gender and History* 29, no. 3 (2017): 1–26.
71. Mgr Jean Lesourd to M. le Chanoine, Nouna, Sept. 23, 1959, AAEA Burkina III.
72. Mgr du Mesnil to P. Charles Tisserant, May 6, 1953. Her birth name was Jeanne-Émilie Dorge, but her religious name is used in most library catalogs. Lavigerie founded the White Sisters in 1869 as a complement to the White Fathers.
73. Marie-André du Sacré-Cœur, *La femme noire en Afrique occidentale* (Paris: Payot, 1939), 222, 225.

74. Ibid., 207, 257.
75. Ibid., 229–230.
76. Marie-André du Sacré-Cœur, *La condition humaine en Afrique noire* (Paris: Grasset, 1953).
77. Charles Tisserant, "Sur le livre de Soeur Marie-André *La Condition humaine en Afrique noire*," enclosed with P. Charles Tisserant to Monsignor, Boukoko, Mar. 25, 1953, AAEA Box 5 / Société.
78. P. Perraud to Mgr, Dakar, July 9, 1957, AAEA Senegal I.
79. Mgr François du Mesnil to Excellence révérendissime, Paris, Dec. 8, 1954.
80. Mgr François du Mesnil to Excellence révérendissime, Paris, Dec. 8, 1955, AAEA Box 7 / Personnel.
81. Pius XII, *Fidei donum,* April 21, 1957, http://w2.vatican.va/content/pius-xii /en/encyclicals/documents/hf_p-xii_enc_21041957_fidei-donum.html.
82. Ibid.
83. See Chanoine M. Leveque to M. le Directeur, Paris, Dec. 15, 1957; Chanoine M. Leveque to M. le Curé, Paris, Dec. 30, 1957, AAEA Box 5 / Animation 1951–1969.
84. He continued to publish one or two issues a year into the 1970s, but in 1961 he decided against making it a quarterly periodical—see *Aide aux missions françaises d'Afrique,* no. 5 (1961): inside cover.
85. Chanoine M. Leveque, "Libération de la femme africaine," *Aide aux missions françaises d'Afrique,* no. 1 (1959): 2.
86. Chanoine Marcel Leveque to Mgr Maury, Aug. 23, 1959, AAEA Senegal I.
87. There had been at least one missionary voice that questioned the focus on slavery earlier in the 1950s. In 1954, Spiritan apostolic vicar of Conakry Michel Bernard argued that the society's antislavery moniker had become increasingly awkward: "you are not unaware, Monsignor, that it is difficult in this day and age to talk of slavery in territories such as those of the French Union, where so-called liberal ideas have been widely disseminated," though Michel definitely thought slavery was an ongoing problem. He likened the status of women in Guinea to that of slaves, and asserted, "the customs and traditions which constitute the social fabric of the country remain pervaded with the spirit of slavery." Mgr Michel Bernard to Mgr, Conakry, Feb. 4, 1954.
88. M. L., "Changement de titre," *Aide aux missionnaires français d'Afrique,* no. 13 (1965): inside front cover.
89. Mgr Paul Zoungrana to Chanoine Leveque, confidential, Ouagadougou, June 21, 1962, AAEA Burkina III.
90. French diplomats described Yaméogo as "very Catholic," but that did not prevent church and state tensions under his rule. Raoul Delaye, Ambassadeur de France en Haute-Volta to Monsieur Maurice Couve de Murville,

Ministère des Affaires étrangères, confidential, Ouagadougou, Feb. 17, 1968, p. 10, ADN 1PO/1/17.

91. Mgr Giovanni Mariani to Chanoine Leveque, Dakar, June 18, 1968, AAEA Senegal I.

92. Mgr Giovanni Mariani to Chanoine Leveque, Dakar, July 23, 1968, AAEA Senegal I.

93. Chanoine M. Leveque to Cardinal Agagianian, July 2, 1968, AAEA Box 6/Correspondance.

94. Ibid.

95. Cardinal Agagianian to Chanoine Leveque, Rome, Sept. 7, 1968, AAEA Box 6/Correspondance.

96. Canon M. Leveque, "Bataille pour l'Afrique," *Aide aux missions françaises d'Afrique*, no. 2 (1960): 2.

97. He felt it was worse among the "évolué" population. Canon M. Leveque, "Ne pas laisser à elle-même l'Église d'Afrique," *Aide aux missions françaises d'Afrique*, no. 5 (1961): 2. See also M. L., "Changement de titre."

98. Chanoine Marcel Leveque to Cardinal Agagianian, Paris, Apr. 18, 1961, AAEA Box 6/Correspondance.

99. Cardinal Agagianian to Chanoine Marcel Leveque, Rome, May 2, 1961, AAEA Box 6/Correspondance.

100. "Quête de l'Épiphanie 1961 = plus de 80 millions de francs distribués entre 65 diocèses en Afrique noire," AAEA Box 6/Correspondance.

101. Back cover of *Aide aux missions françaises d'Afrique*, no. 11 (1964).

102. "Quête de l'Épiphanie," http://www.aea.cef.fr/-Quete-de-l-Epiphanie-.

103. In 1965, Leveque reproduced a graph from the missionary magazine *Spiritus* showing the decline in missionary vocations for men in France between 1951 and 1964. Between 1951 and 1960 there was a 40 percent decline in priestly vocations overall, and a 60 percent drop in missionary vocations. A notable increase in the year 1960 did not stem the overall tide of decline, which resumed afterward. See *Aide aux missions françaises d'Afrique*, no. 12 (1965): inside front cover.

Conclusion: Decolonization and Vatican II

1. For a list of council fathers representing Africa, see Georges Conus, "L'Église d'Afrique au Concile Vatican II," *Neue Zeitschrift für Missionswissenschaft/Nouvelle revue de science missionnaire* 30 (1974): 254–255.

2. John XXIII, "Opening Address to the Council," in *The Encyclicals and Other Messages of John XXIII* (Washington, DC: TPS Press, 1964), 427. On authorship, see Peter Hebblethwaite, *Pope John XXIII* (Garden City, NY: Doubleday, 1985), 430.

3. Pope John XXIII, *Pope John XXIII: Essential Writings,* ed. Jean Maalouf (Maryknoll, NY: Orbis Books, 2008), 111.

4. Adrian Hastings, "The Council Came to Africa," in *Vatican II: By Those Who Were There,* ed. Alberic Stacpoole (London: Geoffrey Chapman, 1986), 316–318.

5. Robert Sastre, "Un Concile à l'heure de l'Afrique," in *Personnalité africaine et catholicisme,* ed. Meinrad P. Hebga (Paris: Présence africaine, 1963), 17; *Tam-Tam,* Apr.-May 1962.

6. Hastings, "The Council Came to Africa," 315–316.

7. Sastre, "Un Concile à l'heure de l'Afrique," 19.

8. On his time in France, see Angelo G. Roncalli, *Souvenirs d'un nonce: cahiers de France (1944–1953)* (Rome: Edizione di Storia e Letteratura, 1963).

9. These are collected in *Un hommage africain à Jean XXIII* (Paris: Présence africaine, 1965), put together by the Société africaine de culture.

10. "Radiomessaggio del Santo Padre Giovanni XXIII ai fedeli di tutto il mondo, a un mese dal Concilio Ecumenico Vaticano II," Sept. 11, 1962, https://w2.vatican.va/content/john-xxiii/it/messages/pont_messages/1962/documents/hf_j-xxiii_mes_19620911_ecumenical-council.html. For the point about drafts, see Hebblethwaite, *Pope John XXIII,* 423.

11. Hebblethwaite, *Pope John XXIII,* 425–426. It was also a bid to shore up the Vatican's ties with the Italian state: Saint Francis was also the patron saint of Italy, and the Italian prime minister and president accompanied John for parts of the journey.

12. "Discours du Pape Jean XXIII au Président de la République du Sénégal Léopold Sédar Senghor," Oct. 5, 1962, https://w2.vatican.va/content/john-xxiii/fr/speeches/1962/documents/hf_j-xxiii_spe_19621005_presidente-senegal.html.

13. "Résumé des questions discutées au cours des deux journées d'études à Rome (26 et 27 mai 1962) sur la présence et l'expression de la personnalité africaine dans la vie catholique," *Présence africaine* N.S. 44 (4e trimestre, 1962): 249–254. See also Claude Prudhomme, "Les évêques d'Afrique noire anciennement française et le concile," in *Vatican II commence . . . approches francophones,* ed. E. Fouilloux (Leuven: Bibliotheek van de Faculteit der Godgeleerdheid, 1993), 165.

14. "A l'occasion du colloque réuni à Rome, M. Alioune Diop précise ce que l'Afrique attend de l'Église," *Informations catholiques internationales* 171 (July 1, 1962): 4–5.

15. Présence africaine, "Deux initiatives," *Présence africaine* N.S. 44 (4e trimestre, 1962): 6.
16. "A l'occasion du colloque réuni à Rome," 4–5.
17. "Discours du Pape Jean XXIII au Président de la République du Sénégal."
18. In 1962, after resigning in Dakar, Lefebvre was elected as Spiritan superior general in a contentious vote that reflected deep generational and philosophical divides in the congregation. Luc Perrin, "Mgr Lefebvre, d'une élection à une demission (1962–1968)," *Histoire et missions chrétiennes* 10 (2009): 139–172.
19. "Évangélisateur et grand organisateur de l'Église en Afrique," *Fideliter* 59 (Sept.–Oct. 1987): 21.
20. Mgr Marcel Lefebvre, "De la pertinacité dans l'erreur ou vers l'apostasie généralisée," *Fideliter* 48 (Nov.–Dec. 1985): 28.
21. "Évangélisateur et grand organisateur," 21–22.
22. John W. O'Malley, *What Happened at Vatican II?* (Cambridge: Belknap Press, 2008), 110–111.
23. Marcel Lefebvre, *J'accuse le Concile!* 2nd ed. (Martigny, Switzerland: Saint-Gabriel, 1976), 75.
24. Ibid., 8–9.
25. "L'épiscopat africain," *Horizons Africains* 148 (Mar. 1963): 13.
26. On francophone African interventions at Vatican II, see Michel Cancouët, *L'Afrique au Concile: journal d'un expert,* ed. Daniel Moulinet (Rennes: Presses universitaires de Rennes, 2013).
27. Agbonkhianmeghe E. Orobator, SJ, "'After All, Africa Is a Largely Nonliterate Continent': The Reception of Vatican II in Africa," *Theological Studies* 74 (2013): 288.
28. Prudhomme, "Les évêques d'Afrique noire," 171, 178.
29. "Rapport de Son Excellence Mgr Gantin sur la première session du Concile," ACSSp 3I 1.19 a5.
30. Prudhomme, "Les évêques d'Afrique noire," 172, 180.
31. There was a subordinate francophone secretariat headed by Jean Zoa, archbishop of Yaoundé in Cameroon. The continent was also divided into nine regional "conferences," each headed by a prelate. Gantin presided over the West African conference, which included Togo, and Zoa led the conference composed of former French Equatorial Africa and Cameroon. Conus, "L'Église d'Afrique au Concile," 250–252.
32. Congar quoted in Conus, "L'Église d'Afrique au Concile," 253.
33. R. P. Chenu, "L'Afrique au Concile," *Tam-Tam,* Jan.–Feb. 1963, 31. See also M.-D. Chenu, "L'Afrique au Concile," *Parole et mission* 6, no. 20 (Jan. 15, 1963): 11–18.
34. Frère Dominique, "L'Afrique et le Concile," *Tam-Tam,* Nov.–Dec. 1962, 21.

35. L.B., "Le nouveau cardinal," *Tam-Tam*, Jan.–Feb. 1965, 27–28.

36. Assisted by Cardinal Quintero of Venezuela and Cardinal Bueno y Monreale from Spain, Zoungrana addressed the workers of the world, professing the church's love for them and interest in their problems, while calling on them to accept its message.

37. Gérard Vieira, *L'Église catholique en Guinée à l'épreuve de Sékou Touré (1958–1984)* (Paris: Karthala, 2005), 263–264, 268.

38. Rachel Kantrowitz, "Triangulating between Church, State, and Postcolony: *Coopérants* in Independent West Africa," *Cahiers d'études africaines* 56 (2016): 220–222.

39. Philip Jenkins, *The Next Christendom: The Coming of Global Christianity*, 3rd ed. (Oxford: Oxford University Press, 2011), 3, 73. On global Christianity with a frequent emphasis on Africa, see also the copious writings of Lamin Sanneh, such as Lamin Sanneh, *Disciples of All Nations: Pillars of World Christianity* (Oxford: Oxford University Press, 2008).

40. Jenkins, *The Next Christendom*, 118. On France see Paul Mercator, *La fin des paroisses? Recompositions des communautés, aménagement des espaces* (Paris: Desclée de Brouwer, 1997).

41. "Prêtres français dans le monde et prêtres étrangers dans les diocèses de France," Statistiques de l'Église catholique, http://www.eglise.catholique.fr /conference-des-eveques-de-france/guide-de-leglise/leglise-catholique -en-france-et-en-chiffres/369948-leglise-catholique-dans-le-monde-et -des-pretres-etrangers-dans-les-dioceses/.

42. An estimated 58,000 French religious (including priests, nuns, and brothers) were working in the French colonies or foreign territory in 1900. J. P. Daughton, *An Empire Divided: Religion, Republicanism, and the Making of French Colonialism, 1880–1914* (New York: Oxford University Press, 2006), 11.

43. "French Church Attack: What We Know," BBC News, July 28, 2016, http://www.bbc.com/news/world-europe-36900761.

44. Adam Nossiter and Hannah Olivennes, "Jacques Hamel, 85, a Beloved French Priest Killed in His Church," *New York Times*, July 26, 2016, https://www.nytimes.com/2016/07/27/world/europe/jacques-hamel-85-a -beloved-french-priest-killed-in-his-church.html. A French government employee of African descent, Brice Wete-Matouba, described Hamel as an "African and a humanist" in the wake of the killing. See http://jci-echanges -afrique-monde.com/index.php/notre-blog/racontez-nous-l-afrique-et -le-congo-brazzaville/585-pere-jacques-hamel-l-africain-avec-l-abbe -auguste-moanda-phuati-francais-congolais-humanistes-de-coeur-plus -de-que-naissance.

45. "Prêtres français dans le monde et prêtres étrangers dans les diocèses de France."
46. "État du personnel—Statistiques—30 June 2016," http://spiritains.org/pays /statist.htm.
47. For statistics, see Hannah Fairfield, Jon Huang, and Amanda Cox, "The 115 Men Who Will Choose the Next Pope," *New York Times* online inter- active feature, Feb. 17, 2013, http://www.nytimes.com/interactive/2013/02/17 /world/europe/pope-cardinals.html?ref=romancatholicchurch.
48. See, for example, his decision to break with Vatican precedent and wash and kiss the feet of prisoners, including two women, on Maundy Thursday 2013. "Pope Francis Washes Prisoners' Feet on Maundy Thursday," BBC News, Mar. 28, 2013, http://www.bbc.co.uk/news/world-europe-21963105. See also Robert Pigott, "Mass Points to Pope's New Priorities," BBC News, Mar. 19, 2013, http://www.bbc.co.uk/news/world-europe-21850067.

ARCHIVES AND KEY PERIODICALS

Archives

FRANCE

Archives Aide aux Églises d'Afrique (formerly Société antiesclavagiste de France), Paris
> Note: After this research was conducted, the AAEA archives moved to the Centre national des archives de l'Église de France in Issy-les-Moulineaux. The materials are intact, but are no longer organized according to the system cited here.
> Boxes:
> 3, 4, 5, 6, 7
>
> Dossiers:
> Benin I, II
> Burkina Faso II, III
> Côte d'Ivoire II
> Guinée / Conakry
> Mauritanie
> Sénégal I, II

Archives de la Congrégation du Saint-Esprit (Spiritans), Chevilly-Larue
> 2F: Relations avec les diocèses
> 2G: Province de France
> 3I: Sénégal

3J: Congo-Brazzaville
6I: Guinée
Salle des Fonds: Fonds Joseph Michel
Salle de Documentation: SD 13 Sénégal

Archives des Missions étrangères de Paris, Paris
DP 100.1: P. Prouvost, Afrique

Archives nationales de France, Pierrefitte-sur-Seine
72AJ / 535–72AJ / 541: Papiers Henri Laurentie

Archives nationales d'Outre-Mer, Aix-en-Provence
Fonds FIDES (Fonds d'investissement pour le développement
économique et social):
1 FIDES
2 FIDES

Fonds 1Affpol (Affaires politiques):
AP 478
AP 2190
AP 2192
AP 2260
AP 2286
AP 3349

Archives de l'Office universitaire de recherche socialiste, Paris
71 APO 1–71 APO 53: Fonds François Méjan

Archives de la Préfecture de Police de Paris, Le Pré-Saint-Gervais
ASS: Associations
G: Renseignements généraux
W: Fonds contemporains

Archives dominicaines, Bibliothèque du Saulchoir, Paris
Province de France:
Photographs; Fiche chronologique du Frère Joseph-Vincent Ducattillon
Province de Lyon:
B 1224 Fonds Nielly
B 1350 Dakar
B 1356 Dakar, Abidjan

Archives de la Société des missions africaines, Strasbourg
    Boxes 50–56: Missions Côte d'Ivoire, Togo
    Dossiers du personnel

Bibliothèque de documentation internationale contemporaine, Nanterre
    Fonds de la Jeunesse étudiante chrétienne internationale

Centre des Archives diplomatiques, Nantes
    Abidjan 1PO/1
    Bamako 62PO/1
    Bobo Dioulasso 101PO/1
    Conakry 163PO/1
    Cotonou 176PO/1
    Dakar 184PO/1
    Rome/Saint-Siège 576PO/1

ITALY

Archives générales de la Société des missionnaires d'Afrique (White Fathers), Rome
    Fonds GEN Mgr Durrieu
    Fonds GEN Père Volker
    Fonds Joseph-Roger de Benoist

Archives de la Société des missions africaines, Rome
    1G 44.3 Statuts clergé indigène
    2D Rapports et circulaires des chefs de mission, correspondance
    2K Évêques africains

SENEGAL

Archives de l'Archidiocèse de Dakar, Dakar
    Dossiers:
    R. P. Bussard
    Mgr Grimault
    Mgr Lefebvre
    Mgr Thiandoum

Archives nationales du Sénégal, Dakar
    Centre de Documentation:
        Dossier Hyacinthe Thiandoum

Fonds AOF:
    2G Rapports périodiques
    O Enseignement et Sciences et Arts
Fonds Fédération du Mali
Fonds Sénégal:
    1G Enseignement

Fonds de Vice-Présidence et Présidence du Conseil de Gouvernement du Sénégal

Key Periodicals

Actualité religieuse dans le monde
Afrique nouvelle (Dakar)
Aide aux missions françaises d'Afrique
Combat
Comprendre
Documentation catholique
Ecclésia: lectures chrétiennes
Echos missionnaires (MEP)
Esprit
Études
Fideliter
Horizons africains (Dakar)
Informations catholiques internationales
La Croix
L'année politique et économique
L'Essor (Bamako)
Le Figaro
Le Monde
Le Soleil (Dakar)
L'Osservatore Romano (Vatican)
Nouvelle revue française d'Outre-Mer
Paris-Match
Parole et mission
Présence africaine
Revue de l'Action populaire
Samedi-Soir
Tam-Tam
Témoignage chrétien

ACKNOWLEDGMENTS

This book has been a joy to research and write, largely because of all of the remarkable people who have helped me along the way. I am deeply grateful for the humbling generosity of many institutions, archivists, mentors, colleagues, family members, friends, and students who made it possible for me to complete it. A Fulbright Scholar Award to France allowed me to launch my research, and I could not have obtained it without the kind invitation of Emmanuelle Sibeud and Philippe Minard at Université Paris 8. A visiting appointment at the Minda de Gunzburg Center for European Studies at Harvard enabled me to make early headway in a vibrant community of scholars, and a summer stipend from the National Endowment for the Humanities supported further archival research. Fellowships from the National Endowment for the Humanities and the American Council of Learned Societies provided additional leave that carried me over the finish line. During that time, a visiting appointment in the Harvard History Department gave me access to essential resources. I would not have benefited from these opportunities without the extraordinary kindness of mentors who have advised me and advocated for me tirelessly for years. My most sincere thanks to Ann Blair, Alice Conklin, Frederick Cooper, and Philip Nord for their steadfast support and encouragement. In addition, I am very thankful for crucial assistance from Dean Bárbara Brizuela, the Faculty Research Awards Committee, and Jonathan Wilson and Khalilah Tyre at the Center for the Humanities, all at Tufts University. Portions of Chapter 3 were first published by the University of Chicago Press as "'Theologies of Colonization': The Catholic Church and the Future of the French Empire in the 1950s," *Journal of Modern History* 87, no. 2 (2015): 281–315. Parts of Chapter 4 are drawn from "'Entirely Christian and Entirely African': Catholic

African Students in France in the Era of Independence," *Journal of African History* 56, no. 2 (2015): 239–259, published by Cambridge University Press. I thank both publishers for permission to reprint the text here.

Many excellent and generous archivists helped me further my research. At the Spiritan archives, Father Gérard Vieira, who passed away in 2014, and Father Roger Tabard were very kind and immensely helpful. I also thank Madame Geneviève Karg and Father Paul Coulon for finding images in the Spiritan photographic collections. At the SMA archives in Rome, I thank Father Pierre Trichet, who has also since passed away, and Father Andrea Mandonico for their friendly welcome and thoughtful assistance. At the SMA archives in Paris, I thank Father Bernard Favier, and at the SMA archives in Strasbourg, I thank Valerie Bisson for her efforts to help me find relevant sources. At the White Fathers' archives in Rome, Father François Richard, Father Fritz Stenger, and Father Dominique Arnauld were generous and accommodating. At the MEP archives in Paris, I thank Brigitte Appavou for receiving me on short notice. At Le Saulchoir, Dominican archivists Fr. Jean-Michel Potin and Fr. Adama Dominique Tapsoba were a great help. I also thank Fr. Jean-Pierre Lintanf for sharing his recollections of Dakar in the 1950s. At Aide aux Églises d'Afrique, I thank Béatrix de Vareilles for a remarkably warm welcome, and her colleagues Stéphanie Genieys and Father Antoine Sondag for their support. At the ADN, Anne-Sophie Cras could not have been more helpful to a researcher with time constraints, and I thank her very much. At the OURS in Paris, I am grateful to Frédéric Cépède for his kind assistance. In Dakar, I extend my most sincere thanks to Madame Fatoumata Cissé Diarra, the director of the National Archives of Senegal, and Albert Diatta. Finally, I am grateful to Madame Coura Sarr at the archives of the Archdiocese of Dakar for welcoming me and for her valiant efforts to put those rich holdings in order.

I would also like to thank generous people who helped me gather or identify sources. Claire Khelfaoui did a wonderful job of tracking down obscure periodicals at the Bibliothèque nationale de France and dossiers at the ANOM. Many thanks to Elizabeth Lehr and Eric Jennings for sending along important bits that I missed in Aix. I thank Suzanne Diop for her assistance with identifications in a key photograph, and Lazare Ki-Zerbo for hunting through his family albums. Andrea Becherucci at the European University Institute, Nancy Jachec, and Kristen Windmuller-Luna all responded helpfully to my queries about particular images.

As the project took shape, I benefited immensely from the advice of a lot of patient, bighearted friends and colleagues. I must first thank Rachel Gillett and Heather Curtis, who read draft after chapter draft, and Dai Ellis, for his careful reading of the entire thing. I am also grateful to Kelly Duke Bryant, Michael

Goebel, Jennifer Johnson, Mary Lewis, Philip Nord, and Miranda Spieler for their suggestions on pieces of it. Many thanks to Jeff Ravel, Dan Smail, Ann Blair, Sarah Shortall, and the members of the Boston Area French History Group for commenting on a chapter, and to my friends and colleagues Rachel Applebaum, Kendra Field, Gary Leupp, Beatrice Manz, Alisha Rankin, and Hugh Roberts for feedback on another. I would also like to thank my editor, Kathleen McDermott, and the readers at Harvard University Press for their thoughts. Every effort has been made to identify copyright holders and obtain their permission for the use of copyright material. Notification of any additions or corrections that should be incorporated in future reprints or editions of this book would be greatly appreciated.

Formal and informal exchanges with colleagues enriched the project. I am grateful for fruitful conversations with and suggestions from Kimberly Arkin, Charles Becker, Jennifer Boittin, Elias Bongmba, Jane Burbank, Edouard Bustin, Jay Carney, Giuliana Chamedes, James Chappel, Olivier Chatelan, Rachel Chrastil, Bruno Dumons, David Ekbladh, Catherine Foisy, Ruth Ginio, Gillian Glaes, Udi Greenberg, Rachel Kantrowitz, Charles Keith, Kate Keller, Heidi Keller-Lapp, Yala Kisukidi, Baz Lecocq, Tim Longman, Kris Manjapra, Greg Mann, Emily Marker, Karen Melvin, Brenna Moore, Sam Moyn, Jessica Pearson, Emmanuelle Saada, Rachel Eva Schley, Berny Sèbe, Matt Stanard, Matt Sutton, Franziska Torma, Charlotte Walker-Said, and Owen White. I still have not fully grasped that Chris Schmidt-Nowara, who helped me think about Catholic antislavery movements and about sports trivia, is no longer with us. I would have loved to have shared the final product with him.

And then there are the lovely people who provided much-needed moral support during a very hectic several years. A big hug of thanks for Annette Lazzara and Lori Piracini, who provided daily encouragement, helped me solve my bizarre technical problems, and listened to my rants on a host of topics. I express my love and appreciation for Alexandra van den Berg Christensen and Alicia D'Abreu—I could not have accomplished my research without their help with childcare during trips to France. A hug, too, for Kathleen Peggar and Giuseppe Grillea, for helping me with Italian and crises in Italy. I am also very grateful to friends who have encouraged me through their scholarly example, sympathy, and perspective, especially Naomi Davidson, Mary Lewis, Alisha Rankin, and Dennis Rasmussen. Special thanks to Kelly Duke Bryant for a great trip to Dakar, to Miranda Spieler for excellent advice right when I needed it, to Jeanne Penvenne for her sunshine, to David Proctor for doing the work of a dozen people, to Ina Baghdiantz-McCabe for her unwavering support, and to Jonathan Wilson for comic relief. I am very grateful for my colleagues in the History Department at Tufts, who make it a real pleasure to come to work, and for my students, some of whom took an interest in my research. Among them, many thanks to Drew DiMaiti and Samantha Travis for their help.

Finally, my deepest gratitude goes to my family. My parents, Timothy and Dorothy Foster, and my brother, Tim, buoy me with unstinting love, unwavering generosity, and wry humor. I could not have finished this book without the help of Peter and Cynthia Ellis, who have been astoundingly generous with their time. Many thanks to Margaret Foster, Catherine West, and Susan Jones for their love and encouragement, and to Benjamin and Karen Foster for ongoing advice in the ways of academe. I am deeply saddened that Richard and Daniel Foster did not live to see this book in print. I know RCF would have read it very carefully, and I wish we could have talked about it over some *fromage* and Sancerre. My most important thank you is, of course, to Dai, for everything he does, every single day, to make my dreams come true.

INDEX